Financial Risk Management

Dr. Vivek
B.Tech. (Civil), M.B.A. (Fin.), Ph.D.
Risk Management Specialist
Finance Professional

Dr. P. N. Asthana
M.Com., LL.B., Ph.D.
Reader,
Deptt. of Applied Business Economics
Faculty of Commerce, St. John's College, Agra.

ISO 9001:2015 CERTIFIED

First Edition : 2008
Second Revised Edition : 2012
Reprint : 2014, 2017, 2021
Reprint : 2026

Published by : Mrs. Meena Pandey
for **HIMALAYA PUBLISHING HOUSE PVT. LTD.,**
Vishal Industrial Estate, 1st Floor, Office No. 63/64,
Bhandup Village Road, Subhash Nagar (Opp. CEAT Tyres),
Nahur (W), Mumbai - 400 078. **Phone:** 022-35131464/65/66/67
E-mail: himpub@bharatmail.co.in; **Website:** www.himpub.com

Branch Offices:

New Delhi : Pooja Apartments, 4-B, Murari Lal Street, Ansari Road, Darya Ganj, New Delhi - 110 002. Phone: 011-23270392, 23278631; Fax: 011-23256286

Nagpur : Kundanlal Chandak Industrial Estate, Ghat Road, Nagpur - 440 018. Mobile: 09325409992, 09325908881

Bengaluru : Plot No. 91-33, 2nd Main Road Seshadripuram, Behind Nataraja Theatre, Bengaluru - 560020. Phone: 08041138821, Mobile: 09379847017, 09379847005

Hyderabad : No. 3-4-184, Lingampally, Besides Raghavendra Swamy Matham, Kachiguda, Hyderabad - 500 027. Phone: 040-27560041, 27550139

Chennai : No. 34/44, Motilal Street, T. Nagar, Chennai - 600 017. Mobile: 09380460419

Pune : First Floor, Laksha Apartment, No. 527, Mehunpura, Shaniwarpeth (Near Prabhat Theatre), Pune - 411 030. Phone: 020-24496323, 24496333; Mobile: 09370579333

Cuttack : Plot No. 5F-755/4, Sector-9, CDA Markat Nagar, Cuttack - 753 014, Odisha. Mobile: 09338746007

Kolkata : 13, S.M. Bose Road, Near Gate No. 5, Agarpara Railway Station, North 24 Parganas, West Bengal - 700 109. Mobile: 09674536325

DTP by : Sri Siddhi Softtek, Bengaluru.

Printed at : Geetanjali Press Pvt. Ltd., Nagpur. On behalf of HPH (P).

This book is dedicated to my father
Late (Dr.) Nand Kishore Gupta

Vivek

PREFACE FOR SECOND EDITION

A decade ago, the concept of Financial Risk Management was confined to Western countries or developed countries. Financial Risk Management was having very little presence in Indian Financial Industry. Basel I forced some big international banks to follow risk management practices. Thanks goes to BIS and BASEL II document for wide acceptance of Financial Risk Management concept by banks and financial institutions worldwide. In India also, implementation of Basel II norms has been satisfactory. However, many financial institutions in India are missing risk culture and risk awareness among their finance managers. Till the time in 2007, RBI forcefully imposed implementation of Basel II norms on Indian banks, it was kept in back burner. RBI had issued a deadline to implement Basel II norms to the Indian banks with the international presence by 31st March'2008 and for the others by 31st March'2009. The challenge of RBI has now increased many fold by introduction of Basel III. The implementation of Basel III will start from 1st January '2013 and needs to be completed by 1st January' 2019.

Focus of the Book

We have written this second edition of Financial Risk management with the following objectives:

1. To create financial risk awareness among young finance managers and students of various professional courses in finance discipline.
2. To demonstrate the readers that the subject of Financial Risk Management is interesting, challenging, simple to understand and very much relevant in practice.
3. To explain the concepts and theories of Financial Risk Management in the simple manner so that the interest of readers is developed in the subject.
4. To provide a comprehensive knowledge about the Financial Risk management at one place to the readers.
5. To attract more students and professional to choose Financial Risk Management as career.
6. To help the risk managers understand the logics of risk management in a better way.

The Financial Risk Management combines theory and practical applications.

Intended Audience

Financial Risk Management is aimed at MBA, CFA, M.Com., CA, MFC, MBE, Risk Professionals, GARP and PRAMIA Aspirants, Managers of FIs and Banks.

Feature of the Book

The financial service industry in India consists of various Financial Institutions (FIs) such as finance companies, commercial banks, securities funds and investment banks, mutual funds and insurance companies, etc. The basic function of these financial institutions involves channelising public money in a profitable manner by bearing sufficient risk and in turn distributing profits by the way of interest and dividends to the investors. In the ***first chapter*** of this book role of financial institution has been discussed.

Few years back in India, the business environment was totally regulated (State controlled) and directed with reference to our banking industry, where the consumer had no or very limited choice. Banks/ FIs operated in an atmosphere where everything was directed and controlled externally (albeit either by RBI, SEBI, NHB or Finance Ministry and other regulatory body). But with dismantling of State control over every sector of economy and with deregulations of supply, demand and prices to shape on the basis of market forces, Indian financial market has now come to face a new challenge. Competition results in the survival of the fittest. In the liberalised environment competing with the high-tech global FIs, the Indian FIs have to re-orient themselves to the changed situation. The new economic regime has not only presented newer opportunities to operate but has exposed Indian financial institutions to newer risk too. Hence the need of risk management arises and accordingly ***second chapter*** of the book is emphasising on need of risk management.

In India, the Financial Market has been opened up recently after which it has seen major financial disasters such as UTI etc. The downtrend interest rate regime is also an outcome of it, which became possible because of a cheaper source of fund available overseas. Most of the Indian FIs went for this option thus exposing them to International Financial Market. A Financial Institution is exposed to various types of risks namely Interest Rate Risk, Market Risk, Credit Risk, Operational & Technology Risk, Off-Balance Sheet Risk, Foreign Exchange Risk, Sovereign Risk and Liquidity Risk, etc. which has been discussed in ***chapter three*** of the book. The measurement of various kinds of the risks has been discussed in ***fourth to tenth chapter*** of this book. These chapters focus has been made on measuring different kinds of risks before its management.

Chapter eleven has been added in this edition of book for various risk management tools being used. The whole Risk Management process covers management of various kinds of risks, as mentioned above, individually and in totality. The management of various kinds of risks has been discussed from ***twelve to eighteen chapter*** of this book. All these risks are interrelated and needs to be managed together. This concept is also known as Enterprise Wide Risk Management (EWRM). For EWRM, a new ***chapter nineteen*** on the subject has been added. For risk reporting and for the knowledge of various accounting standards (IAS, IFRS & SFAS), a new ***chapter twenty*** has been added to this edition of book.

In India, so far the regulators such as RBI and NHB have taken only indicative steps towards effective Risk Management by FIs. RBI issued the guidelines for ALM for the first time in the year 1999 which can be seen as beginning of Risk Management practice in Indian Financial industry. Later on RBI came with various guidance notes on Market Risk, Credit Risk, and Interest Rate Risk etc. in the year 2000 and 2001. These notes proved to be of little help to FIs in the absence of hedging tools in Indian Financial market. In the year 2002, NSE came with some hedging tools i.e. Index Future & Options etc. for market risk. In June 2003, RBI has allowed trading in Interest Rate Futures i.e. a tool for interest rate risk. Recently RBI issued directions for credit default swaps (CDS). The various regulatory issues and Basel I, II & III documents have been discussed in ***chapter twenty-one and twenty-two*** of this book.

It is also important to know the various developments and failures of risk management in India and other parts of the world. To cater to this requirement, ***chapter twenty-three*** of the book covers various famous case studies in the area of risk management including latest addition of subprime cases and financial crises in US in detail. While studying financial risk management, one should be familiar with few concepts such as advance bond concept, time value of money, probability functions and some concepts of statistics, which have been discussed in ***chapter twenty-four*** of this book.

VIVEK

P. N. ASTHANA

Acknowledgement

Our book on Financial Risk Management has come to its final shape because of the contribution of many people. We are thankful to all of them for their support and encouragement. Like most of the textbooks, Financial Risk Management, Second Edition, too has inspiration from a number of authors in the field of finance. We express our sincere gratitude to all of them. As far as possible, they have been fully acknowledged at the appropriate places. We have tried to give credit to all sources from where we have drawn the material in this book. Still there may be remained unintended errors for which we will feel obliged if brought to our notice.

I, Vivek, wish to acknowledge my co-author Dr. P. N. Asthana because of whom this book has come to in existence. Dr. Prem Narain Asthana had always been a source of inspiration for me since my college days.

I, Vivek, specially wish to acknowledge my wife Dr. Rachna Gupta and my children Kaashvi & Krish, who scarified the most valuable years of their childhood by allowing me to write this book at a time when they needed me the most.

We convey our sincere thanks to our colleagues for their support to carry out this valuable assignment.

We are thankful to our family members for their endurance throughout the writing of this book.

Vivek

P N Asthana

Brief Contents

PART E
Case Studies 299 — 344

PART F
Other Important Concepts of Risk Management 345 — 396

Contents

PART A

Introduction of Risk Management

1. The Role of Financial Institutions
2. Need of Risk Management
3. Identification of Risks

Chapter – 1

The Role of Financial Institutions

Chapter Objective

- To understand the functions of banks/FIs
- Understanding the role of banks and FIs in the economy
- To know about various types of financial intermediaries
- Nature of financial services provided by FIs
- Regulatory Environment and its need
- Future trend of FIs

Introduction

The main objectives of this book are need, identification, measurement and management of risk of financial institutions. Financial institutions, i.e. Banks, NBFCs, HFCs, Insurance Companies, specialised banks, Pension Funds and Mutual funds basically work as intermediaries for channelising funds from those who have savings to whom who require funds for business.

In the economy, FIs may be categorised in different groups but all of them face major kind of common risks such as liquidity risk, interest rate risk due to mismatch between its asset and liabilities, credit risk in the form of not honouring contract by counterparty, operational risk arising due to carrying business, external and internal frauds, etc.

The FIs plays an important role in system and carry some inherent risks. They require special attention from regulator to protect business and public interest. Financial institutions exist to improve the efficiency of the financial markets. If savers and investors, buyers and sellers, are able to locate each other to purchase any and all assets without incurring any cost, and make their decisions with freely available information, then financial institutions would have very little scope or business for replacing or mediating direct transactions done by various parties involved in financial transactions. However, this is not the reality of financial world. In actual economies of various countries, market participants seek the services of financial institutions because of the FIs ability to provide market knowledge, transaction efficiency, and contract enforcement. Such FIs operates in two ways. They may discover, underwrite, and service investments made using their own resources, or act as agent for market participants who approach to them to obtain some of these services. In the latter case, investors assemble their portfolios from securities brought to them by these FIs. In light of the two ways in which financial institutions may operate in the financial sector, several issues rise such as, when and under what circumstances should these FIs use their own resources to provide financial services, rather than offering them through a simple agency transaction? Or to the extent that such services are offered through the use of the institution's own resources, how should it be managing its portfolio so as to achieve the highest value added for its stakeholders?

Function of FIs in the Economy

FIs are the sole medium available in the economy to channelise household's savings in lieu of return and to make the funds available to those who require them on the basis of some payment for using that fund. In the absence of these FIs, it would be difficult for savers to supply money to corporates or other party who need money to run business. The difficulty faced by householders would be such as searching corporates, guarantee of return and repayment and timely payments, etc. Individuals also do not have capacity to judge business or projects in which they want to put money. Monitoring of projects and corporates is a very costly affair for individuals because of the involvement of considerable time and expenses to collect correct and relevant information. The lack of monitoring increases the risk in investment made in equity and debt.

Another consideration is of liquidity and pricing. If an individual invests in debt or equity of corporates which is of long term nature, he may not be able to liquidate it as and when required and in turn the individual would like to sit on cash instead of investing. The individuals also carry the risk of pricing of financial products available in the market because of lack of expertise in the subject matter. Investment in debt and equity also attracts various transaction costs, which may make the investment costlier. A model system of functioning of FIs in economy may be understood through Figure 1-1.

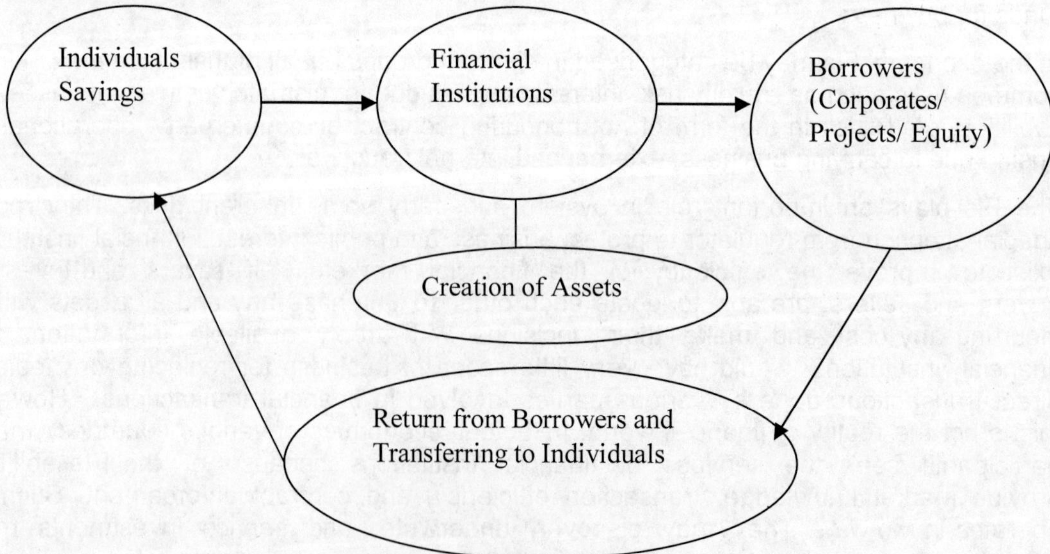

FIGURE 1-1 Basic Functioning of Financial Institution in Economy

The FIs are mainly involved in two kinds of functions, i.e. fee based and fund based. The first function is fee based brokerage function where FIs act as agents for individuals such as investment and research companies, mutual funds, etc. The second function is asset management where FIs manage assets on behalf of households and create assets out of household's savings. In this fund-based function, FI invest savings in corporates' debt, projects or equity directly and generates returns to distribute among depositors on their savings, i.e. commercial banks, specialised lending institutions, etc.

The main objective of these FIs is also to provide financial security and high returns to savers. FIs provide high degree of liquidity for investment in the form of time deposits where principal and guaranteed interest payment is made and the investment may be liquidated any time. The FIs also have the ability to reduce risk by diversifying its investment in a number of securities. The diversification allows FIs to predict accurate return on its assets. FIs which have diversified portfolio in global market as well as the domestic market are better able to manage risk and return on their asset base.

Different Types of Financial Intermediaries

The financial services industry consists of various players such as Depository institutions (commercial banks, saving institutions, NBFCs, para banking companies etc.), Insurance companies, Finance companies, Securities firms, Pension funds and Mutual funds. The products offered by them generally includes payment services, saving products, fiduciary services, lending to business or consumers, underwriting issuance of equity or debt and insurance and risk management products (derivatives), etc.

Commercial Banks

Commercial banks comprise the largest group of depository institution worldwide. The main business of banks involves accepting deposits and making loans. The composition of assets and liabilities of banks differ based on their size, location, etc. The deposit products mainly include current and saving bank accounts, fixed deposits, etc. The loan products include consumer loans, personal loans, working capital loans, housing loans, projects loans, etc. These banks tend to fund themselves in national markets and lend to large corporates in order to earn a spread i.e. the difference between lending and deposit rates. Commercial banks have two major source of funds other than equity provided by owners: deposits and borrowed funds. The equity capital consists mainly of common and preferred stock, surplus or additional paid up capital and retained earnings. Apart from assets and liabilities, banks conduct many off balance sheet (OBS) activities. Off-balance-sheet activities are very important in terms of revenue generated. OBS activities include issuing of various types of bank guarantees, letters of credit, selling loans and derivative transactions such as forwards, futures, options, and swaps.

Insurance Companies

The primary function of insurance companies is to protect individual and corporate policyholders from adverse events causing loss of money or life. Insurance companies promise policyholders compensation if certain specified event takes place in lieu of premium charged to cover the specified risk. The insurance industry is classified in two groups: Life insurance and General insurance covering property loss. The life insurance companies provide protection against the possibility of sudden death, illnesses and superannuation. General insurance protects against personal injury, accidents, theft, fire, earthquake, floods, etc. These days insurance companies are offering products which are very similar to the products being offered by mutual funds and other investment bankers. The life insurance companies offer policies like term life, whole life, endowment life, variable life universal life, etc. Other than this, life insurers also offer policies like group life insurance, industrial insurance and credit life insurance. Few other major activities of life insurance companies involve the sale of annuities, pension plan, and accident & health insurance. Insurance companies have long term nature of their liabilities and in order to generate competitive returns for life insurance products, these companies invest in long term maturity assets e.g. bonds, equities and government securities. The insurance companies in India are regulated by IRDA. The details of various rules and regulations may be obtained from IRDA website www.irda.gov.in.

General insurance involves insurance coverages related to the loss of real and personal property. The form of insurance coverage involves vehicle insurance, property insurance, machinery insurance, project immovable insurance etc. against theft, accident, fire, earthquake, flood, etc.

Investment Banks

Investment banking involves the raising of debt and equity for corporates and governments. This involves the origination, underwriting and placement of securities in money and capital markets for corporate or government issuers. The services also involve assistance in the trading of securities in the secondary markets. Investment banking also includes corporate finance activities such as advising on mergers and acquisition. Trading in securities and underwriting is a financial service that requires no investment in assets or liability and is a profit generating activity that does not require FIs to hold or invest in the securities they trade or issue for their customers. The investment bankers are involved in the activities such as investing, IPO management, private placement, secondary market making, trading, cash management, mergers and acquisitions, etc.

Mutual Funds

Mutual funds pool financial resources of individuals and companies and invest in diversified portfolios of assets. An open-ended mutual fund continuously stands ready to sell new units to investors and to redeem outstanding units on demand at quoted NAV. Mutual funds provide opportunities to the individuals to invest in a pool of securities with diversified risk. Mutual funds also help individuals to reduce transaction costs and commissions. Mutual funds are divided into two categories: short-term funds and long-term funds. The long-term mutual funds comprise bond funds, equity funds and hybrid funds. The short-term mutual funds comprise money market mutual fund. The mutual fund units are also listed in stock exchanges and are frequently traded based on NAV.

Finance Companies

The basic function of finance companies is to make loans to individuals and corporates. The lending function of finance companies is overlapping with commercial banks such as vehicle loans, consumer loan, project loans, commercial loans, etc. Some finance companies are also allowed to raise deposits from corporates and individuals. The major activities of these companies involve consumer durable sales financing, personal loans, business credit, factoring and bill discounting, mortgage based loans (housing loans) etc. In India, this sector comprise NBFCs, HFCs, etc. The major players are such as HDFC, HUDCO, PFC, REC, NABARD, SIDBI, IFCI, etc.

Financial Services Provided by Financial Intermediaries

The services provided by financial intermediaries can be divided into six different activities. These are origination, distribution, packaging, servicing, intermediating, and market making.

1. ***Origination*** involves locating, evaluating and creating new financial claims issued by the financial institution's clients. The originator assembles and evaluates information concerning the transaction. On one hand, if the originator plans to maintain ownership of the new asset, it must set its own standards of acceptable risk and return for it to act as principal as well. On the other hand, if the originator plans to act as an agent and sell the product, it must abide by the underwriting standards of other principals. An example of the latter is a mortgage banker that must originate mortgages in conformance with agency standards to sell such mortgages into an agency sponsored pool of mortgages.

2. ***Distribution*** is the act of raising funds by selling newly originated products to customers that have the resources available to finance them. This activity can be conducted as either a fee based transaction or with the institution acting as principal. In the former, newly originated assets are placed with investors who directly remit to the issuing firm. The financial institution never takes ownership of the asset in question, but merely facilitates its placement into a third party's portfolio. In the latter, the initiating institution purchases the originated assets and sells or distributes them from its own inventory. Most retail sales are made on a brokered basis, while institutional distribution is most frequently conducted with an institution acting as principal.

3. ***Servicing*** involves collecting payments due from issuers and paying the collected funds to claimants. In addition, a servicer maintains payment records, monitors contracts, and pursues action in defaults. In less developed economies, this aspect of financial service provision is relatively invisible. Most assets are originated and held by the same institution, particularly in the fixed income area. Accordingly, the customer service aspect of lending is less obvious. In developed economies, servicing is seen as a distinct business activity in the financial markets.

4. ***Packaging*** is a relatively recent activity. It involves the collection of individual financial assets into pools, and possibly the decomposition of the cash flow from such assets again into different types of financial claims. Such repackaging of financial flows is done with an eye toward increasing liquidity or tailoring cash flows for specific customers.

5. ***Intermediating*** involves the simultaneous issuance and purchase of different financial claims by a single financial entity. It occurs when an institution purchases

one type of financial instrument for its own account and finances the transaction by issuing a claim against its own balance sheet. Three types of such financial intermediation activity are common. These are (i) insurance underwriting whereby the issuer assumes the policy's contingent liability, (ii) loan underwriting, whereby the intermediary uses its own resources in extending credit to a borrower, and (iii) security underwriting which involves buying securities as principal to distribute to investors.

6. ***Market making*** is an activity involving the buying and selling of identical financial instruments by a dealer. The market making firm is usually, but not always, a principal in the transaction. A market maker acts as an intermediary when it finances inventory by issuing its own claims, e.g., security underwriting. Gains and losses associated with the change in inventory value accrue to the market maker's financial benefit or loss. Recently, several commercial auction firms have made markets for loans as the seller's agent. In this case, buyers and sellers take principal risks and the auctioneer gets a commission, acting more as an agent for bringing together buyers and sellers than as a market maker.

Other Special Functions

Apart from its traditional functions of borrowing and lending, FIs also perform certain special functions such as medium of exchange in the economy, i.e. carrier of monetary policy given by the Central Bank, sole credit providers for government predetermined sectors, wealth distribution, transaction and payment services in the country, various support functions, etc. The banks have a big role in M1, M2 and M3 money supply as most of its deposits are covered under the definition of money supply. Money supply has direct impact on inflation, thus the role of FIs increase further in country's economy. The banks also play an important role in buying and selling government securities which give direction to future trend of liquidity and interest rate in financial system.

Need of Regulation for FIs

FIs carry a special character because of its diversified activities and public fund involvement. Failure of FIs may impact economy of country and may have cascading effect on the whole financial system. Thus FIs require a special attention in term of rules and regulations. These regulations are framed by regulatory bodies such as RBI, SEBI, IRDA, NHB, etc. to cover the area of safety and soundness, monetary policy, consumer protection, depositors safety, credit allocation, investor protection, fraud prevention, entry and exit regulations, transactional validity, etc.

To protect depositors and borrowers against risk of FI failure, regulators such as RBI have developed a sound proof mechanism for protection. These mechanisms ensure safety and soundness of the FIs to maintain its credibility among depositors and borrowers. Some of these mechanisms are like not lending beyond certain percentage of its net owned funds to a single borrower, maintaining a minimum level of capita adequacy, various sectoral caps to restrain from taking over exposure in particular sector, providing guarantee on minimum amount of public deposits, proper monitoring and surveillance to prevent fraud and manipulations, etc.

Monetary policy regulation comes in the form of maintenance of minimum level of Cash Reserve Ratio (CRR) and Statutory Liquidity Ratio (SLR). These are the tools in the hand of regulator to maintain liquidity and money supply in the economy.[1]

Credit allocation regulations are imposed to benefit certain unprofitable sectors of the economy, which are important, but not very cash generating such as agriculture, EWS housing, micro financing, etc. These regulations require lending minimum amount at predetermined interest rate, price or fee, which is subsidised by government or cross, subsidised with profitable business line by FIs.

Consumer and investor protection regulations are in force to protect a large population of society, which has directly or indirectly invested its money in FIs or is doing business with them. RBI issues guidelines for consumer protection from time to time. The guidelines for investor protection have been issued by SEBI accordingly. Other regulators such as IRDA and NHB follow the same line.

Future Trends and Global Issues for FIs

The present financial market is not the same as it used to be 30 years back. After the globalisation and opening up of the economy for all, inherent risk in global financial market has also been invited. Before the globalisation of economy, economies of various countries were very closely administered either by regulators or by the government. Thus the risk was minimised to the lowest level with least return. In order to maximize the returns, the banks/FIs have to take risk and expand business. Over the years, banks and FIs have grown enormously in size because of the expansion or mergers and acquisition and consolidation. The economies of countries have also grown many folds at the same time. Diversification in many business lines and in cross countries exposes to various kind of risk in a larger manner which may have never been felt in an administered environment in various countries.

Due to globalisation, the financial markets have also seen a lot of innovation in recent years such as different category of structured financial instruments, methods of borrowing and financing, various derivative products, and various kinds of exchange trading. These innovations and availability of multi-options exposes the system to risks. As the market grows, need of better risk management is felt and in times to come, a lot of regulator initiatives will be taken on risk management front.

Summary

This chapter emphasises on the role of banks/FIs in the economy and the kind of services they provide. Traditionally banks and FIs main concern had been making profit instead of safeguard of public money. Now the scenario has changed completely to making profit while protecting shareholders and depositors money. The banks and financial institutions are required in the financial system to channelise depositors money for better return. The individual depositors may not be able to invest money for better return because of lack of expertise and availability of medium. An individual's main concern is the protection of money along with higher rate of return on the money invested. This individual concern is better taken care of by these banks and financial institution by investing depositors' money in various financial instruments and by creating loans. The depositors' money by these banks are put in very diversified manner, hence minimising the risk to certain extent.

KEY CONCEPTS

NBFC	HFCs	Pension Funds
Mutual Funds	Time Deposit	Money Supply
CRR	SLR	RBI
SEBI	NHB	IRDA

Review Questions and Problems

1. How many types of FIs have their presence in India? What are their specific functions?
2. Why do FIs need special attention? Select any FI and list its activities.
3. Justify the business of FIs investing in high risk assets backed by low risk liabilities.
4. Describe money supply. Differentiate between three types of money supply and its impact on the economy.
5. What is credit allocation and its regulation? Why is this regulation important for the financial system?
6. Study the regulatory framework in force for Indian banks of RBI and divide them in different forms of regulations.
7. List out all the business lines of a scheduled commercial bank in India.
8. Search RBI, SEBI, IRDA and NHB website and prepare a brief write up of each regulator.
9. What are the major assets and liability held by commercial banks?
10. What has the trend in ROA and ROE been in the Indian commercial banking industry over the last decade (2000-2010)?
11. What are the differences between commercial banks, RRBs, UCBs and co-operative banks? Contrast the business activities, location and market of these banks.
12. What strategic changes have banks implemented to deal with changes in the financial services environment?
13. What types of activities are classified as OBS activities? How is an OBS activity classified as asset or liability in balance sheet? Identify OBS activities of any chosen commercial bank.
14. Compare the balance sheet of an insurance company with commercial bank taking into consideration investment and fund raising.
15. What are the profit sources for a life and general insurance company? Kindly prepare an investment profile for a life insurance company.
16. How do the activities of investment banking differ from the activities of commercial bank?
17. List out 5 biggest mutual fund companies in India. How have their funds performed in recent years?

18. List out differences between open-ended and close-ended mutual funds. Also list the names of these funds category wise.
19. What is the difference between asset classification of a MMMF and long term mutual fund?
20. How do finance companies differ from commercial banks?
21. What are the sources of financing for finance companies?
22. Why do finance companies have less regulation in comparison with commercial banks?

Reference:

1. *www.rbi.org.in*

Chapter – 2

Need of Risk Management

Chapter Objective

- What is risk?
- Banks and FIs exposure to risk
- Explain sources of various kind of risks
- Why is risk management needed?
- Understand risk management in an organisation and its framework

Introduction

There is risk in every business activity in this world. One has to understand related risk to its business as risk differs from business to business. The kind of risks that are being faced by a FI/Bank is not the same as faced by an auto manufacturing company or by a hospital. The establishment of the need of risk management for any business is a part of business strategy as risk management has cost involved and sometimes makes product line pricing costlier due to risk cost involved in the business. The sources of various kinds of risks depends on the business environment of an entity, country of business, competitors, political situation, rules and regulation in the parent country, etc. A country where every business is being regulated by government or partially by the government has different gravity of risk when compared to a free economy country. Accordingly, business entity has to decide the framework of risk management and the risk management policy for business. The approach for risk management differs from size and the business of an organisation. A FI/bank of larger size with large number of business lines has greater exposure to risk than the smaller size FI/bank. But smaller size bank having large number of business lines may be exposed to higher risk than the FI/bank of larger size with large number of business lines.

What is Risk?

The term Risk is widely used in the day-to-day business for unknown outcome or the loss arising out of business. Everyone understands the meaning of the word risk in laymen terms. There is some degree of risk involved in every sphere of life. We are exposed to either taking or avoiding various kinds of risks in our daily lives. In a more straight way, the 'risk' can be used to describe any situation in which there is an uncertainty about outcome and the result may be loss.

In the financial market, risk may be defined as "an event or possibility of an event which can impair corporate earnings or cash flow over short/medium/long-term time horizon".[1] Risk can be defined as the impact of a future event that may or may not happen. Corporate earnings or cash flows have a bearing on the wealth of the investors through valuation of the company.

In simple words, the probability for future returns too vary from the expected returns in risk. Risk arises in any business transaction where outcome of input made is not certain. Every business activity has upside and downside risk. If the same returns could be guaranteed under all circumstances, there would be no risk, and financial risk management would be an irrelevant phenomenon for the financial world. However, any such guarantee is not possible in the real financial world; hence, the need for financial risk management arises.

All financial institutions deal with different types of risks, though the nature and magnitude of various risks may differ from institution to institution. This is especially true for banks/financial institutions as they deal with currency and financial instruments. They act as financial intermediaries in any economic system. They mobilise household/ corporate savings and make it available to borrowing entities. Since FIs help in credit creation by means of loans and advances, they face many risks. The risk taking capacity of these FIs in turn gives better return. Taking risk is the core of most of the products and services offered by banks/financial institutions. Certainly, risk management is not a new challenge. Financial institutions have always faced the task of managing their risk exposures while remaining profitable and competitive. But financial innovation, even when it involves well-established products and exposures that are only slightly altered, continues to present new risk-management challenges.

In their role as financial intermediaries, banks and/or financial institutions are involved in the following business lines, which results in various risks:

i. ***Mobilisation of Funds***: Funds are mobilised by accepting term deposits/time deposits, by issuing securities such as bonds, debentures, credit notes, commercial papers, etc.

ii. ***Deployment of Funds/ Credit Creation:*** The funds that are mobilised are first subject to regulatory investment requirements, i.e. banks have to invest a specified proportion of their funds in certain instruments, often government securities to maintain CRR and SLR. The surplus funds are deployed as loans for various segments of corporate and retail borrowers.

iii. ***Transfer of Funds***: Banks and financial institutions are the only vehicles available in the economy for moving funds on behalf of their customers and government. The core competence of banks is to act as service provider for corporations in supporting their business and liquidity needs across the globe. Banks also act as a settlement house for their funds. The banks perform this function with the help of various negotiable instruments. To meet growing demand and complexity of business of corporates, banks had to evolve payment and settlement systems to ensure a fast movement of money in the system.

iv. ***Transfer of Risks***: The bank customers manufacturing and other concerns are exposed to various risks and some of the risks are very crucial to their business. They relate to products, business model, distribution channel, etc. These have to be mainly handled by the companies themselves. However, for risks that arise from financial markets, corporates take expertise of their banks to take them over since it is the latter's core competence to handle them. Along with their own risks, banks also have to handle the risks passed on by their customers. The risks are an integral part of banks existence and its functioning in the financial market.

v. ***Trade Transaction Facility***: Banks facilitate their customers in carrying out trade transactions, both domestic and international. International business transactions involve dealing with a basket of different currencies. The global network of the banking system and its relationships constitute the backbone of global financial trade.

vi. ***Credit Enhancement Facility***: In the course of business, it is quite possible that the concerned business entities may not be familiar with each other. Therefore, suppliers of goods expect the bank's help in evaluating or enhancing the credit-worthiness of its customer. The entire bunch of services offered through letter of credit or guarantees falls under credit enhancement facility.

All these roles of banks/FIs involve dealing with risks of various types. Inadequate financial risk management may adversely affect the net earnings of the bank/FI in the short run and its survival in the long run. This is also true for all business organizations other than banks and financial institutions. The financial performance of most organisations is affected by the change in price that relates to commodities, exchange rates, interest rates of assets and liabilities and equities. Volatility in financial prices is a prime source of major business risk jointly called financial risk. Financial risk may be defined as the probability for cash flows or asset values to vary from expectations due to changes in financial attributes. This definition also gives an indicator of the measurement of risk, i.e., the more volatile the price, the greater is the risk.

Why Risk Management?

Two decades ago, financial risk was apt to be defined as the possibility of suffering financial loss. At that time, neither could anyone think of risk management as a discipline, nor was it likely that many outside of academia or the actuarial business spent much time tinkering with mathematical models in order to weigh different strains of strategic exposure, i.e., a firm's sensitivity to changes in tax rates, interest rates, exchange rates, the price of oil, etc. Globalisation has resulted in pressure on margins. The lower the margin, the greater is the need for risk management. As a result, risk management has become a key area of focus for most of the financial institutions and its top executives. Additionally, due to the failure of many banks/financial institutions in the recent past, it has attracted the attention of regulators also.

The challenge of a modern corporation is to ensure wealth maximisation for their investors that is consistent with their risk preference. A decline in profitability has a more than proportional impact on the firm's fortunes. Financial distress is costly and the cost of external financing increases rapidly when a firm's viability is in question. On one hand, risks have to be managed effectively and on the other hand, adequate consistent returns have to be ensured. There are some risks that can be eliminated, or at least substantially reduced through the technique of risk transfer. With the kind of role that the banks and financial institutions play in the system, they have to look at risks more carefully, since the impact is widespread and contagious and it follows a chain reaction as seen in sub prime issue in US.

An impact on one institution can have fallout for other institutions in the market or economy. Risk in the institutional context, therefore, needs to be understood and dealt with appropriately.

Institutions structured as limited liability corporations involve the separation of ownership and management. The management consists of directors and other functional experts who work on behalf of the investors. Risk management of the business itself has to be more formal and structured in modern corporations. In financial institutions, core business and risk are two sides of the coin. Therefore, they need to be dealt jointly. The risks associated with the provision of financial services differ by the type of service rendered. The number of transactions and the complexity of products traded are increasing every day. In many financial organisations, their entire capital is traded every day. Profit-driven trading requires individuals at various levels of the organisation to be authorised to trade. This implies that these individuals can risk the organisations' capital and even its existence, since the contracts entered into by them are binding for the organisation. Increased volatility around the world and highly leveraged positions in the form of derivatives participation create a further need for risk management in every financial market and system.

The recent spate of banking problems, among more traditional banking organizations in emerging markets, also underscores the importance of maintaining strong capital positions and sound risk management and governance structures in all types of banking organisations. At the same time, it needs to be emphasised that risk management does not imply avoidance but tolerance and transfer of risk. Taking reasonable and well known risks is important in order to earn returns. For that purpose, foolproof policies and procedures should be set up by the organisations to identify, measure, monitor, and control the financial risks.

Sources of Various Risk

In today's world, risk is radically more complicated, intensely more concentrated and devastatingly swift. Risk is any one of a myriad of contingencies that could negatively impact an enterprise, thereby altering its value, cash flow, or future. More globalization, greater interdependence, immediate access to markets of choice, more sophisticated techniques, intensified competition—these are clearly the trends of the future. In a few words, it can be said that the management of risk has become integral to our well-being.

Risks arise from various sources and affect the value of assets held by any institution. Risk arises due to the possibility that the outcome could be different from the expected outcome. The probability of an outcome is governed by the availability of exact information. Due to the asymmetric distribution of information, the correct and up-to-date information is available with only certain economic players. Further, the outcome is dependent on several other drivers. These interrelationships are necessarily known or determinable. Governments play a very important role; their policies may not always be in accordance with expectations. This adds more uncertainty to the possibility. In spite of our best effort to model an outcome, it may not be possible, therefore, to ascertain the exact result.

Some of the factors that can expose any economic entity (more particularly banks or financial institutions) to various risks are economic policies of governments and resultant budget deficits or surpluses, changes in money supply, levels of inflation and interest rates as well as capital formation that takes place concomitantly in the economy. All these, in turn, influence the movement of capital in and out of the country and have an impact on the relative value of currencies and also the value of various debt instruments. Consumption and savings propensities and the preferences of individual consumers result in certain patterns of international trade. In the process, they create trade surpluses in some economies and deficits in others.

Political, social, racial, and ethnic issues impact the availability of or demand for a particular commodity and thus result in upheavals in various commodity markets. Technological factors bring in new products (making other products redundant in the process) and thus have an effect on the fortunes of the corporations which are manufacturing and marketing them. Governance of corporations and their financial performance (which is a result of competitive factors in various markets) as well as the financial structures opted for by the individual organization also plays a role.

In addition to these factors present in the environment, human nature adds to the possibilities in the dynamic situation. An individual may be placed in a situation where his self-interest vis-à-vis his professional responsibility are in conflict. The temptation to opt for self-interest can potentially jeopardize the interests of the corporation that the individual works for and create difficulties for it.

Now we will discuss how the risk arises in different kind of financial business.

For commercial banks, credit or default exposure is a major source of risk because commercial banks are highly leveraged and hold very insignificant amount of capital in comparison with its total asset size and a small default can easily wipe out the equity capital of a bank. Similarly, OBS items are not reflected in balance sheet but may pose great amount of risk if adverse movement is encountered. There are several financial disasters contributed by OBS items only. The notional or face value of OBS activities does not accurately reflect the risk to the bank. The potential for bank to gain or lose is based upon the possible change in market parameters over the life of such agreements. Because of the use of the derivative products, banks have heavily exposed to interest rate risk, credit risk and foreign exchange risk.

Insurance companies have more uncertain payouts on their insurance contracts. Insurance companies charges premium amount much lower than the value of property insured hence in case of major loss to the property, insurance company suffers losses in terms of premium earned to insured the asset.

Risk Management Framework

A good quality risk management system brings various benefits to an organisation such as improving the risk awareness which is actively courted by the company, more objective performance appraisal based on risk-adjusted capital employed, generating proactive approach towards future risks and its timely identification, bringing the system to the process of risk quantification, enabling the assigning of value to estimated risk of loss, e.g. EaR or VaR, increasing the valuation of the company and reduced cost of capital or borrowings, alarming the extreme risk situations for necessary risk mitigation by management.[2]

The risk management policy needs to identify issues in risk management that the business must address. A number of factors need to be agreed on and defined while preparing risk management policy for an organisation. The risk management framework should be well defined taking into account the background and the present & future business of the organization, its regulatory and business environment as well as other organisational factors. The level of the organization to be assessed (strategic, business, operational) at which risk management is expected to be implemented.

Identification of risks and their consequences, clarity of objectives, in particular those situations that the corporation hopes to avoid, and preserving or bringing about risk management needs to be clearly spelt out. Before deciding risk management policy, a risk awareness and risk culture survey must be conducted in the organisation. Internal or external factors that limit application of any risk management strategies also should be clearly identified and ground rules should be established that constitute successful risk management within the system. Tools and techniques to be adopted for the identification and subsequent management, tracking and reporting of the risks are the important area to practice a prudent risk management system in the organisation.

Risk Management in Organisation

As organisations grow larger, one of their major challenges can be described as making sure that the "right hand" knows what the "left hand" is doing. In other words, risks must be recognized and managed across the entire organization. First of all, it needs to be emphasized that the goal of risk management is not to eliminate risk, but to ensure that risk remains at a predetermined level of acceptability. In some cases, firms may be practicing good risk management on an exposure-by-exposure basis, but they may not be paying close enough attention to aggregation of exposures across the entire organization. Also, one should keep in mind that risk and reward often go together. Higher expectations of rewards may expose the organization to a higher level of risk. Similarly, higher levels of risk should provide a higher possibility of return; otherwise, it is not worthwhile to expose the organization to that level of risk. Rapid growth can place considerable pressure on, among other areas, an organization's management information systems, change-management controls, strategic planning, credit concentrations, and asset-liability management.[3]

Given this relationship between risk and returns, there are different approaches to managing risk such as risk avoidance, diversification, risk transfer and retention, risk sharing and loss control. Risk avoidance means avoiding the risk altogether. This is an extreme approach and would even result in least incentive for any activity to take place. Diversification follows a 'Do not put all eggs in one basket' policy. This policy works well when the various business lines in an organization do not involve a high correlation, but sometimes diversification in highly correlated business increases risk manifolds. Under the risk pricing mechanism, the original party that is exposed to risk, transfers the same to another party that is willing to be exposed to that risk. Under the risk retention approach, though the firm is aware about the exposure, it deliberately decides to retain it due to a very high cost of risk transfer. Risk sharing is a combination of the earlier two approaches, where a part of the risk is retained and the other part is transferred out. Loss control is an approach to reduce the possibility or quantum of a loss. For example, to manage liquidity risk, a firm may decide to always keep a certain portion in highly liquid assets.

Summary

In banking business, everyday new risk arises and banks have to mitigate these risks in order to survive. In financial industry, survival of the best managed is the key mantra. There is no financial transaction where banks and financial institutions are not exposed to some kind of risk. It is very important to understand the risk involved in business. Banks and FIs should be able to identify various sources of risks and its origination in order to mitigate these risks. Everybody in the organisation should know the need of risk management in business. The banks should have a proper risk management system in place. A detailed risk management framework needs to be established for each business line of the bank. Ignoring risk management practices may prove a very costly affair for banks. Banks should develop a clear understanding about risk transfer and risk sharing. Every risk cannot be managed or mitigated. Risk can be minimised but cannot be eliminated. Eliminating risk from business may lead to poor profitability or heavy cost. Banks should always remember that risk management in banks has cost involved in it and managing risk is also a risky affair.

KEY CONCEPTS

Risk	Credit Notes	Bonds	Debentures
Commercial Papers	Credit Enhancement	Financial Distress	Commodity Market
EaR	VaR	Asset Liability Management	
Credit Concentration	Risk Transfer	Risk Sharing	

Review Questions and Problems

1. What is risk? Define the risk for at least 10 different corporates.
2. What are the various business lines of banks and the type of risk associated with each business line?
3. What are the various sources of risk?
4. What is the need for risk management in an organization?
5. Why is the risk in present time increasing from past?
6. State the situation where there is no risk in the system.
7. What are the important components of a risk management policy? Why do you think a risk policy is needed by an organization?
8. How is an organisation protected with prudent risk management system in place?
9. Do only banks and financial institutions need risk management? Explain.
10. What are the various risk management approaches that an organization can adopt?

References:

1. *en.wikipedia.org*
2. *www.rbi.org.in*
3. *Value at Risk, Philippe Jorian, 2e*

Chapter – 3

Identification of Risk

Chapter Objective

- Explain various kinds of risks
- Understand various risk exposure to banks
- Learn about various kinds of risks and its nature
- Learn how banks and FIs are exposed to these risks

Introduction

In order to understand the risk in a better manner, it is very important to explore the various types of risks faced by an organisation. Risks can be classified in different ways according to their origin. As the identification of risk is dependent on business lines, there may be an overlapping in various risks. A major objective of FIs is to increase returns for its investors. This involves taking of higher risk for higher return. The various risks faced by FI/Bank are interest rate risk, market risk, credit risk, operational risk, technology risk, foreign exchange risk, liquidity risk, off-balance sheet risk and insolvency risk. The efficient management of these risks is indeed a parameter for the business and FI's performance. The organisations mainly adopt strategies to avoid, transfer or manage the various kinds of risks.

Interest Rate Risk

The assets and liabilities of banks and financial institutions have different maturity and liquidity. This means that they create loan assets and investments and at the same time create deposit or other borrowing liabilities. The investment and loan assets invested in by the bank earn a certain interest return. At the same time, interest cost has to be paid to the lenders of deposit and other borrowings. The mismatches of the maturities of assets and liabilities expose the FIs to interest rate risk. The rate of interest on assets and liabilities are different and is higher on the assets. This difference is the net interest margin, which changes several times in a year. It may happen that the assets in which the firm has invested its money could be of a relatively longer term when compared to the time of maturity of the liabilities. In such a situation, if the movement of interest rate is upward, this will increase the cost of liability at the time of rollover and the same time net interest margin will also come down. On the other hand, if the liabilities have a long-term maturity and funds are deployed for shorter duration at higher rate and there is down trend of interest rate, it may result in a decline in spread.

EXAMPLE : Impact of Interest Rate Increase and Decline on FI's Profitability

Suppose a bank borrows Rs. 100 crores from the market for 2 years @ 10% p.a. and creates an asset of the same amount for 5 years period @ 12% p.a. The mismatch between the two is quite visible. In such a case, the profitability of bank for the year would be Rs. 2 crores (.02 X 100). In case, there is an upward trend of interest rate after 2 years and the cost of liability goes up to 13% p.a., the bank will post a loss of Rs. 1 crore (-.01 X 100).

If the movement in interest rate is downward and comes down to 8% p.a. for liability, bank's profit will increase from Rs. 2 crores to Rs. 4 (.04 X 100) crores in a year.

The above example is true in an ideal situation where other factors are constant but this does not happen in the real world. When a bank holds longer term assets than its liabilities, it exposes itself to refinancing risk. This risk poses threat to profitability for an adverse move in interest rate and increase cost of liability at the time of rollover. If the cost of liability increases and banks also want to increase the cost of asset to maintain the same level of interest margin, it may expose itself to repayment risk. As against this, if a bank holds shorter-term assets in comparison to the liabilities and interest is moving downward, the bank is exposed to reinvestment risk. Bank will face uncertainty of the rate at which funds will be reinvested. Repricing mismatches can also expose a bank to changes in the slope and shape of the yield curve. Yield curve risk arises when unanticipated shifts of the yield curve have adverse effects on a bank's income or underlying economic value. For instance, the underlying economic value of a long position in 10-year government bonds hedged by a short position in 5-year government notes could decline sharply if the yield curve steepens, even if the position is hedged against parallel movements in the yield curve.

At the same time, when FI is exposed to interest rate, repayment, refinancing and reinvestment risks, the market value of FI, i.e. the market value risk, is also at risk. The market value of an FI is the present value of cash flows of its assets and liability at present benchmark rate. In case of rising interest rate scenario, the discounting factor to cash flow increases and reduces the market value of assets and liability and vice-versa. Because of mismatches between assets and liabilities, i.e. assets of longer maturity pose threat to FI and the value of its assets goes down faster than the liabilities. This situation may simply result in insolvency, thus exposing FI to insolvency risk.

FIs/banks have to hedge against interest rate risk by adopting suitable strategy for matching maturity of their assets and liabilities. The interest rate risk may be minimised by adopting the above strategy but cannot be eliminated fully because the interest rate in case of asset and liability never moves uniformly. The hedging against interest rate risk also depends on the capital structure of company such as proportion of finance coming from debt, equity and other sources. The sensitivity of different assets and liabilities towards interest rate change is the main deciding factor for interest rate risk exposure.

Market Risk

Market risk is the risk to which banks/FIs are exposed while trading in financial assets and liabilities due to the movement in interest rates, exchange rates, security prices and market parameters which eventually lead to the changes in the prices of assets and liabilities. Market risk is the risk of losses due to adverse movements in financial market variables. Market risk is the risk of fluctuations in portfolio value because of adverse movements in such market variables. The Bank for International Settlements (BIS) defines market risk as "the risk that the value of 'on' or 'off' balance sheet positions will be adversely affected by movements in equity and interest rate markets, currency exchange rates and commodity prices".[1]

The mismatches of the expectation of prices for security under consideration between buyer and seller pose price risk in the market. Price risk may be seen as an unfavourable movement in the price of a commodity, security or other obligations and result in the overall market risk.

EXAMPLE: Market Risk arising out of Trading Activities

There have been various cases of market risk and one of the most famous is the collapse of Barings Bank, a British Merchant Bank. The bank was expecting that the Japanese stock market index Nikkei would rise if they take position in buying futures. The bank took position of around $8 billion. However, because of a number of reasons and earthquake at Kobe, Nikkei crashed resulting in a $1.2 billion losses to bank in a months time which exceeded banks own net worth. The movement of prices or market index is sometimes driven by some events and this is called event risk.

The above example indicates that very large exposure in one kind of security or in a single market exposes the FIs to concentration risk. This also arises due to non-diversified portfolio of product or business line. Another type of risk which is also associated with market risk, is volatility risk. This risk results not from changes in levels of prices but their volatility. Volatility is measured in terms of degree of unpredictable changes in a financial variable over a period of time.

Credit Risk

Credit risk is the risk due to uncertainty in a counterparty's (also called an obligor's or credit's) ability to meet its obligations. Because there are many types of counterparties from individuals to sovereign governments and many different types of obligations from auto loans to derivative transactions, credit risk takes many forms. A bank or a financial institution enters into a large number of financial transactions. In these transactions, the bank is exposed to a risk linked to the financial strength of the counterparty. Credit Risk originates from the point where FI has completed its transaction and the obligation of counterparty starts. All types of banks and FIs face credit risk. Those banks which are exposed to longer term investment or loans are more exposed to this risk in comparison to the banks having shorter term assets. Credit risk is the risk to each party of a contract that the other will not fulfill its contractual obligation. In most financial contracts, this risk is known as default risk.

The credit risk is linked to the various factors such as performance of the borrower's business, performance of the economy, industry, and management of the specific business. When a FI invests in bonds, the obligation attached to the instrument depends on the financial strength of the issuer.

EXAMPLE: Failure of Obligation by Counterparty Leads to Credit Risk

A famous German Herstatt Bank failed to honour its obligation to counterparty. The bank had received all its foreign currency receipts in Europe in the same business day, but did not honour any of its US Dollar obligation/payments and the situation continued till the end of the business day. Due to this, German banking regulators closed the bank due to insolvency. As a result, the counterparties were left holding unsecured claims against the bankrupt bank's assets.

Sometimes credit risk follows chain reaction in which one FI/bank failing to meet its obligation may pose default situation for another FI which then has to meet its obligation to the counterparty from payment to be received from former. This situation may pose settlement problem in the whole financial system.

Credit risk could occur in case of loans, bonds, debentures, commercial papers, inter corporate deposits, debentures and debt of similar nature. To minimise the chances of default, FIs need to monitor and collect information about borrowers on a continued basis. The managerial monitoring efficiency and credit risk management strategies affect risk and return of loan portfolio.

Credit risk is defined as the possibility of losses associated with diminution in the credit quality of borrowers or counterparties. In a bank's portfolio, losses stem from outright default due to inability or unwillingness of a customer or counterparty to meet commitments in relation to lending, trading, settlement and other financial transactions. Alternatively, losses result from reduction in portfolio value arising from actual or perceived deterioration in credit quality. Credit risk emanates from a bank's dealings with an individual, corporate, bank, financial institution or a sovereign.

Foreign Exchange Risk

The Risk that exchange rate changes can affect the value of the assets and liabilities of an FI located abroad. It is the change in the domestic currency value of assets and liabilities to the changes in the exchange rates. This may be positive or negative. Positive exposure gives rise to gain and negative exposure gives rise to loss. Foreign exchange risk is measured by the variance of the domestic currency value of asset, liability or an operating income, which can be related to unexpected changes in the exchange rates.

Any FI/bank takes exposure in foreign currency assets or liabilities even when taking position in foreign currency has advantage over local currency e.g. raising resources in foreign currency due to lesser interest rate than the domestic market including currency rate fluctuation or lending in those currencies where higher interest are offered. The return on investment in one economy differs from another primarily due to two reasons. The first is the nature of economy in one may be industry based and in another may be a mixed economy, as in India, a mix of agriculture, service and industry. The second reason is the differences in the financial market, saving and consumption habits of inhabitants, resources available and rules & regulations. These factors show imperfect correlation between returns from two different economies. For example, during 2007-08, the US economy was contracting while Indian economy was rapidly expanding.

In global financial market, currencies are like other commodities. It follows simple demand supply theory, as due to the increase in the demand for a currency, the exchange rate tends to go up. On the other hand, if there is an excess supply in the global financial market or demand for the particular currency is low, the exchange rate would tend to move down. The increase in demand due to capital flows arises when investors or lenders seek assets or funds denominated in that currency. The demand and supply of currency may be influenced to some extent by central banks of various countries that are called regulator intervention which may come in various forms such as imposing restrictive ECB norms, cap on FDIs, etc.

The exchange rate fluctuations are not perfectly correlated across countries. This means the dollar-euro exchange rate may be appreciating and at the same time dollar-rupee exchange rate may be depreciating.

EXAMPLE: How Foreign Exchange Risk Arises

A US FI gives a loan to an Indian company in rupee. If the INR depreciates in value relative to USD, the principal and interest payments to US FI would be devalued in dollar terms. If INR depreciates to such an extent that when over the investment period the overall return turn out to be negative, the US FI will get even lesser principal at the time of maturity from the actual lent amount. The situation will get reverse if Indian company takes USD loan. In this case, Indian company will be ending up paying more interest and principal repayment in INR terms.

In banks, foreign exchange risk can arise for a variety of reasons. Assets in the form of foreign currency loans given to customers as well as investments denominates in foreign currency and give rise to this risk. Similarly, a bank's borrowing activities from the overseas market could also expose the bank to the foreign exchange risk.

Sovereign Risk

When any FI holds assets in foreign countries or have exposure in currency of a particular country, apart from traditional risk such as foreign exchange risk and foreign interest rate risk, FI is exposed to additional kind of risk called sovereign risk or country risk. A domestic bank may transform itself into an international one when it starts lending across countries or invests in instruments issued by foreign institutions. When the bank starts doing so, the first risk that it encounters is sovereign risk, risk specific to that country which is governed by a number of factors such as political, social and economic factors, and the legal & regulatory framework. If a domestic company fails or is unwilling to pay the loan, lender usually has recourse to recover the money through various means available such as courts, DRT, SARFESI Act, etc. But if a foreign FI is even willing to repay the loan, it may not do so due to the restriction imposed by its country, shortage of foreign currency or adverse political reasons.

EXAMPLE: Sovereign Risk due to Local Country Policies

In early 80s, Brazilian and Mexican governments announced debt repayment moratorium which delayed debt repayment to the lenders of US. At that period, exposure of US banks to these countries FIs and government was huge and they suffered heavy losses. The Citicorp alone had to provide $3 billion to cover expected losses. The same situation was also encountered by US, Japanese and European banks in early 90s in their exposure to country like Indonesia and Russia. In the year 2001, Argentina also defaulted $130 billion in government issued debt because of an overvalued peso.

The economic position of a country has a significant role on its ability to service the loans availed by the government and its FIs/Banks. The parameters which decide countries position are foreign currency reserves, the current account deficit, the size of external commercial borrowings, FDI, equity exposure of FII in markets, etc. The country's government and its political stability are critical in assessing the country risk. If the government is run democratically with full majority, it indicates country's political maturity. If the country is globally accepted for trade and business, it shows that country will go by universally accepted laws. An established legal framework with suitable legislations is critical for any country's economics progress. Declining returns in fully developed economies forces FIs/banks to move to emerging market for higher return and diversification. At the same time, they are exposed to various kinds of risks of emerging markets such as banking supervision, market regulations legal systems not developed to the international standards, unstable democracies, the policies of the previous government be changed completely by the next government, all resulting in an effect on the business model and assumptions of foreign investors.

In the event of restrictions, rescheduling and prohibition on payment of debt obligations by governments, there is very little room for FIs for recourse to local courts and international courts.

Liquidity Risk

Liquidity risk is the risk that a sudden surge in liability withdrawals may leave an FI in a position of having to liquidate assets in a very short period of time and at low prices.[2] Liquidity risk is the potential inability to meet the bank's liabilities as they become due. It arises when the banks are unable to generate cash to cope with a decline in deposits or increase in assets. It originates from the mismatches in the maturity pattern of assets and liabilities.

An FI may face liquidity crisis if its credit rating is downgraded and experiences sudden, unexpected cash outflows. An FI is also exposed to liquidity risk if markets on which it depends are subject to loss of liquidity. When an asset is illiquid, prices become volatile, sometimes valued at high discounts from at par value. Liquidity risk may lead to other risks. If an FI is not able to liquidate it assets in time or have more of illiquid assets, this may attract market risk. Liquidity risk may also expose to credit risk. If an FI has to meet its loan obligation to other party which is funded by cash to be received from another party and if latter does not meets its obligation, FI will default in its obligation. Hence, liquidity risk may be transformed to credit risk.

Regulators also are equally concerned with liquidity risk of both asset and liability side and various guidelines are issued from time to time to manage liquidity risk. A simple way is to look at future net cash flows on a daily basis. If in a day there is a sizeable negative net cash flow, it deserves attention. This is done through dynamic and structural liquidity statement of all cash outflow and inflow of the organisation.

EXAMPLE: How Liquidity Risk arises?

When liability holders of any FI immediately demands money, FI has to meet its obligation either by selling of assets or additional borrowing from the market. Though the daily movement of cash outflow is predictable from the past behaviour of withdrawals of FI, sudden demand due to some external factors beyond the FI's control may land the FI in liquidity crisis. Maintaining a high cash balance is not a profitable option to meet sudden demand of cash as cash does not earn any interest on it. When there is a liquidity crisis being faced in the overall economy, FI either sell it assets at a discounted price or raise money from market at higher rates to meet its sudden obligation. This in turn reduces FIs profitability and if the situation persists for a longer duration, FI's may be exposed to solvency risk.

Insolvency Risk

Insolvency risk is the risk that a FI may not have enough capital to offset a sudden decline in the value of its assets relative to its liabilities. Insolvency is a consequence or outcome of one or more of the risk described as interest rate, market, credit, foreign exchange, liquidity and country risk. Technically, insolvency occurs when the capital or equity resources of an FI's owner are driven to or near to zero due to the losses incurred as the result of one or more of the risk. The recent development in US in 2007 sub prime loans is the example of insolvency risk where large number of borrowers of mortgage loans started defaulting repayments. At the same time, due to default and recession in the US economy, there were no buyers of securitized assets when FIs wanted to sell to recover losses arising out of heavy provisions. Due to this situation, FI could not meet their obligations and the problem cumulated further when other players in the market refused to lend or roll over the funds to these FIs. The substantial defaults on sub prime loans combined with FIs inability to raise fresh funds resulted in a rapid deterioration of capital position of FIs. Many FIs were unable to survive out of insolvency risk and failed or were bought by other FIs in throwaway valuations. To avoid such a situation, regulators of various countries and Bank for

International Settlement (BIS) in BASEL II document emphasises on the need of adequate capital to cater to the insolvency risk.

Operational Risk

Operational risk is defined as the risk of loss resulting from inadequate or failed internal processes, people and systems, or from external events.[3] Operational risk arises if the internal process and procedures are not properly documented and examined. The check and balances should be incorporated in these procedures and also have to be properly examined to ensure that loopholes are not left so the advantage of it may be taken later on to breach the procedure. Banks and financial institutions have high magnitude of transactions, and identification of operational risks in advance and control processes to mitigate these risks are very critical. Operational risk arises due to inappropriate systems (losses due to inadequate or wrong systems and procedures), settlements (consequences of failed settlements), model risk (losses due to error in model), fraud risk (damage due to internal/external frauds), errors and omissions, legal risk (inappropriate documentation), regulatory risk (non-compliance with regulations), etc.

The following list details some event types with some examples for each category:

- Internal Fraud - Misappropriation of assets, tax evasion, intentional mismarking of positions, bribery, theft and embezzlement, payments without appropriate consideration, falsification of vouchers/records, misuse of vital stationery to create unauthorized documents, employee collusion and fraud.
- External Fraud – Theft of information, hacking damage, third-party theft and forgery, disbursements against false a securities, unauthorized diversion of credits followed by withdrawals.
- Employment Practices and Workplace Safety - Discrimination, workers compensation, employee health and safety, employment law, Industrial action.
- Clients, Products, & Business Practice - Market manipulation, antitrust, improper trade, product defects, fiduciary breaches, account churning.
- Damage to Physical Assets - Natural disasters, terrorism, vandalism, fire, theft.
- Business Disruption & Systems Failures - Utility disruptions, software failures, hardware failures, system capacity, system compatibility, security breach.
- Execution, Delivery, & Process Management - Data entry errors, accounting errors, failed mandatory reporting, negligent loss of client assets, reporting error, settlement/payment error, transaction error, valuation error.

Technology Risk

Technology and operational risks are closely related and is an area of major concern for every FI in techno era. Technology is the backbone of the business of banks and financial institutions. The major objectives of technological expansion are to lower operation cost and increasing operational efficiency of the system in order to capture new market and customers. Technology needs a lot of money, time and effort in order to be implemented. The objective is also to allow banks to exploit its maximum potential economies of scale and economies of scope in rendering services and selling of products. Economies of scale show bank's ability to lower its average costs of operations by expanding its output of financial services. Economies of scope show bank's ability to generate cost synergies by producing more than one output with the same input. Technology risk occurs when investment in some type of technology does not give desired results for good services and cost effectiveness. If the system implementation is too slow or the performance is ineffective due to redundant technology or organisational and bureaucratic inefficiencies, it brings diseconomies of scale. Diseconomies of scope arise when banks fail to achieve synergy or cost savings through new technology investment. In extreme cases, it could result in major losses in competitive efficiency and in longer run, it may have a very negative impact on the survival and growth of the organisation.

Off-Balance Sheet Risk

Due to many financial innovations such as derivatives and guarantee products, many FI's off-balance sheet activities has been growing tremendously in recent years and accordingly there has been an increase in their off-balance sheet risk. In addition to assets and liabilities on a bank's balance sheet, there are various transactions that do not increase the size of asset or liability at present, but could do so in the future. These can be called off-balance sheet items. While all FI's to some extent engage in off balance sheet activities, much attention has been drawn to the activities of banks. Instead, off balance sheet activities affect the future shape of an FI's balance sheet in that they involve the creation of contingent assets and liabilities, which give rise to their potential future placement on the balance sheet. Off balance sheet includes Letter of Credit, loan commitment by bank and positions in forwards, futures, swaps and other derivative securities. Banks also offer underwriting services for the issue of stocks and bonds. No liability arises at the time of underwriting for the bank. In case of a default, bank is required to pay up or subscribe to the under-subscribed portion. These liabilities or losses are not shown in the current balance sheet of the bank and the income arising from the fees for these services is recognised as current period income. Recently, in early 2008, many Indian banks booked heavy losses on derivative products which they had sold to corporates for foreign currency risk hedging. Initially while selling options, all banks charged premium income without taking effects on their balance sheet assets and liabilities. But later on, when products mature or go for premature settlement, banks book huge losses.

Summary

This chapter provides a detailed overview of different types of risks to which banks and financial institutions are exposed to. Banks face interest rate risk in their assets and liabilities mismatch. Banks are also exposed to market risk in their trading book and treasury for any adverse movement in market prices of the tradable securities. Banks main business is lending or investing in corporate bonds and thus face credit risk or default risk from the borrower side. With the heavy use of technology and bigger size organisation, regulatory laws, etc., banks are exposed to operational and technology risk. Banks having exposure in different currencies are also exposed to foreign exchange risk for adverse movement in exchange prices. In recent years, banks are heavily involved in off balance sheet activities thus leading banks to off balance sheet risk. Liquidity risk is another area of concern for banks which may prove costly in tight monetary position in the economy. These days most of the big banks are multinational and hence also carry sovereign or country specific risk. The solvency risk occurs when banks do not have adequate capital and reserves to support sudden financial shocks.

KEY CONCEPTS

Interest rate risk	Market risk	Credit risk
Default risk	Liquidity risk	Sovereign risk
Off balance sheet risk	Insolvency risk	Foreign Exchange risk
Technology risk		

Review Questions and Problems

1. How does a change in interest rates affect the valuation of assets and liabilities?
2. How does credit risk come into play when a bank invests in bonds or debentures issued by a corporate?
3. Is the product diversification a right strategy for credit risk exposure of an FI? Explain.
4. If a bank funds short term assets and long term liabilities, what would be the impact of interest fluctuation on its profitability?
5. One FI claims that it invests only in government securities of various countries which are free from default risk. Is it true? Explain why or why not.
6. State various conditions which have led the FIs to the market risk exposure.
7. Why are the banks lured to off balance sheet business and what are the risks involved in it?
8. What are the various key factors that drive foreign exchange rates?
9. Why are the returns on investments in domestic and foreign country not the same?
10. What are the various foreign exchange risks that a corporate is exposed to?
11. What are the key factors that need to be assessed for sovereign risk?
12. What are the institutional factors that need to be considered in assessing the emerging market risk in addition to the country risk?
13. If an FI is investing in highest rated foreign company, is it subject to sovereign risk? Explain.
14. How can liquidity risk trigger other risks?
15. In a falling interest rate scenario, if the average maturity of assets is longer than average liabilities, would the impact be favourable or unfavourable for the bank?
16. A mutual fund buys a bond of three years maturity few months ago. During this period, the value of bond increased but fund wants to hold the bond for further period of six months. What type of risks is the mutual fund is exposed to for the next six months?

17. What is the difference between technology and operational risk?
18. Why is operational risk gaining importance in different financial services organizations?
19. Will it give fair idea about risk profile of a bank only after studying the balance sheet? Explain.
20. What is credit risk? List the name of the FIs who are more exposed to this risk.
21. What are the internal and external factors for operational risk?
22. How are all risks discussed in chapter interrelated? Explain.

References:

1. *www.bis.org*
2. *www.rbi.org.in*
3. *Basel Committee on Banking Supervision "Overview of the New Capital Accord", BIS.*

PART B

Measurement of Risk

4. Measurement of Interest Rate Risk
5. Measurement of Market Risk
6. Measurement of Credit Risk
7. Measurement of Operational Risk & Technology Risk
8. Foreign Exchange Risk and Sovereign Risk
9. Liquidity Risk
10. Off Balance Sheet Risk

Chapter – 4

Measurement of Interest Rate Risk

Chapter Objective

- Understanding concept of rate sensitive assets and liabilities
- Measurement of interest rate risk through repricing gap model
- Learning the concept of maturity and duration
- Practical working of maturity and duration model
- Understanding the concept of modified duration
- Hedging interest rate risk through duration

Introduction

The FI's strength is measured in terms of Net Interest Income (NII) earned, which is the difference between interest income and interest expenditures. The interest rate fluctuations have direct impact on NII and Market Value of Equity (MVE) which is the net worth. The RBI's monetary policy to the extent decides the movement of interest rates in economy that affects the cost of borrowings and return on assets of an FI. The RBI through its daily open market operations (OMO), such as buying and selling of treasury bills and treasury bonds, controls money supply, inflation and short term interest rates.[1] Changes in interest rates also set pace of the economy of the country. These days, it is quite visible that changes in bank repo/reverse repo rates and Cash Reserve Ratio (CRR) are the measure tools with RBI to set the pace of the economy. For example, in year 2005, Indian economy grew with enormous pace as interest rate were at the lowest to the level of 6% p.a. for the loans. The lower level of interest rates increases the consumption in the economy or the spending level of individuals. At the same time, loans to corporates are available at lower rates which increase its profitability. But the above situation is sometimes followed by inflation and excess money supply in the economy which in turn gives initial sign of hardening of interest rates. The same has been observed in early 2008 when inflation had gone up to 3 years high to the level of 7.33% and interest rates had seen the level of 4 years high. The RBI is also increasing CRR on continuous basis since the last three credit policies.

If interest rate volatility over time is small, all FIs tend to gain from the situation. If interest rate volatility is higher, FIs will observe adverse impact on its NII and MVE. To measure interest rate volatility or risk, various models/methods have been evolved which mainly include the repricing gap model or interest rate sensitivity model, the maturity model and the duration model.

Repricing Gap Model

The repricing gap model is the cash flow analysis of the repricing gap between the interest revenue earned on assets of bank and the interest paid on its liabilities over a period of time. The different time buckets have been set for repricing gaps for assets and liabilities. These time buckets or maturities range from 1 month to 10 years and above. The different buckets are as under:[2]

1. 1 month
2. Above 1 month to 3 months
3. Above 3 months to 6 months
4. Above 6 months to 1 year
5. Above 1 year to 3 years
6. Above 3 years to 5 years
7. Above 5 years to 7 years
8. Above 7 years to 10 years
9. Above 10 years.

As per the requirements of an FI, the buckets may be broken in smaller periods but it is very difficult to manage a large number of buckets.

The following is the example of repricing gap model statement for bank/FI:

Buckets	1 month	Above 1 month to 3 months	Above 3 months to 6 months	Above 6 months to 1 year	Above 1 year to 3 years	Above 3 years to 5 years	Above 5 years to 7 years	Above 7 years to 10 years	Above 10 years
Rate Sensitive Assets (A)									
Rate Sensitive Liabilities (B)									
GAP (A-B)									
Cumulative Gap (CGAP)									

Under the repricing gap model, banks calculate gaps in each maturity bucket for all its Rate Sensitive Assets (RSAs) and Rate Sensitive Liabilities (RSLs). Rate Sensitive Assets and Liabilities means assets and liabilities that are repriced at prevailing market interest rate within the maturity bucket. The GAP points out bank's net interest income exposure to interest rate fluctuation in different buckets.

If for a bank Rate Sensitive Assets (RSAs) are greater than Rate Sensitive Liabilities (RSLs) (RSA>RSL), the gap is positive and if RSLs are less than RSAs (RSA<RSL), then the gap is called negative gap. A bank that has a positive gap will see its interest income rise if market interest rates rise, since more assets than liabilities will give this increase. A bank with a negative gap will be hurt by rising rates and benefit from falling rates. For example, an FI that issues a one year Certificate of Deposit (CD) and invested that fund in a three year AAA bond will see its net interest income eroded if interest rates rise in the first year, because it will have to roll over the CD at a higher rate, while the rate on the AAA bond will remain the same.

The same may also be calculated through the following formula:-

$$\Delta NII_i = (GAP_i)\,\Delta R_i = (RSA_i - RSL_i)\,\Delta R_i$$

Where:

ΔNII_i = Change in net interest income in i^{th} bucket

(GAP_i) = Rupee gap between RSAs and RSLs in maturity bucket i

ΔR_i = The change in the level of interest rate in the ith bucket

EXAMPLE: Calculation of Change in NII

Suppose for a bank, the negative gap in first bucket is Rs. 1,00,00,000.00 and short term interest rates rise by 1 percent, the net change in future interest income will be:

$$\Delta NII_i = (-1{,}00{,}00{,}000.00) \times .01 = -10{,}00{,}000.00$$

In the same manner, Cumulative Gap (CGAP) over various maturity buckets may be taken to see the interest rate change effect over a period of time. Say, CGAP (-ve) for 1 year is Rs. 10 crore and interest rate change is 1 percent:

$$\Delta NII_i = (CGAP)\,\Delta R_i = (-10 \text{ crore})(.01) = -1 \text{ crore}$$

Rate Sensitive Assets and Liabilities

For a FI manager, differentiation between rate sensitive assets & liabilities and non sensitive assets & liabilities is a very important factor while measuring interest rate risk. Few examples of rate sensitive and non-sensitive assets and liabilities are given as follows:

Rate Sensitive Assets	Rate Insensitive Assets	Rate Sensitive Liabilities	Rate Insensitive Liabilities
• Balances with other banks in India in deposit accounts, money at call and short notice and other placements • Investments • Bills of exchange, promissory notes, discounted & rediscounted • Term loans/corporate loans • Short term loans • Reverse Repos/ Forex-rupee swaps (buy/sell)/ Bills rediscounted • Interest rate swaps / FRAs	• Cash • Balance with RBI • Balances with other banks in India in current account • Equity shares, convertible, preference shares, shares of subsidiaries/joint ventures, venture capital units • Fixed assets (excluding assets on lease) • Intangible assets and items not representing cash flows	• Notes, bonds & debentures (Floating and Fixed rate) • Term deposits from public • Certificates of deposits and ICDs • Term-money borrowing • Borrowings from RBI, Government & others • Current liabilities and provisions • Interest payable on bonds/ deposits/borrowings • Repos/ bills rediscounted forex-rupee swaps (sell/buy) / interest rate swaps / FRAs	• Capital, Reserves & Surplus • Gifts, grants & benefactions • Advance income received • Receipts from borrowers pending adjustment • Provisions

Limitations of the Repricing Gap Model

The repricing gap model has few shortcomings like not taking into account the market value of assets and liability due to interest rate changes, cash flows arising out of rate insensitive assets and liabilities, pre mature withdrawal and prepayment and ignoring information regarding assets and liability maturing within the maturities buckets, and cash flows from off balance sheet activities.

The above model takes into account only book value of assets and liabilities while change in interest rates also affects the market value of assets and liabilities. In the buckets where range of period is more say 3-5 years, it may happen that a liability is maturing in the beginning of the bucket and asset is maturing at the end of the bucket. In such a situation, hedging strategy for interest rate risk will go wrong and the change in net interest income cannot be measured correctly. The cash flows arising out of non sensitive assets and liabilities is further reinvested in business at current prevailing rates, hence these are rate sensitive and ignoring these cash flows may give misleading gap information. Changes in interest rate also affects cash flow from Off Balance Sheet (OBS) items and repricing gap model does not consider OBS items. If an FI has taken derivative position to hedge against interest rate risk, the value of derivative product also changes with the changing interest rate. This has daily cash flows either positive or negative.

The Maturity Model

The maturity model originated due to the limitations of repricing gap model which takes only book value of assets and liabilities into account. The market value approach gives real value of assets and liabilities of an FI at which these may be liquidated not at the price these were actually acquired. This method of valuing the securities of an FI at their market value is known as Marking to Market (MTM) method. The maturity model takes into account the effects of interest rate changes on the market values of assets and liabilities of an FI.

EXAMPLE: Effect of interest rate change on the value of asset

Suppose an FI holding a bond of Rs.100 (F) has a coupon of 10% p.a. payable annually (C) and tenure of 1 year. The current yield to maturity (R) of same category of bond is 11%. The market value of bond will fall to:

$$P = (F+C)/(1+R) = (100+10)/1.11 = 99.10$$

i.e. the market value of bond has fallen from its face value of Rs. 100 to Rs. 99.10. The value of FI asset has fallen by 0.90% as interest rate has fallen by 1%.

In the above example, if the tenure of bond is more than 1 year, the value of bond will fall more for any increase to current yield to maturity. Thus maturity of asset has inverse relationship with rise in market yield on asset for value of asset i.e. the longer the maturity and an upward change in market yield will result in greater fall in the value of asset in comparison to the assets of shorter maturities.

CHART: The relationship between maturity of asset and market value of asset

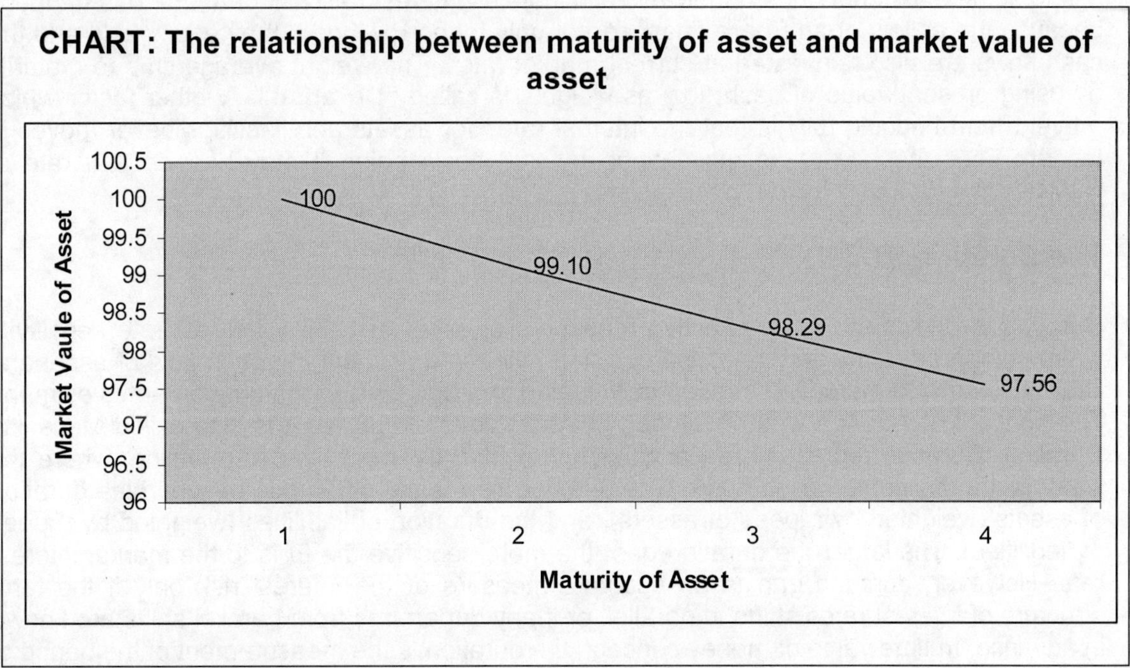

The same relationship is also true for portfolio of assets and liabilities of an FI. The net effect of rising and falling of interest rates on an FI's portfolio depends on the size and nature of mismatches (+ve or –ve) of maturities of its assets and liabilities. The outcome depends on whether **maturity gap (M_A-M_L)**, is greater than, equal to, or less than zero.

In case of banks and FIs, generally their assets are of longer maturities than the liabilities. The difference between the market value of assets (A) and the market value of liabilities (L) of an FI is its net worth or market value of equity MVE (E). The MVE is the true value of an FI if it is liquidated at current market price in the financial market. Hence, change in FI's MVE may be given as follows:

Change in MVE (ΔE) = Change in market value of asset (ΔA) – Change in market value of liabilities (ΔL) i.e. $\Delta E = \Delta A - \Delta L$

From the above formula, the impact of one percentage point change in interest rate on owner's equity may be calculated. With the help of this, interest rate shock analysis on the balance sheet of FI may be carried out to see the impact and risk bearing capacity of FI. Under interest rate shock analysis, the assets and liabilities are put on test for extreme changes in interest rate level in different time horizon to see the changes in FI's MVE at different interest rate levels.

To nullify the effect of maturity mismatches, the best way is to achieve a **(M_A-M_L)** = 0. By minimising the gap between weighted average maturity of assets and liabilities, the effects of interest rate risk may be minimised but may not be eliminated. While a strategy of matching of assets and liabilities maturities may provide hedging to some extent against interest rate risk to some extent but does not always eliminate all interest rate risk of an FI. This happens because the assets of an FI are financed not only by borrowings but by equity also and the cash flows are also reinvested at current market rates. The weight average time to maturity by using present value of cash flow as weights is called **"Duration"**. Another factor which prevent from hedging fully is that the interest rates for assets and liabilities never moves in tandem i.e if the rate of assets change by 200 basis point, it may happen that rate of liabilities changes only by 150 basis points.

The Duration Model

Duration is one of the most effective measures of asset or liability interest rate sensitivity when compared to maturity because duration takes into account the cash flow of asset and liability along with maturity. Duration is weighted average time to maturity on an investment. The concept of duration was developed by Macaulay in 1938, so it is also called Macaulay Duration. Duration represents an account's weighted average time to repricing, where the weights are discounted cash flows. The duration gap is the difference between the duration of assets (weighted by rupees of assets), and the duration of liabilities (weighted by rupees of liabilities). The larger the duration gap, the more sensitive the FI is to the market interest rate. However, duration gap is an accurate measure of the interest risk only if the term structure of interest rates shifts in parallel, or if any departures from parallel shifts are known in advance. In time value of money concept, the duration is the measurement of the period of time required to recover initial investment on the loan. Any cash flow received by FI on loan is treated as repayment of principal till the time it is fully paid and thereafter cash flows are profit or return earned by FI till the maturity.

EXAMPLE: Calculation of Duration for Investment

Suppose an FI invested Rs.100 in bond has a coupon rate of 15% p.a. payable semi-annually along with half of the principal and the maturity of investment is one year. The duration of loan will be:

Duration (D) = $W_{1/2}$ (t/2)+ W_1 (t) where t = 1 year and W is weight of cash flows

$W_{1/2} = (PV_{1/2})/(PV_{1/2} + PV_1)$

$W_1 = (PV_1)/(PV_{1/2} + PV_1)$

Where PV is the present value of cash flow at time ½ and 1.

$PV_{1/2}$ = 57.50/(1.075) = 53.49

PV_1 = $57.50/(1.075)^2 = 46.51$

For above investment, there are two cash flows of Rs.57.50 each paid semi-annually including interest and principal.

$W_{1/2}$ = 53.49/100 = .5349

W_1 = 46.51/100 = .4651

Hence, **Duration(D) = .5349 X (1/2) + .4651 X (1) = .7326 years (approximately 9 months)**

Whereas the maturity of investment is one year.

If the above investment is financed by one year deposit where payment is to be made annually, the duration of deposit would be one year. To understand how an FI is exposed to interest rate risk where maturity of deposit and investment is equal, we have to calculate the duration. In this case duration of deposit is one year and duration of investment is 0.7326. The duration gap is 0.2674. Now it is very clear that maturity gap is not a correct method to measure and hedge interest rate risk and FIs need to rely on duration gap method. Duration equals to maturity where there is no interim payment and the payment is limited to one at the end of maturity.

Formula for Duration for n cash flows:

$$D = \left(\sum_{t=1}^{N} PV_t \times t\right) / \left(\sum_{t=1}^{N} PV_t\right)$$

D = **Duration measured in years**

PV_t = **Present value of cash flow at the end of the period t**

N = **Last period in which cash flow is received**

t = **Time of cash flow**

Characteristics of Duration:

- The duration increases with the maturity of a fixed interest asset or liability but at a decreasing rate.
- The duration increases with falling yield and decreases with increasing yield.
- The higher is the coupon rate of security, the lower is the duration.
- The duration is a measure of interest elasticity that gives the change in the value of security due to percentage change in interest rate. This can be calculated numerically as **$\Delta P = -D (\Delta R/1+R)$**. The relationship also shows that price of bond is inversely proportional to change in interest rate. The equation may also be written as **$\Delta P = -MD \Delta R$**. Here **MD** is called Modified Duration i.e. duration divided by 1 plus the interest rate and is given as **$MD = D/(1+R)$**. The modified duration immediately gives changes in price of security by simply multiplying modified duration with simple change in interest rates rather than the discounted change in interest rate.

FIs may adopt strategy on the basis of duration gap analysis to hedge interest rate risk. Instead of matching maturities of assets and liabilities, the emphasis should be on matching of duration of assets and liabilities. For this purpose, duration of all assets and liabilities should be calculated maturing in different buckets and duration gap should be calculated. The duration of the asset or liability portfolio may be calculated by multiplying duration of individual asset and its proportion in total market value of assets or liability.

EXAMPLE: Interest Rate Risk Hedging through Duration Gap

The efforts of FIs is to minimize ΔE (change in net worth) due to interest rate shock, which may be calculated as under:

$\Delta E = -(D_A - D_L k) \times A \times (\Delta R/1+R)$

where

$k = L/A$ = Liabilities/Assets

$(D_A - D_L k)$ = Adjusted duration gap

$(\Delta R/1+R)$ = Interest Rate Shock

Suppose for an FI D_A = 5 years and D_L = 3 year, ΔR = 1%, R = 10%, k= 0.9, A = 100 crores and L = 90 crores.

$\Delta E = -(5-0.9*3)x100x(.01/1.1) = -2.09$ crore

It means a percentage change in interest rate from 10 to 11% will result in change in net worth of FI by Rs. 2.09 crore. FI has to minimize ΔE or bring $\Delta E = 0$ by rearranging its assets and liability size or duration. If FI reduces its D_A = 2.7 years, then $\Delta E = 0$ and if FI increases its D_L = 5.55, then $\Delta E = 0$, or reduce D_A = 4 and increase D_L = 4.44, then $\Delta E = 0$, or change k = 0.95 and increase D_L = 5.26, then $\Delta E = 0$. Various such strategies may be worked out on the basis of duration gap analysis.

Global Interest Rate Risk

Different fixed income markets are exposed to their own sources of risk. The Japanese government bond market is exposed to yen interest rates. The price and yield volatilities are different in different countries market. The yields of bond are primarily driven by inflationary expectations, which is a similar concept across all markets. Central Banks across all countries have common determination to keep inflation in check. As recently US Federal Reserve Bank Chairman, Ben Bernanke, has announced that they will not change policy rate for another two years and will keep it at minimum, posing a straight challenge to Subba Roa, Governor, RBI who has revised its key rate i.e. Repo and Reverse-Repo 4-5 times in last one-year's time. This great dividing difference in interest rate policy of two major countries propels waves of global interest rate risk.

Summary

This chapter deals with three methods of measuring of interest rate risk exposure of bank and FI, i.e repricing gap model, maturity model and duration gap model. The repricing model measures interest rate risk exposure of bank by considering gap between rate sensitive assets and liabilities. The maturity model measures interest rate risk by using difference between maturity of assets and liabilities. Both these models have difficulty in measuring interest rate risk exposure accurately. The repricing model does not take interest rate change in account while assessing exposure. The maturity model does not take into account the timing of cash flows of assets and liabilities. These two difficulties are overcome to a large extent by using duration gap model. The duration gap model takes care of timing of cash flows of assets and liabilities and also takes care of interest rate sensitivity. By using duration gap method, banks can hedge whole balance sheet against interest rate risk exposure.

KEY CONCEPTS

OMO	NII	MVE	CRR
RSA	RSL	Maturity Gap	Repricing Gap
CGAP	Maturity Buckets	MTM, Duration	Duration Gap
Modified Duration			

Review Questions and Problems

1. In what ways RBI monetary policy affects interest rate scenario in the economy?
2. Work out the rate sensitive assets and liabilities of four different nature of FIs with the help of balance sheet.
3. What do you mean by maturity bucket in the repricing model?
4. What is difference between book value and market value of assets and liabilities?
5. What are the various limitations of repricing model and how can these be overcome?
6. Is it possible to hedge perfectly by matching maturities of assets and liabilities?

7. What is the maturity gap? How can the maturity gap model be utilized for hedging against interest rate risk?
8. What is the price of bond with a face value of Rs.1 lac with 10% annual coupon rate? The current market yield is 14%.
9. Why is duration considered as a more effective method for interest rate sensitivity than maturity model?
10. What is the duration of a five-year Rs.1 lac bond with a 15 percent coupon payable quarterly and principal at maturity? What is the duration if current market yield is 12%?
11. A 5 years deposit of Rs.10000 pays interest of 8% p.a. payable annually. What is the duration of deposit? What is the duration of deposit, if period is extended to 7 years and market yield to maturity is 10%?
12. How is duration an indicator of interest rate elasticity? What is the relationship between duration and maturity?
13. The price of a bond fell from Rs.10000 to Rs.9500 when market yield rose from the level of 10% to 12%. What is the duration of bond?
14. Identify the strategies being used to hedge interest rate risk in duration gap model.
15. A 10 year, 10% annual coupon bond is traded at a YTM 8%. What is the duration and modified duration of bond?
16. What is the advantage of calculating modified duration and how is this useful for hedging of interest rate risk?
17. Calculate the repricing gap and the impact on NII of a 2% decrease in interest rates for (i) RSAs of Rs. 300 crores and RSLs of Rs. 200 crores; (ii) RSAs of Rs. 200 crores and RSLs of Rs. 300 crores; (iii) RSAs of Rs. 500 crores and RSLs of Rs. 500 crores.
18. Calculate the impact on NII of the above situation, assuming 3% increase in interest rates. Also, draw the conclusion for above repricing models.
19. Assume a 10 years, 10% annual coupon bond with a required return of 12%. The bond has a face value of Rs.10000. Calculate (i) price of the bond; (ii) If interest rate rise to 15%, price of bond; (iii) percentage change in price of bond if ROI increases by 2%; (iv) recalculate (i), (ii) & (iii) for a bond having maturity of 25 years; (v) What reference you draw in change of price of bond?
20. Assume a 7 years, 15% annual coupon bond with a face value of Rs.50000 is trading at a market yield to maturity of 10%. Calculate (i) the price of the bond; (ii) if YTM increases by 2%, what will be the new price of bond.
21. A commercial bank has Rs. 200 crores in cash and Rs.1800 crores loan portfolio. On the liability side bank has Rs.180 crores demand deposits, Rs.1620 crores corporate deposits and Rs. 200 crores equity capital. The loan portfolio has maturity of 5 years, earns interest @ 10% p.a., and amortise quarterly. The bank pays 8% on corporate deposits having maturity of 3 years and the payment of

interest is made at the time of maturity. Calculate (i) maturity gap for bank; (ii) Assess interest rate sensitivity for bank; (iii) change in MVE if there is decline or increase of market rate of interest by 2%.

22. A mutual fund company has invested in the following fixed income securities: (i) Rs. 50 crores of 5 years T-Notes @5% p.a. selling at par in the market; (ii) Rs. 52 crores of 10 years bonds paying 8% interest with par value of Rs. 50 crores and (iii) Rs. 60 crores of 12 years debentures paying 10% interest with par value of Rs. 55 crores. Calculate (a) weighted-average maturity of portfolio of assets; (b) change in weighted-average maturity for a decline or increase of yield on securities by 2%; (c) effect on MVE of company for interest rate movement given at (b).
23. XYZ bank had issued a 2 years Rs.100 crores CD paying 8% to make a loan for 2 years paying an interest rate of 10%. The principal of loan will be repaid in four half-yearly installments of Rs.25 crores each. Calculate (i) maturity gap of the bank; (ii) NII at the end of every year; (iii) effect on annual NII of a 3% interest rate increase or decrease immediately after loan is disbursed.
24. Two bonds are available in the market for investment. The first bond is a 5 years Rs. 50000 bond carrying 10% p.a. rate of interest and the second bond is a 5 years zero coupon bond of Rs. 50000. Calculate duration of above bonds for YTM of 8%, 10% and 12% p.a.
25. A 5 years Rs.100 crores loan carries a market rate of interest of 15%. The repayment of loan to be made on quarterly basis in 20 installments along with interest due every quarter. Calculate (i) duration of loan; (ii) the cash flow at the end of each year; (iii) the present value of each cash flow at the market rate of 12%; (iv) present value of loan at market rate of 18%; (v) the proportion of cash flow occurs at the end of each year.
26. A mutual fund company wants to invest in three bonds, which have 5 years maturity and trade at a YTM of 10%. The coupons of these bonds are 8%, 10% and 12%. Calculate (i) duration of each bond; (ii) plot the relationship between the duration and coupon of these bonds.
27. A borrower wishes to obtain a loan of Rs.100 lacs @12% for 5 years. He has a choice of paying principal at the end of 5 years or paying installment of interest and principal in equal payments at the end of each year for 5 years. Calculate the duration of the loan under both the methods of payment and analyse the difference in the two results.
28. Calculate the duration of 3 years, Rs.10000 bond that pays an annual coupon of 12% and trades at a yield of 10%. What would be the change in the price of bond if rate of interest increase or decrease by 1%?

References:

1. *www.rbi.org.in*
2. *RBI Guidelines on ALM for Banks.*

Chapter – 5

Measurement of Market Risk

Chapter Objective

- Understand market risk exposure
- Concept of DEAR, VaR, CFAR
- Value at risk methodology
- Methods and formulas of calculation of VaR
- Compare different methods of VaR calculations
- Back Testing VaR
- Discuss model of market risk measurement like RiskMetrics
- Focus on various tests for market risk measurement

Introduction

The immense trading activities and worldwide FIs and banks participation in trading activities in big way have attracted everybody concerned with the financial market be it analysts, regulators or investors. Major FIs worldwide incurred heavy losses due to trading activities and some of them even had faced bankruptcy or insolvency. Few examples of those who faced major losses are JP Morgan, Citigroup, Merrill Lynch etc. FIs in different countries are not an exception to these and they virtually faced bankruptcy due to trading activities. The famous case in this category is Barings, the British merchant bank which was forced into insolvency due to losses arising out of trading activities. The list does not end here, Daiwa Bank and one of the largest loss ever of $2.6 billion incurred by Sumitomo Corporation, Japanese Bank, LTCM and Bank of America etc. are among the banks/FIs who suffered major losses due to trading activities. The major concern of market risk is insolvency threat to FIs/banks due to trading losses.

Generally, FIs/banks maintain two kinds of books for their investments, one is trading book and the other is banking book. Under the trading book, those assets, liabilities and derivative contracts are kept which are being bought or sold in the market quickly. The tradable assets and liabilities under trading book are hold generally for a period of less than one year. For some banks, this period may be more shorter depending on the banks policy. The assets and liabilities in trading book are of highly liquid nature which may be bought or sold quickly and may be converted in cash. Contrary to this, under banking book, assets and liabilities are held for a longer period (generally more than one year) and consist of less liquid assets and liabilities. The banking book mostly contains all loans and deposits of the banks.

Financial innovations in recent years have made every asset and liability tradable in the market such as securitisation. Hence, there is a thin line differentiation between trading and banking book on the basis of time horizon for holding assets and liabilities. The terminology used for trading and banking books is Held for Trading (HFT) or Available for Sale (AFS) and Held till Maturity (HTM) category respectively.

The market risk is the risk arising due to changes in market parameters such as market volatility, liquidity, currency fluctuation, interest rates change or economic slowdown, etc. impacting FI's earnings out of its trading activities or changing value of assets and liabilities. The market risk arises for trading and not for banking book where assets and liabilities are kept for longer period and not for trading purposes. For an FI, more reliance on the earnings through trading activities rather than traditional activities of borrowing and lending is more exposed to market risk.

The market risk measurement is very important for financial solvency of an FI because it provides various vital information to management for decision making such as risk exposure vis-à-vis capital resources of an FI. This also gives information regarding activity wise risk exposure and resources allocated so that the management may reduce resource allocation to risky activity and may divert resources to profitable and less risky activity. The market risk is measured in terms of **Value at Risk (VaR) or Earnings at Risk (EaR) and Daily Earnings at Risk (DEAR)**. There are six common approaches to measure market risks, which are RiskMetrics, Historic or Back Simulation, Monte Carlo Simulation, Stress Testing, Scenario Analysis and Sensitivity Analysis.

The RiskMetrics Model[1]

The main objective of market risk management model is the prediction of next day losses if tomorrow is a bad day for business activities in a single number. With this objective, J P Morgan in 1994 first developed RiskMetrics. The RiskMetrics initially made the risk measure available for 300 financial instruments across 14 countries. The data represent an elaborate variance/covariance matrix of risk and correlation measures that evolved through time. The RiskMetrics is available for free and user need computer software to integrate the RiskMetrics system with own positions. RiskMetrics takes a pragmatic approach to modelling risk. Variances are modeled using exponentially weighted moving average (EWMA) forecast. The exponential model is particularly easy to implement because it relies on one parameter only. RiskMetrics provides risk forecasts over monthly horizons, defined as 25 trading days. The one-day exponential model is used to extrapolate volatility over next day, then the next, and so on until the twenty-fifth day ahead. The RiskMetrics is not the substitute for good management, experience and judgment. It is a toolbox, not a black box.

The market risk exposure of an FI on a daily basis may be measured by using RiskMetrics approach. The FI's main concern is that how much it can potentially lose if market conditions move adversely tomorrow. It means market risk is equal to estimated potential loss under adverse circumstances.

The market risk in the terms of FI's Daily Earning at Risk (DEAR) has three measurable components:

Daily Earnings at Risk (DEAR)	**=**	**(Rupee market value of the position)**	**×**	**(Price sensitivity of the position)**	**×**	**(Potential adverse move in yield)**

Since price sensitivity multiplied by adverse yield move measures the degree of price volatility of an asset, the equation above may be written as:

Daily Earnings At Risk (DEAR) = (Rupee market value of the position) × (Price volatility)
Daily Price Volatility = (Price sensitivity to a small change in yield) x (Adverse daily yield move) = (-MD) x (Adverse daily yield move)

EXAMPLE: The Market Risk of Fixed Income Securities

Suppose a bank has a Rs. 68.06 crore market value position in deep discount bonds of 5 years maturity with a face value of Rs.100 crore. The current market yield is 8% p.a. and potential adverse move in yield is 0.00165 (5% chances (1 bad day in 20 days) of yield change at 90% level of confidence following normal distribution with standard deviation of 10 basis point). The bank wants to measure daily earnings at risk on above bond due to an adverse move in interest rate next day.
Modified Duration = D/(1+R) = 5/(1.08) = 4.63
Price Volatility = (-4.63) x (0.00165) = - 0.00764 = 0.764%
DEAR = (Rs.68.06 crore) x (-0.00764) = -Rs.0.52 crore
Hence bank may lose Rs.52 lac if tomorrow is a bad day in next 20 days.

The same may be extended to N days. If assumption is drawn that yield shock is independent, the bond is not illiquid, daily volatility will remain constant and bank will hold the asset for N number of days, then N-day market value at risk will be:

VaR = DEAR x √N

DEAR = (Rupee value of position) X (β) X 1.65σ

β = the systematic risk of the security;

1.65 σ = standard deviation at 90th percentile

If N = 10, for the above example VaR = Rs.52 lac x √10 = Rs.164.44 lac

There is need of calculating VaR in place of DEAR because illiquid market conditions may increase losses as it may take many days in offloading the positions.

Value at Risk (VaR)

The term Value at Risk (VaR) was coined by Guldimann in late 1980s. In the year 1993, the Group of Thirty (G-30)[2] found VaR as a best practice for dealing with risk. Since then, VaR has revolutionized market risk measurement for financial institutions. Later on, this concept has been extended to other risks such as credit risk, foreign exchange risk and operational risk.

VaR is defined as an estimate of potential loss in a position or asset/liability or portfolio of assets/liabilities over a given holding period at a given level of certainty. Risk is defined as the probability of the unexpected happening minus the probability of suffering a loss. VaR is an estimate of the loss likely to be suffered, not the actual loss. The actual loss may be different from the estimate. It measures the potential loss, not the potential gain. Risk management tools measure potential loss as risk has been defined as the probability of suffering a loss. VaR measures the probability of loss for a given time period over which the position is held. The given time period could be one day, few days, few weeks or an year. VaR will change if the holding period of the position changes. The holding period for an instrument/position will depend on the liquidity of the instrument/market. With the help of VaR, we can say that with varying degrees of certainty, the potential loss will not exceed a certain amount. This means that VaR will change with different levels of certainty.

The following table describes the three main methodologies to calculate VaR:

Methodology	Estimation	Appropriateness
Parametric	Estimates VaR with equation that specifies parameters such as volatility, correlation, delta, and gamma	Accurate for traditional assets and linear derivatives, but less accurate for non linear derivatives
Monte Carlo simulation	Estimates VaR by simulating random scenarios and revaluing positions in the portfolio	Appropriate for all types of instruments - linear and nonlinear
Historical simulation	Estimates VaR by reliving history	Takes actual historical rates and revalues positions for each change in the market

VaR is a method of assessing risk using standard statistical techniques. It is the maximum loss over a target horizon such that there is a low, predetermined probability that the actual loss will be larger. VaR has a scientific basis and provides users with a summary measure of market risk. For instance, an FI says that the daily VaR of its trading portfolio is INR 5 crore at the 99% level of confidence, it means that there is only one chance in a hundred under normal market conditions, that a loss greater than this amount will occur. This number summarises the bank's exposure to market risk as the probability of an adverse move. It measures risk using the same units as the bank's domestic currency.

There are three main approaches for measuring VaR:

1. The Variance/Covariance matrix approach
2. Historical or Back simulation approach
3. Monte Carlo simulation approach

All three approaches require a statement of three basic parameters:

- Holding period,
- Confidence interval, and
- The historical time horizon over which the asset prices are observed.

The Variance/Covariance Matrix Approach

Variance-Covariance approach is a method that calculates the parameters underlying a profit and loss distribution, i.e. mean and standard deviation, in order to come up with the potential loss of an asset or portfolio, given a holding period and confidence level. After deriving the mean and standard deviation, statistical theory is applied to come up with a VaR estimate. This is the reason it is referred to as Variance-Covariance approach. Depending on the type of instruments comprising a portfolio, Variance-Covariance approach could further be broken down to the delta-normal and delta-gamma approaches. The delta-normal approach takes on a linear relationship between the risk factor movements and the changes in the value of the portfolio. On the other hand, the delta-gamma approach recognizes the presence of non-linearities, e.g., options, and takes additional factors into consideration via second-order derivatives.

Delta-Normal Method

The delta-normal method is a Variance-Covariance approach that arrives at the VaR after building a distribution of profit and loss values based on an assumption of a linear relationship between the value of a position and the movements of underlying risk factors. A further assumption is that such risk factor movements follow a normal distribution. Consequently, the resulting distribution of values is also normal. This denotes the effect of a change in one unit of the risk factors. Arriving at the total value changes and their mean will require further operations. The task involved in VaR calculation is the determination of the mean and variance of these values. The mean of the distribution should be the sum of all the expected portfolio value changes. Risk mapping, for instance, is a Risk Metric's methodology that reduces the instruments within the portfolio into simple, approximating instruments, whose sensitivities are estimated. This avoids the task of computing numerous variances.

Given the assumptions, parametric VaR is relatively fast and easy to compute and not too prone to model risk. The data requirements are also considerably attainable. The standard deviation provides far more information than mere quantiles based on values taken from history or a random generation function. Moreover, in terms of utility theory-based analysis, this is the only VaR approach that does not violate the rational ranking of choices based on expected utility value.

Delta-Gamma Method

The delta-gamma method is a Variance-Covariance approach that recognizes non-linear relationships in an instrument or portfolio by adding additional factors into the profit/loss equation that capture non-linear behavior. Under the delta-gamma method, the non-linear relationships are first estimated and then inputted into the linear equation as an approximation of the non-linearities. Non-linear relationships are for example present in portfolios containing options. The value of the portfolio is thereby dependent on the underlying value of the variable upon which the contained option is dependent. These non-linearities are captured by means of a Taylor expansion. Not just the delta or the sensitivity of the portfolio of the risk factor is required, the option gamma or its second order term is also calculated.

Historical or Back Simulation Approach

Historical or Back Simulation is a numerical approach of calculating the VaR of an asset or portfolio for a specified holding period and confidence level that takes past data on the movements of underlying risk factors to determine the probable returns. The whole calculation process arrives at a series of profit and loss figures. The value at the specified quantile is the absolute VaR.

If, for example, VaR is to be calculated for a portfolio, given a 95% confidence interval and using a historical simulation of risk factor movements covering 100 days, then the historical simulation VaR would be the value of the 95th percentile of all the derived values. In other words, it is the 96th worst value of the portfolio returns calculated. To arrive at this, the risk factors are first inputted into the valuation formula of the portfolio to yield hypothetical mark-to-market values of the portfolio. This could include an exchange rate, an interest rate, etc. Meanwhile, the current value of the portfolio at the analysis date is also derived. This current value is then subtracted from each of the 100 historically simulated values. These are ranked from highest to lowest. The 96th worst value of the ranked values is the potential loss that should not be exceeded with 95% certainty.

The generalized procedure is as follows:

1. Take a portfolio and determine its current value at the analysis date by inputting the actual parameters of the identified risk factors into the appropriate valuation formula.

2. Choose a confidence level and holding period for which the potential loss will be determined.

3. Take a set of historical risk factor values appropriate or significant for the holding period chosen. Input these historical values into the valuation

formula of the portfolio. As a result, hypothetical mark-to-market values will be calculated.

4. Subtract the current value of the portfolio from the hypothetical mark-to-market values. This yields the profit and loss values of the portfolio.
5. Rank the profit and loss values. The value at the chosen confidence level is the VaR per historical simulation.

Historical simulation is relatively easy to implement and takes on a full valuation of all positions in its VaR computation, while using only one sample path. There is no modeling or approximation of some sort. But the calculation could quickly become complicated for large portfolios with complex structures. On the other hand, if the sample size is too small, then an estimation error could ensue. Another point against its credibility is the use of historical data to forecast future risk factor movements. It is assumed that historical risk factor movements would capture future risk factor movements, and thus, taking historical data is justifiable. There is an element of realism here because historical trends could actually repeat. But taking a sample of values arbitrarily will also have its effects. The results depend heavily on the set of variables chosen. Moreover, an analyst is lucky if all the values corresponding to the number of days chosen are available.

Monte Carlo Simulation Approach

Also a numerical approach, Monte Carlo simulation bears some similarities with the approach applied by historical simulation. The difference is that historical data are not taken. A random generator of variables is instead made use of to come up with data on risk factor movements. Thus, Monte Carlo simulation is a method that calculates the potential loss of an asset or portfolio for a defined holding period and confidence level by introducing randomly generated risk factor movements to come up with profit and loss values.

For example, a random set of 100 risk factor values is taken that will be inputted into the valuation formula of a portfolio, whose VaR is to be calculated with a 95% confidence level. After subtracting the current value of the portfolio from the resulting simulation values, a series of profit and loss values is derived. The Monte Carlo VaR would be the value at the 95th percentile. In other words, it is the 96th worst value of the portfolio returns that we have calculated. This is the potential loss that should not be exceeded with 95% certainty.

The general procedure is summed up as follows:

1. Take a portfolio and determine its current value on the analysis date by inputting the actual parameters of the identified risk factors into the appropriate valuation formula.
2. Choose a confidence level and holding period for which the potential loss will be determined.
3. Run the random generator and value the portfolio using a number of parameters that is appropriate for the holding period chosen. As a result, hypothetical values of the portfolio will be yielded.
4. Subtract the current value of the portfolio from the simulated values. This yields the profit and loss values of the portfolio.

5. Rank the profit and loss values. The value at the chosen confidence level is the VaR per Monte Carlo simulation.

This is said to be the most powerful method to compute the VaR. If non-linear relationships are involved in the portfolio, the use of Monte Carlo simulation will better accomplish the VaR estimation. If the number of variables were large enough, the resulting values would capture the profit and loss distribution well. Unlike other VaR analysis that provide only a static consideration of value changes, Monte Carlo simulation allows for dynamic developments in the variables as well as the portfolio composition. It is a very open and comprehensive approach in measuring market risk, if the modeling were correct. The calculation is however tedious (but less tedious than non-VaR-based methodologies). Since it involves several variables, it requires resources, e.g., computer power, that could tackle this effortlessly.

VaR is used as a MIS tool in the trading portfolio to "slice and dice" risk by levels/ products/geographic/level of organisation etc. It is also used to set risk limits. In its strategic perspective, VaR is used for decisions like what business to do and what not to do. However VaR as a useful MIS tool has to be "back tested" by comparing each day's VaR with actuals and necessary re-examination of assumptions needs to be made so as to be close to reality. VaR, therefore, cannot substitute sound management judgement, internal control and other complementary methods. It is used to measure and manage market risks in trading portfolio and investment portfolio.

VaR should be used in combination with "stress testing" to take care of event risks. Stress test takes into account the worst case scenario.Backtests compare realized trading results with model generated risk measures, both to evaluate a new model and to reassess the accuracy of existing models. Although no single methodology for backtesting has been established, banks using internal VaR models for market risk capital requirements must backtest their models on a regular basis. Banks should generally backtest risk models on a monthly or quarterly basis to verify accuracy. In these tests, they should observe whether trading results fall within pre-specified confidence bands as predicted by the VaR models. If the models perform poorly, they should probe further to find the cause (e.g., check integrity of position and market data, model parameters, methodology).

Comparison of Methods

	Variance/ Covariance Matrix Approach	Historical or Back Simulation Approach	Monte Carlo Simulation Approach
Holding period and confidence level	Determined as required by the analysis; results are thereby affected by the choice	Determined as required by the analysis; results are thereby affected by the choice	Determined as required by the analysis; results are thereby affected by the choice
Risk factor movements	Normally distributed	Based on historical values	Based on a random generation function

VaR calculation	The value at the specified quantile of the profit and loss distribution; the difference between the mean and the chosen quantile value of the assumed normal distribution	The value at the specified quantile of the profit and loss distribution; the difference between the current value and the chosen quantile value of the historical distribution of values	The value at the specified quantile of the profit and loss distribution; the difference between the current value and the chosen quantile value of the simulated distribution of values
Communicability	Easy	Easy	Easy
Level of difficulty of calculation	Easy; complication arises when the number of assets increase	Easy; complication arises for complex structures	Easy; complication arises for complex structures
Infrastructure/ data requirements	Surmountable	Surmountable	Requires powerful calculation systems

Other VaR Formulas

1. VaR = Market value of position X Modified Duration X Worst yield increase

For example, market value of an asset of Rs.100 crores having modified duration of 13.5 and if the worst increase in yield at 95% level is 1.65%, VaR of asset would be

VaR = 100 X 13.5 X 0.00165 = Rs.22 crores

It means the worst loss at the 95% confidence level is approx. Rs.22 crores.

2. If we know one day VaR of any security or portfolio, the VaR for n days may be calculated by using formula given below:

VaR (N days) = VaR (1 day) X $\sqrt{N}$

3. The Basel Committee allows 10-day VaR at 99% confidence interval based on one-year historical data to decide for market risk capital charges. The formula to calculate 10-day VaR is given below:

VaR (10 days,99%) = VaR (1 day,99%) X $\sqrt{10}$

Shortcomings of Value at Risk

- It does not describe the worst loss; for example, in VaR calculation with 99% confidence, there is a one in hundred possibility that actual loss will exceed VaR estimates.

- It does not describe the distribution of losses.
- VaR itself is subject to some sampling variation; a different sample period or a period with a different length could lead to different VaR numbers.

Cash Flow at Risk

Cash Flow at Risk (CFAR) measures worst shortfall in cash flow due to unfavourable movement in market risk factors. This involves quantities, Q, unit revenue, P, and unit cost, C. In equation form, we can write:

$$CF = Q \times (P-C)$$

If we take exchange rate, S, as market risk factor, each of these variables may be affected by S. Revenue and cost may be denominated in the foreign currency, partially or wholly. Quantities can also be affected by the exchange rate through foreign competition effects. Because quantities are random, this creates quantity uncertainty. The relationship between quantities and risk factors needs to be established. Once this is done, simulations can be used to project the cash flow distribution and identify the worst loss at some confidence level. Accordingly, FI may decide whether to hedge, and if so, the best instrument to use for hedging.

Example of the above is the value of a farmer's harvest. At the beginning of the year, cost are fixed and do not contribute to risk. The price of wheat and the size of harvest are unknown if price movements are driven by supply shocks, such as the weather. If there is a drought during summer, quantities will fall and price will rise. Conversely, if there is an exceptionally abundant harvest, quantities will increase and prices will fall. Because of negative correlation between Q and P, total revenues will fluctuate less than when the quantities were fixed. Such relationships need to be factored into the risk measurement system because they will affect the hedging program.

Stress testing

Stress testing can be considered over longer horizons—a week, two weeks, a quarter or even a year. Stress testing has been adopted as a generic term describing various techniques used by banks to gauge their potential vulnerability to exceptional, but plausible, events. Stress testing addresses the large moves in key market variables, which lie beyond day-to-day risk monitoring but can potentially occur. The process of stress testing, therefore, involves first identifying these potential movements, including which market variables to stress, how much to stress them by, and what time frame to run the stress analysis over. Once these market movements and underlying assumptions are decided upon, shocks are applied to the portfolio. Revaluing the portfolios allows one to see what the effect of a particular market movement has on the value of the portfolio and the overall profit and loss. Stress test reports can be constructed that summarise the effects of different shocks of different magnitudes. Stress testing is mostly used in managing market risk, which deals primarily with traded market portfolios. These portfolios include interest rate, equity, foreign exchange, and commodity instruments and are amenable to stress testing because their market prices are updated on a regular basis. Stress tests produce information summarising the firm's exposure to extreme, but possible, circumstances.

Stress testing achieves very different risk management objective as compared to VaR. Its purpose is to examine the impact of extreme events on the portfolio. This test thus deals with the ability of the business to survive extreme conditions and implement changes in strategy. It provides a deeper understanding of the risk and thereby prepares a ground for better protection. This can also be better assessed before the business becomes involved. Risk management must envisage extreme events and factor the risks caused by them. Stress testing deals with these events. There are various events and factors on which stress test may be conducted. A crisis in one market gets passed on to other markets and normal correlations go haywire. All markets get highly correlated with each other and accentuate the risk. Under normal circumstances, concentration allows market leadership. However, in extreme conditions, it creates the risk of a near fatal loss. Stress tests are carried out with reference to some extreme events such as shifts in yield curve, interest rate differential, currency devaluation, volatility, price shift, liquidity and credit tightening.

Under stress test, historical event analysis is also put on test as extreme event may occur again. A scenario based on historical events is developed and the outcome for such scenarios is examined. Scenarios are also developed based on the events relevant to the bank or institutional portfolio. Extreme standard deviation scenarios are also tested to know what could happen if the returns vary by 5σ, 6σ, 10σ standard deviations. Extreme incremental events and tail risk and quantitative evaluation of tail events are also examined to see if there is any pattern in the tail events and uses the results in scenario analysis.

Scenario Analysis

A scenario analysis specifies the shocks that might plausibly affect a number of market risk factors simultaneously if an extreme, but possible, event occurs. It seeks to assess the potential consequences for a firm for an extreme, but possible, state of the world. A scenario analysis can be based on an historical event or a hypothetical event. Historical scenarios employ shocks that occurred in specific historical episodes. Hypothetical scenarios use a structure of shocks thought to be plausible in some foreseeable, but unlikely circumstances for which there is no exact parallel in recent history. Scenario analysis is currently the leading stress testing technique. Scenario stress tests are generally based on either a portfolio-driven approach or an event-driven approach. In event-driven scenarios, the scenario is formulated based on plausible events and how these events might affect the relevant risk factors in a firm's portfolio. These scenarios are often formulated at the request of senior management and are sometimes motivated by recent news, such as a run-up in oil prices. Correlations across asset classes are normally implicit, although some firms will also examine the implied correlations in order to ensure that the results are not overly conservative.

Historical scenarios rely on a significant market event experienced in the past, whereas a hypothetical scenario is a significant market event that has not yet happened. The choice of historical or hypothetical scenario depends on a number of factors, including the relevance to the portfolio of historical events, as well as the resources - particularly in terms of time and labour - that can be devoted to a particular exercise. Historical scenarios tend to be more fully articulated as they reflect an actual stressed market environment but they may not reflect the background of interest and the new ways in which financial risk is being packaged.

Hypothetical scenarios are potentially more relevant to the risk profile of the firm, but they are labour-intensive and involve considerably more judgment. Accordingly, management and business level support for hypothetical scenarios is particularly important. Sometimes macroeconomic models are also employed. At the enterprise level, this broader participation also goes some way to ensure that cross-business correlations are taken into account. In practice, hybrids are quite common, i.e., hypothetical scenarios which are informed by historical market moves but which are not necessarily linked to a specific crisis. The use of historical episodes assist in the calibration of the size of price changes and other hard-to-set factors, such as the possible effects on market liquidity.

The following steps are taken in scenario analysis:

1. Choose 5-10 scenarios that would adversely affect the markets in which the bank operates
2. Estimate the changes in each risk factor(s) given the scenario
3. Value the portfolio under the given scenario
4. Test the portfolio on a daily basis to estimate the probable loss under each scenario
5. Review and update the scenarios periodically

Sensitivity Analysis

Sensitivity Analysis is also known as the 'what if' analysis. It is a useful tool to determine how the changes in the market could affect the value of the portfolio. The market risk factors are market variables like interest rates, credit spreads, equity prices, exchange rates, etc. A simple sensitivity test isolates the short-term impact on a portfolio's value of a series of predefined moves in a particular market risk factor. For example, if the risk factor was an exchange rate, the shocks might be exchange rate changes of ± 2 percent, 4 percent, 6 percent and 10 percent. Firms also run a large number of sensitivity stress tests. The most straightforward type of test is a simple sensitivity test whereby risk parameters are moved instantaneously by a unit amount, such as a 10% decline or a 10 basis point rise.

A second group of sensitivity tests examines historical movements in a number of factors. These tests can take several forms. One type is based on worst case movements for each risk factor over a set historical period, eg the worst change in the last 10 years for interest rates and equities. This is objective and provides a maximum loss, but the unrealistic combination of risks - the time periods for each risk factor do not have to be coincident - may result in a loss that is overly pessimistic.

Back Testing Value-at-Risk

Back Testing is a technique used to reconcile forecasted losses from VaR with actual losses at the end of the time horizon (generally 1 day, 1 week, 2 weeks, 1 month, 1 quarter, 6 months or 1 year). VaR estimates with a given probability (generally 1% or 5%) the loss that a given portfolio may experience by the end of the analysis horizon under normal market conditions. For instance, if a portfolio has a weekly VaR of Rs.10 crores at 99% confidence level, this means that the portfolio has a 1% chance of experiencing a loss of at least Rs.10 crores by the end of the week under normal market conditions. At the end of the week, if the portfolio experiences a loss greater than Rs.10 crores, then it is conclude that the VaR model has not been accurate in forecasting the potential loss and risk of the portfolio. On the other side, if the portfolio has made a gain or a loss lower than Rs.10 crores, then the VaR methodology used might have been appropriate and seems to have been accurate in predicting the potential loss exposure for that particular portfolio.

If there have been too many failures, then the VaR model may not be adequate for the instruments composing the portfolio. For instance, if we run a Back Testing every day (therefore, requiring daily VaR computations) at 99% confidence level, then there should theoretically be one violation over a window of 100 trading days. If we conduct a monthly Back Testing on a VaR (irrespective of the frequency it is calculated since we will only compare the values at the beginning and end of the month) at a 95% confidence level, then we could expect to have a maximum of five violations over the next 8.33 years. If a portfolio has registered more violations that it was supposed to have, then one should review the pricing models used for each instrument, the volatility clustering models, the VaR methodology, the number of simulations, the state of the economy, and so on and so forth, to identify the source(s) of the breach.

There are basically two main approaches to perform Back Testing on VaR: dirty and clean. We describe the two techniques as well as provide some pros and cons for each.

Dirty Back Testing

Dirty Back Testing consists of comparing the VaR estimates with the actual P&L values at the end of the time horizon. Similarly, to Stress Testing, Back Testing starts with a given portfolio and heavily relies on the assumption that this portfolio will not evolve too much. First, we check the number of derivatives, which can exhibit sudden jump in prices, and further check the weight of all derivatives compared to the fund NAV. Second, we also look at the number of instruments that have an individual VaR much higher than the VaR of the portfolio (very risky assets, so therefore very volatile). One solution would be to perform Back Testing and eventually the VaR computations more often, thus reducing the number of incremental trades that may affect the portfolio too drastically.

Dirty Back Testing can be implemented on an Excel spreadsheet, where we can store the VaR estimates in one column and in another column the actual P&L after removing any cashflow effects (redemptions/subscriptions). A third column would simply indicate if the VaR estimate is higher or lower than the actual P&L, and therefore if there has been a breach of VaR or not.

Clean Back Testing

Clean Back Testing consists of comparing, still at the end of the time horizon, the VaR estimates with some hypothetical P&L values of the portfolio, having kept its composition unchanged. In that case, we simply re-price the same portfolio at the end of the time interval, calculate the returns and then compare them with the ex-ante values of VaR. If the VaR model has failed to foresee a loss greater than VaR, then irrespective of the trading activity that may have taken place between these two points in time, clean Back Testing tells us that there may be something wrong with the VaR model that would require further investigation. The main advantage of this type of Back Testing is that it respects the fundamental assumption that when we compute VaR, the portfolio must remain unchanged over the selected time period.

Back Testing is not the panacea to identify flaws in a VaR model but rather a required technique that indicates whether a VaR methodology is being used appropriately or not for a given portfolio. As the composition of the portfolio evolve, Back Testing lies in a constant reminder that the VaR model should also be reviewed and eventually readjusted if VaR has lost a bit of its predictive power. When applicable, it would be best practice to perform both Clean and Dirty Back Testing as they bring to light different flaws in the VaR computations.

Summary

In this chapter, various methodologies have been discussed to assess market risk exposure of banks and FIs. The banks assets and liabilities are rate sensitive, hence their price is subject to any change in interest rate level. The volatility of underlying securities dependes on price sensitivity or price volatility. The volatility is measured through DEAR or VaR or CFAR. In this chapter, various methods of calculation of VaR have been discussed and compared. The formulas of calculation of VaR have also been discussed. The important aspect of back testing of VaR has been detailed. The model developed by J P Morgan, i.e. RiskMetrics, has been analysed in detail. The techniques available for measuring extreme events such as stress test, sensitivity analysis and scenario analysis have also been discussed. These are the techniques used to assess extreme risk in market risk exposure.

KEY CONCEPTS

AFS	HTM	VaR
DEAR	EaR	EWMA
Price Sensitivity	Price Volatility	Historical Simulation Monte
Carlo Simulation	Variance	Covariance
Stress Testing	Scenario Analysis	Sensitivity Analysis

Review Questions and Problems

1. What is the objective of market risk measurement models?
2. What does DEAR mean? What are the various measurable components of DEAR?
3. A Bank has a Rs.10 lac, 5 years zero coupon bond with face value of Rs.14.03 lac. The bond is trading at YTM of 7%. What is the modified duration of bond?
4. What does VaR mean? How is VaR related to DEAR for RiskMetrics model?
5. The DEAR for a bank is Rs.10 lac. What is the VaR for 10 days period?
6. Why is VaR of 20 days period not the twice of 10 days period?
7. How is the duration a measure of market risk?

8. An FI has bond with market value of Rs.100 crore. The bond has an estimated price volatility of 0.95%. What is the DEAR and 10 days VaR of this bond?
9. What are the advantages of using back simulation approach to estimate market risk?
10. What are the advantages of using Monte Carlo simulation approach to estimate market risk?
11. How is Monte Carlo approach more useful than back simulation approach in measuring market risk?
12. What are the various methods for computing VaR and how do they differ?
13. What precautions should be taken while using the VaR model?
14. Draw the comparisons of various methods of VaR.
15. What are the steps followed in scenario analysis?
16. What are the various methods for back testing VaR and how do they differ?
17. Compare stress test, sensitivity analysis and scenario analysis for market risk measurement. Which of the technique is best among three? Draw a conclusion.
18. A bank has an investment in 15 years bond carrying coupon of 12% having face value of Rs.10 lacs. The bond is currently traded at 8% market rate. Calculate (i) modified duration of bond; (ii) price volatility if potential adverse movement in yield is 50 basis points; (iii) DEAR.
19. A bank's portfolio has market value of Rs.100 crores. The beta of the portfolio is one whose standard deviation is 1.5%. Calculate 10 days VaR for the portfolio at 99th percentile.
20. A bank has its estimated VaR for the previous 90 days to be Rs. 25 crores. DEAR for the previous day was Rs.18 crores. Calculate the amount of capital required to be held for market risk as per Basel Committee standards.

References:

1. *www.riskmetrics.com*
2. *www.bis.org*
3. *www.jpmorgan.com*

Chapter – 6

Measurement of Credit Risk

Chapter Objective

- Understand credit risk exposure of banks
- Familiarise with concepts like Probability of Default (PD), Exposure At Default (EAD) and Loss Given Default (LGD)
- Focus on Credit Scoring Model
- Explain concepts of expected and unexpected losses
- Discuss various models used for credit risk exposure measurement such as CreditRisk, CreditMetrics and KMV Portfolio Manager

Introduction

Lending is the main business of FIs and banks and is also a major source of income. Loans have a major share in bank's balance sheet. The performance of banks is decided on the basis of asset quality and level of default. The FI is exposed to credit risk while extending credit facilities to corporations, individuals and governments. The FI takes risk on these loans for a better return to its lenders and stakeholders. The FIs price loans to cover the cost of borrowings, the spread and the credit risk involved in lending. There are various sources of credit risk. The amount of credit risk depends upon the structure of the agreement between the bank and its borrowers. For example, the amount of loan that the borrower owes to a bank is fixed, whereas in a line of credit, the borrower decides the periodicity of withdrawal. The clauses in the loan agreement executed between a bank and its borrower gives complete structure of loan and the risk involved on the basis of embedded option in agreement.

Recently, US FIs have suffered major losses from sub prime lending such as Citibank, Barclays Bank, New Century Financial Corporation, Bear Stearns, BNP Paribus, etc. The sub prime lending were made to low rated borrowers by rating agency at higher rate of interest. Because of low rating, credit risk was higher in sub prime lending which exaggerated by slow down in mortgage market of US. The majority of US banks, hedge funds and FIs are reporting losses as a result of having to write off these loans. There are various credit risk measurement models which are being used such as default risk model, credit scoring models, term structure of credit risk approach, mortality rate approach,

RAROC models, option models or KMV credit monitor model, CreditMetrics and Credit Risk+.

Characteristics of Loans

Before going to these models, it is important to understand the credit quality concept and types of loans. The credit quality of assets of banks is the major area of concern. Extending the credit facility to different segment of the society without assessing credit worthiness of borrower may lend banks in high number of bad loans. The banks lend to low rated customer for higher returns and credit risk. The bad loans have been a major area of concern for regulators and stakeholders in banks and FIs. The credit off-take in the country is growing at an enormous pace and credit quality of these loans is going down. Since the introduction of risk management concept in banks and FIs, the ratio of non-performing loans to total loans has seen a decline from 2006 onwards. Credit quality problem in case of sub prime lending caused many FIs to become insolvent. The credit risk is not only limited to traditional lending activities but has expanded to off balance sheet items and other commitments of banks.[1]

The banks offer a variety of loans and its features differ. The major kind of commercial loans offered by banks are short term loans, term loans, syndicate loans, secured & unsecured loans, commercial papers, mortgaged loans, real estate loans, etc. The nature of these loans differs from loan to loan. The short term commercial loan is generally taken by corporates for working capital need. The long term loans or term loans are taken for capital expenditure or business expansion. The risk involved in both loans differs as the tenure and the end usage of loans differs. The higher is the tenure, more the bank is exposed to risk. If loan is extended to start a business, it carries more risk than when the loan is given to existing business. The loan syndication is a financial innovation to finance corporate and big projects where it is not feasible for a single bank or FI to lend. Under loan syndication, loan is provided by a group of banks and FIs. The lead FI act as financial agent of borrower and arrange finances from others banks and FIs. Through this kind of loan, credit risk associated with big projects is diversified among various lenders.

The credit risk involved in loans also depends on the security available with loan. On the basis of security, loan may be divided in two categories - secured and unsecured loans. A secured loan is backed by specific asset of borrower and in case the borrower defaults, immediate recourse is available to bank. In case of unsecured loan, if default occurs, its claim is subordinate to other claims. The disbursal of loan is also a decisive factor for credit risk exposure. The loan may be drawn in one go or in different tranches. If a loan is taken in one go, the credit risk exposure may be mitigated otherwise bank is exposed to credit risk till the time full amount is not disbursed.

The corporates also raise money through issuance of commercial paper which is an unsecured short term debt instrument. This instrument is either sold directly by corporates or through an underwriter to buyers in financial markets. The banks also take exposure in real estate financing. In this type of loan, bank faces two kinds of risks, one is credit risk out of exposure to corporates and another is market risk associated with real estate market. Some other features which change the magnitude of credit risk are fixed rate loans, floating rate loans, revolving loans, ceilings on maximum rate, prepayment of loan, etc. These are the embedded options which make loans different from other loans. Hence banks or FIs have to give different treatment to different kinds of loans. The credit risk may not be generalized to all kind of loans.

The Default Risk Models

This model is qualitative model of credit risk measurement. On the basis of a set of borrower and market specific information, the credit decision is taken. According to FI's profile, certain weights are assigned to these factors to take an overall credit decision. The borrower specific factors are like reputation of borrower, borrower-lender relationship, the borrower leverage or capital structure, volatility of earnings and security available. The market specific factors are business cycle, interest rate level, etc.

In borrower specific factors, weights are assigned to credit worthiness of the borrowers. A credit history of borrowers for timely repayment and honouring the contract is prepared. That gives credit behaviour of borrower towards its obligations. The borrower capital structure and the debt equity ratio also affects its probability of default (PD). If borrower is more dependent on debt for its financial needs it means it carries more interest burden and this enhances credit risk involved. The more dependency on debt fund stress Debt Service Coverage Ratio (DSCR). A little uncomfortable situation may lead to default. A highly volatile earnings from project may increase probability of defaults that the borrower is not able to meet repayment of principal and interest. The industries with high earning variance over time are more credit risky. A debt backed by security reduces risk of recovery of principal in consideration than the unsecured loan. Unsecured debt is riskier because in case of default, lender is left to general course of recovery and thus carry more credit risk.

The market specific factors such as business cycle phases are very important for the assessment of the probability of borrower default. Recession in economy may affect corporate badly as their profitability goes down and in turn probability of default increases. Similarly, the level of interest rates also affects probability of default. If loans are given on floating rate basis and interest rate due to tight monetary policy goes up, the burden of interest rate on corporates will increase which may lead to default. The high interest rate is highly correlated with higher credit risk.

Credit Scoring Model

In contrary to default risk model, this model is quantitative in which borrower characteristics are quantified to get a score giving probability of default. Under this model, emphasis is on evaluation of those factors which are important in default risk. To employ credit scoring model, factors like cash flow information and financial ratios are important. After data identification, default risk probability is scored with the use of statistical techniques. There are generally two methods which are followed for credit scoring - one is linear probability model and another is linear discriminant model.

Under linear probability model, historical data for important factors such as financial ratios are used as input in the model to examine repayment experience on old loans. On the basis of this, forecast for repayment on new loans are made. The old loans are divided in two categories: those that defaulted and those that did not default.

Altman's Z Score Model

Under linear discriminant model, borrowers are divided in two categories: high and low default risk on the basis of past observed experience of defaulting and non defaulting borrowers. This model is widely known as Altman's Z Score Model[2]. The indicator variable Z is an overall measure of the default risk classification of a commercial borrower. This variable depends upon values of various financial ratios of the borrower and weighted importance of these ratios. The weighted importance of these ratios has been fixed on the basis of intense research on past behaviour of borrowers for loan repayments.

$$Z = 1.2 X_1 + 1.4 X_2 + 3.3 X_3 + 0.6 X_4 + 1.0 X_5$$

Where

X_1	=	Working capital/total asset ratio
X_2	=	Retained earning/total asset ratio
X_3	=	EBIT/total asset ratio
X_4	=	MVE/book value of long-term debt ratio
X_5	=	Sales/total asset ratio

The higher is the value of Z, the lower is the default risk from borrower. The value of Z less than 1.81 is considered as high default risk. The bank may take decision to lend to the borrower where Z is less than 1.81 either by charging risk premium or to wait till the time score is improved.

EXAMPLE: Decision making by using Z Score Model

Suppose the financial ratios of a borrower are as under:

$X_1 = 0.40$
$X_2 = 0.05$
$X_3 = 0.10$
$X_4 = 0.15$
$X_5 = 1.50$

The $X_1 = 0.40$ shows that the company is more dependent on working capital and $X_5 = 1.50$ means company is maintaining good sales level. These two ratios together show that company liquidity position is good. $X_4 = 0.10$ means company is highly dependent on debt for its financial needs. The other ratios as $X_2 = 0.05$ and $X_3 = 0.10$ show a comfortable profit and reserve and surplus for company. Simply looking at these ratios, the financial soundness of the company may be seen. The same may be applied to Altman's Z score model.

Altman's Z score for above company is :

$$Z = 1.2 (0.40) + 1.4 (0.05) + 3.3 (0.10) + 0.6 (0.15) + 1.0 (1.5)$$

$$Z = 0.48 + 0.07 + 0.33 + 0.09 + 1.5$$

$$Z = 2.47$$

Hence Z = 2.47, which is above specified Z score of 1.81, means company is low on credit risk.

Limitations of Z Score Model

There are a number of limitations of Z score model which are as follows:

1. The model is based on two extreme events: default or no default. The events falling between two extreme events have not been considered. Using this model either company is eligible for loan or not. There is no other remedy suggested.
2. The model is limited to certain financial ratios only whereas the consideration of other ratio for some companies may be important in credit risk assessment. The time horizon has not been given any consideration in assessing credit risk. The same model is to be applied for short term loans and long term loans.
3. The model misses behavioural aspects of the borrowers which are crucial for default or no default situation such as borrower willingness to pay, its market reputation, management of the company, etc.
4. The authenticity of data used in this model is not verified. The ratios are calculated on the basis of company's result. In case of small or medium company, the information provided in annual report may be misleading.

RAROC Model

This model was developed with the objective to use market data to assess credit risk by Banker Trust.[3] The RAROC means Risk Adjusted Return On Capital. The model includes default risk in pricing of loan. In this model, return on asset (ROA) is calculated on the basis of loan at risk at the time of default, because if loan becomes NPA, provision have to be made out of bank's capital.

RAROC	=	One Year Income on Loan (I) / Loan Risk or Capital at Risk (ΔL)

A loan is sanctioned if RAROC is higher than the benchmark rate of bank for return on capital (ROC). For example if bank's ROC is 12%, a loan should only be made if estimated RAROC for loan is higher than 12%, otherwise risk premium should be increased. There are two methods that are adopted to calculate loan at risk, the denominator of the RAROC model. The adoption of method differs from FI to FI based on its database and availability of information required for the calculation.

Under the first method, capital risk exposure or loss amount is calculated on the basis of duration of loan and credit risk premium shock or credit quality shock.

Rupee capital Risk Exposure or loss = Duration of Loan x loan amount x (expected change in credit premium or risk on loan)

$$\Delta L = -D_L \times L \times (\Delta R/1+R)$$

The main feature of this method is to calculate the maximum change in the credit risk premium on loan by next year. The premium changes are available publicly for AAA, AA, A and other rated loans. The risk premium changes give the number if a loan changes rating from AAA to AA or to other category.

Under the second method, if very good loan default database is available with bank, then the unexpected loss rate and exposure at the time of default is calculated on the basis of previous pattern of such category of loans. The denominator is calculated on the basis of three factors, which are Probability of Default (PD), Loss Given Default (LGD) and Exposure At Default (EAD).

Probability of Default (PD)

What is the likelihood that the borrower will default on its obligation either over the life of the loan or over some specified horizon, such as a year? Calculated for a one-year horizon, this may be called the Expected Default Frequency (EDF).

Exposure at Default (EAD)

This is also known as the Loan Equivalence (LEQ). It is the outstanding amount at the time of default. In the event of a default, it indicates the amount of outstanding loan.

Loss Given Default (LGD)

In the event of a default, the certain fraction of exposure can be recovered through bankruptcy proceedings or some other form of settlement. The proportion of the loan lost or not recovered on default is called the loss given default.

The expected and unexpected loss is given by the equations:

Expected Loss (EL) = PD x EAD x LGD

Unexpected Loss (UL) = PD x CAR x LGD

Here, CAR is Credit at Risk (Maximum credit at risk in worst case scenario)

Expected loss is covered through pricing of the bank's products and services. Unexpected loss is the variability about this mean loss, which should be covered through adequate capital allocation or provisioning. Thus risk adjusted return on capital under this method is:

RAROC = One year income per rupee loan (I) / PD x LGD

EXAMPLE : Calculation of RAROC on a Loan Exposure

Under First Method:

Suppose a bank wants to calculate RAROC for a loan of Rs.100 crore earning net income including a fee of Rs.1.5 crore, with duration of 3.2 years. The current market rate of interest for such loans is 12% and change in risk premium is 3.5%.

$$\Delta L = -D_L \times L \times (\Delta R/1+R)$$

ΔL = -(3.2)(Rs.100 crore)(.035/1.12) = -Rs.10 crore

Then

RAROC = 1.5 / 10 = 15%

If internal benchmark RAROC is less than 15%, the loan may be approved, otherwise loan will be rejected or higher risk premium will be charged.

Under Second Method:

Suppose default rate of borrower (PD) is 10 percent and loss given default (LGD) is 90 percent. Then

RAROC = 0.015/(0.10) (0.90) = 16.67%

The process of measuring credit risk for a portfolio of credit assets is different from the one used for a single loan because of the correlations between loans in a portfolio. Correlation reflects the extent to which loans tend to default simultaneously. This may happen because of macroeconomic factors like recession or interrelationships between the various credit assets (e.g. default by the parent company may trigger defaults by its subsidiaries or default by the manufacturer may result in a default by the company's suppliers). The effects of correlation may result in highly skewed loss distributions—many years of low loss followed by a few years of extremely high loss. However, these correlation effects are difficult to observe because defaults are few and far between. As a result, some models have been developed for measuring the credit risk of a portfolio. They are based on some financial assumptions and can be used with fewer data points. These models are:

- The CreditRisk+ Model
- The CreditMetrics Model
- The KMV Portfolio Manager Model
- The Modern Portfolio Theory

The CreditRisk+ Model

In this model, the statistics of historical losses are directly used. The Credit Risk+ model developed by Credit Suisse Financial Products (CSFP) is based on the actuarial model. The process is quite complex. The focus of this approach is to estimate the expected loss of loans and the distribution of those losses to calculate FI's required capital reserve to meet the losses above a certain point. This model is generally used for analyzing default risk on a large portfolio with small loans rather than portfolios that contain small number of big loans. The main steps in the calculation process are:

- Determining the probability of default for each company
- As the probability of default on loans is small, the frequency distribution of default rate is modeled by a Poisson distribution of losses, given the mean probability of default for all loans in the portfolio

- Using Gamma distribution to create uncertainty in the mean probability of default
- Calculating the inverse binomial distribution of losses, given the uncertainty in the mean probability of default
- Aggregating the groups independent results

However, the actuarial approach suffers from two major drawbacks:

1. Defining the standard deviations of the Gamma functions that drive correlations
2. Linking the credit risk with market risks

The CreditMetrics Model and KMV Portfolio Manager Model helps in overcoming these difficulties.

The CreditMetrics Model

This model helps is simulating the correlating defaults for a portfolio of loans. The model generates random values for each company's assets; if the value is too low, the model simulates a default. Since loans are not traded actively in the market, it is difficult to calculate loan's market value and the volatility of loan value over one year period. On the basis of credit rating, probability of change in rating in next one year, recovery rate on defaulted loans and yield spread in bond market, a hypothetical loan's market value and volatility may be calculated. The estimation of the portfolio Value-at-Risk due to Credit (Credit-VaR) through CreditMetrics is summarised in the figure below:

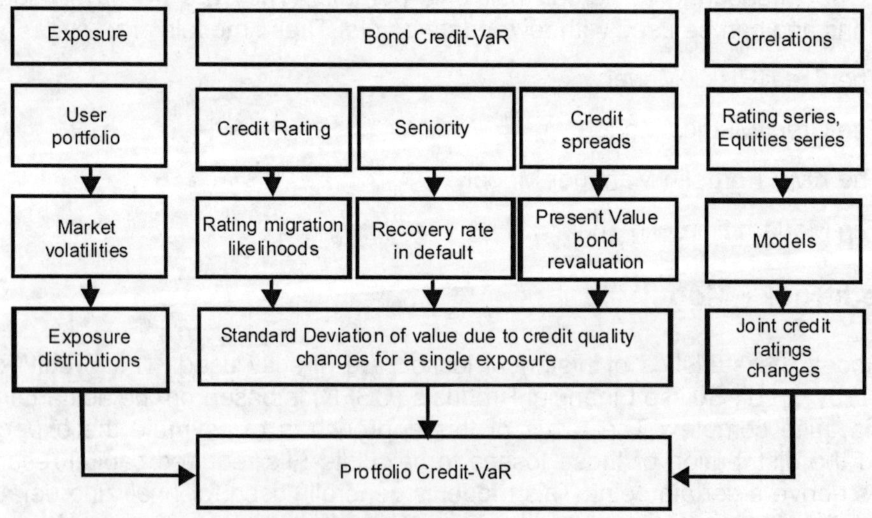

Source: JP Morgan/Presentation: Ronald Domingues.com

Fig 1: Credit Metrics Framework

A rating system with probabilities of migrating from one credit quality to another over a given time horizon (transition matrix) is the key component of the credit-VaR proposed by JP Morgan. The specified credit risk horizon is usually one year.

The main steps in this process are:

- Determine the probability of default for each company and rating migration probability table
- Determine the value of loans on the basis of future cash flow discounted by risk free return and annual credit spread for entire tenure of loan on an yearly basis
- Determining the value of loan at the end of year under different rating class
- Calculate the mean of loan's value or expected value at the end of year one
- Calculate the VaR based on normal distribution of loan values and the actual distribution of loan values because value of loan is not symmetrically distributed
- Asses the capital requirement on the basis of above calculated VaR.

The KMV Portfolio Manager Model

This model developed by KMV Corporation is called portfolio manager. Under this model, banks need to determine and measure three things: the expected return on loans (R), the risk of loan (σ) and the correlation of default risks between loans (ρ). KMV measures each of these as follows:

$R = AIS - E(L) = AIS - (PD \times LGD)$

$\sigma = UL = \sqrt{PD} \times (1\text{-}PD) \times LGD$

ρ = correlation between two borrowers

The return on loan is measured by All-In-Spread (AIS) which is measured on the basis of fees paid on loan and spread on loan. The risk of loan reflects the volatility of loan default rate. On the basis of this unexpected loss is calculated. The expected return for loans and variances are calculated and then risk and return of the portfolio is calculated.

The Modern Portfolio Theory

If the portfolio of banks and FIs have widely traded assets or loans and it is easy to calculate loan return, portfolio diversification model is used to measure credit risk exposure. The main steps in this process are:

1. Estimate the expected return on each loan in the portfolio
2. Calculate variance of returns or risk of the portfolio

On the basis of the above theory, bank can diversify credit risk as long as returns on different assets are not correlated. The negative correlation between return of two loans in the portfolio reduce overall risk of portfolio. With the use of modern portfolio theory, banks may create minimum risk portfolio where variance of portfolio return is reduced to lowest possible level.

If expected return (R_i) of each loan is known in the FI's portfolio, the FI can compute the expected return (R_p) on a portfolio asset as:

Expected Return:

$$\mathrm{E}(R_p) = \sum_i w_i \mathrm{E}(R_i)$$

where R_p is the return on the portfolio, R_i is the return on asset i and w_i is the weighting of component asset i (that is, the share of asset i in the portfolio)

In addition to this, the variance of returns or risk of the portfolio can be calculated as:

Portfolio return variance:

$$\sigma_p^2 = \sum_i w_i^2 \sigma_i^2 + \sum_i \sum_{j \neq i} w_i w_j \sigma_i \sigma_j \rho_{ij},$$

where ρ_{ij} is the correlation coefficient between the returns on assets i and j. Alternatively, the expression can be written as:

$$\sigma_p^2 = \sum_i \sum_j w_i w_j \sigma_i \sigma_j \rho_{ij}$$

where $\rho_{ij} = 1$ for i=j.

Summary

In this chapter, various models and approaches have been discussed to measure credit risk or default risk. The concept of lending by banks and how they are exposed to credit risk, have also been detailed. The parameters used in assessing credit risk exposure of banks such as probability of default, loss given default and exposure at default have been explained. The practical models such as RAROC have been discussed. The other models such as CreditRisk, CreditMetrics, KMV Portfolio Manager and Modern Portfolio theory have been discussed in detail.

KEY CONCEPTS

Default Risk	PD	EAD
LGD	DSCR Credit Scorers	RAROC
Expected Loss	Unexpected Loss	CreditRisk
CreditMetrics	KMV Portfolio Manager	Modern Portfolio Theory

Review Questions and Problems

1. What is credit quality and how does this affect the profitability of a bank?
2. What are the various types of loans that are made by banks and FIs? How are these loans different from each other on the basis of credit risk exposure?
3. Develop a checklist for extending loan to a company for credit risk assessment.
4. Why is credit risk analysis an important component of FI risk management?

5. Differentiate between secured and unsecured loans on the basis of credit risk exposure.
6. What are the purposes of credit scoring models? Identify one credit rating model being used by Indian bank.
7. What changes can be made to Altman's Z score model to make it suitable to Indian companies credit assessment? Suggest some other financial ratios which may be considered for scoring.
8. A bank has made a loan @10% p.a.. Bank expects a probability of default of 5% and if loan is defaulted, it expects to recover 50% of its money through security sale. What is the expected return on loan?
9. What is RAROC? How does this model use the concept of duration to measure the risk exposure of loan? How is the expected change in the credit premium measured?
10. How does CreditRisk+ differ from CreditMetrics model?
11. How does KMV measure return on loan?
12. How does loan portfolio risk differ from individual loan risks?
13. Explain how modern portfolio theory can be applied to lower the credit risk of an FI's portfolio.
14. What is minimum risk portfolio? What are the various steps are taken to create such a portfolio?
15. If EDF = 0.10% and LGD = 50 %, what is unexpected loss on the loan?
16. A bank offers one-year loan @ 10% p.a. but as per condition bank requires deposit of an amount equivalent to 10% of loan. Calculate the true cost of loan to the borrower. Also calculate the effect on true cost of loan if deposit amount is raised to 20% and 25%.
17. A bank has made a loan @ 12% p.a.. The expected probability of defaultof this loan is 5%. In case of loan default, bank expects to recover 60% amount through sale of mortgaged asset. Calculate the expected rate of return on loan.
18. A bank is appraising a proposal of loan of Rs.100 crores to a firm. The upfront fee charged by bank is 1.5% of the loan amount. The loan has a maturity of 8 years and duration of 7.5 years. The cost of fund for the bank is 10%. The maximum change risk premium for the sector would be approx. 4%. The current prevailing rate of interest for such loan is 12%. By using RAROC model, decide whether bank should make this loan or not. How much additional interest and fee income should be collected in order to make the loan? What should be duration in order to approve the loan?
19. A firm has assets of Rs. 500 crores and total debt of Rs.450 crores. The implied volatility of the firm is estimated at Rs. 10 crores. Under the KVM method, what is the expected default frequency?
20. A bank has two loans of Rs. 50 crores each, where loan X has an expected rate of return of 10% with a standard deviation of return of 10% and loan Y has an expected rate of return of 12% with a standard deviation of return of 15%. Calculate (i) expected rate of return and standard deviation of the portfolio at given covariance of 2% between loan X & Y; (ii) expected rate of return and

standard deviation of the portfolio at given covariance of (–ve) 2.5% between loan X & Y. Assess the role of covariance and standard deviation in risk reduction attribute of MPT.

21. A bank uses the KMV portfolio manger model to evaluate credit risk of loans in its balance sheet. A loan X earns 3% fee every year and loan is priced at 5% spread over the cost of funds for the bank. If the borrower defaults, the loss of 20% will be on face value of loan because of weak mortgage value. The expected probability of default is 5%. Calculate return on loan and the risk of the loan.

References:

1. *www.rbi.org*
2. *Altman's "Managing the commercial Lending Process" (1985).*
3. *RAROC at BOA : From Theory to Practice.*

Chapter – 7

Measurement of Operational & Technology Risk

Chapter Objective

- Know the sources of Operational and Technology Risk
- Understand various types of Operational and Technology Risk
- Focus on different approaches for measurement of Operational and Technology Risk
- Discuss various Operational and Technology Risk
- Impact of Technology in Financial Services

Introduction

Operational risk is the most important risk for an organization. Operational risk may result from inadequacy or failure of people, processes, systems or external factors. The risk is important because, unlike credit risk or market risk, where the variables are known and can be quantified, in assessing operational risk it may be difficult to do so. This is why even the top ten internationally active banks (which are doing the credit and market risk measurement) find it difficult to come to terms with operational risk.

The Basel Committee in its reports stated that informal survey highlights the growing realization of the significance of risks other than market and credit risks, such as operational risk, which has been at the heart of some important banking problems in recent years. Some of these problems are:-

1. Banker Trust ($150m loss), the bank becomes embroiled in a high profile lawsuit with a customer that accuses it of improper selling practices. The reputation of bank was badly damaged and later on bank bought by Deutsche Bank (1994).
2. Sumitomo ($2.6 billion loss), A copper trader amasses unreported losses over 3 years (1996).
3. Morgan Grenfell Asset Management ($720m loss), A fund manager exceeds his guidelines leading to huge loss. Later Deutsche Bank agrees to compensate the investors (1996).
4. NatWest ($127m loss), A trader deliberately covers up losses by mispricing and overvaluing option contracts. Later NatWest was taken over by the Royal Bnak of Scotland (1997).

5. Allied Irish Bank ($691m loss), A trader hides three years of losing trades on the yen/dollor exchange rate at the US subsidiary (2002).

These failures involves operational risk i.e. failure to supervise. The largest of these failures can be traced to a case of internal fraud by employees. The operational losses in some cases are even higher than those mentioned above.

The Sources of Operational Risk

There are various sources of operational risk that have been identified by different banks and FIs. The major sources of operational risks are as under:

- Employee (Internal frauds and human error)
- Technology (Technology failure and obsolete technology)
- Capital Assets (Destruction by natural calamities or other reasons)
- Customer relationship (customer services or legal disputes)
- External (External frauds and theft)
- Transaction (Execution and booking)

The factors responsible for operational risk needs to be identified meticulously in order to minimize loss arising out of operational risk. Some of the originating factors are listed below:[1]

Source of Risk	Originating Factors
Employee Risk	• Employee turnover • Key personnel risk • Fraud risk • Error • Rouge trading • Money laundering • Confidentiality breach
Technology Risk	• Programming error • Model risk • Mark-to-market error • Management information • IT system outage • Telecommunication failure • Contingency planning
Capital Asset Risk	• Safety

	• Security • Operation cost • Fire/flood or other natural calamities
Customer Risk	• Contractual disagreement • Dissatisfaction • Default
External Risk	• External fraud • Taxation risk • Legal risk • War • Collapse of market • Reputation risk • Relationship risk
Transaction Risk	• Execution error • Booking error • Settlement error • Commodity delivery • Documentation risk

The major operational risk these days are faced by technology risk. Technology becomes obsolete very fast and involves heavy capital outflow. To reduce the operational cost, technology adoption has become a backbone of banking operations. More the banks are exposed to technology, more they are exposed to operational risk. Technology is important because selection of right technology increases banks profitability. The technology plays an important role in managing high volume of customers and diversified range of products and services. The technology plays an important role in banks and FIs following activities such as controlled disbursement, accounts reconciliation, electronic fund transfer, treasury management, e-commerce, electronic billing, etc. For customer relationship, the following services are offered such as ATM, debit or credit card, on line banking, etc. which involves heavy use of technology on both the ends, i.e. at the bank's and at the customer's end.

A product based on technology turns out to be negative for bank if the revenue generated out of product line is not sufficient enough to take care of expenditure made in technology of that product.

Measuring Operational Risk

The approaches available for measuring operational risk are:

- Quantitative approach

- Structural approach
- Historical approach
- Modern approach

Quantitative Approach

Quantitative approach is based on quantifying losses arising out of various sources of risk. The judgment is based on information collected through internet or commercial database and tries to gather information on historical events and current state of affairs. Historical events include any financial losses, write offs that have resulted in actual losses and near misses, which could have resulted in losses but did not happen or were controlled but did not cause any losses, for example, advertising expenses being recorded as repairs expenses. The collection of data for such events is very difficult. Even when the events are recorded, it is difficult to quantify losses from such event or misses. Quantification of losses of such events differ from location to location as the implication of legal cases in India differ from US. A database of such events along with monetary loss is prepared. Then the bank identifies its line of business where such event may take place and accordingly sets aside the required capital for such losses. Information about the current state of affairs tends to focus on two issues—reliability and stress. The factors affecting reliability of the system include level of automation and quality of personnel. Reliability may be at risk if there is more manual intervention or recording is not done meticulously or is done by an inexperienced personnel. The other factors that may also risk reliability are high employee turnover, increased overtime and complexity of the operation. This information can be used to judge the credit scoring of each department and allocate capital on the basis of these scores.

Structural Approaches

These approaches use a model of causality that defines a set of linkages between various processes and the probability of loss events. This helps banks in concentrating their efforts on those links or the array of events in the process which have a high probability of loss. It may not be possible to use this approach for all operational risk. This approach may be useful only for the well defined operational risks such as process risk or business risk. In the structural approach, the flow chart of the process is constructed. Then, the bank tries to identify the weak links in the process and the expected losses in such an event. The probability of each link failing can be estimated to quantify the loss for any given event. For less frequent events, this estimate may be based on bank's judgment. On the basis of probability and quantum of losses, the risks are arranged.

Historical Approach

This approach is based on historical events which are used to extrapolate the future outcome. This approach is statistical in nature and hence make minimal assumptions about the causes and method of loss. Under this approach, efforts are made to estimate the parameters of the loss distribution, i.e. they do not identify the sources of risks but include all of them. Hence, they are better than quantitative approach where the management identifies the sources of risk. In the latter, there is a possibility that an important source of risk might be overlooked.

Modern Approach

This approach is a combination of all the above. This approach use judgement, structure and loss experience to measure the operating risks. Even the Basel Committee has recommended such an approach to measure operational risk. Two main approaches in this category are historical loss mapping and key risk indicators. In historical loss mapping, the probability distribution of loss is estimated on the basis of historical data. The steps in this method are:

1. Historical data on operating loss events are collected at the organization, industry and country levels. For industry level data, the information may either be obtained from various sources in the public domain or the date from various players may be pooled by a nodal agency and made available to all players on an anonymous basis (i.e. data is shared without disclosing the names of the organizations, the corresponding loss events and the loss suffered). The country level data is gathered from published report of such events from that country or reports published by investigating agencies.
2. The loss data is classified on the basis of the type of event that caused the loss, the type of business unit process in which the loss occurred and the country in which the event had taken place. The place of event is very important as various parameters of business differ from location to location.
3. The processes and business units of a particular bank are similarly classified and the loss data for the industry is used to estimate the expected/unexpected loss for the bank. Sometimes to fine tune the risk exposure, different locations of business have to be given a different treatment.

KRIs are quantifiable measures of the performance of the bank's processes. If these indicators have been well chosen, the changes in KRIs should be in line with the probability of loss. Key risk indicators for operational risk may include volume of trades processed, volatility in profit and loss account, employee turnover rate, average overtime per employee, etc. KRIs are very useful as a management tool. However, till historical data that supports their connection to loss has been gathered correctly, their usage to determine the capital charge for operational risk will remain restricted. One of the biggest controversy regarding operational risk is that the big banks are more exposed to risk in comparision with small banks but they are more reluctant in providing capital for operational risk. The big banks perceive their systems and procedure more efficiently as compared to the small banks or locally present banks.

Technology Risk

Risk arising out of adoption of latest technology and intense use of technology in financial transaction is becoming major source of operational risk. The technology includes computers, data transferring, audio-video communication systems, software for online transactions and other related usage of information technology. In recent time, banks and financial institutions are heavily investing in upgrading themselves from manual work to work through use of information technology in India. The increased dependence on technology usage for financial transactions has inbuilt operational risk. Technology is an important phenomenon for banking industry as it increases both the FI's NIM and other non-interest income.

Impact of Technology on Financial Services

The most important area where technology has impacted financial services is Cash Management Services (CMS). CMS includes collection, transfer and disbursement of funds anywhere for corporates and individuals. Apart from this, various other services such as maintaining disbursement accounts, account reconciliation, making float available against clearing instruments, fund transfer to centralized location, electronic fund transfer like SWIFT, RTGS, etc., deposit services, electronic initiation of letter of credit, treasury management services, electronic data transfer and interchange, facilitating business to business e-commerce, electronic billing, assisting e-commerce, ATMs, Point of Sale debit cards (POS), home banking, credit cards, online payment of bills, online banking, smart cards, online security trading, etc. All these services are technology based and have inherited risk such as date theft, hacking of vital information, online fraud transactions, etc. For the safeguards of its customers, FIs have to spend big amount of money to create safe environment for online financial transactions. A small incident may put high operational losses to FIs. Thus, FIs providing all these services are highly exposed to operational risk. In case of loss of vital customer information, customer may sue FIs and the compensation to be paid may be more than the equity capital of the FI.

While providing these services, FIs also have to analyse cost and benefit (Cost-Benefit Analysis CBA) in providing such services. Based on CBA, the decision for providing services to the clients is taken. Not every service is profitable to the banks because of inherited risk involved in providing a service.

FIs based on historical data develop models to work out operational risk involved in different line of business.

Summary

In this chapter, various sources of operational risk have been discussed. The major factors that expose banks to operational risk have been detailed out. The factors have been classified on the basis of its character and nature such as employee related factors, technology related factors, customer related factors, external factors and transactional factors, etc. The various approaches to measure operational risk exposure have been discussed. Operational risk arising out of technology use have also been covered to the extent possible.

KEY CONCEPTS

Internal Fraud	External Fraud	Technology Failure
Employee Risk	Technology Risk	Capital Asset risk
Customer Risk	External Risk	Transaction risk

Review Questions and Problems

1. What are the advantages of an efficient technology base for a bank? Does the size of bank matter in technology selection and exposure to operational risk?
2. What are the various examples of operational risk arising from its various sources?
3. Identify a bank or FI and assess the operational risk exposure to it.
4. What is the operational risk involved in introducing technology based new product?
5. What is the link between operational and technology risk?
6. What are the various approaches for measurement of operational risk? How do they differ from each other?
7. How does the operational risk exposure differ on the basis of location of business?
8. Develop a real time case study for operational losses faced by an FI due to operational risk exposure.
9. List the types of operational risk defined by Basel II along with sources of each type of risk.
10. How are crime and fraud risk and avoidance of banking regulations getting easier and frequent with the improvement in technology innovation in financial transactions?

Reference:

1. Measuring and Managing Operational Risk in Financial Institution : Marshall (2001).

Chapter – 8

Measurement of Foreign Exchange & Sovereign Risk

Chapter Objective

- Trading activities in Forex
- Understand Foreign Currency Risk Exposure
- Exchange Rate Volatility
- Explain positions in Forex Market such as Long and Short Position
- Discuss the concept of Exchange Rate Shock
- Focus on Interest Rate Parity theory
- Sources of Sovereign Risk
- Evaluation of Sovereign Risk

Introduction

Foreign Exchange Risk

The globalisation of Indian economy and expansion of banks and FIs to other countries have exposed them to foreign exchange risk. Banks and FIs are exposed to foreign exchange risk if they are holding positions of assets and liabilities in foreign currency. The trading in foreign currency also exposes to the foreign exchange risk on daily basis. The foreign exchange risk exposure is more in trading in foreign currency in comparison with holding foreign currency assets and liabilities. There are various examples of foreign currency risks such as depreciation of Russian ruble and Thai baht in late 90s led to currency devaluation of most of the Asian currency against US dollar. Due to this fluctuation in currency across Asia, many banks and FIs worldwide booked heavy exchange losses. Many FIs deal directly in currency trading by taking various positions in spot and forward foreign currency market. These FIs are greatly exposed to foreign exchange risk even on an hourly basis. Playing foreign exchange derivative is a very risky affair as even a small position in any currency derivative may turn out to be so big that the entire net worth of FI is wiped out. A famous case of LTCM is witness of such situation it had faced due to devaluation of Russian ruble.

The forex markets have enormous trading activities. According to BIS, as of April' 2010, average daily turnover in global foreign exchange markets is estimated at $3.98 trillion.

The $3.98 trillion break-down is as follows:

$1.490 trillion in spot transactions

$475 billion in outright forwards

$1.765 trillion in foreign exchange swaps

$43 billion currency swaps

$207 billion in options and other products

Trading Activities in Foreign Exchange

A bank's position in the forex market reflects four types of trading activities:-

1. The sale and purchase of foreign currencies for customers to complete overseas commercial transactions
2. The sale and purchase of foreign currencies to allow customers to to take position in foreign investments
3. The sale and purchase of foreign currencies for hedging purposes to offset customer's exposure in any other currency
4. The sale and purchase of foreign currencies for speculative and arbitrage purposes in anticipation of future favorable move in forex rates.

Sources of Foreign Exchange Risk Exposure

All major commercial banks, private and foreign banks in India are major players in foreign exchange market. These banks trade and deal in foreign currency and take heavy positions in foreign currency assets and liabilities. The trading position taken in spot or forward market in the form of buying spot and forward contracts is called a long position and by selling contracts is called a short position. The foreign exchange risk is measured on the basis of net exposure of banks and FIs in foreign currency. The net exposure in foreign currency is the sum of difference between assets and liabilities positions and difference between buying and selling contracts in foreign currency. The net exposure is calculated separately for each designated currency. Banks can hedge against foreign currency exposure by matching its assets and liabilities position and buy and sell position in designated currency and thus making net exposure zero. The exposure can be hedged by having cross positions in trading and banking book i.e. mismatches of banking book may be covered by taking inverse position in trading book. The following terms should be known in order to measure the foreign exchange risk exposure of any bank or FI:

Net Long Position = Foreign Currency Bought > Foreign Currency Sold

Net Short Position = Foreign Currency Sold > Foreign Currency Bought

EXAMPLE: Foreign currency exposure in Banks

Suppose a bank is net long in currency exposure i.e. USD. The bank will face risk if the value of USD falls against INR. If the bank is net short in exposure of USD, the bank will face risk if the value of USD rises against INR. This may be explained numerically also, suppose banks net long exposure in USD is 10 million and the exchange rate is 1 USD = INR 40. The bank had to shell out INR 400 million to take exposure. If the value of USD falls to INR 35, the bank will loose INR 50 million. In the same manner, if bank has net short exposure of same amount in USD and value of USD rises to INR 45, bank will loose INR50 million.

Exchange Rate Volatility

The fluctuation in foreign exchange portfolio of bank is linked to volatility of exchange rate in designated currency.

INR loss or gain in currency = (Net exposure in foreign currency in INR) x Exchange rate shock

Net exposure in foreign currency = (FX Assets – FX Liabilities) + (FX bought - FX sold)

The first major source of foreign exchange risk is the trading activities in foreign currencies which is one of the largest activities of financial markets. The turnover of this market in one day is more than the GDP of many countries in the world. Another major factor adding to foreign exchange risk is that the foreign exchange market is 24 hours market unlike other financial market, which operates in certain timings. The forex market never sleeps. There are various trading activities which exposes banks to risk like buy and sell of foreign currencies on behalf of customers, buying financial assets overseas, hedging against exposures or a simple speculative purpose for short term gains. The activity that the banks perform on behalf of their customers does not have any forex risk. But other activities such as banks hedging itself for their exposure or taking open position for speculative gains, faces forex risk directly.

The second source of foreign exchange risk is forex exposure arising out of mismatches in assets and liabilities held in foreign currencies.

Net Long Position = Foreign Currency Assets > Foreign Currency Liabilities

Net Short Position = Foreign Currency Liabilities > Foreign Currency Assets

The above positions are taken by borrowings in foreign currency through ECB route and lending in foreign currency to overseas borrowers or by buying bonds in different currencies.

Foreign Exchange Risk and Hedging

The profitability on foreign assets depends on two factors - one is contractual rate of interest payable on loan or investment which is generally linked with London Inter Bank Rate (LIBOR) plus some spread and another is exchange rate fluctuation in designated currency.

As the economic condition changes, the interest rate and exchange rate also changes, thus impacting profitability and in extreme cases profits may result in loss.

EXAMPLE: Impact of Foreign Exchange Fluctuation on FI's Profitability on Investment

Suppose an FI has invested USD 100 million in US AAA rated company @ LIBOR (5.75) plus 100 basis point for one year and the exchange rate 1 USD = INR 43. If at the time of payment on maturity exchange rate is 1 USD = INR 40 and LIBOR is 2.75, then total payment including principal and interest would be INR 4150 million against the initial investment of INR 4300 million. FI will face a loss of INR 150 million due to exchange rate and interest rate change, if position is left unhedged.

The bank and FI cannot know the future currency rate in advance. Only a fair amount of estimation or a rough predictions about future rates can be made. Bank can hedge its position in two ways - first through on balance sheet hedging and second through off balance sheet hedging. Through on balance sheet hedging, bank may alter its exposure in assets and liabilities to match gap and protect bank's profit. The off balance sheet hedging involves buying or selling of forward or other currency derivative products to hedge forex risk.

The off balance sheet hedging involves cost of hedging in the form of premium paid to buy derivative products such as forward cover, currency swaps, etc. The banks also hedge exposure by taking cross currency exposure to different currency which has less volatility in comparison with the present currency position.

Interest Rate Parity Theorem (IRPT)

Forward rates are a function of the spot rate currently prevailing between two currencies and the interest rate differentials that are prevailing in the respective countries. If the forward rates are not linked to the interest rate differential, there is an arbitrage opportunity to make money by borrowing in one currency and lending in another, and at the same time eliminating the risk of currency movement by entering into a forward contract. The currency carrying a lower rate of interest would be at a forward premium and that carrying a higher rate of interest would be at a forward discount to the extent of the differential in interest rates. If interest rate parity does not hold well, arbitragers will take advantage of risk-free arbitrage.[1]

The interest rate parity may be expressed as under:

$$1 + R_{INR} = (1 + R_{USD}) \times F_t \times (1/S_t)$$

Where

R_{INR} = Interest rate offered in India (INR)

R_{USD} = Interest rate offered in US (USD)

S_t = Spot exchange rate between currencies at time t (INR/USD)

F_t = Forward exchange rate at time t (INR/USD)

EXAMPLE: How Interest Rate Parity Theorem works

Suppose interest rate offered in AAA bond by an Indian company @ 9% and by US company @ 5%. The spot INR/USD rate is INR 40/$. The forward exchange rate would be:

$1 + 0.90 = (1 + 0.05) \times F_t \times (1/40)$

$F_t = 40 \times (1.09)/(1.05) = 41.52/\$$

If forward rate is not matching with the above at time t, an arbitrage opportunity exists.

Recently, there are significant inflows of foreign currencies in India either on account of portfolio investment and foreign direct investment (FDI), with the result that INR is strengthening against the US Dollar and appreciated by 10% in a year's time. On the strength of rupee, exporters who are likely to receive export earnings in the future may cover their receivable by entering into forward contracts while importers may chose not to the cover their payments. When currency is sold in the forward market to a bank, the bank sells currency in the spot market to remain hedged and that results in a weakening of the dollar in the spot market as well as a softening of the dollar premium in the forward market. It would work in an opposite manner if there are strong outflows of dollar from India.

Sovereign Risk

The cross country loans are generally made without the judgment regarding credit quality of the sovereign country in which the borrower resided or government organization of that country or a private corporation. Countries meet their demand for funds beyond those provided by WB & IMF through cross country borrowings. When sovereign country due to unforeseen reasons or internal disturbance or aggression or war or due to some uncontrollable development defaults the repayment of its foreign debts, this originates sovereign risk or frequently called country risk.

The debt repayment problem was first observed in 1980 with Poland and other European countries. Similarly, in 1982, a debt moratorium was announced by Brazil and Mexican government. A debt moratorium means delay in repayment of loan installments due in future. Due to these defaults, worldwide many banks had to provide for bed loans created out of sovereign defaults. Further, the same situation was experienced in 1994 when Mexico devalued its currency which lasted till 1997 when Mexico paid all its loans to US.

Measurement of Sovereign Risk

For measurement of country risk, an FI may use various options available such as international rating agencies report and country ratings assigned by them, domestic rating agencies rating assigned to various countries, developing its own assessment model for country risk, etc. In order to make final decision in assessment of country risk, all these options may be clubbed to get the best possible result. The methods for sovereign risk assessment may be based on quantitative techniques as well on qualitative techniques as the risk in question cannot easily be quantified or assessed. There are various factors posing country risk which are of subjective nature as sudden internal disturbance, war, etc. The quantitative techniques may support the possible prediction of country risk arising out of currency movement, country debt position, country's inflation or money supply, etc which are of financial nature.

In US, three country risk assessment services are available to the outside investors and FIs: the Euromoney Index, The Economist Intelligence Unit and the Institutional Investor Index.

The Euromoney Index is based on a large number of economic and political factors having different weights as per their relative importance in assessing country risk.

The Economist Intelligence Unit rates country risk in combination of economic and political risk on a 100 point scale. The higher number of index signifies higher amount of risk.

The Institutional Investor Index is based on surveys of loan officers of various major multinational banks. A subjective score based on credit quality of countries is assigned by loan officers on 100 point scale signifying high score means higher security.

Statistical Model

The Country Risk Analysis model consists of identifying those variables which are important in assessment of country risk. Some common variables are:

1. Debt Service Ratio (DSR) = Debt repayment (Interest and Principal)/ Exports, if the ratio value is less than one, there is a possibility that the country will have to reschedule its debt repayment. For comfort zone, number has to be more than one.
2. Import Ratio (IR) = Total Imports / Total foreign exchange reserves, if there is greater need of imports arises, there is a possibility of depletion of foreign exchange reserve very fast, leaving country in defaulting mode for repayment of its foreign debt. Hence, to rule out the possibility of loan rescheduling, the value of IR should be greater than one.
3. Investment Ratio (INVR) = Real Investment / GNP, the IVNR measures the degree to which a country is allocating resources to real investment rather than to consumption. The higher number signifies the more productive economy in future and the lower possibility of reschedulement of country's debt.
4. Variance of Export Revenue (VAREX) = σ^2_{ER}, the export of a country is influenced by two parameters, surplus product availability in domestic market for export and competitive pricing of export good in international market. These risks are categorized as quantity risk and price risk. The volatility in export earnings and any downside turn in earnings may result in probability of debt reschedulement.
5. Domestic Money Supply Growth (MG) = ΔM / M where ΔM is change in money supply from initial level M. The higher rate of inflation makes country's currency weaker in international markets. If country's currency loses credibility in international market as a medium of exchange, then country has to depend upon other acceptable currencies in international market which adversely impact the real output. The persistent inflation and money supply growth increases the probability of debt reschedulement.

Here by summing up these variables, we may calculate probability of rescheduling (p) as:

p = f(DSR, IR, IVNR, VAREX, MG......................)

The list of variables is not exhaustive but depends upon the domestic and international circumstances influencing debt repayments of country assessing country risk. The validity of this model depends upon the various factors such as measurement of key variables, population groups, political risk factors, corruption perceptions, etc.

Summary

In this chapter, the sources of forex risk faced by banks and financial institutions have been discussed. Such risks arise due to fluctuations in various currency exchange rates and the position hold by banks in their balance sheet in foreign currency. Banks are also exposed to forex risk arising due to mismatches of assets and liabilities in their balance sheet. The exchange rate volatility has been discussed to measure exchange rate shock. The interest rate parity theory has been discussed to measure the behaviour of various currency vis-à-vis domestic currency based on market parameter such as interest rate.

KEY CONCEPTS

Long Position	Short Position	Exchange Rate Shock
LIBOR	FDI	Spot Rate
Forward Rate	Interest Rate Parity	

Review Questions and Problems

1. List the various kinds of currency risks faced by banks.
2. If a bank has taken a long position in $, will it gain or lose if the Rupee appreciates in value against dollar.
3. An FI has $100 millions in assets and $50 millions in liabilities. It has also taken a position of $150 million in forex trading. What is its net exposure in dollar?
4. A bank has $100 million in liabilities and JPY 1 billion in assets and has sold JPY 500 million and bought $200 million in foreign currency market. Discuss the long and short position of bank. How is the bank exposed to exchange rate fluctuation in either currency?
5. What are four forex trading activities of a bank?
6. What is major source of most profit or loss on foreign exchange trading?
7. Study a case of loss due to forex exposure in India and list out the failures in measuring forex risk.
8. What are the various factors that affect banks profitability from its positions in forex?
9. Find out the various trading activities performed by banks and FIs and the risk associated with these activities.

10. What are the various factors, which force banks/FIs to take currency risk?
11. How does the interest rate parity theorem work? Test the results of the theorem with inputs from current market rates.
12. What are the various opportunities available if IRPT does not hold good?
13. A bank wants to invest in securities and consider the following one year rates: Indian security ROI = 10%, US security ROI = 4%, Spot INR/$ rate = INR 40/$, forward exchange rate = INR 42/$. In which country's security, should the bank invest?
14. The cost of one year paper in India is 10%, the yield of one year loan is 12% and dollar loan yield is 6%. The spot exchange rate is Rs. 45/$ and the one year forward rate is Rs. 48/$. Assess which loan is attractive rupee or dollar.
15. The following are the foreign currency position of a bank, expressed in INR in crores:

Currency	Assets	Liabilities	FX Bought	FX Sold
Dollar	150	75	85	65
Pound	225	175	130	65
Euro	75	65	90	75

(i) What is bank net exposure in dollar?
(ii) What is bank net exposure in pound?
(iii) What is bank net exposure in euro?
(iv) What is expected loss or gain if euro exchange rate appreciates by 1%?
(v) What is expected loss or gain if pound exchange rate depreciates by 2%?
(vi) What is expected loss or gain if dollar exchange rate appreciates by 3%?

16. Assume that annual ROI in India is 10% and 4% in US. A bank can borrow or lend at these rates. The spot rate is Rs. 45/$. (i) If the one year forward rate is Rs. 48/$, how could the bank arbitrage using a sum of Rs.100 crores? (ii) What forward rate will siege an arbitrage opportunity?
17. What are various risks occurred while making loans to foreign country's borrowers?
18. What are sovereign risk assessment models available to investors? Explain in details using internet or websites for detailed information.
19. Define the ratios used in CRA model and explain how each ratio is interpreted in assessment of country risk?

20. Calculate the probability of loan reschedulement based on the data given below:

Variables	Country Value	Weight
DSR	1.50	0.10
IR	1.76	0.15
INVR	0.54	0.29
VAREX	0.12	0.33
MG	0.05	0.13

Make the decision of loan if probability of acceptance is below 0.45 and probability of refusal is above 0.70.

21. Nepal and Sri Lanka have export of $7 billion and $16 billion respectively. The debt repayment of foreign loans for both the countries is $3 billion and $5 billion respectively. Calculate (i) DSR for both countries; (ii) Which country is safe for lending between two; (iii) Is the decision taken on the basis of DSR alone is correct? Explain why?

Reference:

1. *http://som.gmu.edu/sba/irp*

Chapter – 9

Measurement of Liquidity Risk

Chapter Objective

- Understand Liquidity Stress in different Institutions
- Discuss Liquidity Gap Model
- Measurement of Bank's Liquidity Exposure/Risk
- Explain limitations of Liquidity Gap Model

Introduction

The management of liquidity is daily business of banks and financial institutions. The day begins with the liquidity position assessment for future business. Liquidity in simple terms is the easy flow of money for repayment of loans and deposits, daily transaction cash, disbursement of loans, etc. The extreme event in liquidity ends with solvency problem for banks and FIs. Apart from normal business of banks, liquidity stress is also faced by external events such as panic created out of natural disasters, political instability, war, financial market crash etc. The liquidity risk depends on the nature of FIs and it is not the same for all kinds of institutions. The liquidity risk depends on the factors such as size of the bank, business lines of the bank, geographical locations of the bank, reputation of the bank, etc. The size of the bank is a very important factor for liquidity risk as big banks sometimes survive extreme liquidity risk in comparison with small banks. For small banks, it is difficult to arrange sudden liquidity at the time of crisis, hence these are more vulnerable to extreme liquidity risk. For example, in comparison with banks, the insurance companies have less liquidity risk.

Liquidity risk arises with the sudden heavy cash outflows and with the bank not having enough cash to meet its obligations. The bank funds are generally locked in long-term assets because of higher return on these. All banks keep minimum amount of cash because of no return on this. Though in crisis situation, assets may be unlocked by bank but at discounted price or further fund may be raised at a very high cost to meet obligations which may hamper bank's profitability or may lead to insolvency. The liquidity risk also arises out of off balance sheet commitments. In banks, loan sanction to disbursement ratio is around 60% and this increases sudden demand of disbursements.

Liquidity Risk in Different Institutions

Liquidity risk is not same for banks, insurance company or for a mutual fund. It depends on the nature of business being performed by FIs.

Liquidity Risk in Banks: Banks liabilities are of short term nature and assets are of long term nature. While return on assets is also exposed to various other risks such as interest rate risk and credit risk. The repayments of liabilities of banks are fixed and bank has to honour these. Because of low return on deposit, banks may find it difficult to raise further deposits at the time of maturity of its old deposits. At the same time, sudden loan disbursement may tighten liquidity position. The demand deposit account holders are the major source of fund for banks. Deposit holders are free to withdraw their deposit at any given day and entitle of immediate repayment of deposit amount and interest due on deposit. All banks assumes that on any given normal day only a small portion of total demand deposit will be withdrawn and accordingly banks plan their liquidity position. To manage liquidity position banks continuously monitor the net deposit amount, i.e. fresh deposit minus repayment of deposits. On the basis of historical data, the behavioural pattern of withdrawal of deposit and fund raising through fresh deposit may easily be predicted for each business cycle. Adversities in liquidity position are very hard to mitigate and often leads to failure of a bank or FI. Sudden withdrawal of deposit from bank triggered due to some uncontrollable event may create serious repayment problems to its account holders. The problem may cumulate if there is liquidity crunch in the money market. The same may be experienced on asset side also in case borrowers exercise their loan commitments in tight liquidity position or at the time of liquidity crunch.

Liquidity Risk in Insurance Company: In case of insurance companies, generally two types of liquidity risk may be seen - one is sudden policies cancellation and another is sudden rise in claims. For normal maturity of policies, insurance companies have provisions but the above two conditions are also not ruled out. Suppose if government withdraws IT Act Section 80 C benefits for investing in life insurance policies, there would be sudden withdrawal of money from insurance companies and these companies have to honour the surrender value of policies. Similarly, any natural clamity or accident may also put pressure on insurance company for settling a large number of claims. Usually insurance companies invest premium income in long term bonds or provide long term loans to corporates, banks and other FIs.

Liquidity Risk in Mutual Fund: There are two types of mutual funds - one is closed-end fund and another is open-end fund. The close end fund offers a limited option to buy mutual shares at the issue price or from the market at NAV. The open end fund offers unlimited number of share or buyback at NAV. To make the offer attractive, mutual fund offer instant liquidity facility which may expose them to sudden drain of cash in adverse market conditions for which mutual funds have to liquidate its holding in depressed market conditions.

Liquidity Risk in FIs/ Non Banking Finance Companies: Liquidity risk in these institutions is relatively less than the banks. The main concern of these institutions is sudden cash outflow due to downgrading of rating or loss and losing investor confidence overnight. The downgrading of rating or losing investors faith in the institution is directly governed by asset quality and the management. In such a situation, it is very difficult for them to infuse fresh liquidity into the company because no lender is available. Thus NBFCs/FIs may face immediate insolvency.

Liquidity Risk Measurement

Liquidity Gap Model

The liquidity gap model is cash flow analysis of the liquidity gap between the cash inflows on assets of bank and the cash outflows on its liabilities over a period of time. The different time buckets have been set for liquidity gaps for assets and liabilities. These time buckets or maturities range from 1 month to 10 years and above. The different buckets are:[1]

1. 1 month
2. Above 1 month to 3 months
3. Above 3 months to 6 months
4. Above 6 months to 1 year
5. Above 1 year to 3 years
6. Above 3 years to 5 years
7. Above 5 years to 7 years
8. Above 7 years to 10 years
9. Above 10 years.

As per the requirement of an FI, the buckets may be broken in smaller period but it is very difficult to manage a large number of buckets.

The following is the example of liquidity gap model statement for bank/FI:

Buckets	1 month	Above 1 month to 3 months	Above 3 months to 6 months	Above 6 months to 1 year	Above 1 year to 3 years	Above 3 years to 5 years	Above 5 years to 7 years	Above 7 years to 10 years	Above 10 years
Cash Inflows (Maturing Assets) (A)									
Cash Outflows (Maturing Liabilities) (B)									
GAP (A-B)									
Cumulative Gap (CGAP)									

Liquidity Classification of Assets and Liabilities

For a FI manager, cash flow classification of assets & liabilities on the basis of timing of cash flows and the nature, i.e. highly liquid or less liquid, is a very important factor while measuring liquidity risk. Few examples of bucketing of future cash flows of assets and liabilities on the basis of maturity profile are:

Cash Inflows (Assets)	Time Bucketing Assets	Cash Outflows (Liabilities)	Time Bucketing Liabilities
• Balances with other banks in India in deposit accounts, Money at call and short notice and other placements.	1 month bucket Deposits as per residual maturity	• Notes, bonds & debentures (Floating and Fixed rate) • Term deposits from public • Certificates of deposits and ICDs	Mainly as per residual maturity or as per embedded option, if any or on the basis of behavioral analysis of payments
• Investments • Bills of exchange, promissory notes, discounted & rediscounted	As per residual maturity for banking book and in first three buckets as per holding period for trading book	• Term-money borrowing • Borrowings from RBI, Government & others	As per residual maturity
• Term loans/corporate loans • Short Term Loans	As per residual maturity and timing of cash flows	• Current liabilities and provisions • Interest payable on bonds/ deposits/borrowings	As per likely timing of cash flow or due date
• Reverse Repos/ Forex-rupee swaps (buy/sell)/ Bills rediscounted	As per residual maturity	• Repos/ bills rediscounted forex-rupee swaps (sell/buy) / interest rate swaps / FRAs	As per residual maturity
• Interest rate swaps / FRAs	As per residual maturity	• Capital, Reserves & Surplus • Gifts, grants & benefactions	Over 10 years Bucket
• Cash	1 month bucket	• Advance income received • Receipts from borrowers pending adjustment	Over 10 years bucket
• Balance with RBI	1 month bucket	• Provisions on assets	May be netted out from gross value of assets
• Balances with other banks in India in current account	Minimum required amount in 1-3 years bucket and rest in 1 month bucket		

• Equity shares, convertible, preference shares, shares of subsidiaries /joint ventures, venture capital units • Fixed assets (excluding assets on lease) Intangible assets and items not representing cash flows	Over 10 years bucket Over 10 years bucket		
• NPAs (Sub Standard)	All repayment for 3 years in 3-5 years bucket and rest in the respective buckets as per timing of repayment by adding 3 years		
• NPAs (Doubtful Assets)	All repayment for 5 years in 5-7 years bucket and rest in the respective buckets as per timing of repayment by adding 5 years		
• Contingent Cash flows such as letter of credit, guarantees, loan commitments, undisbursed amount	As per past behavioral analysis or drawdown request or timing		

In addition to the above, banks also prepare Short Term Dynamic Liquidity (STDL) statement for a period of six months which is a further break up of above statement to keep a watch on immediate liquidity risk. The format of STDL is as follows:-

Buckets	1-14 days	15-28 days	29 days-2 months	3 months	Above 3 months-6 month's
Cash Inflows (A)					
Cash Outflows (B)					
GAP (A-B)					
Cumulative Gap (CGAP)					

Limitations of the Liquidity Gap Model

The liquidity gap model has few shortcomings like it ignores information regarding assets and liability maturing within the maturities buckets, does not takes into account pre mature withdrawal and prepayment and ignores cash flows from off balance sheet activities. The assets and liabilities with embedded options may be captured correctly in this model, hence may build a pressure on liquidity position if options are exercised.

Measuring Bank's Liquidity Exposure

The bank's liquidity risk may arise from outflow of deposit or demand of undrawn loans. Bank meets these demands either by borrowing fresh funds or by unlocking its investments. The bank must be able to measure its liquidity position on real time basis. A liquidity gap statement has already been discussed in previous topic. A bank can manage its liquidity position in three ways:

1. It can sell its liquid assets, government bonds etc. carrying low price risk; or
2. It can borrow money for short term from money market; or
3. It can use excess reserves maintained than the regulatory requirements.

A method of measuring liquidity risk by using liquidity index was developed by Jim Pierce at the Federal Reserve. This index measures potential losses bank may suffer from sudden disposal of its assets under distressed conditions rather than at fair market value. The greater the difference between immediate distress sale asset price (P_i) and fair market price under normal market conditions (P^*_i), the liquidity of bank's assets are treated on lesser side.

The equation of index ***I*** may be written as :-

$$I = \sum_{i=1}^{N} [(W_i)(P_i / P^*_i)];\ 0 <= I <= 1$$

where w_i is the percent of each asset in the bank's portfolio

$$\sum_{i=1}^{N} (w_i) = 1$$

Example: Calculation of the Liquidity Index

Assume a bank has two investments: 50% in government security for one month and 50% in AAA bond. If bank sells its investment today to meet out urgent liquidity need, it will fetch Rs.99 of Rs.100 face value for government security and Rs.85 of Rs.100 face value of AAA bond. The AAA bond at the end of one month will fetch a price of Rs.92. Thus, one-month liquidity index for bank's investment would be:

$$I = (0.5)[(99/100)] + (0.5)[(85/92)]$$

$$= 0.957$$

Summary

Liquidity risk arises out of unexpected cash outflow from banks and financial institutions. This kind of situation may be triggered by many factors such as liquidity crunch, panic among depositors, bank credibility loss or the huge losses faced by banks. Regulators from time to time framed various policies to maintain adequate liquidity to meet abnormal withdrawal. Banks cash is locked in financing long term assets whereas the liabilities are of short term nature and may be recalled at a very short notice.

KEY CONCEPTS

Liquidity Stress	Liquidity Gap	CGAP
Liquidity Gap Buckets	Liquidity Gap Model	Liquidity Index

Review Questions and Problems

1. What are the various sources of liquidity risk? Identify on the basis of nature of FIs?
2. What are three major sources of bank's liquidity?
3. How does liquidity risk differs for different types of FIs?
4. What are the various reasons for liquidity risk? How does the liquidity risk of asset side differ from liquidity risk of liability side?
5. What could be immediate source of liquidity for an insurance company when premium income is not enough to meet claims?
6. Define the situations where banks, insurance companies, mutual funds and NBFCs may face solvency risk due to liquidity risk.
7. Perform the bucketing of assets and liabilities from annual accounts of selected FI/Bank and find out the liquidity gap.
8. For a listed mutual fund, what are the various situations where it may face liquidity risk?
9. If assets and liabilities are maturing at the same time, is there any liquidity risk?
10. A bank has following balance sheet and expect a loan of Rs.100 crores and repayment of deposit of Rs.120 crores:-

Assets		Liabilities	
Loans & Advances	Rs.1200 crores	Equity	Rs.300 crores
Investments	Rs.500 crores	Deposits	Rs.1500 crores
Cash at Bank	Rs.100 crores		
Total assets	Rs.1800 crores	Total liabilities	Rs.1800 crores

Prepare the bank's balance sheet if (i) bank create further liability to make deposits repayment; (ii) bank use investments to make deposits repayment; (iii) bank create further liability to make loan; (iv) bank use investments to make loan.

11. A bank has the following balance sheet and expect a loan release of Rs.500 crores:-

Assets		Liabilities	
Loans & Advances	Rs.1000 crores	Equity	Rs.100 crores
Investments	Rs.100 crores	Deposits	Rs.900 crores
Cash at Bank	Rs.10 crores	Borrowed Funds	Rs.110 crores
Total assets	Rs.1110 crores	Total liabilities	Rs.1110 crores

Prepare the bank balance sheet by adopting asset management liquidity risk strategy and by adopting liability management liquidity risk strategy.

12. A bank has Rs.100 crores in government T-Bills, have tie-ups for raising Rs.50 crores from market and maintaining Rs. 40 crores excess in cash reserve with RBI. The bank has borrowed Rs. 50 crores from RBI and Rs. 20 crores from call market to meet its short term demand of funds. Calculate (i) Bank's total available sources of liquidity; (ii) Bank's total use of liquidity; (iii) Net liquidity position of bank, and (iv) Write down your conclusion made from above results.

13. An FI has the following assets in its balance sheet: Rs.100 crores in cash reserve with RBI, Rs.150 crores in Govt. T-bills, security based loans of Rs.100 crores and Rs.50 crores invested in fixed assets. Assume that assets need to be liquidated today, FI will receive only 90% of the fair market price of security based loans and 98% of the fair market value of T-bills. Calculate the Liquidity Index for bank.

14. A bank has Rs. 300 crores cash in hand, Rs. 900 crores in loans and Rs.750 crores in demand deposits. Calculate (i) the financing gap; (ii) financing requirement, and (iii) How can the bank use financing gap for its day-to-day liquidity management?

15. A bank wishes to liquidate certain investments after a period of one year. Calculate present and one-year liquidity index of these investments as per information provided below:

Investments	Face Value	Liquidation Values	
		t = 0	t = 1
X company shares	Rs.100	Rs.120	Rs.150
AAA corporate bonds	Rs.10000	Rs.8500	Rs.9100
T-bills	Rs.100000	Rs.80000	Rs.90000

Also calculate present and one-year liquidity index, if percentage of each investment in books has been given as 30% for X company shares, 40% for AAA corporate bonds and 30% for T-bills.

16. Discuss the model used for measurement of liquidity exposure of banks.

References:

1. *RBI Guidelines on ALM for Banks (1999).*
2. *www.investopedia.com*

Chapter – 10

Measurement of Off-Balance-Sheet Risk

Chapter Objective

- Understand Off-Balance-Sheet items
- Understand Off-Balance-Sheet Risk
- Focus on OBS items types
- Types of OBS Risks
- Measurement of OBS Risk

Introduction

The Off-Balance-Sheet (OBS) activities involve risks that cumulate the overall risk exposure of a bank or FI. The failures of various banks and FIs such as Barings bank, Bankers Trust, etc. has been due to OBS activities in derivative products. OBS activities are used to hedge or reduce other risk such as credit risk, market risk, interest rate risk and foreign exchange risk etc. but OBS activities has both the tendencies of risk reducing and risk enhancing. The banks and FIs are tending to deal in OBS activities as it is an important source of their fee-based income.

OBS activities generally appear as footnotes or in notes of accounts in financial statements and are hence, less visible to investors or regulator. Off-balance-sheet items are classified as contingent assets and liabilities that have a futuristic impact on balance sheet rather than current reflection. These have major impact on future profitability and solvency of banks. The management of OBS activities effectively gives a leading edge in controlling overall risk exposure of an organisation. OBS assets and liabilities may transform in positive or negative cash flow in future. Due to this nature of OBS activities, the real value of capital or net worth of an FI cannot be assessed. Based on future event and its occurrence, the OBS items move onto asset or liability side of balance sheet.

Types of OBS Activities

There are various types of OBS activities which are as follows:-

- Loan Commitments
- Future and Forward Contracts

- Credit Derivatives
- Guarantees
- Letter of Credit
- Option Contracts
- Interest Rate Swaps
- Sale of Bed Assets with Recourse

Loan commitment is a contractual obligation for providing loan to borrower at a future date. The FIs/banks charge up front fees and commitment charges if loan is not withdrawn at a future date.

Line of credit or letter of credit is a kind of guarantee extended to buyer of guarantee for the performance of the borrower. In case borrower's performance or obligations are not upto the mark, the FI is liable to pay on behalf of buyer of letter of credit. Letter of Credit is an insurance against future performance of its customers and also against the severity of an event may occur in future. These are used for both domestic and international trade.

Derivative contracts are discussed in detail in Chapter 11.

The measurement of OBS item risk may be made on the basis of a behavioural pattern of obligations occurred from OBS items such as letter of credit, guarantees and loan commitments. On the basis of this analysis, a suitable fee structure may be designed and risk premium over normal interest may be loaded. For example, a bank has loan commitment of Rs.100 crores @ 10% p.a. and from the past analysis it gathers that 50% of the amount may not be withdrawn at the same rate and at the likely time of withdrawal, the rate will be 9%. The bank has two options in this case, either to charge a high upfront fee or to load risk premium to mitigate interest rate risk.

Types of Off-Balance-Sheet Risks

The various risks are associated with OBS activities some of which are being discussed in this chapter. Other associated risks have already been dealt in respective chapters of this book.

Interest Rate Risk is a contingent risk arising from the fact that a bank offering loans to its customers on some pre-specified interest rate on fixed basis for entire tenure or on floating basis. For example a loan is made @15% and cost of fund of FI rises. The cost of corresponding liability crosses the rate on which loan was made resulting in negative earning on this loan. This risk may be tackled by offering loan on floating basis linked to the prime rate which is based on cost of liability. Even this does not fully cover interest rate risk as the cost of fund and price of loan are not perfectly correlated. For example, the cost of fund may rise by 150 basis points but the prime rate is only increased by 100 basis points. This spread risk is also called Basis Risk.

Loan Drawl Risk is arising out of customer drawl of loan out of maximum loan sanctioned. For example, a borrower has been sanctioned a loan of Rs. 1000 crores but borrower takes disbursement of only Rs. 550 crores. Undisbursed portion Rs. 450 crores of loan becomes a contingent asset which may turn as real asset if borrower takes remaining amount. This exposes bank with the liquidity risk as during the commitment period borrower may any time demand remaining amount. However, some bank charges commitment fee to take care of such events but it is not sufficient at the time of tight liquidity position in money market.

A bank is also exposed to contingent credit risk arising out of loan commitment to a AAA borrower on 1% discount over the prime rate of bank. But during the commitment period, if borrower's rating is down to AA to which bank provides loans at 1% above the prime rate, the bank may face credit risk or default risk.

Multiple Funding Risk is also a contingent risk as big corporates generally tie up with many banks and FIs for their future loan requirements. At the time of credit crunch due to market conditions or monetary policy, banks and FIs become restrictive in extending loans as cost of fund increases and pricing of loan become difficult due to inherent default risk which is most likely at the time of higher rates. In such credit crunch time, big corporate having multiple tie-ups are likely to exercise their commitments with banks and FIs. In order to meet commitment, banks and FIs have to raise fund at higher cost.

Settlement Risk is one to which a bank or an FI is exposed to a within-day or intraday credit risk that does not appear on its balance sheet. The intraday settlement risk is an additional OBS risk to which every bank and FI is exposed those participating in settlement of daily fund transfers or setting off trades. Bank on the basis of receipts during the day make further commitments for its disposal, may face settlement risk if even one of its receipt fails to settle as it will disturb whole chain of settlements. One single failed settlement may pose settlement risk to many transactions.

Subsidiary Company Risk is also a contingent risk as all its commitments are not reflected in parent company's balance sheet. But it may happen that the commitments of subsidiary company become obligatory on the part of parent company at the time of failure of subsidiary company. The regulator may also impose penalty on parent company for unfulfilled commitments of its holding company. In some countries, it is legally obligatory on part of parent company for misdeeds of holding company as corporate separateness are not legally supported.

Measurement of Off-Balance-Sheet Risk

The off-balance-sheet (OBS) activities on both assets and liabilities side may pose risk to banks and FIs. Many times in this book, we have discussed the failure of many banks and FIs worldwide due to exposure in derivatives, a main constituent of off balance sheet item. The OBS activities are mainly performed to hedge various kinds of risks but the instruments involved in hedging have both the nature of reducing and increasing risk. A lesson may be learnt from disasters taking place worldwide in financial market that OBS activities may not be ignored or under considered while working on risk management practices. The implication of these activities may be threatening to the solvency of the institution.

The derivative products will be discussed later in different chapters.

Summary

The off balance sheet items have big impact on banks balance sheet and hence require special attention of banks. The risks involved in various OBS items have been also discussed.

KEY CONCEPTS

Off-Balance-Sheet Activities	Loan Commitments	Future Contracts
Forward Contracts	Credit Derivatives	Guarantees
Letter of Credit	Option Contracts	Interest Rate Swaps
Sale of Bed Assets		

Review Questions and Problems

1. Study Annual Report of a bank and list out contingent assets and liabilities disclosed in annual statements.
2. The market value of assets and liabilities of a bank is Rs. 15000 crores and Rs. 12500 crores respectively. Bank also has contingent assets and liabilities valued at Rs. 350 crores and Rs. 600 crores respectively. What is real net worth of the bank?
3. What are the various OBS activities? Kindly write a para on each along with the risk associated with each.
4. What are the other purposes of OBS activities besides speculation or hedging?
5. What are the various contingent risks arising out of OBS activities?
6. How can you distinguish between an off-balance-sheet asset and an off-balance-sheet liability?
7. How is a bank exposed to various types of contingent risks and how can these risks be controlled?
8. How is an FI exposed to loan drawl and multiple funding risks? Are these risks related to each other?
9. How do different types of contingent risks increase the insolvency risk of a bank?
10. How does settlement risk arise in interbank payments and why has it been classified as contingent OBS risk?
11. How can the failure of a subsidiary company affect the parent company?
12. Explain how OBS activities not only expose FIs to various other risks but also hedge risks of FIs?

PART C

MANAGEMENT OF RISK

11. Risk Management Tools
12. Interest Rate Risk Management
13. Market Risk Management
14. Credit Risk Management
15. Operational Risk Management
16. Foreign Exchange & Sovereign Risk Management
17. Liquidity Risk Management
18. Management of Capital Adequacy
19. Enterprise Wide Risk Management
20. Risk Reporting

Chapter – 11

Risk Management Tools

Chapter Objective

- Overview of Derivatives
- Understanding of Forward Contracts
- Understanding of Future Contracts
- Understanding of Various forms of Options
- Understanding of Various forms of Swaps
- Understanding of Caps, Floors and Collars

Introduction

Derivatives are being used worldwide as risk management tools to manage interest rate risk, market risk, credit risk and foreign exchange risk. In this chapter, we will discuss various types of derivatives. The use of these derivatives in hedging/management of different kind of risks will be dealt in respective chapters.

Derivatives are financial contracts and drive their value from some underlying asset/index. Movements in the value of the derivatives depend on price of underlying asset or index. The derivatives are contract between two parties and run on zero sum game. For any gain made by one party, the other party must have suffered loss of equal amount. The size world's derivative market is the $1.2 quadrillion as of 2010 and its notional value is 20 times the size of the world economy.

The most commonly used derivatives contracts are forwards, futures options, swaps, caps, floors and collars. Now we will discuss these types of derivatives in detail.

Forwards and Futures

Forward Contract

Forward contract is an agreement between two parties to exchange underlying asset against cash at a fixed date in future. The terms of the contract include quantity, date and price at which contract will mature. For example, a farmer having crop production perceive that by the time crop is available for sale, the price will fall from its current price. Farmer enters in a forward agreement with the counterparty to deliver fixed quantity of crop in future at today's rate, thus hedging himself from future price fluctuation in underlying commodity.

A forward contract or simply a forward is a non-standardized contract between two parties to buy or sell an asset at a specified future time at a price agreed today. This is in contrast to a spot contract, which is an agreement to buy or sell an asset today. It costs nothing to enter a forward contract. The party agreeing to buy the underlying asset in the future assumes a long position, and the party agreeing to sell the asset in the future assumes a short position. The price agreed upon is called the delivery price, which is equal to the forward price at the time the contract is entered into.

The price of the underlying instrument, in whatever form, is paid before control of the instrument changes. This is one of the many forms of buy/sell orders where the time of trade is not the time where the securities themselves are exchanged.

The forward price of such a contract is commonly contrasted with the spot price, which is the price at which the asset changes hands on the spot date. The difference between the spot and the forward price is the forward premium or forward discount, generally considered in the form of a profit or loss by the purchasing party.

Forwards, like other derivative securities, can be used to hedge risk (typically currency or exchange rate risk) as a means of speculation, or to allow a party to take advantage of a quality of the underlying instrument which is time-sensitive. The forwards are not normally traded on exchange. Forwards with certain standardized (by exchange) features are called futures. Futures are traded on exchange.

Payoffs

The value of a forward position at maturity depends on the relationship between the delivery price (K) and the underlying price (S_T) at that time.

For a long position, payoff is:

$$f_T = S_T - K$$

For a short position, payoff is:

$$f_T = K - S_T$$

Example: How forward prices is agreed upon

Suppose the initial price of farmer's goods is Rs.1,00,000/- and that merchant enters into a forward contract to buy the goods one year from today. But since farmer knows that he can immediately sell for Rs.1,00,000/- and places the proceeds in the bank, he wants to be compensated for the delayed sale. Suppose that the risk free rate of return R (the bank rate) for one year is 4.5%. Then the money in the bank would grow to Rs.1,04,500/- risk free. So farmer would want at least Rs.104,500/- one year from now for the contract to be worthwhile for him - the opportunity cost will be covered.

Another example, let us say the current price of the stock is Rs. 800 and we entered in forward contract to buy this stock in 3 months time for Rs. 810 (that means we hope that price will not fall lower than Rs. 810). If after three months, price is more than Rs. 810, let us say Rs. 830, than we can buy the same stock for Rs. 810 (as stated by forward contract) and after reselling it on the market our payoff will be

P = Rs.830 – Rs.810 = Rs.20

If at forward maturity, the stock price falls to Rs.780, then our loss will be

P = Rs.810 – Rs.780 = Rs.30

The graphs below illustrate the forward contract payoff patterns for long and short positions.

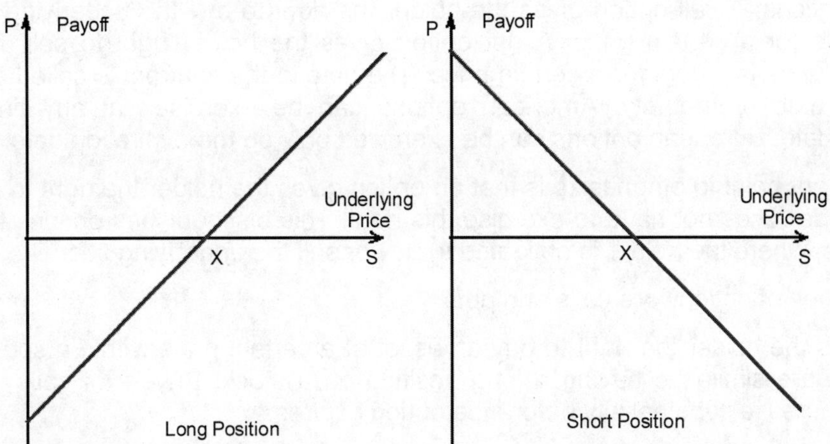

Futures Contract

A futures contract is a standardized contract between two parties to exchange a specified asset of standardized quantity and quality for a price agreed today (the futures price or the strike price) with delivery occurring at a specified future date, the delivery date. The contracts are traded on a futures exchange. The party agreeing to buy the underlying asset in the future, the "buyer" of the contract, is said to be "long", and the party agreeing to sell the asset in the future, the "seller" of the contract, is said to be "short". The terminology reflects the expectations of the parties -- the buyer hopes or expects that the asset price is going to increase, while the seller hopes or expects that it will decrease.

In many cases, the underlying asset to a futures contract may not be traditional commodities at all – that is, for financial futures the underlying asset or item can be currencies, securities or financial instruments and intangible assets or referenced items such as stock indexes and interest rates.

While the futures contract specifies a trade taking place in the future, the purpose of the futures exchange institution is to act as intermediary and minimize the risk of default by either party. Thus the exchange requires both parties to put up an initial amount of cash i.e., the margin. Additionally, since the futures price will generally change daily, the difference in the prior agreed-upon price and the daily futures price is settled daily also. The exchange will draw money out of one party's margin account and put it into the other party's account so that each party has the appropriate daily loss or profit. If the margin account goes below a certain value, then a margin call is made and the account owner must replenish the margin account. This process is known as marking to market. Thus on the delivery date, the amount exchanged is not the specified price on the contract but the spot value (since any gain or loss has already been previously settled by marking to market).

Options

An option is a stipulated privilege of buying or selling a stated security, commodity, or property at a given price (called strike price) within a specified time. There are two basic types of options. A call option gives the holder the right to buy the underlying security by a certain date for a certain price. A put option gives the holder right to sell the underlying security by a certain date for a certain price. The date in the contract is called exercise date, expiration date or maturity. American options can be exercised at any time up to the expiration date. European options can be exercised only on the expiration date.

The important point to emphasize is that an option gives the holder the right to do something but the holder does not have to exercise this right. This distinguishes options from forwards and futures, where the holder is obligated to buy or sell the underlying security.

The two types of options are calls and puts.

A call gives the holder the right to buy an asset at a certain price within a specific period of time. Calls are similar to having a long position on a stock. Buyers of calls hope that the stock will increase substantially before the option expires.

A put gives the holder the right to sell an asset at a certain price within a specific period of time. Puts are very similar to having a short position on a stock. Buyers of puts hope that the price of the stock will fall before the option expires.

There are four types of participants in options markets depending on the position they take:

1. Buyers of calls
2. Sellers of calls
3. Buyers of puts
4. Sellers of puts

Here is the important distinction between buyers and sellers:

- Call holders and put holders (buyers) are not obligated to buy or sell. They have the choice to exercise their rights if they choose.
- Call writers and put writers (sellers), however, are obligated to buy or sell. This means that a seller may be required to make good on a promise to buy or sell.

Long Call

Payoff from Buying a Call

A trader who believes that a stock's price will increase might buy the right to purchase the stock (a call option) rather than just purchase the stock itself. He would have no obligation to buy the stock, only the right to do so until the expiration date. If the stock price at expiration is above the exercise price by more than the premium (price) paid, he will profit. If the stock price at expiration is lower than the exercise price, he will let the call contract expire worthless, and only lose the amount of the premium. A trader might buy the option instead of shares, because for the same amount of money, he can control (leverage) a much larger number of shares.

If S is a final price of the option underlying security, X is a strike price and OP is an option price, then the profit is

Long Call: P = S - X - OP

Long Put

Payoff from Buying a Put

A trader who believes that a stock's price will decrease, can buy the right to sell the stock at a fixed price (a put option). He will be under no obligation to sell the stock, but has the right to do so until the expiration date. If the stock price at expiration is below the exercise price by more than the premium paid, he will profit. If the stock price at expiration is above the exercise price, he will let the put contract expire worthless and only lose the premium paid.

If S is a final price of the option underlying security, X is a strike price and OP is an option price, then the profit is

Long Put: P = X - S - OP

Short Call

Payoff from Writing a Call

A trader, who believes that a stock price will decrease, can sell the stock short or instead sell, or "write," a call. The trader selling a call has an obligation to sell the stock to the call buyer at the buyer's option. If the stock price decreases, the short call position will make a profit in the amount of the premium. If the stock price increases over the exercise price by more than the amount of the premium, the short call position will lose money, with the potential loss unlimited.

If S is a final price of the option underlying security, X is a strike price and OP is an option price, then the profit is

Short Call: P = X - S + OP

Short Put

Payoff from Writing a Put

A trader who believes that a stock price will increase can buy the stock or instead sell, or "write", a put. The trader selling a put has an obligation to buy the stock from the put buyer at the put buyer's option. If the stock price at expiration is above the exercise price, the short put position will make a profit in the amount of the premium. If the stock price at expiration is below the exercise price by more than the amount of the premium, the trader will lose money, with the potential loss being up to the full value of the stock.

If S is a final price of the option underlying security, X is a strike price and OP is an option price, then the profit is

Short Put: P = S - X + OP

The following graphs illustrate the option contract payoff patterns for long and short positions.

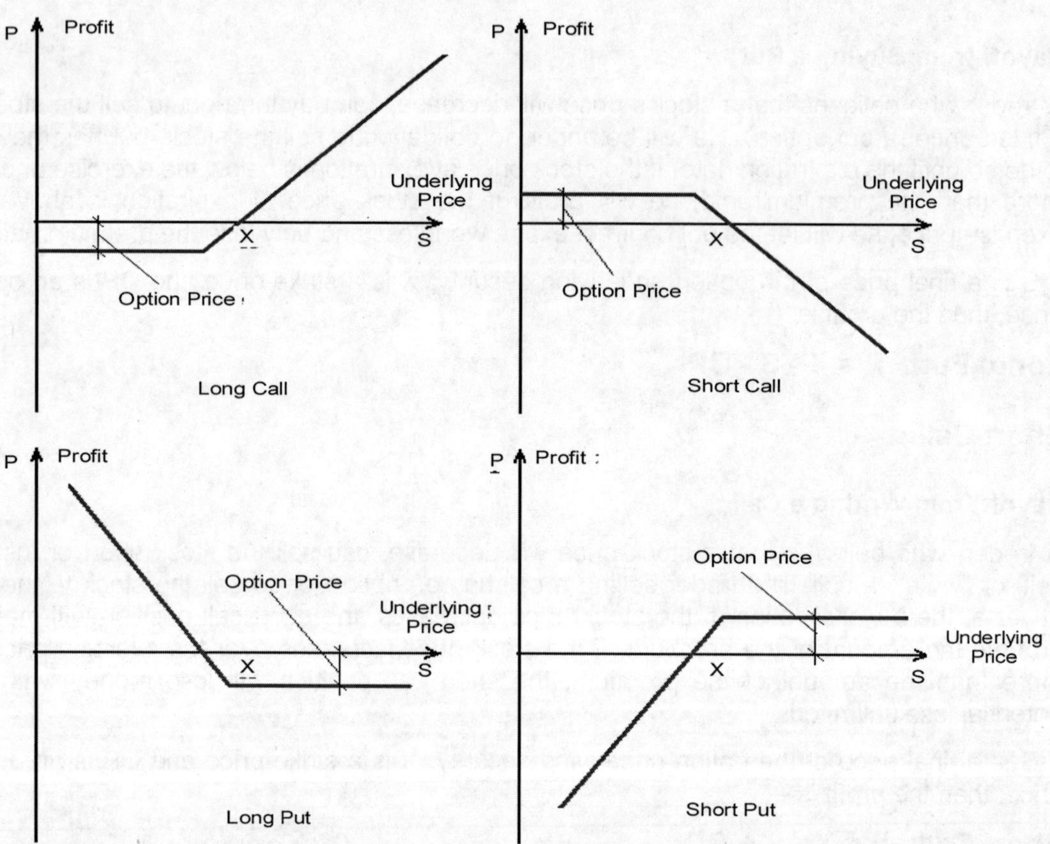

For example, let us say the stock price is Rs. 50, we bought European call option with strike Rs. 53 and paid Rs. 2 for this option. If option price is less than Rs.53, we will not exercise the option to buy the stock, because it does not make sense to buy security for higher price than it costs on the market. In this case, we lose all initial investment equal to the option price Rs. 2. If stock price is more than Rs. 53, we will exercise the option. For example if the stock price is Rs. 56, after exercising the option and immediately reselling the acquired stock, our profit will be:

P = Rs. 56 – Rs. 53 – Rs. 2 = Re. 1

If the stock price is Rs. 54, then the profit is:

P = Rs.54 – Rs.53 – Rs.2 = - Re.1

As we see, in latter case, we lose money. The reason is that increase of stock price just by Re.1 above the strike (Rs.53) does not cover our initial investment of Rs.2, although we still exercise the option to recover at least Re.1 of initial investment. If the stock price at exercise time is Rs. 55, then we exercise the option to cover our initial expenses(equal to option price):

P = Rs.55 – Rs.53 – Rs.2 = 0

Option Strategies

Combining any of the four basic kinds of option trades (possibly with different exercise prices and maturities) and the two basic kinds of stock trades (long and short) allows a variety of options strategies. Simple strategies usually combine only a few trades, while more complicated strategies can combine several.

Strategies are often used to engineer a particular risk profile to movements in the underlying security. For example, buying a butterfly spread (long one X1 call, short two X2 calls, and long one X3 call) allows a trader to profit if the stock price on the expiration date is near the middle exercise price, X2, and does not expose the trader to a large loss.

An Iron Condor is a strategy that is similar to a butterfly spread, but with different strikes for the short options – offering a larger likelihood of profit but with a lower net credit compared to the butterfly spread.

Selling a straddle (selling both a put and a call at the same exercise price) would give a trader a greater profit than a butterfly if the final stock price is near the exercise price, but might result in a large loss.

Similar to the straddle is the strangle which is also constructed by a call and a put, but whose strikes are different, reducing the net debit of the trade, but also reducing the risk of loss in the trade.

Put-Call Parity

One well-known strategy is the covered call in which a trader buys a stock (or holds a previously-purchased long stock position) and sells a call. If the stock price rises above the exercise price, the call will be exercised and the trader will get a fixed profit. If the stock price falls, the call will not be exercised, and any loss incurred to the trader will be partially offset by the premium received from selling the call. Overall, the payoffs match the payoffs from selling a put. This relationship is known as put-call parity.

Payoffs from Buying a Butterfly Spread

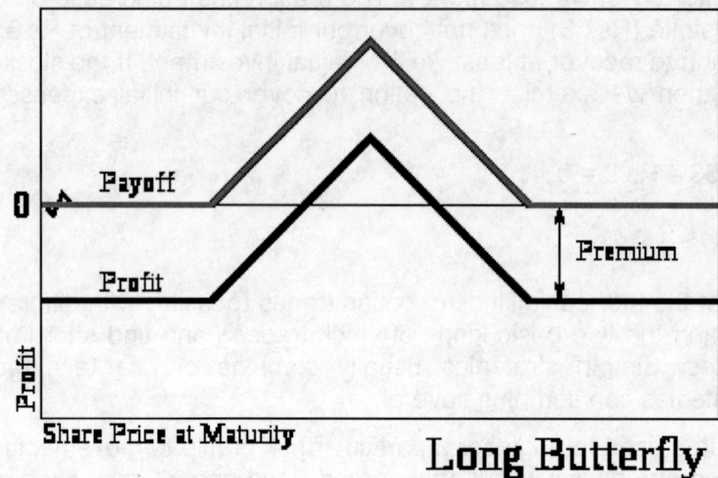

Payoffs from Selling a Straddle

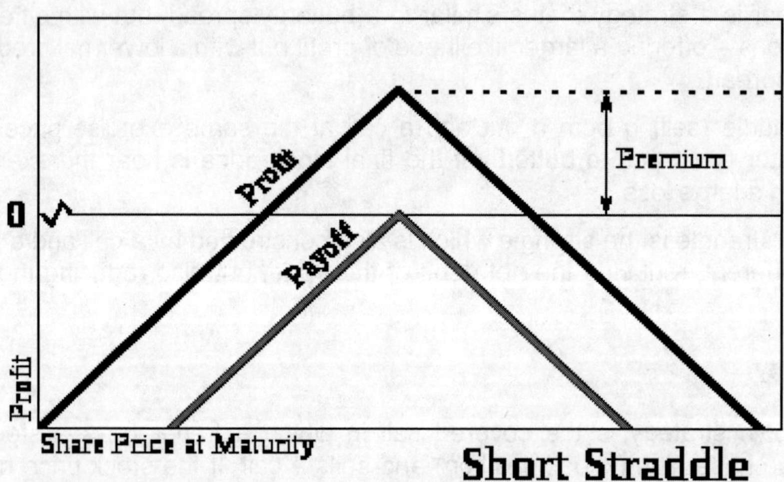

Payoffs from a Covered Call

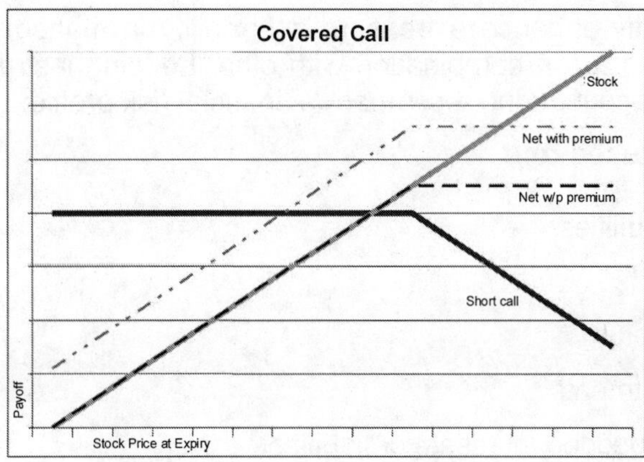

Swap

A swap is a derivative in which counterparties exchange certain benefits of one party's financial instrument for those of the other party's financial instrument. The benefits in question depend on the type of financial instruments involved. For example, in the case of a swap involving two bonds, the benefits in question can be the periodic interest (or coupon) payments associated with the bonds. Specifically, the two counterparties agree to exchange one stream of cash flows against another stream. These streams are called the legs of the swap. The swap agreement defines the dates when the cash flows are to be paid and the way they are calculated. Usually at the time when the contract is initiated at least one of these series of cash flows is determined by a random or uncertain variable such as an interest rate, foreign exchange rate, equity price or commodity price.

The cash flows are calculated over a notional principal amount, which is usually not exchanged between counterparties. Consequently, swaps can be in cash or collateral.

Swaps can be used to hedge certain risks such as interest rate risk, or to speculate on changes in the expected direction of underlying prices.

Today, swaps are among the most heavily traded financial contracts in the world. The total amount of interest rates and currency swaps outstanding was more than $426.7 trillion in 2009, according to International Swaps and Derivatives Association (ISDA).

Caps, Floors and Collars

Caps and floors are essential tools in managing floating rate liabilities while minimizing hedging and opportunity costs. They protect against adverse rates risk, while allowing gains from favourable rate movements. Caps and floors are forms of option contracts, conferring potential benefits to the purchaser and potential obligations on the seller. When purchasing a cap or floor, the buyer pays a premium- typically up-front. The premium amount depends on the specified cap or floor rate and time period covered, which may range from a few months to several years.

Benefits of Caps, Floors and Collars

Caps and floors greatly enhance a treasurer's flexibility in managing financial assets and liabilities. Used together or in combination with other hedging instruments, caps and floors are efficient tools for reconfiguring a company's financial risk profile.

Caps and Floors are used to:

Hedge floating-rate liabilities

Reduce borrowing costs

Increase investment returns

Create synthetic investments

Neutralize options embedded in assets or liabilities

Interest Rate Caps

A cap creates a ceiling on floating rate interest costs. When market rates move above the cap rate, the seller pays the purchaser the difference. A company borrowing on a floating rate basis when 6 month LIBOR is 3% might purchase a 5% cap, for example, to protect against a rate rise above that level. If rates subsequently rise to 8%, the company receives a 3% cap payment to compensate for the rise in market rates. The cap ensures that the borrower's interest rate costs will never exceed the cap rate.

Interest Rate Floors

A floor is the mirror image of a cap. When market rates fall below the floor rate, the seller pays the difference. A 9% floor triggers a payment to the purchaser whenever market rates drop below 9%. Asset managers buy floors to guarantee a minimum return on floating rate assets. They sell floors to generate incrementally higher returns. Debt managers buy floors to protect against opportunity losses on fixed rate debt when rates fall. They may sell floors as a component of a hedge strategy involving other derivative instruments.

Combining Caps and Floors to Create Collars

A collar is created by purchasing a cap or floor and selling the other. The premium due for the cap (floor) is partially offset by the premium received for the floor (cap), making the collar an effective way to hedge rate risk at low cost. In return, the hedger gives up the potential benefit of favourable rate movements outside the band defined by the collar. A borrower who purchases an 10% cap and sells a 8% floor guarantees a 8-10% base rate on a floating rate loan. An investor in floating rate CD's might do exactly the opposite, buying a 8% floor and financing it with the sale of an 10% cap. A costless collar is created when the cap and floor levels are set so that the premiums exactly offset each other.

Caps, floors and collars are a simple but very effective way to control risk and manage hedge costs. The option characteristics of caps and floors offer unique opportunities to minimize borrowing costs or achieve higher investment returns.

For detail study on derivatives, an exclusive book on derivatives (futures and options) may be referred. However, these days various computerized models are available for pricing of derivatives.

Summary

The various kinds of risk management tools are used by FIs as per their need of hedging risk. In this chapter, the use of forwards and futures contracts by FI has been discussed. The various option strategies are also discussed which are widely used by FIs. New option strategies may be devised by FIs as per need and requirement of type of hedge required. Swap is also widely used derivative product for hedging interest rate risk, credit risk and foreign exchange risk. The use of caps, collars and floors has also been discussed to have an understanding of derivative products.

KEY CONCEPTS

Forwards	Future	Option	Long Call
Long Put	Short Call	Short Put	Swaps
Caps	Collars	Floors	Interest rate caps
Interest rate floors			

Review Questions and Problems

1. What are derivative contracts? What is the importance of derivative contracts for banks?
2. Prepare an analysis for worldwide trade of derivatives including types of derivatives, size of trade and country of trade.
3. What are the various types of derivatives? Which type of derivative has highest volumes of trade worldwide?
4. What is the difference between a forward contract and a future contract?
5. What is the difference between a spot contract and a forward contract?
6. Write a note on long and short position in future contract along with example and graphical representation.
7. A bank purchases a T-bill future contract at Rs.94.
   (i) What is the bank's obligation at the time the future contract is purchased?
   (ii) What is the loss or gain if T-Bill future price falls to Rs.93?
   (iii) What is the loss or gain if T-Bill future price rises to Rs.97?
8. Should an FI should buy or sell a future contract to hedge risk in the following cases:
   (i) A bank plans to issue CDs in three months;
   (ii) An insurance company plans to buy bonds in three months;
   (iii) A NBFC is going to sell T-bill in one month;
   (iv) An Indian bank lends to a US company and loan is payable in dollar.

9. How does use of options differ from use of forward or future contracts?
10. What is call and put option?
11. What are four types of participants in options markets? What is the payoff from each type of participant in options markets?
12. What are the various option strategies? Explain with the use of graphs.
13. Explain the similarity between a swap and a forward contract.
14. If FIs were already using forwards, futures and options as hedging instruments, why is there a need of swaps?
15. Differentiate between swap buyer and swap seller. In which markets does each have the competitive advantage?
16. What are caps? What are the circumstances in which buyer of a cap receive a payoff?
17. What are floors? What are the circumstances in which buyer of a floor receive a payoff?
18. What are collars? What are the circumstances in which a bank uses collar?
19. How is buying a cap similar to buying a call option on interest rates?
20. Under what circumstances would it be desirable to sell a floor to help finance a cap? When would it be desirable to sell a cap to help finance a floor?

Reference:

1. *http://en.wikipedia.org*

Chapter – 12

Interest Rate Risk Management

Chapter Objective

- Know Hedging of interest rate risk
- Understand use of Derivatives for interest rate risk hedging such as interest rate futures and options
- Discuss Duration based hedging Strategy
- Explain various Hedging strategies for interest rate risk
- Understand use of Interest rate swaps for hedging

Introduction

The interest rate risk is managed by using derivatives such as interest rate forward contracts, interest rate future contracts, options, Interest rate swaps and other interest rate derivatives. These derivatives are meant for hedging assets and liabilities but very often we see that derivatives are being used for speculation of profit making purpose. Derivatives though are risk management tools for hedging financial risks but may prove very risky if used for purposes other than hedging. There are various examples of financial disasters, which took place because of use of derivatives for speculative purposes such as Barings Bank, LTCM, etc.

Interest rate risk management signifies need of insulating banks or FIs NII from market fluctuation or from change in market parameters. Unhedged interest rate positions may lead to decreasing interest income and in long run affecting MVE of banks. Banks and FIs usually lend to its customers on both fixed and floating interest basis and also invest in bonds with fixed or floating rate of interest. At any time, increase in the interest will result in decreasing value of assets and investment. So, on one hand, the banks have to protect their net interest income and, on the other hand, the value of investments also needs to be protected. There are various exchange traded and over the counter (OTC) derivatives that are available to hedge interest rate risk.

Hedging Interest Rate Risk by using Forward Contracts

The forward contract is a contractual agreement between buyer and seller at current date to buy and sell at a future date for certain price. The contract is between two banks or financial institutions or with their customers. The forward contract is the simplest form of derivative. This is normally not traded in exchange. The hedging of interest rate risk depends on the future movement of interest rates.

Suppose a bank holding a bond investment of Rs.100 crores with 10 years maturity with present value of investment is Rs.95 crores. The bank expects rise in interest rate by 300 basis points in next 6 months from its current level of 7%. If the rate of interest rises, it means value of investment will go down and bank has to book losses on investment by marking it to market. The first step that the bank will take is to assess the loss in next six months time and formulate the hedging strategy accordingly. The calculation of loss arising out of 300 basis point interest rate change is shown in following example:

Example: Calculation of Loss in Investment due to Interest Rate Change

The bank can calculate the value of loss by using duration method for any interest rate change. The value of bond is Rs. 95 crores and duration of bond is 5 years. The loss will be:

$$\Delta P/P = -D\,(\Delta R/1+R)$$

Where:

ΔP = Loss on bonds

P = Market price of bonds

D = Duration of bond

ΔR = Expected change in interest rate

R = Current market yield of bonds

$$\Delta P = -5 \times 95 \times (.03/1.07) = -13.32 \text{ crores}$$

As a result of increase in interest rate by 3%, the capital loss to bank on bond investment would be Rs.13.32 crores. In percentage terms, the value of investment will go down by 14% from its current market price to Rs.81.68 crores.

To hedge this loss, bank has to buy a forward contract from such a buyer who is willing to buy the bonds for Rs.96 crores in six months time at the current date. The premium paid for the deal is say Rs.1 crores. If after six months time, banks expectation of rising of interest rate proved true, then the same bonds will be available in the market for Rs.81.68 crores. To honour the forward contract, bank will buy the bonds from the market for Rs.81.68 crores and deliver it to the buyer at the price of Rs.96 crores. The bank will gain Rs.13.32 crores after adjusting the cost incurred in premium payment for forward contract. In this way, bank is able to perfectly hedge capital loss by buying interest rate derivative.

Hedging Interest Rate Risk by using Future Contracts

Like a forward contract, a future contract is a contractual agreement between buyer and seller to buy or sell an asset at a certain time in future for a certain price. Future contracts are widely traded in exchange. An interest rate future contract is a future contract on an asset whose price is dependent on the level of interest rates. There are generally two kinds of approaches being adopted by banks while hedging against interest rate risk. One approach is to hedge the balance sheet instrument wise, like the bank wants it's cost of fund constant over a period of time and it hedges its liability taking sell position in future contacts for possible rise in interest rate. The bank tries to match assets or liabilities by buying forward or future contract whose underlying securities exactly matches with bank's assets or liability. This approach is often called microhedging. The second approach focuses on hedging of entire balance sheet instead of hedging it instrument wise. Bank uses future contracts to hedge entire balance sheet duration gap. This approach works at macro level in the bank and is hence called macroheding. Both the approaches may be used by bank depending upon bank's risk perception and priorities.[1]

The hedging strategy differs from bank to bank. Some banks go for full hedging of interest rate risk on a daily basis and others opt for selective hedging, thus leaving some portion unhedged. Hedging also involves some cost in terms of premium paid for buying derivatives and this reduces the expected return on assets or results in excess cost paid for liabilities. The number of future contracts that bank buys or sells depends upon the size and directions of its interest rate exposure. The interest rate shock on banks balance sheet depends upon the duration mismatch between assets and liabilities. The impact of interest rate shock on bank's market value of equity may be measured as follows:

Example: Measurement of Change in MVE of Bank due to Interest rate Shock

$$\Delta E = -(D_A - D_L k) \times A \times (\Delta R/1+R)$$

where

ΔE = Change in MVE

k = L/A = Liabilities to Assets Ratio

$(D_A-D_L k)$ = Adjusted Duration Gap

$(\Delta R/1+R)$ = Interest Rate Shock

Suppose for a bank D_A = 6 years, D_L = 4 years, A = 100 crores, L= 90 crores, E = 10 crores and it is expected that interest rate will rise from 8% to 10% over one year horizon. The change in MVE of bank will be:

$$\Delta E = -(6 - 0.9 \times 4) \text{ X } 100 \text{ X } (.02/1.08)$$

$$= -(2.4) \text{ X } 100 \times (0.0185)$$

$$= -4.44 \text{ crores}$$

If in one year horizon, interest rate goes up by 2%, bank may lose 4.44% of its MVE, which is 44.44% of its capital of Rs. 10 crores. The impact of interest rate risk may be so intense that bank may lose half of its equity.

In the above example, bank's strategy is to fully hedge the balance sheet exposure with the use of interest rate future. Banks will enter in such future contracts where its gain is a minimum of Rs. 4.44 crores after adjustment of hedging cost.

The value of future contract also changes along with the changes in interest rates because the value of future contract is derived from underlying security. The value of underlying security changes with interest rate changes and accordingly value of future contracts also change. The prices of future contract are marked to market, hence require daily settlement of loss or gain arising out of contract.

Duration Based Hedging Strategy using Future Contract

The expected loss in MVE may be hedged by using duration-based method using duration of future contracts and duration of assets and liability. As explained earlier, the price of future contract changes in the same manner as that of underlying security, hence same may be given as:

$$\Delta F/F = -D_F (\Delta R/1+R)$$

or

$$\Delta F = -D_F (FP \times N) (\Delta R/1+R)$$

Where:

ΔF = Change in Value of Future Contract

F = Market price of Future contracts

D_F = Duration of Underlying security

ΔR = Expected change in interest rate

R = Current market yield of bonds

F = FP X N = Price of future contract X Number of Contract

The higher duration assets or liabilities are more rate sensitive than the lower duration ones. By using the above equation, the gain arising out of future contract should be equal to loss of MVE due to rate change. Hence the equation may be rewritten as :

$$\Delta E = -(D_A - D_L k) \times A \times (\Delta R/1+R) = -D_F (FP \times N) (\Delta R/1+R) = \Delta F$$

$$N = (D_A - D_L k) \times A / D_F \times FP$$

Example : Calculation of Number of Future Contract required for hedging

In continuation with the above example, if the current future price of underlying bond of Rs.100 bond is Rs.95 and the duration of this bond is 8 years and the minimum lot size is 10000 bonds. The bank is having loss on MVE and it has to be set off against gain of future contract for rising in interest rate, hence bank has to sell future contract. The number of future contracts to be sold is:

$$N = (D_A - D_L k) \times A / D_F \times FP$$

$$N = (2.4) \times 100{,}00{,}00{,}000 / 8 \times 950000$$

N = 316 contracts

If bank sells 316 future contracts of above bond, then gain from future contract would be:

$$\Delta F = -D_F (FP \times N)(\Delta R/1+R)$$

$$\Delta F = -8 (950000 \times -316)(.02/1.08)$$

$$\Delta F = 4.44 \text{ crores}$$

Comparing the above two examples, it is seen that the loss arising from interest rate rise is fully hedged by gain from selling interest rate futures.

The number of contracts may be changed depending upon the future contract and underlying security. If underlying security is of lesser duration, more number of future contracts have to be sold.

Another kind of interest rate future is Forward Rate Agreement (FRA). A FRA is a forward contract where two parties agree that a certain interest rate will apply to a certain principal during a specified future period of time.

Hedging Interest Rate Risk by using Options

There is a wider variety of option products available in the financial market, which includes exchange-traded options, over the counter options, embedded options, and caps, collars and floors. The use of options also protect banks from MVE loss in the manner forwards and future does, but options if not used wisely can lead to huge losses for banks. There are generally four strategies that are used for options, i.e. buying a call option, selling (writing) a call option, buying a put option and selling (writing) a put option. Buying a call option (long position) means buyer has the right but not the obligation to buy underlying security at a prespecified strike price in return of call premium paid to seller or writer of call option. In case buyer exercise call option, writer of call option has to oblige buyer, the seller may not refuse.

Suppose a bank buys a call option for bond at a strike price of Rs.105 by paying a premium of Rs.5. The buyer will exercise option only when market price goes beyond Rs.105 otherwise option will not be exercised and will result in Rs.5 loss to buyer. Suppose, in the meanwhile the price rises to a level of Rs.120, the buyer will exercise call option and will make profit of Rs.10 after adjusting call premium. In this case, writer of call option will buy bond from market and deliver it to buyer at the rate of Rs.105 thus losing Rs.10 on deal. The option runs on zero sum game i.e. someone's loss is other's gain. Generally options are settled on a daily basis in the form of margin. One thing to be noticed here is that the gain to the option buyer is unlimited as price of the bond goes beyond Rs.105 to any higher level but gain to option writer is limited to call premium it receives. The loss to call writer is unlimited as it has to honour the contract irrespective of the price of bond by buying from the market.

The opposite of the above strategy is writing a call option (short position) where bank acts as a writer of call option and the other party as buyer. This means that the writer has an obligation to the buyer of call option to sell underlying asset at exercise price but the buyer of call option has right to refuse or accept it in return of premium paid to buy option. Writing a call option is a very risky affair as losses are unlimited and the gains are limited to premium fee.

Buying a put option (long position) means that the buyer of put option has the right to sell but not the obligation to sell the underlying security to the seller or writer of put option at agreed exercise price in return of put premium paid by the buyer to writer. In this situation, if the interest rate goes up, the price of bond will decrease and the buyer of put option will exercise the put option. The writer of put option has to buy bond at prespecified rate even though the market price is much lower than the exercise price. The gain of put option buyer is unlimited but to the writer of put option gain is limited put premium paid with unlimited loss liability. The opposite of this strategy is writing a put option (short position) which means writer of put option has an obligation to buy underlying security in return of premium paid by buyer.

The above mentioned four strategies are shown below in a tabular form:

Strategy	Buyer	Seller (writer)
Buying a call option (Long Position)	Buyer has right to buy underlying security but not the obligation at strike price	Seller has an obligation to sell underlying security at strike price
Writing a call option (Short Position)	Buyer has right to buy underlying security but not the obligation at the strike price	Seller has an obligation to sell underlying security at strike price
Buying a put option (Long Position)	Buyer has right to sell underlying security but not the obligation at strike price	Seller has an obligation to buy underlying security at strike price
Writing a put option (Short Position)	Buyer has right to sell underlying security but not the obligation strike price	Seller has an obligation to buy underlying security at strike price

The interest rate risk hedging through buying and selling of different option may be done in the following ways:

1. When bank is long in a bond portfolio, it may hedge against interest rate risk by writing a call option. This strategy works when interest rates fall and the value of bond portfolio rises. The gain from value of portfolio may be offset against loss in writing a call option. But if reverse happens, banks gain would be limited to premium income earned on writing the call option whereas losses from bond portfolio value would be significant.
2. In the same situation, if bank hedge by buying a put option and the interest rate rises, the loss arising from value of bond portfolio may be offset against profit from put option exercise. If reverse happens, the value of portfolio will increase and losses from buying a put option will be limited to option premium paid.

The fair value of an option may be calculated by using Binomial method and Black-Scholes model. Various softwares are available to calculate option price by using the above methods.

Other kinds of derivatives are Cap, Floors and Collars. Buying a cap means buying a call option with multiple exercise dates. If the interest rate rises above a certain level, writer of call will compensate the buyer of interest rate call option in return of call premium paid. Buying a floor means buying a put option on interest rate. If interest rate falls below the floor rate specified in the deal, the writer of put option will bear the loss to the buyer in return of the premium paid. A collar is a combination of the above two types of options. This kind of strategy is adopted when bank wants to hedge against rising interest rate and earn premium to be paid through writing a floor or vice versa. These derivatives are used in different combination depending upon the mode of financing of bank such as fixed rate or floating rate assets and liabilities.

Numerical Representation:

Suppose an FI wants to hedge against interest rate rise, affecting its net worth, by using put options, FI will buy put options to make profits, which are enough to offset the loss in net worth due to interest rate shock. For deciding the number of options to be bought, the following equation may be used:

$$\Delta P = (N_p \, X \, \Delta p)$$

Where

ΔP = total change in the value of put options position

Δp = change in rupee value of put option position

N_p = number of put option to be purchased

The equation may be rewritten as:

$$N_p = (D_A - kD_L) \times A / (D \times B \times \delta)$$

Where

δ = change in the value of a put option for each rupee change in the underlying security, the value of δ lies between 0 and 1

B = current market value of underlying security for which put option is to be taken

D = duration of underlying security for put option

For a hedge involving a call option, the equation is:

$$N_c = (D_A - kD_L) \times A / - (D \times B \times \delta)$$

For put options, the delta has negative sign since the value of the put option falls when bond price rise. This happens because the price of bond and interest rate has inversely proportionate relationship. While applying modified duration formula, which also has negative sign, the formula of put option number gives positive sign and call option formula gives negative sign as delta for call option has a positive sign since the value of call option rises when bond prices rise.

The result of call option number to be purchased will give positive result as the duration gap of FI **(D_A - kD_L)** will be negative, i.e. FI will use call option if duration gap is negative means **(D_A - kD_L) < 0** duration of its assets is shorter than that of its liabilities.

For calculating the number of put option to buy for hedging interest rate risk on an asset, the duration gap of FI may be replaced by duration of asset. The equation will look like:

$$N_p = D_A \times P / (D \times B \times \delta)$$

where **P** *= initial value of an asset*

Accordingly, the total premium cost of buying a put or call option may be calculated as:

Total premium cost = N_p or N_c X Put or Call premium per contract

Hedging Interest Rate Risk by using Interest Rate Swaps

Swaps are contractual agreement between two entities to exchange cash flows in future as per the deal. The simplest form of interest rate swap is a plain vanilla interest rate swap. In this, one bank B agrees to pay to other bank cash flows equal to the interest at predecided fixed rate on a notional principal for contractual period. At the same time, bank A agrees to pay bank B cash flows equal to interest at a floating rate on the same notional principal for the same contractual period. The interest rate swaps are available on both over the counters and through exchange. The IRSs are used by banks and other entities where their assets and liabilities are financed through mix of fixed and floating rate of interest. Suppose a bank has a floating rate liability through which it has financed a fixed rate asset. If interest rate rises, bank has to pay more on liability whereas its return from asset is fixed. Strategically, bank would prefer to transform its liability from floating to fixed rate and sell the swap to receive fixed rate payment and will pay floating rate payment to swap buyer. If a bank is having floating rate assets and these are financed through fixed rate liabilities, bank would like to transform its liabilities from fixed to floating rate if there is a fall in interest rates. In a swap agreement, swap buyer agrees to pay fixed rate payment to swap seller for floating rate payment from swap seller. Both buyer and seller of swap have competitive advantages in their respective mode of payment, i.e. fixed and floating rate of interest.

The change in market value of swap contract (**ΔS**) may be obtained from the following equation:

$$\Delta S = -(D_{FX} - D_{FL}) \times N_s \times (\Delta R/1+R)$$

The notional value of interest rate swaps may be determined by using following formula:

$$N_s = (D_A - kD_L) \times A / (D_{FX} - D_{FL})$$

Where

N_s = Notional value of swap contracts

(D_{FX} - D_{FL}) = Difference between durations of a government bond that has same maturity and coupon as the fixed and floating side of the swap

The total number of swaps contracts to be entered to hedge interest rate risk may be obtained as per following equation:

$$N = N_s / N_{vs}$$

Where

N = number of swap contracts to be entered

N_{vs} = value/size of each swap

Example: Calculating the number of swap contract to be entered for hedging

Assume $D_A = 5$, $k = 0.9$, $D_L = 3$ and A = Rs.10 crores. Also assume that the duration of fixed rate T-bill having maturity of 10 years is $D_{FX} = 7$ years and the duration of a floating rate bond repricing annually is $D_{FL} = 1$. The size of each contract is Rs.1 lac.

then

$N_s = (D_A - kD_L) \times A / (D_{FX} - D_{FL})$

N_s = Rs.23 crores / (7 - 1) = Rs.3.83 crores

Now

$N = N_s / N_{vs}$

N = Rs.3,83,00,000 / Rs.1,00,000

N = 383 contracts

If from the above-obtained values, gain on interest rate swap (**ΔS**) is calculated, it will be equal to change in net worth (**ΔE**) of FI for any upward change in interest rate.

Summary

Interest rate risk may put threat to future earning of banks as well as market value of equity. In this chapter, various strategies have been discussed for interest rate risk hedging with the use of derivatives such as interest rate forwards, interest rate futures and interest rate options. Duration based hedging is very important and accurate for bank and FI which is also explained in detail. The other method of hedging interest rate risk is with the use of interest rate swaps which is also detailed in the chapter. With the use of interest rate derivatives, interest rate risk in the balance sheet of bank may be minimized but the use of these derivatives should specifically be for hedging purpose otherwise it may prove risky.

KEY CONCEPTS

OTC	NII	MVE
Interest Rate Forward Contract	Interest Rate Future Contract	Interest Rate Option Contract
Micro-hedging	Macro-hedging	Short Position
Long Position	Interest Rate Swaps	

Review Questions and Problems

1. What are the different kinds of derivative contracts that are available for interest rate risk hedging?
2. Identify the banks and FIs in India offering interest rate derivatives and the nature of their deals.
3. A bank invests Rs.10 crores in 10 years bond of Rs.100 at par at a price of Rs.105 having YTM 8%. The bond has duration of 5 years and bank plans to sell it after 6 months. The rate of interest is expected to rise from 8% to 10% in next six months. The bank wants to hedge the interest rate risk by buying a forward and future contract. How much would the loss be if interest rate rises by 200 basis points in next 6 months?
4. If a bank buys a future contract of Rs.90 on a bond, what is the bank's obligation at the time of purchase of contract and in what kind of hedge is it engaged?
5. If a bank has assets of longer-term maturities and liabilities of shorter term maturities, how will an interest rate future help bank's interest rate risk?
6. What are the reasons due to which an FI can go for selective hedging of its portfolio?
7. What is the full balance sheet hedging and how is it done?
8. Why is the writing of an option risky?
9. Why do the banks prefer to choose buy options instead of writing?
10. Suppose a bank has assets of Rs. 200 crores and liabilities of Rs.175 crores with equity capital of Rs. 25 crores. The duration of assets is 7 years and the duration of liabilities is 5 years. The rise in interest rate is expected by 100 basis from 10% to 11% in next three months. A future contract price is quoted at Rs. 98 per Rs. 100 face value for 10 years bond with 8% coupon and the minimum lot size is Rs.1 crores. The duration of bond is 5 years. Calculate the loss of bank's net worth for expected rise in interest rate. How many number of future contracts should the bank buy or sell to hedge the net worth loss?
11. How does the option differ from future and forward contracts?
12. A bank is purchasing a call option on a bond. What can be the bank's expectation in near future about interest rate changes?
13. A bank is buying a put option on a bond. What should be the interest rate in order for the bank to book the profit from this option?
14. Even when the derivatives such as forward, future and options are available, why do the banks need swaps for interest rate risk hedging?
15. Identify an interest rate swap deal that has taken place between two banks.
16. An FI holds a 10-year, par value, Rs.10 crores bond that is priced at 105 with a yield to maturity of 8%. The bond has a duration of 7 years, and the FI plans to sell it after three months. The FI predicts that interest rates will be 10% after three months. Market is not anticipating any change in rates, hence three-month forward contracts for 10-year bonds are available at 105. The FI

would like to hedge against the expected change in interest rates with an appropriate position in a forward contract. What will be this position? Verify that if rates rise 2% as forecast, the hedge will protect the FI from loss.

17. A bank has assets that consist mostly of 20 years mortgage loans and liabilities that are short-term time and demand deposits. Will an interest rate futures contract the bank buys add to or subtract from the bank's risk?

18. A bank has the following balance sheet (Rs. in crores):

Assets	500	Liabilities	400
		Equity	100
Total	500	Total	500

The duration of the assets is 7 years and the duration of the liabilities is 5 years. The bank is expecting interest rates to fall from 12% to 10% over the next year.

i. What is the duration gap for bank?
ii. What is the expected change in net worth for bank if the forecast is accurate?
iii. What will be the effect on net worth if interest rates increase 200 basis points?
iv. If the existing interest rate on the liabilities is 7% , what will be the effect on net worth of a 1.5% increase in interest rates?

19. What is fully hedged balance sheet of an FI?

20. A Bank has assets of Rs.400 crores, liabilities of Rs.300 crores, and equity of Rs.100 crores. The asset duration is 8 years, and the duration of the liabilities is 5 years. Market interest rates are 12 percent. Bank wishes to hedge the balance sheet with Treasury bond futures contracts, which currently have a price quote of Rs.97 per Rs.100 face value for the benchmark 10 years, 7.6% coupon bond underlying the contract.

i. Suggest the bank whether to go short or long on the futures contracts to establish the full hedge of balance sheet.
ii. Calculate the number of contracts necessary to fully hedge the bank.
iii. Verify that the change in the futures position will offset the change in the balance sheet position for rise of interest rate by 2% and fall by 1%.

21. If a bank hedge with T-bill futures contracts having market value of Rs.97 per Rs.100 of face value, how many futures contracts are necessary to fully hedge the balance sheet?

22. An FI planning to use bond options to hedge interest rate risk in its bond portfolio.

i. How does writing call options hedge the risk when interest rates decrease?
ii. Will writing call options fully hedge the risk when interest rates increase? Explain.
iii. How does buying a put option reduce the losses on the bond portfolio when interest rates rise?

23. An FI has Rs.100 crores portfolio of 10 years bonds that have an 10% rate of interest. The bonds are trading at par and have duration of 6 years. The FI is planning to hedge the portfolio with T-bond options that have a delta of -0.625. The underlying long-term Treasury bonds for the option have duration of 9 years and trade at a market value of Rs.97 per Rs.100 of par value. Each put option has a premium of Rs.0.50.
    i. How many bond put options are necessary to hedge the bond portfolio?
    ii. If interest rates increase 200 basis points, what is the expected gain or loss on the put option hedge?
    iii. What is the expected change in market value on the bond portfolio?
    iv. What is the total cost of placing the hedge?
24. A Bank has Rs. 2000 crores of assets with duration of 15 years and liabilities worth Rs.1600 crores with duration of 10 years. Bank is planning to hedge the portfolio for interest rate change. The call and put options have a delta (δ) of 0.5 and –0.5, respectively. The price of an underlying T-bond is 105 and its modified duration is 8 years.
    a. Calculate the number of options to be purchased.
    b. What is the effect on the economic value of the equity if interest rates rise 100 basis points?
    c. What will be the effect on the hedge if interest rates rise 150 basis points?
    d. How much must interest rates move against the hedge for the increased value of the bank to offset the cost of the hedge?
25. An FI has Rs. 400 crores assets having duration of 9 years and liabilities of Rs. 360 crores liabilities having duration of 6 years. The FI is planning to use put options on T-bonds to hedge against unexpected interest rate increases. The average delta (δ) of the put options has been estimated at -0.6, and the average duration of the T-bonds is 6.5 years. The current market value of the T-Bonds is Rs. 96. How many put option contracts should it purchase to hedge its exposure against rising interest rates? The face value of the T-bonds is Rs.100.
26. An FI has Rs. 5000 crores of assets having duration of 10 years and Rs4600 crores of liabilities having duration of 7 years. The FI is planning to hedge its balance sheet with a swap that has fixed-rate payments with duration of 5 years and floating rate-rate payments with a duration of 3 years. What is the optimal amount of the swap to hedge against the adverse effect of a change in interest rates on the value of the FI's equity?

Reference:

1. *Option, Future & Other Derivatives, John C. Hull, 3e, pg -78.*

Chapter – 13

Market Risk Management

Chapter Objective

- Discuss strategies for Market Risk Management
- Understand use of Greeks such as Delta, Gamma, Vega and Rho
- Know calculation of VaR
- Explain Capital Charge for Market Risk
- Calculating Optimal Hedge Ratio
- Optimal Hedge by using Duration & Beta

Introduction

The financial institutions and banks those sell derivatives to a customer in the over the counter market is faced with the problem of management of market risk. If the same derivatives sold by banks or FIs are traded in the exchange, bank may hedge its position by buying the derivatives from the exchange. The derivatives are mostly structured as per customers needs and do not match with standard derivative products that are being traded in stock exchange. Hence, hedging the exposure becomes difficult for seller of derivative products. There are mainly two approaches for managing market risk - one involves quantifying and controlling each risk separately and the other involves carrying out scenario analysis where impact on option position of alternative future scenarios is evaluated.

There are two different positions that are being taken by FIs in derivative market. Naked position is when FIs do not hedge its position with counter derivative. Covered position is taken when FIs buy the underlying security as soon as derivative is sold and thus FIs cover its risk arising out of exercise of option by buyer. This method is an expensive way of doing the hedging. Both the positions mentioned above do not provide satisfactory way of hedging, as loss to option writer is unlimited.

The traditional approach to market risk management includes hedging. Hedging consists of taking positions, which lower the risk of the portfolio. Two kind of hedging strategies are followed: one is static hedging and the other is continuous hedging. The hedging through derivatives is also exposed to basis risk. Basis risk arises when changes in payoffs on the hedging instrument do not perfectly offset changes in the value of portfolio. It means the future contracts do not reflect the characteristics of underlying securities.

Stop Loss Method of Hedging

This above method is also known as stop loss strategy. Under this method, FI writes a call option at some strike price (S_P). The hedging strategy is such that if the price of underlying security rises above S_P , FI buys security at strike price and as soon as prices fall below S_P, FI sells the security. The main objective of the strategy is to hold naked position whenever price is below strike price and to hold a covered position when price is above strike price. The strategy ensures that the FI owns the stock at a time when option close in the money and does not own it when the option closes out of the money. At the end, it gives same gain as in the case of option. There are a few criticisms of this strategy as mentioned below:-

1. The cash flows occur at different times and must be discounted.
2. Purchases and sales cannot be made exactly at the strike price. There may be some differences between the strike price or the execution price which increases the cost of hedging.
3. Because of continuous sell and purchase of stock, the strategy involves high hedging cost.

There are few more advanced strategies of hedging that are used by using Greeks. The Option Greeks are mathematical outputs from an Option Valuation Model, which predicts possible future movement in option values based on underlying parameters. Greeks used in the prediction of option values help in buy/sell/hedge decisions. The common Greeks used are Delta, Gamma, Vega, Theta and Rho. The details of Greeks are as follows:[1]

Delta (Δ)

Delta stands for rate of change in an option value for a given movement in the price of underlying assets.

$$\Delta = \delta f / \delta S$$

Where

***f* = The price of the option**

S = The price of the underlying asset

For example, if the Δ of a Call option is 0.70, it means that if the price of underlying asset moves up by Re 1.00, the Call option will rise by 0.70. Call option Deltas give positive relationship, indicating that a rise in price of underlying asset will result in rise in the option value. Put option Deltas give negative relationship, that means a rise in underlying asset price will result in a fall in the Put option value.

Delta Hedging Strategy

Suppose the option price of an asset is Rs. 20 and the stock price is Rs.150. An investor has sold 20 option contracts to buy 2000 units of assets (lot of 100 units). If the delta of asset is

0.70, investor position may be hedged by buying 1400 units of asset. The gain (loss) arising out of option position would be offset by the loss (gain) on the asset position. For example, if the stock price goes up by Rs.10, it will produce a gain of Rs.14000 on the asset purchased and at the same time, the option price will also increase by Rs.7, thus resulting in a loss of Rs.14000 for selling 20 option contracts. Similarly, if the asset price goes down by Rs. 10, investor will gain on option written and lose on an asset position.

In the above example, the delta of the investor's option position is -14000, i.e. investor loses 1400 x change in asset price, when asset price move up by ΔS. Hence the delta of stock is 1. The long position on asset has a delta of +1400. The delta of investor's total position is zero. The delta of position held on underlying asset offsets the position held in option. This strategy is also known as Delta Neutral position.

It is very important to know that behavior of delta depends upon two factors - one is change in the price of underlying asset and the other is the passage of time. As the time passes, the value of delta also gets changed. When delta hedging is adopted by any FI, it is required to hedge the position on a continuous basis. This is called rebalancing of delta hedging and is also known as dynamic hedging strategy.

Theta (θ)

$$\Theta = -\frac{\partial V}{\partial \tau}$$

Earlier, it was shown that option values will decrease with the passage of time. The time value component of the option will gradually move towards zero as it nears expiry day. The theta of a portfolio of derivatives is the rate of change of the value of the portfolio with respect to time assuming all other parameters remains same. It is also referred as time decay of the portfolio. For example, if the theta of an option is –0.10, it means the value of this option will decrease by 0.10 at the end of one day. Theta is usually negative for an option. This is because as the time to maturity decreases, the option tends to become less valuable. Theta is not the same type of hedge parameter as delta. This is because there is uncertainty about the future asset price but there is no uncertainty about passage of time. There is no usage of hedging against the effect of the passage of time on an option portfolio.

Theta is usually negative for long calls and puts and positive for short (or written) calls and puts. An exception is a deep in-the-money European put. The total theta for a portfolio of options can be determined by summing the thetas for each individual position.

The value of an option can be analysed into two parts: the intrinsic value and the time value. The intrinsic value is the amount of money you would gain if you exercised the option immediately, so a call with strike Rs. 50 on a stock with price Rs. 60 would have intrinsic value of Rs.10, whereas the corresponding put would have zero intrinsic value. The time value is the value of having the option of waiting longer before deciding to exercise. Even a deeply out of the money put will be worth something, as there is some chance the stock price will fall below the strike before the expiry date. However, as time approaches maturity, there is less chance of this happening, so the time value of an option is decreasing with time. Thus if you are long on an option you are short at theta and your portfolio will lose value with the passage of time (all other factors held constant).

Gamma (Γ)

$$\Gamma = \frac{\partial \Delta}{\partial S} = \frac{\partial^2 V}{\partial S^2}$$

The Gamma of a portfolio of derivatives on an underlying asset is the rate of change of the portfolio's delta with respect to the price of the underlying asset. If the gamma is small, delta changes only slowly and less frequent interventions are required to make portfolio delta neutral. But if gamma is large, delta is highly sensitive to the price of underlying asset. It requires dynamic hedging strategy and may prove risky if portfolio is kept unhedged for a long time. For example. for a given asset price, the delta of an option is currently 0.70. The gamma at the moment is 0.03. This indicates that if the asset price moves up by Re 1.00, the option value will move up by Rs. 0.70. When this happens, the delta itself will become 0.73(i.e.0.70 as earlier, plus 0.03). Thus, the gamma predicts movements in delta, given the changes in the underlying share price.

Vega ($\mathcal{V}$)

$$\nu = \frac{\partial V}{\partial \sigma}$$

The value of derivative also changes with movement in volatility and volatility change over time. Vega of a portfolio of derivatives ($\mathcal{V}$) is the rate of change of the value of the portfolio with respect to the volatility of the underlying asset. If Vega is high, the portfolio value is very sensitive to small change in volatility. If Vega is low, volatility changes have very little impact on the value of the portfolio. Vega determines the increase or decrease in value with precision. For example, if Vega is 0.10, it means that the option value will rise by Rs 0.10 for 1% increase in volatility. Assume the current volatility of an asset is 20% and the value of an option is Rs.11, the implication is that if the volatility moves up to 25%, the option value would rise to Rs.11.50. If volatility were to fall, the option value would decrease correspondingly.

Rho (ρ)

$$\rho = \frac{\partial V}{\partial r}$$

The Rho of a portfolio of derivatives is the rate of change of the value of the portfolio with respect to change in interest rate. It measures the sensitivity of the value of a portfolio to interest rates. For example, if Rho is 0.20, it means that the call option value will rise by 0.20 for increase of interest rate by 1% and the value of put option will decrease by 0.20 for change in interest rate by 1%.

The Optimal Hedge Ratio

The optimal hedge ratio is the minimum number of future contracts required to hedge investment position. The optimal hedge ratio (N*) may be defined as under:

$$N^* = -\beta_{sf} \times Q \times s / Q_f \times f$$

Where

β_{sf} = Coefficient of regression of percentage change in investment position and percentage change in future price

Q = Quantities of underlying asset to be hedged

s = Unit price of underlying asset in spot market

Q_f = Notional value of each contract

f = Future price

The N* is also expressed with the help of the following equation, if correlation between future and spot price change is known:

$$N^* = -\rho_{SF} \times \sigma_S \times Q \ / \ \sigma_F \times Q_f$$

Where

ρ_{SF} = Correlation between future and spot price change

σ_S = Standard deviation of spot price over time horizon of hedge

σ_F = Standard deviation of future price

Optimal hedging using duration

The optimal hedge ratio is simply minus the ratio of the rupee duration of cash related to the rupee duration of the hedge. The optimal hedge using duration is given by the ratio of rupee duration of the position and rupee duration of the hedging instrument. The equation of duration based optimal ratio is as follows:

$$N = -(D^*_s \times S) / (D^*_f \times F)$$

Where

D^*_s = Modified duration of portfolio

D^*_f = Modified duration of future

Optimal hedging using Beta

Beta is a measure of the exposure of the rate of return on a portfolio to the movement in the market. It also represents systematic risk. The optimal hedge with index future is given by beta of the cash position times its value divided by the notional value of the futures contract. The equation of duration based optimal ratio is as under:

$N^* = -(\beta S)/F$

Where

S = Value of the portfolio

F = Value of the notional amount of the futures contract

Calculation of VaR

Suppose VaR is to be calculated for Rs.100 crores portfolio over 10 days at 99% confidence level of normal distribution. The VaR will be computed as follows:[2]

1. Step1: Establish market value of the portfolio, say 120 crores
2. Step2: Calculate standard deviation of the portfolio (σ) say 10%
3. Step3: Set the time horizon or the holding period of asset (N) say 10 days and divide it by total number of trading days (say 252 days)
4. Step4: Set a confidence level, say 99%, assuming normal distribution α = 2.33
5. Step5: Calculate VaR by multiplying all of the above

VaR = Market value of portfolio X σ X $\sqrt{N/252}$ X α

VaR = 120 X .10 X $\sqrt{10/252}$ X 2.33

VaR = Rs. 5.57 crores

VaR gives the expected maximum loss over a target horizon within a given confidence interval.

Capital Charge for Market Risk

The BIS allowed large banks to use their internal model to calculate market risk. The following things should be taken into account while calculating capital charges for market risk:

1. The bank must define an adverse change in rates at 99% confidence level i.e. multiply σ by 2.33
2. The bank should assume minimum holding period of 10 days

The bank must consider capital charges higher of the following:

1. The previous day's VaR
2. The average daily VaR over period of 60 days times a multiplication factor with minimum value of three, i.e. capital charges = 10 days VaR X 3

For the above example, the capital charges would be Rs.5.57 crores X 3 = Rs.16.71 crores.

Summary

Market risk arises in trading book of banks. Banks usually invest in securities for two purposes - one is for Hold Till Maturity (HTM) and the other for Available For Sale (AFS). The former is classified as banking book and the latter as trading book. The bank has to hedge its position on a daily basis as position in trading book needs to be Mark to Market (MTM). In this chapter, various strategies have been discussed by using derivatives. The use of greeks such as Delta, Gamma, Theta, etc have also been discussed, which are used for option pricing. The calculation of VaR for calculation of capital charge is also explained.

KEY CONCEPTS

Naked Position	Strike Price	Greeks
Delta	Theta	Gamma
Vega	Rho, VaR	Capital Charge

Review Questions and Problems

1. What does it mean to say that the delta of a call option is 0.50? How can a short position of in 1500 call option be made delta neutral when delta option is 0.50?
2. What do you mean by theta of an option position being -0.10? If a bank feels that neither asset price nor its volatility will change, what type of strategy should be adopted?
3. What is gamma position of an option position? In a situation for put option seller when gamma is large and negative and delta is zero, what are the risks?
4. What is delta neutral hedging strategy? In which all circumstances, it cannot be used?
5. What is stop loss strategy? What would happen if transaction cost is very high? Would banks prefer the strategy if cost of transaction is very high?
6. What does it mean by vega of a call option being 0.20? How is the calculation of vega beneficial for banks?
7. What you mean when rho of a put option is -0.40? What would happen to the value of the portfolio if interest rate goes down by 200 basis points?
8. Calculate VaR for a portfolio value of Rs. 200 crores with standard deviation of portfolio as 20% at 95% level of confidence for a holding period of 15 days. The total number of trading days is 252.
9. Calculate the capital charge required for market risk using the above question.
10. A silver producer will sell 2000 metric ton of silver in next 3 months at prevailing market price after 3 months. The silver future contract is for 50 metric ton of silver. The value of $\rho_{SF} = 0.78$, $\sigma_S = 3\%$ and $\sigma_F = 3.5\%$. The silver producer wants to hedge its position by using 3 months silver

futures. To hedge the price of silver, how many future contracts should be purchased by silver producer?

11. A company will buy 2 million gallons of crude oil in next 3 months at prevailing market price after 3 months. The oil future contract is for 10000 gallons of oil. The value of ρ_{SF} = 0.81, σ_S = 15% and σ_F = 20%. The buyer wants to hedge its position by using 3 months oil futures. To hedge the price of oil, how many future contracts should be purchased by buyer?
12. A steel company needs to purchase 5000 metric ton of iron ore in next 3 months at prevailing market price after 3 months. The notional value of one contract is 10000 kilograms. The current price of iron ore is Rs. 30000 per metric ton and the futures price of iron ore is Rs.3 per kg. The value of β_{sf} = 0.94. The buyer wants to hedge its position by using 3 months iron futures. Calculate optimal number of futures contract to buy/sell.
13. Company's portfolio having modified duration of 7 years is valued at Rs. 250 crores. The current notional of futures contract is Rs. 3 crores having modified duration of 9 years. Calculate the number of contracts to buy/sell for optimal protection.
14. A bank wants to hedge Rs.150 crores corporate deposit having duration of 150 days. The current rupee value of the future contract is Rs.10 crores having duration of 90 days. Calculate the number of futures contracts required for optimal hedging.
15. An FI holds a portfolio of Rs.240 crores with a beta of 1.2 related to NIFTY 50. The current notional of the futures contract is Rs.5.5 crores. Calculate number of contracts for optimal hedging.

References:

1. *Option, Future & Other Derivatives, John C. Hull, 3e, pg –308-333.*
2. *Philippe Jorion, Value at risk, 2e, pg 108-109.*

Chapter – 14

Credit Risk Management

Chapter Objective

- Understand approaches to credit Risk Management
- Understand structure of Credit Risk Rating System
- Explain use of Credit Derivatives
- Focus on types of Credit Derivatives such as CDS, TOR Swaps, CDS, CLN, CDO, CBO etc.
- Discuss Credit Rating concept
- Focus on Hedging Strategy for Credit Risk
- Loan Sales as Credit Risk Management Technique

Introduction

One of the oldest identified risk is credit risk. The regulators also mention about credit risk measurement and management. Till the time Basel introduced market risk, the credit risk was the main concern of regulators and banks/FIs. The capital adequacy was maintained only on credit risk associated with various assets on the basis of risk weight. Risk weights were the measurement of the credit risk associated with assets/loans usually decided by regulator of the country. Later on at the time of Basel II, various other models have been introduced to measure credit risk. The credit risk is managed through use of internal monitoring systems and credit derivatives.

Through internal monitoring system, credit risk is managed by setting up internal credit monitoring process, appraisal system, loan review mechanism, credit approving powers, prudential limits on large credit exposures, standards for loan collaterals, portfolio management, risk concentration, risk monitoring and evaluation, pricing of loans, ratings of loans, rating review, provisioning, regulatory/legal compliances, etc.

Through the use of credit derivatives, different methods have been evolved to manage credit risk such as credit default swaps, total return swaps, credit spread forwards & options, credit linked notes, securitization, etc.

Credit Risk Management

Credit risk management of the banks and FIs is reflected through three main parameters, which are profitability of bank, liquidity position of bank and level of Non Performing Assets (NPAs). The main function of banks in managing credit risk is to maximize Risk Adjusted

Return On Capital (RAROC) and at the same time maintaining credit quality and quantity. The management of NPAs is one of the biggest challenges for banks and FIs because with increasing business, the risk of default also increases. The banks are exposed to credit risk on individual loan and also on whole portfolio. The biggest source of credit risk for banks is loans but some other sources such as off balance sheet items like corporate guarantee, line of credit, etc. also expose bank to credit risk to some extent.

Every bank and FI needs to have credit risk management process in place which should cover the following:-

1. Identifying and measuring credit risk on the basis of credit scoring models and other internal mechanism for individual loans and for whole portfolio.
2. Pricing of loans on the basis of risk associated with each loan or sector wise pricing or loan size wise pricing.
3. Assessment of adverse impact of assets exposure on banks financials such as NPA assessment.
4. Choosing right approach for credit risk mitigation such as selection of credit derivatives.
5. Hedging the credit risk by using appropriate derivative product.
6. Continuous monitoring and review of hedging strategy in changing scenario of the market of loan profile.

Approaches to Credit Risk Management

There is no standard approach available to manage credit risk. Banks and FIs devise different models as per the profile of their business and the nature of its assets. Most of the banks in India have developed credit scoring models for each category of loans such as working capital finance, trade finance, retail loans including mortgage financing, agriculture credit, corporate finance, term loans, SME financing, microfinance, project finance, export finance, food credit, infrastructure finance, etc. In these credit scoring models, scores have been assigned to different credit parameters. Every loan's information is put into the credit scoring model and the total score is calculated. If total score of loan falls in acceptance region, the loan is granted otherwise the loan is rejected. These models are also used for charging risk premium on loan if score is not falling under a very comfortable zone. The different approaches are as follows:

1. ***Credit Appraisal and Approval Process:*** FI/bank should have a detailed credit appraisal system in place including parameters such as borrowers profile, income, borrower's assets and liabilities, annual cash flow, repayment capacity, previous credit repayment record, credit record available with CIBIL, project financials, project's financial viability, etc. On the basis of credit appraisal and score obtained during appraisal, approval of loan is granted. Delegation of loan approval is also to be in place on the basis of sector and/or size of loan. On the basis of size of bank/FI, approving authority may be decided. If the size of the bank or FI is big, multi-tier approving system may be in place based on the size of loan and the sector in which exposure is being taken.

2. ***Credit Concentration and Sectoral Cap:*** Generally, regulators talk about the credit concentration and sectoral cap. The regulator set the maximum limit for sectoral cap and credit concentration, this does not mean that any bank or FI may take exposure to the maximum. Bank has to devise a policy for sectoral exposure and exposure size on the basis of risk estimation for each sector. More risky sectors may be capped for less exposure and credit risk may be covered by levying risk premium. Credit concentration generally means giving a large credit to a particular corporate or group of companies. Taking large exposure on a single party or a group increases default risk manifold which sometimes may not be hedged by any means. Sometimes it is also referred as open risk.

3. ***Credit Scoring Model and Risk Rating of Loans:*** Credit scoring model is a scientific method which has been evolved from the analysis of past behaviour of loans. Various parameters which contribute to the quality of assets have been closely studied and then scores are assigned to these parameters. Credit scoring model is used for rating of individual loans and on the basis of this, the cumulative score for the whole portfolio may be obtained. Credit scoring model is used for knowing the likely possibility of default. Parameters for scoring models are decided on the basis of nature of loans. Say for retail loans, parameters like personal income, age, job profile, number of dependents, residential status, number of years of experience, qualification etc are considered. For a corporate loan, various ratios such as Inventory Turnover Ratio, Debtors Turnover Ratio, Creditors Turnover Ratio, Debt Equity Ratio, Financial Leverage, Interest Coverage Ratio, Gross Profit Margin, Net Profit Ratio, Expenses Ratio, Return on Capital employed, Return on Net Worth, Dividend Payout, etc. are taken into consideration while devising scoring model.

4. ***Pricing of Loan:*** The pricing of different loan products in banks is done on the basis of risk associated with each type of assets. The credit risk in all the assets is not same hence there may not be a common pricing for all kind of loan products. The basis of risk estimation and probability of default on particular type of loan is the decisive factor in loan pricing. The method of deciding risk premium has been discussed in chapter of credit risk measurement i.e. RAROC. The pricing of loan does not only depend on risk profile of loan product but also on factors such as cost of borrowings, servicing of loans, cost of capital to be provided to create a loan, etc. In most of the investment products, banks have to follow market driven prices and it is not possible for bank to devise its own pricing due to price competitiveness. While lending on market driven price, bank may be exposed to credit risk which cannot be covered by charging risk premium. These kinds of exposure may be hedged by using credit derivatives.

5. ***Loan Review Mechanism:*** Once loan is finally disbursed, the repayment of loan starts. The timely repayment of loan gives comfort to banks against credit and liquidity risk. The steps taken while sanctioning and pricing of loans are not sufficient enough to mitigate credit risk fully. Sometimes it happens that even when all the risk mitigation steps are followed, the defaults on loans are observed. Banks/FIs should have a well designed system in place for loan monitoring on a continuous basis covering the following:

- Periodic scoring of loans on the basis of annual performance of borrowers and if need arises loan may be recalled or repriced based on revised parameters.
- Validation of projected cash flows on annual basis and revision of projected cash flow on the basis of present performance.
- Verifying the end usage of fund which means that the fund is used for the purpose for which it has been disbursed and there is no deviation of funds. It is a proven fact in the banking industry that by and large if fund use is diverted, the probability of likely default also increases.
- Ensuring the compliance of various sanction conditions and completion of loan documents including legal compliance and creation of security.
- In case any of the above deviation is observed, there should be a clear reporting system to management about likely default situation. Such accounts are also named as special mention accounts which may fall under NPA category in near future.

Structure of Credit Risk Rating System

Credit Risk

1. **Internal**
   a. Business Risk
      i. Current Market Share
      ii. Market Standing
      iii. Operating Efficiency
      iv. Growth Perspective
      v. SWOT Analysis
   b. Financial Risk
      i. Past Financial Record
      ii. Quality of Past Financial Records (Performance)
      iii. Projected Financials
      iv. Financial Structure
      v. Cash Flow Positions
   c. Management Risk
      i. Management Track Record
      ii. Repayment History of previous loans
      iii. Quality of Management

d. Credit Facility Risk
    i. Availability of Security
    ii. Past Payment Record
    iii. Directors/Corporate Guarantee
e. Project Risk
    i. DSCR Adequacy
    ii. Tenure of Loan
    iii. Asset Coverage Ratio
    iv. Future Cash Flows
    v. Financial Leverage

2. External

a. Industry Risk
    i. Nature of Industry
    ii. Competitors and other players in the industry
    iii. Industry prospects
    iv. Industry SWOT

Credit derivative[1]

In finance, a credit derivative is a "financial instrument or derivative whose price and value derives from the creditworthiness of the obligations of a third party, which is isolated and traded". Credit default products are the most commonly traded credit derivative product and include unfunded products such as credit default swaps and funded products such as synthetic Collateralized Debt Obligations (synthetic CDOs).

Credit derivatives, in their simplest form, are bilateral contracts between a buyer and seller under which the seller sells protection against certain pre-agreed events occurring in relation to a third party (usually a corporate or sovereign) known as a reference entity. These events are called credit events and they relate to the creditworthiness of the reference entity. The reference entity will not (except in certain very limited circumstances) be a party to the credit derivatives contract, and will usually be unaware of the contract's existence.

The parties will select which credit events apply to a transaction and these usually consist of one or more of the following: bankruptcy (the risk that the reference entity will become bankrupt), failure to pay (the risk that the reference entity will default on one of its obligations (e.g. a bond or loan)), obligation default (the risk that the reference entity will default on any of its obligations), obligation acceleration (the risk that an obligation of the reference entity will be accelerated e.g. a bond will be declared immediately due and payable following a default), repudiation/moratorium (the risk that the reference entity or a government will declare a moratorium over the reference entity's obligations), and restructuring (the risk that obligations of the reference entity will be restructured).

Where credit protection is bought and sold between bilateral counterparties, it is known as an unfunded credit derivative. If the credit derivative is entered into by a financial institution or a special purpose vehicle and payments under the credit derivative are funded using securitization techniques such that a debt obligation is issued by the financial institution or SPV to support these obligations, this is known as a funded credit derivative. This synthetic securitization process has become increasingly popular over the last decade, with the simple versions of these structures being known as synthetic CDOs, credit linked notes, single tranche CDOs, to name a few. In funded credit derivatives, transactions are often rated by rating agencies, which allows investors to take different slices of credit risk according to their risk appetite.

Market Size and Participants

The ISDA reported in April 2007 that the total notional amount on outstanding credit derivatives was $35.1 trillion with a gross market value of $948 billion. Although the credit derivatives market is a global one, London's market share rests at about 40 percent, with the rest value of Europe standing at about 10 percent. The main market participants are banks, hedge funds, insurance companies, pension funds, and other corporates. The main inter-dealer brokers are Creditex, Tullett-Prebon, GFI Group and ICAP.

Types of Credit Derivatives

There are many types of credit derivatives. Credit derivatives are fundamentally divided into two categories of product, funded credit derivatives and unfunded credit derivatives. An unfunded credit derivative is a bilateral contract between two counterparties, where each party is responsible for making its payments under the contract (i.e. payments of premiums and any cash or physical settlement amount) itself without recourse to other assets. In a funded credit derivative, the credit derivative will be embedded into a bond (which will usually either be issued by an SPV or a financial institution), and bondholders will (ultimately) be responsible for the payment of any cash or physical settlement amounts.

Unfunded credit derivative products include the following products:

- Single name Credit Default Swap (CDS)
- Total return swap
- First to Default Credit Default Swap
- Portfolio Credit Default Swap
- Secured Loan Credit Default Swap
- Credit Default Swap on Asset Backed Securities
- Credit Default Swaption (CDSw)
- Recovery lock transaction
- Credit Spread Option
- CDS index products
- Constant Maturity Credit Default Swap (CMCDS)

Funded credit derivative products include the following products:

- Credit Linked Note (CLN)
- Synthetic Collateralised Debt Obligation (CDO)
- Constant Proportion Debt Obligation (CPDO)
- Synthetic Constant Proportion Portfolio Insurance (Synthetic CPPI)

Credit Default Swap

The credit default swap or CDS has become the cornerstone product of the credit derivatives market. This product represents over thirty percent of the credit derivatives market. A credit default swap, in its simplest form (the unfunded single name credit default swap), is a bilateral contract between a protection buyer and a protection seller. The credit default swap will reference the creditworthiness of a third party called a reference entity, this will usually be a corporate or sovereign. The credit default swap will relate to the specified debt obligations of the reference entity: perhaps its bonds and loans, which fulfill certain pre-agreed characteristics. The protection buyer will pay a periodic fee to the protection seller in return for a contingent payment by the seller upon a credit event affecting the obligations of the reference entity specified in the transaction. The relevant credit events specified in a transaction will usually be selected from amongst the following: the bankruptcy of the reference entity, its failure to pay in relation to a covered obligation, it defaulting on an obligation or that obligation being accelerated, it agreeing to restructure a covered obligation or a repudiation or moratorium being declared over any covered obligation.

If any of these events occur and the protection buyer serves a credit event notice on the protection seller detailing the credit event as well as (usually) providing some publicly available information validating this claim, then the transaction will settle. This means that in the case of a physically settled transaction, the protection buyer can deliver an amount of the reference entity's defaulted obligations to the protection seller in return for their full face value (notwithstanding that they are now worth far less). In the case of cash settled transaction, a relevant obligation of the reference entity will be valued and the protection seller will pay the protection buyer the full face value of the reference obligation less its current value (i.e. compensating the protection buyer for the decline in the obligation's creditworthiness).

Credit default swaps have unique characteristics that distinguish them from insurance products and financial guaranties. The protection buyer does not need to own an underlying obligation of the reference entity. The protection buyer does not need to suffer a loss. The protection seller has no recourse to and no right to sue the reference entity for recovery. The product has many variations, including where there is a basket or portfolio of reference entities, although fundamentally, the principles remain the same. A powerful recent variation has been gathering market share of late credit default swaps which relate to asset-backed securities or Credit Default Swaps on Asset-Backed Securities.

The Reserve Bank of India (RBI) in May' 2011 came out with a credit default swap (CDS) guideline that would allow corporate entities including insurers, FIIs and mutual funds (MFs) to hedge risk against default in corporate bonds to which they subscribe. The guidelines will come into effect from 24th October' 2011. As per guidelines, foreign institutional investors

(FIIs), banks, insurers, NBFCs, listed companies, housing finance companies, provident funds and primary dealers can buy credit protection under the scheme. It further said that banks, primary dealers and NBFCs with sound financial and good track record will be allowed to act as market makers or facilitators (for buying and selling of such swaps). The bonds for the purpose of CDS would include unlisted and unrated debt instruments, including those issued by the infrastructure companies engaged in sector like road, port and telecommunication, and power, among others. Elaborating on the guidelines, the RBI said that beside banks, the NBFCs and primary dealers with a net owned fund of Rs. 500 crores would be permitted to act as market makers. The guidelines further said that entities would only be allowed to buy CDS contracts to hedge credit risk and not for speculation.

With the help of diagrams, Credit default swap is explained below:

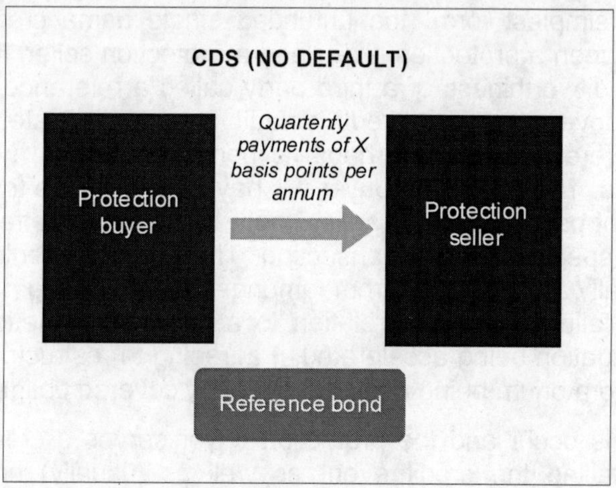

If the reference bond performs without default, the protection buyer pays quarterly payments to the seller until maturity.

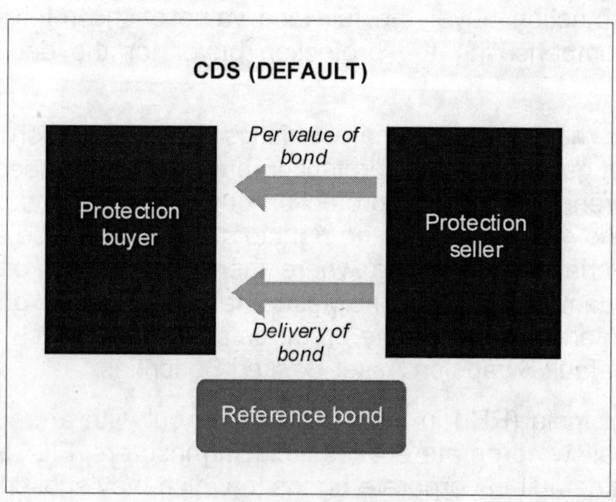

If the reference bond defaults, the protection seller pays par value of the bond to the buyer, and the buyer physically delivers the bond to the seller.

Buyer purchased a CDS at time t_0 and makes regular premium payments at times t_1, t_2, t_3, and t_4. If the associated credit instrument suffers no credit event, then the buyer continues paying premiums at t_5, t_6 and so on until the end of the contract at time t_n.

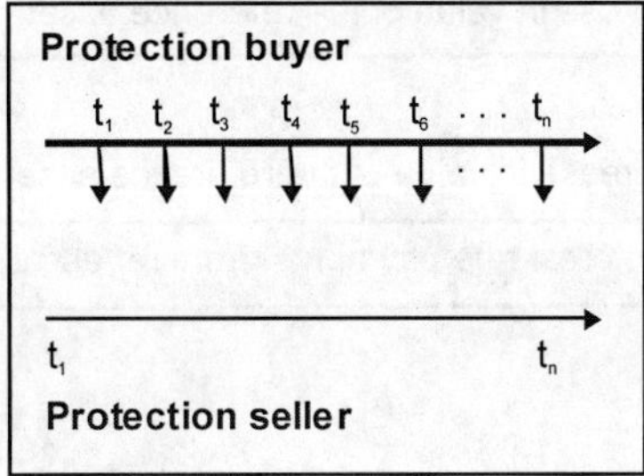

However, if the associated credit instrument suffered a credit event at t_5, then the protection seller pays the buyer for the loss, and the buyer would cease paying premiums.

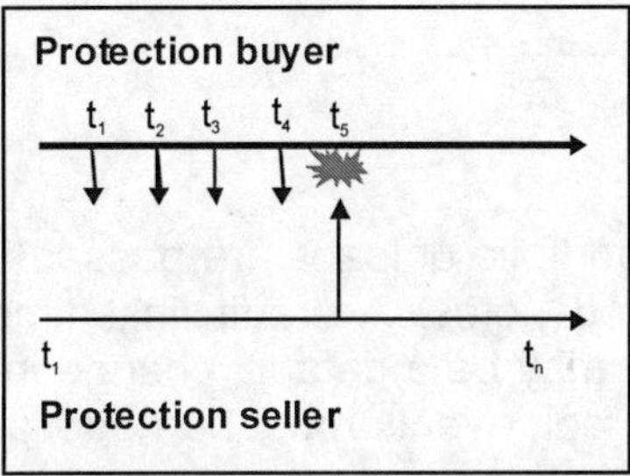

Total Return Swap

A Total Return Swap (also known as Total Rate of Return Swap) is a contract between two counterparties whereby they swap periodic payments for the period of the contract. Typically, one party receives the total return (interest payments plus any capital gains or losses for the payment period) from a specified reference asset, while the other receives a specified fixed or floating cash flow that is not related to the creditworthiness of the reference asset, as with a vanilla interest rate swap. The payments are based upon the same notional amount. The reference asset may be any asset, index or basket of assets. The TRS is simply a mechanism that allows one party to derive the economic benefit of owning an asset without the use of the balance sheet, and which allows the other to effectively "buy protection" against loss in value due to ownership of a credit asset. The essential difference between a total return swap and a credit default swap is that the credit default swap provides protection against specific credit events. The total return swap protects against the loss of value irrespective of cause, whether default, widening of credit spreads or anything else i.e. it isolates both credit risk and market risk.

In the figure given below, it is explained how total return swap works:

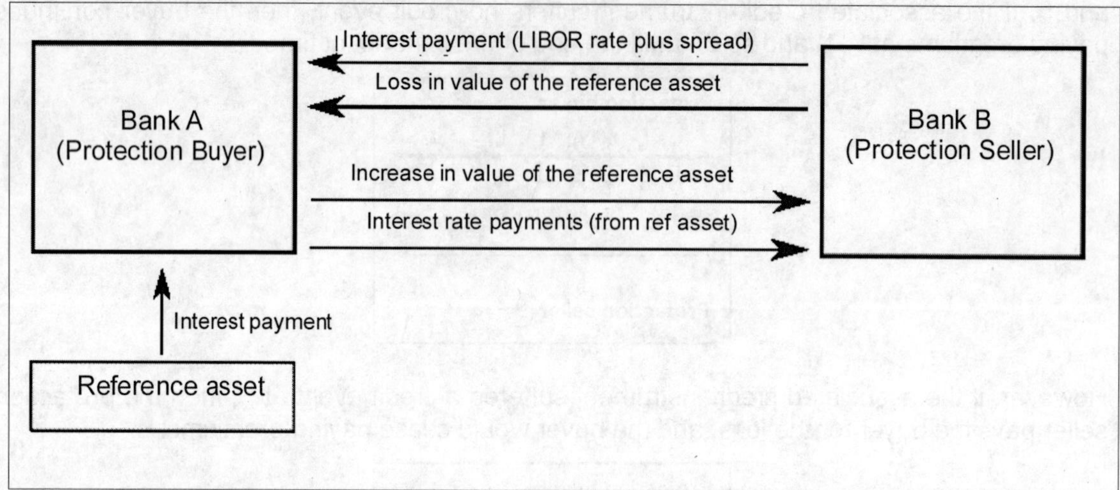

Credit Linked Notes (CLN)

The coupons from the bank's portfolio of loans are passed to the SPV, which uses the cash flow to service the credit linked notes. A credit linked note is a note whose cash flow depends upon an event, which may be a default, change in credit spread, or rating change. The definition of the relevant credit events must be negotiated by the parties to the note. A CLN in effect combines a credit-default swap with a regular note (with coupon, maturity, redemption). Given its note like features, a CLN is an on-balance-sheet asset, in contrast to a CDS. Typically, an investment fund manager will purchase such a note to hedge against possible downgrades, or loan defaults. Numerous different types of Credit Linked Notes (CLNs) have been structured and placed in the past few years. The most basic CLN consists of a bond, issued by a well-rated borrower, packaged with a credit default swap on a less creditworthy risk.

For example, a bank may sell some of its exposure to a particular emerging country by issuing a bond linked to that country's default or convertibility risk. From the bank's point of view, this achieves the purpose of reducing its exposure to that risk, as it will not need to reimburse all or part of the note if a credit event occurs. However, from the point of view of investors, the risk profile is different from that of the bonds issued by the country. If the bank runs into difficulty, their investments will suffer even if the country is still performing well. The credit rating is improved by using a proportion of government bonds, which means the CLN investor receives an enhanced coupon. Through the use of a credit default swap, the bank receives some recompense if the reference credit defaults. There are several different types of securitized product, which have a credit dimension. CLN is a generic name related to any bond whose value is linked to the performance of a reference asset, or assets. This link may be through the use of a credit derivative, but does not have to be.

Collateralized Debt Obligation (CDO)

Collateralized Debt Obligations or CDOs are a form of credit derivative offering exposure to a large number of companies in a single instrument. This exposure is sold in slices of varying risk or subordination - each slice is known as a tranche. In a cashflow CDO, the underlying credit risks are bonds or loans held by the issuer. Alternatively in a synthetic CDO, the exposure to each underlying company is a credit default swap. A synthetic CDO is also referred to as CSO. Other more complicated CDOs have been developed where each underlying credit risk is itself a CDO tranche. These CDOs are commonly known as CDOs-squared.

Collateralized bond obligations (CBO): Bond issued against a pool of bond assets or other securities. It is referred to in a generic sense as a CDO.

Collateralized loan obligations (CLO): Bond issued against a pool of bank loan. It is referred to in a generic sense as a CDO.

Collateralized Mortgage obligations (CMO): The cash flows on mortgage loans are bundled and sold to investors by issuing pass through certificates carrying specific coupons based on loans cash flow. The pass through certificates are backed by mortgage created on loans.

Mortgage backed bonds (MBB): In this kind of securitization, the loans are removed from the books of an issuer unlike done in case of CMO. To issue MBB, a bank segregates a group of mortgage assets on its balance sheet and pledges these assets as collateral against MBB issue.

Loan sale as Credit Risk Management Technique

The loan sale among banks is a very old practice. In fact, few small banks create loans in their books but due to various reasons such as capital requirement, default risk, etc., these banks sell loans to big banks. The loans are also sold among banks with or without recourse. Loan sold with recourse carry the default risk to the seller instead of buyer whereas in loan sold without recourse basis, the default risk is also transferred from seller to buyer of loan. Loans sold on recourse basis create a contingent liability on seller's balance sheet. The various types are loans usually sold among participants such as short term loans, mortgage loans, highly leveraged loans created for mergers and acquisitions, loans to finance leveraged buyouts, distressed loans where default has already occurred, etc.

Reasons of Loan Sale by FIs

The five major reasons for which FIs sell their loans are described below:

1. ***To manage credit risk:*** This is the major reason why FIs sell their loan. Through loan sales, assets are removed from FI's books and allow FIs to reduce risk and helps for better diversification of its assets. By selling distressed assets, FI reduces its provisioning requirements and create way for creation of new loans. FI's also unlock funds involved in making provisions for bad loans.

2. ***Source of fee income:*** Not every FI has ability to create loans in the market. In such a case, big FIs and banks create loans in their books and later sell to small banks and FIs in return of a fee income.

3. ***To mange adequate capital and statutory reserves:*** As per regulatory requirement, banks have to maintain certain reserves with RBI, which also has cost to banks. Apart from this, for creation of each loan, bank has to bring capital to meet CAR as stipulated by RBI. In order to maintain above two statutory requirements, banks sell the loans without recourse that allows them rightsizing the assets and repayment of high cost debts.

4. ***Cost of Capital:*** The capital adequacy requirement imposed by RBI differs from loan to loan based on risk weight assigned to these loans as per Basel II norms. Hence, for loans having higher risk weight, banks have to bring more capital in comparison with loans having lower risk weight. During the currency of loans, the rating of loans also downgraded which increase risk weight of such loans means higher capital requirement. In order to keep cost of capital checked, banks sell these loans to the buyers who are having higher CAR.

5. ***To manage liquidity risk:*** Banks liabilities are more liquid in comparison with its assets. Holding illiquid asset in books may increase liquidity risk at the time of liquidity crunch. To mitigate liquidity risk, banks sell some of their illiquid loans in the market.

CREDIT RATINGS

A credit rating assesses the credit worthiness of an individual, corporation, or even a country. Credit ratings are calculated from financial history and current assets and liabilities. A credit rating indicates a lender or investor, the probability of the subject being able to pay back a loan. However, in recent years, credit ratings have also been used to adjust insurance premiums, determine employment eligibility, and establish the amount of a utility or leasing deposit. A poor credit rating indicates a high risk of defaulting on a loan, and thus leads to high interest rates, or the refusal of a loan by the creditor.

The credit rating of a company is a financial indicator to potential investors of debt securities such as bonds. These are assigned by credit rating agencies such as Standard & Poor's, Moody's or Fitch Ratings and have letter designations such as AAA, B, CC. The Standard & Poor's rating scale is as follows: AAA, AA, A, BBB, BB, B, CCC, CC, C, D. Anything lower than a BBB rating is considered a speculative or junk bond. The Moody's rating system is similar in concept but the verbage is a little different. It is as follows: AAA, Aa1, Aa2, Aa3, A1, A2, A3, Baa1, Baa2, Baa3, Ba1, Ba2, Ba3, B1, B2, B3, Caa1, Caa2, Caa3, Ca, and C.

Credit scores for individuals are assigned by credit bureaus (US; UK: credit reference agencies, CIBIL). Credit ratings for corporations and sovereign debt are assigned by credit rating agencies. In the United States, the main credit bureaus are Experian, Equifax, and TransUnion. A relatively new credit bureau in the US is Innovis. In the United Kingdom, the main credit reference agencies for individuals are Experian, Equifax, and Callcredit. There is no universal credit rating as such, rather each individual lender credit scores based on its own wish-list of a perfect customer. In Canada, the main credit bureaus for individuals are Equifax, TransUnion and Northern Credit Bureaus/ Experian. In India, the main credit bureaus are CRISIL, CARE, FITCH and ICRA. The largest credit rating agencies (which tend to operate worldwide) are Moody's, Standard and Poor's and Fitch Ratings.

Table: Credit ratings employed by Standard and Poor's for rating bonds

AAA	Best credit quality—Extremely reliable with regard to financial obligations
AA	Very good credit quality—Very reliable
A	More susceptible to economic conditions—still good credit quality
BBB	Lowest rating in investment grade
BB	Caution is necessary—Best sub-investment credit quality
B	Vulnerable to changes in economic conditions—Currently showing the ability to meet its financial obligations
CCC	Currently vulnerable to nonpayment—Dependent on favorable economic conditions
CC	Highly vulnerable to a payment default
C	Close to or already bankrupt—payment on the obligation currently continued
D	Payment default on some financial obligation has actually occurred

Hedging of Credit Risk

By Using Credit Forwards and Futures

A credit forward is an agreement that hedges against an increase in default risk on a loan. The credit forward agreement specifies a risk premium above the risk free rate to compensate for default risk on a benchmark bond issued by bank borrower. Suppose a bank invests in AA rated bond of some company at the rate of G Sec rate of same maturity plus 300 basis points. In this case, 300 basis points is credit spread and this is the rate at which credit forward contract is written. The credit forward buyer bears the risk of an increase in credit risk on the bond of a company and credit forward seller hedge itself against an increase in the borrower's credit risk. If the borrower credit rating decreases, it means higher credit spread is required in the market, in this case the credit forward buyer compensate the credit forward seller. The gain in credit forward to seller may be used to offset the loss in the market value of loan due to downgrading of the rating of the bond borrower. If the credit rating of the borrower does not decrease, the seller of credit forward will pay premium to the credit forward buyer.

Payoffs in Credit Risk Hedging with Forward Contracts

The table below gives a payoff mechanism while hedging credit risk with credit forward contracts:-

Credit Spread at the Maturity of Forward Agreement	Credit Spread Seller (FI)	Credit Spread Buyer (Counterparty)
$S_t > S_f$	**Receipt:** $(S_t - S_f) \times MD \times A$	**Payment:** $(S_t - S_f) \times MD \times A$
$S_f > S_t$	**Payment:** $(S_f - S_t) \times MD \times A$	**Receipt:** $(S_f - S_t) \times MD \times A$

In the above table, S_t is actual credit spread on the loan when credit forward matures and S_f is the credit spread on which the credit forward contract is sold. The credit forward seller, i.e. lender bank/FI hedge itself against the increasing default risk of borrower and the buyer of credit forward hedge itself against the increasing default risk on loans of borrowing company. When at the time of maturity of credit forward, default risk of borrower increases, a higher spread will be required than the originally agreed to in forward contract ($S_t > S_f$). In this event, the credit forward buyer will compensate credit forward seller by amount equal to $(S_t - S_f) \times MD \times A$.

For example, suppose credit spread between AA bonds and T-bill widened to 4% from 3% over the year and the modified duration of the benchmark AA bond was 5 years. The size of the forward contract was Rs.100 lacs. In this case seller of contract will gain Rs.5 lacs i.e. (4% - 3%) x 5 x 100. In case borrower's default risk increases, the market value of loan decreases that may be offset by the gain of contract seller from forward contract.

However, if borrower's default risk decreases at the time of maturity of forward contract ($S_f > S_t$), the credit forward seller will pay the credit forward buyer an amount equal to $(S_f - S_t) \times MD \times A$.

By using Credit Spread Call Option

A credit spread call option is a call option whose payoff increases as default risk increases than the predecided credit spread. If a bank expects credit risk on some bond, it may purchase a credit call option to hedge the credit risk. If credit risk on a loan increases, the value of loan decreases and bank's net worth too decreases. If credit risk on a loan increases, the call option will not be exercised and bank will suffer loss equal to premium paid which can be offset against the gain in portfolio.

By using Caps, Floors, and Collars

These derivatives are in use in the absence of exchange traded future and option for credit risk. These derivatives are available over the counter and also carry counterparty credit risk. Only banks which are more creditworthy should write such derivatives.

By Credit Swaps

Credit Risk is the most important risk to be managed in comparison with interest rate risk or forex risk because due to this a bank may fail. Generally two types of credit swaps are used - one is total return swap and the other is credit default swap.

Summary

Credit risk occurs when counterparty defaults its timely obligation such as repayment of interest and principal. Credit risk is one of the most important risk for banks as it occurs in its main business of lending. Most of the banks mainly focus on this risk under risk management perspective. In this chapter, various credit risk management approaches have been detailed. The credit risk, also termed as default risk, may be hedged through credit derivatives. Most of the credit derivatives are not traded in exchange and are available over the counter. The various types of credit derivatives such as credit default swaps, total return swaps, etc. have been detailed and their use in hedging has also been explained. Most of the banks in India use credit risk rating system to grade the loans in different credit grades and on the basis of which pricing of loan is done. The credit risk rating system tells the likely default scenario for loans. The concept of credit rating by external agencies such as Standard and Poor has been given. In this chapter, various other strategies of credit risk hedging by using options, cap, floor and collar has been discussed in brief.

KEY CONCEPTS

NPA	RAROC	Credit Appraisal	Credit Approval
Credit Concentration	Sectoral Cap	Credit Scoring Model	Risk Rating of Loans
Pricing of Loans	Credit Risk	Business Risk	Management Risk
Loan Review Mechanism	Credit Facility Risk	Project Risk	Industry Risk
ISDA	Credit Rating	Credit Forward	Caps
Credit Spread Call Option	Floors	Collars	Credit Swaps
Loan sales			

Review Questions and Problems

1. What is the credit risk management? What are the various factors involved in bank's credit risk?
2. Study credit risk management process in any selected bank/FI.
3. What are the various approaches of credit risk management in any organisation?
4. Study and define the credit risk rating structure for any Indian bank.
5. What are the credit derivatives? How many kinds of credit derivatives are available in Indian market?
6. List the credit derivatives traded in exchange worldwide.
7. Identify at least five CD deals that took place recently including nature of industry and financial transactions involved.

8. Prepare a brief of rating agencies internationally available and also gives its different coding used for rating along with the meaning of rating codes.
9. As per RBI recognition, how many rating agencies are operating in India? What are the various instruments being rated by them and the rating used for these instrument?
10. What is the rationale behind the rating used by these credit rating agencies?
11. Explain credit default swaps for default and no default situation with help of diagram.
12. What is total return swap? How TRS works, explain with the help of diagram?
13. What is a credit forward? Explain its payoff table.
14. Calculate the gain on the purchase of a Rs.100 crores credit forward contract with a modified duration of 5 years if the credit spread between a benchmark bond and loan of borrowing firm decreases by 2%.
15. Calculate the gain on the sale of a Rs. 200 crores credit forward contract with a modified duration of 6 years if the credit spread between a benchmark bond and loan of borrowing firm decreases by 1.5%.
16. Discuss loan sales technique used by bank for credit risk management.

Reference:

1. *http://en.wikipedia.org*

Chapter – 15

Operational Risk Management

Chapter Objective

- Discuss various measures in Operational Risk Management
- Understand Moody's Analytical Framework for Operational Risk Management
- Explain methodology of Moody's Framework

Introduction

The operational risk is being overlooked in recent years even when the size of the financial industry and the size of various banks and FIs is growing. Operational risk management is gaining importance, particularly when large losses can be attributed to the failure of internal and external controls. The Basel II proposals require banks to keep capital aside for operational risk arising out of losses due to failure of internal and external controls. Operational risk management can be achieved through preventive as well as damage limiting controls. The preventive controls are necessary to decrease the probability of loss incurred by the occurrence of an event.

Management of Operational Risk

The following are the suggestive measures for managing operational risk:-

1. As per the nature of business of financial institution and the size of organisation, the kinds of operational risk and various areas where organisation is exposed to, operational risk should be clearly defined. If the areas and risks are not clearly defined, mitigation of operational risk is difficult.

2. A proper operational risk management committee should be in place to take policy decision on operational risk identification and timely decision on its mitigation. Some type of operational risk look small in nature but needs immediate attention of the management of banks and FIs.

3. The priority of different kinds of operational risk needs to be set on the basis of probability and quantum of financial losses expected to arise. The operational risk having more capital loss may be addressed first.

4. Though quantifying the financial losses in different kinds of operational risk is not a easy task due to non availability of the losses from risk events. The losses arising from similar types of risk event may be used to quantify after applying certain error elimination techniques.

5. Proper check and balance are required for each process being adopted in business. The proper validation of risk mitigation techniques is also required from time to time. Operational risk techniques change along with time and need to be adjusted as per change in technology and legal framework of the respective country.

6. Each business line identifies the nature and size of operational risk. It is necessary to identify high impact events as well as their probabilities. Events when combined could have a significant impact and require appropriate monitoring.

7. An audit of the financial transactions and controls by an external agency is an essential risk control. The audit can take the form of concurrent audit or even pre-audit. With the use of technology, information systems audit has also become necessary. The various bodies have also started giving certification to professionals in the area of system audit such as CISA etc.

8. In line with credit metrics and risk metrics, operational risk matrics may be developed including the parameters such as early risk warning signals, likely occurrence scenario, etc.

9. There has to be a clear demarcation of duties at various levels in the organisation so that the financial transactions are not dealt by only a single employee. The separation of functions can be seen in treasury offices in the form of front office, mid-office, and back office. The function of these three offices should be independent from each other, i.e. there should not be any common interest and reporting.

10. Once the operational risks in the organisation are identified, operational risk management committee should try to know the root cause of arising of that risk before suggesting any risk mitigation techniques.

11. The delegation of authority and span of control at all levels of the organisation should be clearly defined. This is particularly important in terms of the authority for financial transactions or policy decisions having big financial implications etc.

12. Technology brings consistency in processing and minimises human errors. Wherever straight through processing is possible, systems should be allowed to talk to each other without human intervention. Technology, however, also involves operational risk and this needs to be controlled.

13. Transferring the risk is not a new concept. If the management of a risk is a costly affair than transferring it to the third party, there is no need to expose to that risk. These kinds of risks may be identified and transferred to third party.

14. The system input should be independently checked and approved. This reduces the possibility of errors within the system. Often organizations insist on joint authorization for activities such as cheque payments and procurement orders to ensure an independent application of mind.

15. Financial and accounting reconciliation of records is an important control.

16. Every procedure and process should be properly documented in the form of operation manuals. If possible for the organisation, ISO certification should be taken in order to classify each and every activity and its process. They provide the steps involved in various processes and the responsibility of carrying them out within the set time framework. The ownership of each process and step should be clearly defined and communicated.
17. There should be proper alerts for important and vital events of the organisation. A proper event diary may be prepared at the beginning of financial year for each business line or the department.

Operational Risk Management (ORM) implies the importance of non-quantifiable loss events to the businesses and its managers. Operational risk in certain extreme situations threatens with a loss of magnitude not comparable with any other risks challenging a business enterprise just because the amount involved cannot be estimated and retraction and recovery is almost impossible and also importantly happens in an unexpected quarter at an unexpected time.

Moody's Analytical Framework for Operational Risk

Management of Banks[1]

Moody believes that the assessment of operational risk is becoming increasingly central to the fundamental analysis of a rated bank. Operational risk management improves the quality and stability of earnings, thereby enhancing the competitive position of the bank and facilitating its long-term survival. The financial services sector has seen considerable advances in the field of risk management, with operational risk now receiving greater prominence and being recognised as a separate, although impinging, category in its own right. Over a comparatively short period of time, a significant number of high-impact losses, some of which have resulted in institutional failure, have clearly demonstrated the significance of operational risk. This has resulted in change to the business environment. The control of operational risk is fundamentally concerned with good management, which involves a tenacious process of vigilance and continuous improvement. This is a value-adding activity that impacts, either directly or indirectly, bottom-line performance. It must, therefore, be a key consideration for any business. Since operational risk will affect credit ratings, share prices, and organisational reputation, analysts will increasingly include it in their assessment of the management, their strategy and the expected long-term performance of the business.

Key considerations in the field of operational risk, which both analysts and bank management will need to take into account, are:

i. Determination of the overall risk profile of the bank

ii. Identification of main risks, showing how they impact on profitability and the quality and stability of earnings

iii. Optimisation of the risk-reward relationship

iv. Verification and validation of underlying factors

Moody's Methodology

Moody's Methodology considers the assessment of operational risk within a bank to be an ongoing process. Their assessment is based upon an in-depth analysis, structured around a series of discussions with the bank's management. The outline framework for this thorough review is provided below. A holistic approach is adopted and is based on consideration of four inter-related areas.

The framework recognises that, when assessing any business, a primary consideration is the quality of management and its leadership capability. Ultimately, the success of management can be determined from the results achieved, which are a function of how efficiently and effectively the various resources have been applied, together with how effectively external threats have been mitigated.

Framework

1. **General Background:**
   - 1.1 Definition and Boundaries of Operation Risk
   - 1.2 The Driving Forces and Limitations (Regulatory & Commercial)
   - 1.3 Management
   - 1.4 Stages of Development and Organisation Structure
   - 1.5 Key Risks - Their significance and impact
   - 1.6 Operation Risk Profile Document, Reports and Indicators
2. **Leadership:**
   - 2.1 Corporate Governance
   - 2.2 Culture
   - 2.3 Ethics
   - 2.4 Strategy
   - 2.5 Management
3. **Organisational Efficiency & Effectiveness:**
   - 3.1 Operation Risk Framework (including organisation structure)
   - 3.2 Development Stages
   - 3.3 Key Risks and Priorities
4. **External Factors:**
   - 4.1 Contingency Planning
   - 4.2 Outsourcing
   - 4.3 Insurance

5. **Reports and Results:**
   - 5.1 Reports
   - 5.2 Performance Assessment
   - 5.3 Data, Quantification and Modelling
   - 5.4 Validation and Verification

Moody wanted to know the key operational risks faced by the bank and how these may impact upon the quality and stability of its earnings. As a principle, Moody does not adopt a checklist approach for the determination of ratings. This framework provides background information to support future risk assessment meetings and is not meant to be comprehensive. In this framework, Moody has designed a series of question's covering all the aspects given above.

Summary

The assessment of operational risk is very difficult in the absence of historical date of the events related to operational risk. Hence its management is also a very subjective process. All the banks manage this risk as per their developed procedures and there is no standard available for this. Moody's has developed a framework for operational risk management for banks which has been discussed in this chapter in brief. The various measures of operational risk management strategies have also been discussed.

KEY CONCEPTS

Basel II	System Audit	CISA
Operational Risk	Operational Risk Framework	

Review Questions and Problems

1. What are the various operational risks to which banks are exposed due to use of technology and its mitigation?
2. What are the various parameters that need to be considered while managing operational risk?
3. Explain the role of audit in operational risk management.
4. How does the operational risk arise out of regulatory issues? What may be the strategy to mitigate risk arising out of regulatory issues?
5. Explain Moody's analytical framework for operational risk management.
6. What methodology is adopted in Moody's framework?
7. By using Moody's analytical framework, kindly prepare operational risk management document for any selected FI/bank.

Reference:

1. www.gloriamundi.org

Chapter – 16

Foreign Exchange & Sovereign Risk Management

Chapter Objective

- Understand Forex Risk Management
- Understand nature and magnitude of Forex Risk
- Know tools and techniques for Managing Forex Risk
- Explain use of Forex Derivatives
- Calculation of Hedge Ratio
- Discuss Forex Risk Management Strategies
- Understand Option Strategies and Low Cost option Strategies
- Management of Sovereign Risk Exposure

Introduction

Foreign Exchange Risk may be defined as the risk that a bank may suffer losses as a result of adverse exchange rate movements during a period in which it has an open position, either spot or forward, or a combination of the two, in an individual foreign currency. The banks are also exposed to interest rate risk, which arises from the maturity mismatching of foreign currency positions. Even in cases where spot and forward positions in individual currencies are balanced, the maturity pattern of forward transactions may produce mismatches. As a result, banks may suffer losses as a result of changes in premia/discounts of the currencies concerned. The fluctuation in exchange rate may be positive or negative. Positive change gives rise to gain and negative change gives rise to loss. Foreign exchange risk hedging refers to strategy, where one protects the price of assets and liabilities at a date in the future by taking an opposite position in the present by using currency derivatives such as Currency Options, Currency Futures, Forward Contracts, Currency Swaps, etc. These are safeguard strategies of protecting the financial exposures in the underlying asset or liability due to fluctuations in the exchange rates by taking positions through currency derivatives to offset the losses in the cash market i.e. change in the value of asset or liability, by gain in the derivatives market. The forex risk management involves the identification of foreign exchange exposure, the value of exposure, holding positions through currency derivatives to offset losses, estimating and maintaining minimum hedge ratio, risk limit setting acceptable to management, estimation of future movement of exchange rates i.e. calculation of currency VaR etc.

Foreign Exchange Risk Management[1]

In the forex business, banks also face the risk of default of the counterparties or settlement risk. While such type of risk crystallisation does not cause principal loss, banks may have to undertake fresh transactions in the cash/spot market for replacing the failed transactions. Thus, banks may incur replacement cost, which depends upon the currency rate movements. Banks also face another risk called time-zone risk or Herstatt risk which arises out of time-lags in settlement of one currency in one centre and the settlement of another currency in another time-zone. The forex transactions with counterparties from another country also trigger sovereign or country risk. The three important issues that need to be addressed in this regard are:

- Nature and magnitude of exchange risk
- The strategy to be adopted for hedging or managing exchange risk
- The tools of managing exchange risk

Nature and Magnitude of Risk

The risk inherent in running open foreign exchange positions have been heightened in recent years by the pronounced volatility in forex rates, thereby adding a new dimension to the risk profile of banks' balance sheets. The first aspect of management of foreign exchange risk is to acknowledge that such risk does exist and that it must be managed to avoid adverse financial consequences. Many banks refrain from active management of their foreign exchange exposure because they feel that financial forecasting is outside their field of expertise or because they find it difficult to measure currency exposure precisely. However not recognising a risk would not make it go away. Nor is the inability to measure risk any excuse for not managing it. Having recognized this fact, the nature and magnitude of such risk must now be identified.

The basic difficulty in measuring exposure comes from the fact that the available accounting information which provides the most reliable base to calculate exposure (accounting or translation exposure) does not capture the actual risk a bank faces, which depends on its future cash flows and their associated risk profiles (economic exposure). Also there is a distinction between the currency in which cash flows are denominated and the currency that determines the size of the cash flows.

Another dimension of exchange risk involves the element of time. In the very short run, virtually all local currency prices for goods and services (although not necessarily for financial assets) remain unchanged after an unexpected exchange rate change. However, over a longer period of time, prices and costs respond to price changes. It is therefore necessary to determine the time frame within which the bank can react to (unexpected) rate changes.

For a bank, being a financial entity, it is relatively easier to gauge the nature as well as the measure of forex risk simply because all financial assets/liabilities are denominated in a currency. A bank's future cash streams are more predictable than those of a non-financial firm. Its net exposure, or position, completely encapsulates the measure of its exposure to forex risk. In order to manage forex risk, some forex market relationships need to be understood well. The first and most important of these is the covered interest parity relationship. If there is free and unrestricted mobility of capital, the interest differential between two currencies will equal the forward premium/discount for either of the currency. This relationship must hold under the assumptions, otherwise arbitrage opportunities will arise to restore the relationship. However, in the case of rupee, since it is not totally convertible, this relationship does not hold exactly. Although interest rate differentials are the driving factor for the dollar premium against the rupee, it also is a factor of forward demand / supply factors. This brings in typical complications to forward hedging which must be taken into account.

From the above it can easily be determined that a currency with a lower interest rate will be at a premium in comparesion to a currency with a higher interest rate. The other relationships in the forex market are not as deterministic as the covered interest parity, but need to be recognised to manage forex exposure because they are the theoretical tools used for predicting exchange rate movements, essential to any hedging strategy particularly to economic risk as opposed to accounting risk. The most important of these is the Purchasing Power Parity relationship which says exchange rate changes are determined by inflation differentials. The Uncovered Interest Parity theory says that the forward exchange rate is the best and unbiased predictor of future spot rates under risk neutrality. These relationships have to be clearly understood for any meaningful forex risk management process.

Managing Foreign Exchange Risk

For a bank, therefore, the first major decision on forex risk management is for the management to fix its open foreign exchange position limits. Although typically this is a management decision, it could also be subject to regulatory capital and could also be required to be in tune with the regulatory environment that prevails. These open position limits have two aspects, the daylight limit and the overnight limit. The daylight limit could typically be substantially higher for two reasons, (a) It is easier to manage exchange risk when the market is open and the bank is actively present in the market, and (b) the bank needs a higher limit to accommodate client flows during business hours. Overnight position, being subject to more uncertainty and therefore being more risky, should be much lower.

Having decided on the overall open position limits, the next step is to allocate these limits among different operating centres of the bank (in the case of banks which hold positions at multiple centres). Within a centre there could be a further allocation among different dealers. It must, however, be ensured that the bank has a system to monitor the overall open position limit for the bank on a real time basis.

Tools and Techniques for Managing Forex Risk

There are various tools, often substitutes, available for hedging of foreign exchange risk like over the counter forwards, futures, money market instruments, options and the like. Most currency management instruments enable the bank to take a long or a short position to hedge an opposite short or long position. In equilibrium and in an efficient market, the cost of all will be the same, according to the fundamental relationships. The tools differ to the extent that they hedge different risks. In particular, symmetric hedging tools like futures cannot easily hedge contingent cash flows where risk is non-linear: options may be better suited to the latter. Foreign exchange forward contracts are the most common means of hedging transactions in foreign currencies. However, since they require future performance, and if one party is unable to perform on the contract, the hedge disappears, bringing in replacement risk which could be high. This default risk also means that many banks may not have access to the forward market to adequately hedge their exchange exposure. For such situations, futures, if available, may be more suitable, since they are exchange traded and effectively minimise default risk. However, futures are standardised and therefore may not be as versatile in terms of quantity and tenor as over the counter forward contracts. This, in turn, gives rise to assumption of basis risk.

Currency Derivatives

The following currency derivatives are largely used to hedge foreign exchange risk:

- Money Market Hedge
- Currency Options
- Forward Contracts
- Currency Futures
- Roll Over Contracts
- Currency Swaps

Money market borrowing to invest in interest-bearing assets to offset a foreign currency payment, also serves the same purpose as forward contracts. This follows from the covered interest parity principle. Since the carrying cost of a position is the same in both, the forex or the money market hedging can also be done in either market. For instance, let us say a bank has a short forward dollar position. It can, of course, hedge the position by buying forward dollars. Alternatively it can borrow rupees now, buy dollar with the proceeds, and place the dollars in a forward deposit to meet the short dollar position on maturity. The rupees received on the sale on maturity are used to pay off the rupee borrowing. The cost of this money market hedge is the difference between the rupee interest rate paid and the US dollar interest rate earned. According to the interest rate parity theorem, the interest differential equals the forward exchange premium, the percentage by which the forward rate differs from the spot exchange rate. So the cost of the money market hedge should be the same as the forward or futures market hedge.

Currency options are another tool for managing forex risk. A foreign exchange option is a contract for future delivery of a currency in exchange for another, where the holder of the option has the right to buy (or sell) the currency at an agreed price, the strike or exercise price, but is not required to do so. The right to buy is a call and the right to sell is a put. For such a right, the holder pays a price called the option premium. The option seller receives the premium and is obliged to make (or take) delivery at the agreed-upon price if the buyer exercises his option. In some options, the instrument being delivered is the currency itself; in other words, a futures contract on the currency. American options permit the holder to exercise option at any time before the expiration date whereas European options only on the expiration date.

Futures and Forwards are contracts in which two parties oblige themselves to exchange something in the future. They are thus useful to hedge or convert known currency or interest rate exposures. An option, in contrast, gives one party the right but not the obligation to buy or sell an asset under specified conditions while the other party assumes an obligation to sell or buy that asset if that option is exercised. Options being non-linear instruments are more difficult to price and therefore their risk profiles need to be well understood before they can be used. For example it needs to be understood that the value of a currency changes not just when exchange rate changes (the event for which the bank usually hedges using forwards/futures) but also if the underlying volatility of the currency pair changes, a risk which banks are not directly concerned with while hedging.

Hedging Foreign Exchange Risk with Currency Future

If a bank wants to hedge using currency future, it has to decide that how many future contracts it should sell which produce a sufficient profit on future contracts to offset any losses arising out of adverse change in exchange rates. The spot and future market may or may not be moved in perfect correlation. When it is expected that spot and future prices are not perfectly correlated, hedge ratio helps in deciding the number of future contracts to be sold to hedge perfectly. With the help of formulas given below, we may calculate the number of future contracts required to hedge and the payoffs out of future contracts.

N_f = Size of long position / Size of a future contract

Loss on exchange rate = Size of long position x ΔS_t

Where $\Delta S_t = S_t - S_{t+1}$; S_t is spot exchange rate and S_{t+1} spot exchange rate after a year

Gain on Future Contracts = (N_f x size of a future contract) x ΔF_t

Where $\Delta F_t = F_t - F_{t+1}$; F_t is future price on contract and F_{t+1} future price after a year

If $\Delta S_t \neq \Delta F_t$, loss on exchange rate will not be equal to gain on future contracts. In such a case, hedging is done by using Hedge Ratio by multiplying with number of future contract to be sold.

H (Hedge Ratio) = (ΔS_t / ΔF_t)

N_f = Size of long position x H / Size of a future contract

Roll over contracts are similar to forward contract but rolled over after specified period at premium or discount.

Currency Swaps is the exchange of one set of financial obligation i.e. in one currency to another and second currency for specific period. These are mainly currency swap or interest rate swap in designated currencies.

The primary treasury operation of a bank is that of catering to customer needs, both in the spot as well as forward market. This lands the bank with net foreign exchange positions which it needs to manage on a real time basis. If the bank needs to sell dollars forward to an importer, the bank has a short dollar position. It can offset the position by buying matching forward dollars in the market in which case all risks apart from the profit element are covered for the bank. However, it may be easier for the bank to immediately cover the forex risk with a purchase of dollars in the spot market. Here again the exchange risk is fully covered except for the profit element. However, the bank now has a swap position. This is called a gap. The bank has a gap risk which affects it if the interest rates change affecting the forward premia for dollar. In the case of our domestic markets, in addition, premia could also change due to forward demand/supply factors. However, gap risks are easier to manage than exchange risks. So the bank can build up gaps, subject to the management mandated gap limits, and do offsetting swaps to reduce gap risks if it so desires periodically.

The bank's treasury might also do transactions to take advantage of disequilibrium situations, subject to such transactions being permissible. For instance, if the forward premium for 6 months is, say, 5% while the 6-month interest differential between rupee and dollar is, say, 4%, the bank can receive in the forex market (buy spot, sell 6-month swap to earn 5% annualised for 6 months) and finance the transaction by borrowing in the money market (money market cost being 4% annualised for 6 months).

The bank can also do transactions to take advantage of expected interest rate changes. It can then use either the money market route (mismatched cash-flow maturities) or the forex market route (by running a gap risk). The bank, of course, also trades on currency movements with a view to make profits. Here, the management must keep in place systems stop loss discipline, proper monitoring and evaluation of open positions, etc. The management of the bank need to lay out clear and unambiguous performance measurement criteria, accountability norms and financial limits in its treasury operations. Management must specify in operational terms the goals of exchange risk management. It must also clearly recognise the risks of trading arising from open positions, credit risks, and operations risks. The bank must also keep in place a system to independently evaluate the net positions taken through marking to market. Marking to market should ideally be based on objective market prices provided by an external agency. All position limits should be made explicit and expressed in simple terms for easy control.

While hedging against foreign exchange risk, the corporates must choose the currency preference. The currency in which exposure is more and the market volatility is higher should be taken up first. The priority of hedging must be set for all currency exposures based on position and expectation of rate fluctuation. Generally INR quotes are not the true market quotes because these are derived from other currencies. In international currency market, INR quotes vis-à-vis other widely acceptable currencies such as USD, British Pound, Euro, JPY, AUD, NZD and CHF are not available. Hence while hedging Forex, quotes should be invited from various banks and financial institutions. It is observed that there is price difference in quotes from banks to banks. The knowledge of bid rate, i.e. price at which currency is sold, and ask rate, i.e. price at which currency is bought, is very important. The company taking forex position should be capable of buying or selling currency at any point of time. The difference between ask and bid rate is called spread. The spread is the arbitrage opportunity for traders.

Foreign exchange hedging should not be restricted to only one currency because if there is adverse movement in specific currency due to currency specific reasons, chances of suffering major losses are increased. The exposure should be taken in multicurrency to the extent possible and suitable to business profile and need. Firms should shift from one 'instrument' to another or one currency to another depending upon the changing market conditions or changing economy indicators. Based on economic forecasting models (PPP,

Relative Purchasing Power Parity, Balance of Payment, Interest Rate Parity), exchange rate may be predicted and acted accordingly. Other methods like economic indicators, oscillators, currency and other investment ratings may also be used to predict or forecast the currency rates.

Hedging decision is strategically very important for the organisation because hedging against foreign exchange risk involves cost to the organisation. Based on intense research and use of technical models for making prediction of currency price movement in future is the key to hedging strategy. Suppose if one bank feels that the movement of certain currency will be stable in shorter term, it may leave positions unhedged in that currency or vice versa. There is no 'set of rules' that can provide perfect hedging strategies, and thereby guarantees that there would be no wild fluctuations in company's cash flows. However, by using non-speculative strategies, with the calculation of optimal hedge ratios, one can hedge its risk. Additionally, with the increased volume of international trade and financing, increase in volatility of exchange rates and increased exposure of foreign exchange gain and losses, hedging foreign exchange risk has gained importance.

Handling Forex with Risk Management Strategies[2]

The enormous size of the forex market gives it the speed and liquidity like no other financial world market. Losses exist, but profits are even higher! But just like any other speculative trade, amplified risks are involved along with the probability for a higher profit/loss.

Exit the market at profit targets

Limit orders let the Forex investors stop further trading and leave the market at preset profit objectives. Creating a disciplined trading methodology, limit orders allow the traders to fix a limit of the profits which they want to make, and then exit the market. Also, they are free from the work of continuously monitoring the market sitting in front of their computers all day.

Limit your losses

Stop/loss commands also follow the same motive as that of the limit orders, by allowing the investors to set an exit point for a loss. By limiting your losses to a pre-set position, stop/loss orders help investors control their risk conditions. By placing them well in advance, one can get an almost accurate idea of how much loss will be incurred, in case the stop/loss order is hit.

Accurate placing of stop and limit orders

Where does the investor place his stop and limit orders respectively, determines the amount of risk he is taking up. It is advisable not to place the stop/loss orders too close to the normal market price, as a little fluctuation in the market, can then trigger the order. Likewise, limit orders should also reflect a rational hope of profits one is expecting, based on the market's trading activity. They should be set at the rate which is not overexposed to the trade, and also not too close to the market. 'Stop-loss' and 'limit' orders can lower an investor's exposure to risk by a large proportion.

Analyse while trading Forex

The things to know about forex comprehending all the intricacies of the basics behind an investment, and an understanding of the major market trading, is the right way to go about trading forex. Skilled technical analysis and good money management skills are the basic essentials to trade well. Analyse the market and create a position, establishing rational stop loss and profit taking levels.

BASIC OPTION STRATEGIES

With the help of puts and calls, certain option strategies have been developed which are as follows:-

- SPREADS: Bull Spread, Bear Spread, Box Spread and Butterfly Spread
- STRADDLE
- STRIP AND STRAPS
- STRANGLE

SPREADS

A spread trading strategy involves taking a position in two or more options of the same type (i.e. two or more calls or two or more puts).

BULL SPREAD **:** This can be created by buying a call option with a certain strike price and selling another call option with a higher strike price, for same maturity. In this, the maximum loss is restricted to the net premium paid and maximum profit is the difference between the strike prices less the net premium paid.

BEAR SPREAD: This can be created by buying a put option with a certain strike price and selling another put option with a lower strike price, for same maturity. Here, the maximum loss is restricted to the net premium paid and maximum profit is the difference between the strike prices less the net premium paid.

BOX SPREAD: A box spread is a combination of a bull call spread with strike prices K1 and K2, and a bear put spread with the same two strike prices. The payoff from the box spread is always K2 – K1, the value of the box spread is therefore always the present value of this payoff or (K2 – K1)e-rT. If the market price of the box spread is too low, it is profitable to buy the box and vice versa.

BUTTERFLY SPREAD: A butterfly spread involves positions in options with different strike prices. It can be created by buying a call option with a relatively low strike price K1, buying a call option with a relatively high strike price K3 and selling two call options with a strike price, K2, averaged between K1 and K3. A butterfly spread leads to a profit if the price of the underlying asset is close to K2 and gives rise to a small loss in case of significant movements in the price of the underlying asset.

STRADDLE

One popular combination is a straddle, which involves buying a call and put options with same strike price and maturity date. If the spot price on maturity is close to the strike price, the trader will make small loss, whereas in case of significant movement of prices of underlying asset in either direction, significant profit will result.

STRANGLE

This strategy involves buying a put and call option with different strike prices but with same maturity. The call strike price is higher than the put strike price.

STRIPS

This is created by buying one call option and selling two put options with the same strike price and expiration date. In a strip, an investor is betting that there will be a big movement in the price of the underlying asset and considers a decrease in the price to be more likely than an increase, in which case it leads to windfall profits.

STRAPS

This is created by buying two call option and selling one put options with the same strike price and expiration date. In a strip an investor is betting that there will be a big movement in the price of the underlying asset and considers a increase in the price to be more likely than an increase, in which case it leads to windfall profits.

LOW COST OPTION STRATEGIES

An option buyer can reduce his premium cost by selling another option. The combination can reduce the cost as the premium received on the option sold could either partially or fully offset the cost of option bought. As per Indian regulations, one cannot be a net receiver of premium. Different strategies are Range Forward, Participating Forward, Seagull, Leverage Forward and Inverse Range.

ZERO COST RANGE FORWARD: Range Forward involves buying an out of the money call/put option with the worst case rate as the strike price and selling an out of the money put/call option with such a strike price (best case rate) that the net premium is zero. If price at maturity is beyond the 'wcr', the bought option will be exercised. If the price at maturity is beyond 'bcr', the sold option will be exercised and if price at maturity is between the 'wcr' and 'bcr', you buy or sell at spot.

ZERO COST PARTICIPATING FORWARD: Participating forward involves buying an out of the money call/ put option with the worst case rate as the strike price and selling an in the money put/call option for a reduced amount and with the same strike price so that the net premium is zero. In effect, there is a synthetic out of the money forward contract for the amount of the in the money option sold and a free out of the money option for the balance amount.

ZERO COST SEAGULL: Involves buying an out of the money call/put option (X) and selling an out of the money put/call option (Y) and also selling a far-of-the-money call/put option (Z), so that the net premium of the whole portfolio is zero. If price at maturity is between the strikes of X and Z, only X will be exercised. If the price at maturity is beyond the strike of Y, only Y will be exercised. If the price at maturity is beyond the strike of Z, both X and Z will be exercised. If price at maturity is between the strikes of X and Y, you buy or sell at spot. This is a variant of the range forward as a far-out-of-the-money call/put is sold with the range forward to improve the best case rate or the strike of Y.

ZERO COST LEVERAGED FORWARD: Leveraged forward involves buying an in the money call/ put option and selling an out of the money put/call option for an increased amount and with the same strike price so that the net premium is zero. In effect, there is a synthetic in the money forward contract for the full amount with a leveraged loss beyond the synthetic in the money forward rate (strike price).

Here are a few examples of derivative transactions executed by companies:

1. Forward Contracts taken by Financial Institutions:

During the last quarter of 2007 and early 2008, various short- term forward contracts were taken in USD by a leading FI to hedge its lending. At the time of maturity, USD depreciated substantially to the extent of Rs.3.75 per USD, below the rate at which forward contracts were taken. It resulted in opportunity loss for the FI, inspite of the fact that the FI had hedged its exposure. In the above case, FI may have taken currency call options or currency long futures as a hedging instrument to hedge its lending. Currency call options provide downside protection against risk and upside benefit from favourable movements. Alternatively, forward contracts may have been cancelled, when exchange rate has started moving in opposite direction for minimising the loss. So selection and timing of right hedging strategy Is of utmost importance and it should be in line with the exchange rate movement.

2. Currency Call options taken by an FI

During the first quarter of 2008, an FI had taken call options to buy USD and sell INR, to hedge its USD payments. The options were taken at a higher strike rate to save call premium and since there is a negative relationship between call premium and strike rate, as strike rate increases call premium decreases. The other motive of the FI was to earn profits, since it expected USD to depreciate against rupee. But USD appreciated against rupee, instead of depreciating, unlike the FI's expectation. FI lost heavily in terms of opportunity loss of Rs. 3 per USD, since it remained exposed to risk by selecting a very higher call option strike rate. The FI, instead of doing hedging by selecting a call option strike rate equivalent to forward contract rate for the same maturity period, speculated by selecting a very high call option strike rate.

3. Buying Call Option and Selling Put Option at Different Strike Prices to Hedge Payments

A leading FI bought currency call option and sold put option to hedge its dollar payments. The FI expected the USD to appreciate. For example in January 2007, a FI bought 3 month currency call option contract to buy USD call, sell INR @ 42.80 at a premium of 30 paise. It sold a 3-month currency put option @ 42.90, at a premium of 20 paise.

There were twin fold objectives of the FI to adopt this strategy, firstly to reduce the premium from 30 paise to 10 paise and secondly it expected the USD to appreciate. But actually, the USD depreciated to Rs. 42.50 on the maturity date, and the firm lost an additional 60 paise per USD, instead of reducing its premium cost from 30 paise to 10 paise. Ideally, the firm may have kept its put strike price less than Rs. 42.30. It adopted an aggressive speculative strategy to bring down its premium cost.

Hedging Foreign Exchange Risk using Option Strategies

Few forex risk-hedging strategies and commonly used terms are being discussed below. However, the list of strategies is not exhaustive but these strategies are being used widely in forex market.

ITM: In the Money Option

The intrinsic value of an option is the value of exercising it today. Thus if the spot price of the underlying security is above strike price, a call has positive intrinsic value and is called "in the money" while a put has zero intrinsic value. The time value of an option is a function of the option value less the intrinsic value and is also taken as the value of not exercising the option immediately. In the case of a European option, one cannot choose to exercise it at any time, so the time value can be negative whereas for an American option if the time value is ever negative, one can exercise it. An in-the-money option has positive intrinsic value as well as time value. A call option is in-the-money when the strike price is below the spot price. A put option is in-the-money when the strike price is above the spot price.

ATM: At-the-money Option

An option is at-the-money if the strike price is the same as the spot price of the underlying security on which the option is written. An at-the-money option has no intrinsic value, but has only time value.

OTM: Out-of-the-money Option

An out-of-the-money option has no intrinsic value. A call option is out-of-the-money when the strike price is above the spot price of the underlying security. A put option is out-of-the-money when the strike price is below the spot price.

Bull Call Spread

A bull call spread is created with the help of two call option, first by buying a call option with a low exercise price and selling another call option with a higher exercise price.

Payoffs from a Bull Call Spread

The call option having lower exercise price will always be at-the-money while the call option with the higher exercise price is out-of-the-money. Both the call options must have the same underlying security and maturity. For example, IDFC share currently priced at Rs.100 and every option contract size is of 100 shares. Suppose next month, a call option with a strike price of Rs. 100 costs Rs. 3 per share, or Rs. 300 per contract, while a call option with a strike price of Rs. 115 is selling at Rs.1 per share, or Rs. 100 per contract. An FI can then buy a long position on the Rs. 100 strike price option for Rs. 300 and sell a short position on the Rs. 115 option for Rs. 100. The net debit for this trade then is Rs. 300 - 100 = Rs. 200. This trade results in a profitable trade if the stock closes on expiry above Rs. 102. If the stock's closing price on expiry is Rs. 110, the Rs. 100 call option will end at Rs. 10 per share, or Rs. 1000 per contract, while the Rs. 115 call option expires worthless. Hence a total profit of Rs. 1000 - 200 = Rs. 800. The trade's profit is limited to Rs. 13 per share, which is the difference in strike prices minus the net debit (15 - 2). The maximum loss possible on the trade equals Rs. 2 per share, the net debit.

Bull Put Spread

A bull put spread is created by selling higher striking in-the-money put options and buying the equal number of lower striking in-the-money put options on the same underlying security with the same maturity. The FI employing this strategy hopes that the price of the underlying security will increase enough so that the written put options expire worthless. For example IDFC is currently priced at Rs.100 and standard contract size is of 100 shares. Suppose next month, a put option with a strike price of Rs.105 costs Rs. 8 per share, or Rs.800 per contract, while a put option with a strike price of Rs.125 is selling at Rs.27 per share, or Rs. 2700 per contract. An FI opens a long position on the Rs.105 strike put option for Rs.800 and open a short position on the Rs.125 put option for Rs.2700. The net credit for this trade then is Rs. 2700 – Rs. 800 = Rs.1900. This trade will be profitable if the stock closes on expiry above Rs.106. If the stock's closing price on expiry is Rs.110, the Rs.105 put option will expire worthless while the Rs. 125 put option will end at Rs.15 per share, or Rs.1500 per contract. Hence a total profit of Rs. 1900 – Rs. 1500 = Rs.400. The trade's profit is limited to Rs.19 per share, which is equal to the net credit. The maximum loss on the trade is Re. 1 per share which is the difference in strike prices minus the net credit (20 - 19).

Bear Call Spread

A bear call spread is a limited profit strategy and limited risk options trading strategy that can be used when the FI is moderately bearish on the underlying security. It is entered by buying call options of a certain strike price and selling the same number of call options of lower strike price (in the money) on the same underlying security with the same expiration month. For example share of bank costs Rs.100 per share, with a call option with a strike price of Rs.105 for Rs.2 and a call option with a strike price of Rs.95 for Rs.7. To implement a bear call spread, one buys the Rs.105 call option, paying a premium of Rs.2, and sells the Rs.95 call option, making a premium of Rs.7. The total profit after this initial options trading phase will be Rs.5. At the time of expiration, the options may be exercised. If the stock price ends at a price X below or equal to Rs.95, neither option will be exercised and total profit will be the Rs.5 per share from the initial options trade. If the stock price ends at a price X above or equal to Rs.105, both options will be exercised and total profit per option is equal to the sum of Rs.5 from the original options trading, a loss of (X - Rs.95) from the sold option, and a gain of (X - Rs.105) from the bought option. Total profits will be (Rs.5 - (X - Rs.95) + (X - Rs.105)) = -Rs.5 per share (i.e. a loss of Rs.5 per share). The loss is due to speculation that the price would go down but it actually did not.

Bear Put Spread

A bear put spread is a limited profit and limited risk options strategy that can be used when the FI is moderately bearish on the underlying security. It is entered by buying higher striking in-the-money put options and selling the same number of lower striking out-of-the-money put options on the same underlying security and the same maturity. The FI hopes that the price of the underlying security will decrease, maximizing its profit when the underlying security price decreases drops below the strike price of the written option, netting the difference between the strike prices minus the cost of entering into the position.

Long Straddle

A long straddle is created going long, i.e., purchasing, both a call option and a put option on some stock, interest rate, index or other underlying security. The two options are bought at the same strike price and expiry. The owner of a long straddle makes a profit if the underlying price moves a long way from the strike price, either above or below. Thus, an FI may take a long straddle position if FI feels that the market is highly volatile, but does not know in which direction it is going to move. This position is a limited risk, since the most a purchaser may lose is the cost of both options. At the same time, there is unlimited profit potential. For example, AB Bank is set to release its quarterly financial results within a fortnight. An FI believes that the release of these results will cause a large movement in the price of AB Bank share, but does not know whether the price will go up or down. FI can enter into a long straddle, where it gets a profit no matter which way the price of AB Bank share moves, if the price changes enough either way. If the price increases much, FI uses the call option and ignores the put option. If the price decreases, FI uses the put option and ignores the call option. If the price does not change, FI loses money up to the total amount paid for the two options. The risk is limited by the total premium paid for the options, as opposed to the short straddle where the risk is virtually unlimited.

Short Straddle

A short straddle is a non-directional options trading strategy that involves simultaneously selling a put and a call of the same underlying security, strike price and expiry. The profit is limited to the premiums of the put and call, but it is risky because if the underlying security's price increase substantially or correct substantially, the potential losses are virtually unlimited. The deal breaks even if the intrinsic value of the put or the call equals the sum of the premiums of the put and call. This strategy is also called "non-directional" because the short straddle profits when the underlying security changes little in price before the expiration of the straddle. The short straddle can also be classified as a credit spread because the sale of the short straddle results in a credit of the premiums of the put and call. A short straddle position is highly risky, because the potential loss is unlimited due to the sale of the call and the put options which expose the FI to an unlimited losses (on the call) or losses equal to the strike price (on the put), whereas profitability is limited to the premium gained by the initial sale of the options.

Management of Sovereign Risk Exposure

There are few methods which have been suggested for managing sovereign risk. These methods may be used on alternative basis as the nature of sovereign risk. The methods are discussed below:

1. ***Converting Sovereign Loans into Equity***: Certain countries offer conversions of loans into equity in case of loan repayment default. When a country defaults in the payment of its debt obligation, it offers lender an opportunity to convert outstanding loan into equities of some priority sector investments areas or to engage in long-term equity partnership. With this arrangement, the lender gets rid of bad loans from its books and converts same into investment, however lending FI has to absorb some losses it faces out of devaluation of loan's market value. At the same time, the borrowing country saves itself from immediate payment of loan installments or repayment of entire debt.
2. ***Restructuring of Loans:*** If a country fails in honouring its loan obligations and the lender because of some reasons wants to keep the loan in its books instead of converting it into equity or outright sale, the borrowing country and the lender may enter into a restructuring agreement. The restructuring of loans provides some moratorium to the borrowing country. However, the lending FI has to forgo interest on loan for sometime but that may be compensated by charging some fee for restructuring of loan. The loan usually restructured by resetting of loan at the current rate or converting loan into concessional loans and increasing the tenure or maturity of loan.
3. ***Outright Loan Sale:*** Under this method, the FI sales loans of defaulting country to some other market maker willing to buy loans on some discount. By doing this, FI removes loans completely from its books and saves itself from making bad loans provisions as per the requirements of parent country banks/FIs regulator. However, during this exercise, FI suffers losses because of discount offered during sale of loan over its book value. That is the difference between the book value of loan minus market value of loan. Some losses arising out of loan sale are compensated from tax saving by FIs as the losses are offset against the profit of FIs.
4. ***Swapping Loans for Bonds:*** The loan may be swapped for highly liquid bonds available in defaulting country market such as Government bonds, treasury bonds, etc. This enables FI to receive regular payment of interest and comfort of liquidity.

Conclusion

So deciding to hedge is one thing and getting it right is quite another. Hedging should also be done without speculation. Further, application of hedging strategies along with no trade off between uncertainties associated with exchange rate and opportunity loss, makes a hedging foreign exchange risk itself a risk.

Summary

In this chapter, various strategies for managing forex risk have been discussed. The magnitude and nature of risk is very important to know before its mitigation. Various tools and techniques are available to manage forex risk, some of which have been detailed in this chapter. The strategies to manage forex risk differ from bank to bank based on the size of bank and its exposure to the forex market. The use of derivatives for forex risk management has also been explained. Most of the forex derivatives are traded in exchange. Various option strategies to hedge forex risk have also been discussed in brief in the chapter.

KEY CONCEPTS

Currency Forward	Currency Future	Currency Option
Currency Swap	Hedge Ratio	Currency VaR
Herstatt Risk	Currency Derivatives	Money Market Hedge
Roll Over Contract	Strip	Strap
Strangle	Seagull	Bull Call Spread
Bull Put Spread	Bear Call Spread	Bear Put Spread
Long Straddle	Short Straddle	Sovereign Risk

Review Questions and Problems

1. How is an FI exposed to foreign exchange risk? List out the various possible financial transactions involving foreign exchange risk.
2. How is the nature and magnitude of foreign exchange risk decided?
3. What are the various types of currency derivatives that are available for foreign exchange risk management?
4. List out the exchange traded currency derivatives along with exchange names and denominated currencies.
5. What are the various things that need to be considered while hedging against forex risk?
6. How do the currency derivatives differ from each other in view of their usage?
7. What are the risk management strategies available to handle forex?
8. Discuss the option strategies for foreign risk management by citing practical examples of such strategies.
9. Write a note on knockout option recently used by corporates and sold by banks in which corporates like Haxaware booked heavy losses.
10. Discuss the low cost option strategies. Are they really low or zero cost?
11. A bank has an asset investment in dollars. The bank expects the exchange rate of INR/$ to increase by the maturity of the asset.
    i. Is the INR appreciating or depreciating against the dollar?
    ii. To fully hedge the investment, should bank buy or sell $ futures contracts?
    iii. If there is perfect correlation between changes in the spot and futures contracts, how should bank determine the number of contracts necessary to hedge the investment fully?
    iv. If there is imperfect correlation between changes in the spot and futures contracts, how should bank determine the number of contracts necessary to hedge the investment fully?

12. What is the hedge ratio and how it is measured? Under which conditions, hedge ratio is valuable in determining the number of futures contracts necessary to hedge fully an investment in another currency?
13. Calculate the number of future contracts required to hedge the investment, loss on exchange rate and gain on future contracts for the given values:

    S_t = Spot exchange rate (INR/$) Rs.45.25

    F_t = Future price 3 months (INR/$) Rs.44.50

    S_{t+1} = Spot exchange rate after one year (INR/$) Rs.45

    F_{t+1} = Future price after one year (INR/$) Rs.44.25

    Value of investment = Rs.1000 crores

    One future contract = Rs.150 lacs
14. Calculate the number of future contracts required to hedge the investment, loss on exchange rate and gain on future contracts for the given values:

    S_t = Spot exchange rate (INR/Euro) Rs.66.25

    F_t = Future price 3 months (INR/Euro) Rs.67.50

    S_{t+1} = Spot exchange rate after one year (INR/Euro) Rs.65.50

    F_{t+1} = Future price after one year (INR/Euro) Rs.66.75

    Value of investment = Rs.750 crores

    One future contract = Rs.500 lacs
15. Calculate the number of future contracts required to hedge the investment, loss on exchange rate, gain on future contracts and hedge ratio for value given above in question no.14 where S_{t+1} = Spot exchange rate after one year (INR/Euro) Rs.65.25 & F_{t+1} = Future price after one year (INR/Euro) Rs.66.75.
16. Discuss the various option strategies along with suitable examples. Also search for real time deal made by FIs/banks using these strategies.
17. What are the various methods used for management of sovereign risk? Discuss a real time case on the subject recently taken place.
18. What do you mean by In the Money Option, At the Money Option and Out of the Money Option? Explain with suitable examples.

References:

1. *http://www.geocities.com/kstability/inbank/risk/fex-risk.html*
2. *http://www.marketforex.net/forex_risk_management.html*
3. *http://en.wikipedia.org*

Chapter – 17

Liquidity Risk Management

Chapter Objective

- Understand Liquidity Risk Management and Liquidity Management Policy (LMP)
- Discuss Contingency Funding Plan for Liquidity Management
- Discuss events which trigerres Liquidity Risk
- Explain Volatility Index for Liquidity Risk Management
- Focus on Foreign Currency Liquidity Risk

Introduction

Liquidity risk is the potential inability to meet the bank's liabilities as they become due. It arises when the banks are unable to generate cash to cope with a decline in deposits or increase in assets. It originates from the mismatches in the maturity pattern of assets and liabilities. Measuring and managing liquidity needs are vital for effective operation of commercial banks. By assuring a bank's ability to meet its liabilities as they become due, liquidity management can reduce the probability of an adverse situation developing.

The bank and financial institutions are highly exposed to liquidity risk because their assets are illiquid in comparison to their liabilities. The liabilities may be withdrawn at a shorter notice and banks have to honour it. Suppose all the depositors start withdrawing deposits from bank and bank has financed long term loan, bank will fall short of money and to fulfill the requirements of depositors, bank will borrow from market. In the tight liquidity position, it may happen that bank is not able to get money or get it on exorbitantly higher rate. In case bank is not able to get money, it will default. Future cash flows are to be analysed under "what if" scenarios so as to assess any significant positive / negative liquidity swings that could occur on a day-to-day basis and under bank specific and general market crisis scenarios. Factors to be taken into consideration while determining liquidity of the bank's future stock of assets and liabilities include their potential marketability, the extent to which maturing assets /liability will be renewed, the acquisition of new assets / liability and the normal growth in asset / liability accounts.

Analysis of liquidity risk involves the measurement of not only the liquidity position of the bank on an ongoing basis but also examining how funding requirements are likely to be affected under crisis scenarios. Net funding requirements are determined by analysing the bank's future cash flows based on assumptions of the future behaviour of assets and liabilities that are classified into specified time buckets and then calculating the cumulative net flows over the time frame for liquidity assessment. To reduce the liquidity risk, banks can insulate their balance sheet from liquidity risk by managing liquidity gaps in assets and liability maturity. The management of banks or regulator of the country may decide the minimum level of liquidity gap between assets and liabilities based on past event or behavioural patterns of withdrawal.

Factors affecting the liquidity of assets and liabilities of the bank cannot always be forecast with precision. Hence they need to be reviewed frequently to determine their continuing validity, especially given the rapidity of change in financial markets. The liquidity risk in banks manifest in different dimensions:

Funding Risk - need to replace net outflows due to unanticipated withdrawal/non-renewal of deposits (wholesale and retail);

Time Risk - need to compensate for non-receipt of expected inflows of funds, i.e. performing assets turning into non-performing assets; and

Call Risk - due to crystallisation of contingent liabilities and unable to undertake profitable business opportunities when desirable.

The liquid assets are those which can easily be converted into cash such as T-Bills, T-Notes and T-Bonds and are actively traded in market. These assets usually carry low credit risk. Banks liquidity risk can be reduced by holding a major portion of theses assets but at the same time return on these assets are very low compared to market return.

Liquidity Risk Management[1]

The first step towards liquidity management is to put in place an effective Liquidity Management Policy (LMP). The LMP should spell out the funding strategies, liquidity planning under alternative scenarios, prudential limits, liquidity reporting / reviewing, etc. The LMP should also cover the areas such as delegation of power, responsibility, exposure and risk limit. Liquidity measurement is quite a difficult task and can be measured through stock or cash flow approaches. The key ratios, adopted across the banking system are Loans to Total Assets, Loans to Core Deposits, Large Liabilities (minus) Temporary Investments to Earning Assets (minus) Temporary Investments, Purchased Funds to Total Assets, Loan Losses/Net Loans, etc.

While the liquidity ratios are the ideal indicator of liquidity of banks operating in developed financial markets, the ratios do not reveal the intrinsic liquidity profile of Indian banks which are operating generally in an illiquid market because most of their investments and loans are not traded in the market. Experiences show that assets commonly considered as liquid like Government securities, other money market instruments, etc. have limited liquidity as the market and players are unidirectional. Thus, analysis of liquidity involves tracking of cash flow mismatches. For measuring and managing net funding requirements, the use of maturity ladder and calculation of cumulative surplus or deficit of funds at selected maturity dates is recommended as a standard tool. The maturity gap method has been discussed in detail in the chapter on measurement of liquidity risk The format prescribed by RBI in this regard under ALM System should be adopted for measuring cash flow mismatches at different time bands. The cash flows should be placed in different time bands based on projected future behaviour of assets, liabilities and off-balance sheet items. In other words, banks should analyse the behavioural maturity profile of various components of on/off-balance sheet items on the basis of assumptions and trend analysis supported by time series analysis. Banks should also undertake variance analysis, at least, once in quarter to validate the assumptions. The assumptions should be fine-tuned over a period which facilitate near reality predictions about future behaviour of on/off-balance sheet items. Apart from the above cash flows, banks should also track the impact of prepayments of loans, premature closure of deposits and exercise of options built in certain instruments which offer put/call options after specified times. Thus, cash outflows can be ranked by the date on which liabilities fall due, the earliest date a liability holder could exercise an early repayment option or the earliest date contingencies could be crystallised.

The difference between cash inflows and outflows in each time period, the excess or deficit of funds, becomes a starting point for a measure of a bank's future liquidity surplus or deficit, at a series of points of time. The banks should also consider putting in place certain prudential limits as detailed below to avoid liquidity crisis:

- Cap on inter-bank borrowings, especially call borrowings
- Purchased funds vis-à-vis liquid assets
- Core deposits vis-à-vis Core Assets i.e. Cash Reserve Ratio, Statutory Liquidity Ratio and Loans
- Duration of liabilities and investment portfolio
- Maximum cumulative outflows across all time bands
- Commitment Ratio - track the total commitments given to corporates/banks and other financial institutions to limit the off-balance sheet exposure
- Swapped Funds Ratio, i.e. extent of Indian rupees raised out of foreign currency sources.

Banks should also evolve a system for monitoring high value deposits (other than inter-bank deposits) say Rs.10 crore or more to track the volatile liabilities. Further, the cash flows arising out of contingent liabilities in normal situation and the scope for an increase in cash flows during periods of stress should also be estimated. It is quite possible that market crisis can trigger substantial increase in the amount of draw downs from cash credit/overdraft accounts, contingent liabilities like letters of credit, etc.

The liquidity profile of the banks could be analysed on a static basis, wherein the assets and liabilities and off-balance sheet items are pegged on a particular day and the behavioural pattern and the sensitivity of these items to changes in market interest rates and environment are duly accounted for. The banks can also estimate the liquidity profile on a dynamic way by giving due importance to:

- Seasonal pattern of deposits/loans
- Potential liquidity needs for meeting new loan demands
- Unavailed credit limits
- Potential deposit losses
- Investment obligations
- Statutory obligations, etc.

Contingency Funding Plan

All banks are required to produce a Contingency Funding Plan. These plans are to be approved by ALCO, submitted annually as part of the Liquidity and Capital Plan, and reviewed quarterly. The preparation and the implementation of the plan may be entrusted to the treasury.

Contingency Funding Plans are liquidity stress tests designed to quantify the likely impact of an event on the balance sheet and the net potential cumulative gap over a 3-month period. The plan also evaluates the ability of the bank to withstand a prolonged adverse liquidity environment. At least two scenarios require testing: Scenario A, a local liquidity crisis, and Scenario B, where there is a nationwide name problem or a downgrade in the credit rating if the bank is publicly rated (see Exhibit).

The bank's contingency funding plans should reflect the funding needs of any bank managed mutual fund whose own Contingency Funding Plan indicates a need for funding from the bank. Reports of Contingency Funding Plans should be performed at least quarterly and reported to ALCO. If a Contingency Funding plan results in a funding gap within a 3-month time frame, the ALCO must establish an action plan to address this situation. The Risk Management Committee should approve the action plan. At a minimum, Contingency Funding plans under each scenario must consider the impact of accelerated runoff of Large Funds Providers. The plans must consider the impact of a progressive, tiered deterioration, as well as sudden, drastic events. Balance sheet actions and incremental sources of funding should be dimensioned with sources, time frame and incremental marginal cost and included in the Contingency Funding plans for each scenario. Assumptions underlying the Contingency Funding plans, consistent with each scenario, must be reviewed and approved by ALCO.

Exhibit: Events	
A. Bank Specific/ Local Liquidity Crisis Is a consequence of the problems affecting the bank	**Assumptions** • Flight of volatile deposits, some of the core deposits may be prematurely closed • Interbank borrowings may not be rolled over • Money market lines may be snapped • Substantial share of assets would have turned non-performing and become illiquid • Cost of maintaining liquidity may escalate
B. Market Crisis Market crisis may be due to industry specific problems or regulator's actions **Industry specific crisis** May be due to deterioration in the risk profile of the banking system. Market disruptions, contagion, failure of one or more market players, like it happened when banks in the cooperative sector wobbled **Regulators' Actions** Crisis due to extreme tightening of liquidity conditions arising out of monitoring stance of RBI	• Crisis triggers flight of volatile deposits • Increase in drawing from current accounts, overdraft accounts, loan accounts, contingent liabilities • No roll-over of high-value customer deposits • Loan repayments stop forthcoming • Increase in reserve requirement (CRR,SLR) • Cut in refinances • Liquidity crunch • Restriction on lending, increase in margin requirement
Source: Treasury Management Journal, May' 2004	

Volatility Index[2]

The liquidity risk management may be done by using volatility index. Volatility index is calculated on the basis of core and volatile amount of deposits and other liabilities based on historical data and behavioural analysis of withdrawal pattern. On the basis of core and volatile portion of deposits and certain abnormal withdrawal at the time of liquidity crisis, volatility grid is prepared.

Volatility Grid
Contingency Plan should be for : 5/4 [S (a+b+c)]+d+e-f Where a = Volatile portion of current account ranges between 10 to 20% of balances held in current account b = Volatile portion of savings bank account ranges between 10 to 20% of balances held in saving bank account c = Fixed deposit due to mature within three months together with accrued interest d = Additional outflow from current, savings bank accounts and fixed deposits due to mature in three months i.e. 25% of a+b+c e = Other outflow include inter-bank borrowings recalled by lenders, panic withdrawals by loanees etc. f = Fixed deposits kept in bank as security against which loans have been availed

The Chief Executive / Chairman must be advised as soon as a decision has been made to activate or implement a Contingency Funding Plan. Either the Chief Executive or the Risk Management Committee may call for implementation of a Contingency Funding Plan. The ALCO will implement the Contingency Funding Plan, amending it with the approval of the Risk Management Committee, where necessary, to meet changing conditions; daily reports are to be submitted to the Treasury Head, comparing actual cashflows with the assumptions of the Contingency Funding Plan.

Foreign Currency Liquidity Management

For banks with an international presence, the treatment of assets and liabilities in multiple currencies adds a layer of complexity to liquidity management for two reasons. First, banks are often less well known to liability holders in foreign currency markets. Therefore, in the event of market concerns, especially if they relate to a bank's domestic operating environment, these liability holders may not be able to distinguish rumour from fact as quickly as domestic currency customers. Secondly, in the event of a disturbance, a bank may not always be able to mobilise domestic liquidity and the necessary foreign exchange transactions in sufficient time to meet foreign currency funding requirements. These issues are particularly important for banks with positions in currencies for which the foreign exchange market is not highly liquid in all conditions.

Banks should, therefore, have a measurement, monitoring and control system for liquidity positions in the major currencies in which it is active. In addition to assessing its aggregate foreign currency liquidity needs and the acceptable mismatch in combination with its domestic currency commitments, a bank should also undertake separate analysis of its strategy for each currency individually.

When dealing in foreign currencies, a bank is exposed to the risk that a sudden change in foreign exchange rates or market liquidity, or both, could sharply widen the liquidity mismatches being run. These shifts in market sentiment might result either from domestically generated factors or from contagion effects of developments in other countries. In either event, a bank may find that the size of its foreign currency funding gap has increased. Moreover, foreign currency assets may be impaired, especially where borrowers have not hedged foreign currency risk adequately. The Asian crisis of the late 1990s demonstrated the importance of banks closely managing their foreign currency liquidity on a day-to-day basis.

The particular issues to be addressed in managing foreign currency liquidity will depend on the nature of the bank's business. For some banks, the use of foreign currency deposits and short-term credit lines to fund domestic currency assets will be the main area of vulnerability, while for others it may be the funding of foreign currency assets with domestic currency. As with overall liquidity risk management, foreign currency liquidity should be analysed under various scenarios, including stressful conditions.

Summary

Liquidity Risk Management is one of the most important function of banks. Most of the banks monitor their liquidity position on a daily basis. The regulators of the banks and financial institutions prescribe various measures to maintain adequate liquidity to meet sudden outflow of cash. Apart from these measures, banks also devise certain strategies to manage liquidity position. Bank generally use contingency funding plan or volatility index to measure requirement of liquidity in extreme conditions. In this chapter, these methods have been discussed. The various crisis situations have also been discussed which create liquidity crisis.

KEY CONCEPTS

Funding Risk	Time Risk	Call Risk
Liquidity Management Policy	Contingency Funding Plan	Volatility Index

Review Questions and Problems

1. Why do regulators set minimum liquidity requirement for banks?
2. What are the various securities that are treated as most liquid or at par with cash?
3. How do the regulators manage liquidity in the financial system? What are the various tools used by regulators for liquidity management in the system?
4. Discuss the liquidity management policy of any selected FI.
5. What do you understand by contingency funding plan?
6. What are the various prudential limits banks that should adhere to avoid liquidity crisis?
7. What are the scenarios which impact banks liquidity?
8. What is volatility index and how is it used to measure the liquidity requirement of banks? Can the parameters defined in the model be changed as per bank's size and business?
9. How can you manage foreign exchange liquidity? What are the parameters that are required to be considered for forex liquidity?

References:

1. *http://www.geocities.com/kstability/inbank/risk/liquidity-risk.html*
2. *Treasury Management Journal, May' 2004*

Chapter – 18

Management of Capital Adequacy

Chapter Objective

- Understand concept of Capital Adequacy
- Discuss constituent of Capital Adequacy Ratio (CAR)
- Explain calculation of CAR

Introduction

The primary source for a bank to protect it from risk of insolvency and failure is bank's adequate capital. The capital may be used by bank to absorb unanticipated losses. The adequate capital also provides a level of confidence among other player to transact business with each other. The capital protects depositors, bondholders, and creditors at the time of liquidation of a bank. The adequate capital is very essential for a bank to survive from a financial unexpected shock and if it survives, then only the bank may improve its performance in time to come.

Capital Adequacy of Financial Intermediaries (FI)/Bank[1]

Need for Capital

Financial Intermediaries need capital for two reasons:

- To run operations of their business
- To safeguard against the losses, that may arise

Adequate capital helps financial intermediaries to survive even during substantial losses. It gives time to re-establish the business and avoid any break in operations. To ensure the good performance of FIs, the regulatory authority (RBI) has specified the minimum capital for the FI. This requirement is called Capital Adequacy, and it is specified for Banks and Non Banking Financial Corporations (NBFCs).

Computation of Capital Adequacy Ratio (CAR) of banks

For computation of CAR, we need to calculate:

- Tier I capital
- Tier II capital
- Risk Weighted Assets (RWA)

Step 1: Compute Tier I capital:

Tier I capital is the most permanent and readily available support against unexpected losses. It consists of-

1. Paid up equity capital
2. Statutory reserves
3. Capital reserves
4. Other disclosed free reserves

Less:

1. Equity investments in subsidiaries
2. Intangible assets
3. Current and Accumulated Losses, if any

Step 2: Compute Risk Weighted Assets

Step 3: Compute Tier II capital

These are not permanent in nature or, are not readily available. Tier II capital consists of:
1. Undisclosed reserves and cumulative perpetual preference shares- Cumulative preference shares should be fully paid and should not contain clauses which permit redemption from shareholders.

2. Revaluation Reserves (RR)- 45% of RR is only taken in calculation of Tier II capital.

3. General Provisions and Loss Reserves (GPLR)- Actual GPLR or 1.25% of Risk Weighted Assets, whichever is lower, is taken.

4. Hybrid Debt Capital Instruments- These combine characteristics of both equity and debt. As they are more or less similar to equity, they are included in the Tier II capital.

5. Subordinated Debts- These must be fully paid up, unsecured, subordinated to the claims of other creditors and also there should be no such clause which permits redemption. The amount of subordinate debts to be taken as Tier II capital depends upon the maturity of debt. Subordinate Debt Instruments will be limited to 50% of Tier I capital.

Remaining term to maturity	Discount Rate (%)	Amount to be taken in %
1.Where the date of maturity is above 5 years	0	100
2.Where the date of maturity is above 4 years but does not exceed 5 years	20	80
3.Where the date of maturity is above 3 years but does not exceed 4 years	40	60
4.Where the date of maturity is above 2 years but does not exceed 3 years	60	40
5.Where the date of maturity is above 1 year but does not exceed 2 years	80	20
6.Where the date of maturity does not exceed 1 year	100	0

Note: Tier II capital cannot be more than Tier I capital.

Capital Adequacy Ratio

Tier I Capital Ratio = Tier I capital / Risk adjusted assets

Capital Adequacy Ratio = (Tier I capital + Tier II capital) / RWA

According to the present norm, the Capital Adequacy Ratio of bank as defined earlier should be at least 9%.

Example:

Following are the details of the bank for the year ending 2007-2008	Rs. in crores
Equity Capital	130
Statutory reserves	40
Undisclosed reserves	50
General provision and loss reserves	50
Subordinated debt	
Maturity between 2 and 3 years	30

Maturity between 4 and 5 years	30
Maturity within one year	10
Equity investments in subsidiaries	20
Revaluation reserves	40
Cash in hand	20
Balance with RBI	30
Loans and advances guaranteed by GOI	150
Loans and advances guaranteed to PSU's of Central Government	70
Furniture and fixtures	100
Buildings and equipments	75
Underwriting facility provided to public sector undertaking	20
Other Risk Weighted Assets	1500

Computation of Capital Adequacy Ratio

Step 1: Compute Tier I capital	
Equity capital and reserves (a)	130
Statutory reserves (b)	40
Equity investments in subsidiaries (c)	20
Tier1= a+b-c	150.00

Step 2: Calculation Of RWA

Calculation of Risk weighted Assets

Balance sheet items assets	Amount	% of Risk weights	Risk weighted
Cash in hand	20	0	0
Balance with RBI	30	0	0
Loans and advances guaranteed by GOI	150	2.5	3.75
Loans and advances guaranteed by PSUs of central government	70	100	70
Furniture and fixtures	100	100	100
Building and equipments	75	100	75
Total(A)		**248.75**	

Off balance sheet items	Amount	% of Risk weights	Conversion Factor	RWA
Underwriting facility provided to PSU	20	100	1	20
Total (B)				**20**

Other risk weighted assets are (C) 1500

Total RWA (A+B+C) = 1768.75

Step 3: Compute Tier II Capital

Computation of Tier II capital

Particulars	Amount	Discount Rates	Amount
Undisclosed reserves	50	0	50
General provision and loss reserves (1.25% of RWA or 50 whichever is minimum)	50	--	22.11
Revaluation reserves	40	55	18

Subordinated debt			
Maturity between 2 and 3 years	30	60	12
Maturity between 4 and 5 years	30	20	24
Maturity within one year	10	100	0
Tier II capital			**126.325**

Step 4: Compute Capital Adequacy Ratio	**Rs (in Crore)**
Tier I capital (A)	150
Tier II Capital (B)	126.11
Total RWA(C)	1768.75
CAR= (A+B)/C	0.1561

Therefore, we see that Capital Adequacy Ratio of the bank is 15.61%.

Summary

The banks and financial institutions are required to maintain adequate capital. The adequate capital is some percentage of banks risk weighted assets. As per Basel II, banks have capital also for market and operational risk in comparison to earlier norm where capital was required for only credit risk. On the basis of risk weights assigned to various assets, RWAs are calculated and then certain percentage of capital needs to be maintained by banks. The percentage of capital adequacy ratio prescribed by Basel II is 8% whereas in India, banks are required to maintain CAR of 9%. In this chapter, simplest method of calculating CAR has been discussed.

KEY CONCEPTS

Capital Adequacy	CAR	Tier I Capital
Tier II Capital	Risk Weighted Assets	Paid Up Capital
Statutory Reserves	Capital Reserves	Intangible Assets
Revaluation Reserves Hybrid	Debt Capital	Subordinate Debts

Review Questions and Problems

1. Why does a Bank become economically insolvent, if its networth turns negative?
2. What is the difference between Tier I and Tier II capital? What are the regulatory caps regarding Tier I and Tier II capital?

3. Identify assets in each risk weight category.
4. Why is capital adequacy ratio required for banks?
5. Identify and discuss the important functions of a banks capital.
6. Take the financial report of a bank and calculate its capital adequacy.
7. What are the components used in the calculation of risk weighted assets?
8. What are various limits prescribed by RBI for different FIs?
9. A bank has the following balance sheet (in crores):

Liabilities		Assets	
Equity Capital	100	Loan & Advances	1900
Reserves and surplus	2000	Investments	300
Debentures and bonds	500	Government Bonds	200
Deposits	900	Other loans	150
Other liabilities	100	Cash	50
Total Assets	2600	Total Liabilities	2600

Calculate:

i. Tier I capital ratio

ii. Capital Adequacy Ratio

10. A bank has the following balance sheet (in crores):

Liabilities		Assets	
Equity Capital	600	Loan & Advances	13500
Reserves and surplus	5000	Investments	1000
Debentures and bonds	2000	Government Bonds	1000
Deposits	7000	Other loans	500
Other liabilities	1500	Cash	100
Total Assets	16100	Total Liabilities	16100

Calculate:

i. Tier I capital ratio

ii. Capital Adequacy Ratio

The following changes in assets and liabilities take place in balance sheet during the year:

i. Increase deposit base by Rs.1000 crores

ii. Increase mortgaged loans Rs.800 crores

iii. Investment Rs. 200 crores in PSU bonds

iv. Sale of Rs. 200 crores of government bonds

v. Repays Rs. 300 crores debentures

vi. Repayment of other loans of Rs. 100 crores

Calculate new:

i. Tier I capital ratio

ii. Capital Adequacy Ratio

Reference:

1. *http://www.investopedia.com/*

Chapter – 19

Enterprise Wide Risk Management

Chapter Objective

- Explain the concept of EWRM
- To understand Enterprise Wide Risk Management Model
- To understand Risk Management Policy Objectives
- To understand about Risk Management Committee (RMC) and various subcommittees such as MRMC, CRMC and ORMC
- To know about roles and responsibility of RMC
- Need & roles and responsibility of Risk Management Department (RMD)
- Concept of Economic Research & Analysis Cell
- Concept of MIS & Model Back Testing Cell
- Concept of Risk Based Internal Audit

Introduction

Enterprise Wide Risk Management (EWRM) has emerged as an important new business trend. EWRM is a structured and disciplined approach aligning strategy, processes, people, technology, and knowledge with the purpose of evaluating and managing the uncertainties the enterprise faces as it creates value. Enterprise wide Risk Management means the removal of traditional functional, divisional, departmental, or cultural barriers. A truly holistic, integrated, future-focused, and process-oriented approach helps an organization manage all key business risks and opportunities with the intent of maximizing shareholder value for the enterprise as a whole. Leaders face a variety of new challenges in their drive to maximize value. Globalization, e-business, new organizational partnerships, and the increasing speed of business activity are rapidly changing and expanding the risks organizations face. One significant result is that risk management must now extend well beyond traditional financial and insurable hazards to encompass a wide variety of strategic, operational, reputation, regulatory, and information risks. As a means of identifying, prioritizing, and managing such risks across an enterprise or division and linking them to value creation, EWRM has the potential to provide organizations with a new competitive advantage. Most organizations, however, are uncertain about how exactly to translate the concept of EWRM into concrete action steps that will help them enhance shareholder value. Leaders agree that as important as EWRM might be in theory, it will never be valuable in practice unless it enables organizations to use risk information to drive business value in a way they could not do otherwise.[1]

Enterprise Wide Risk Management Model

The structure of risk management and control system of an FI is given below:

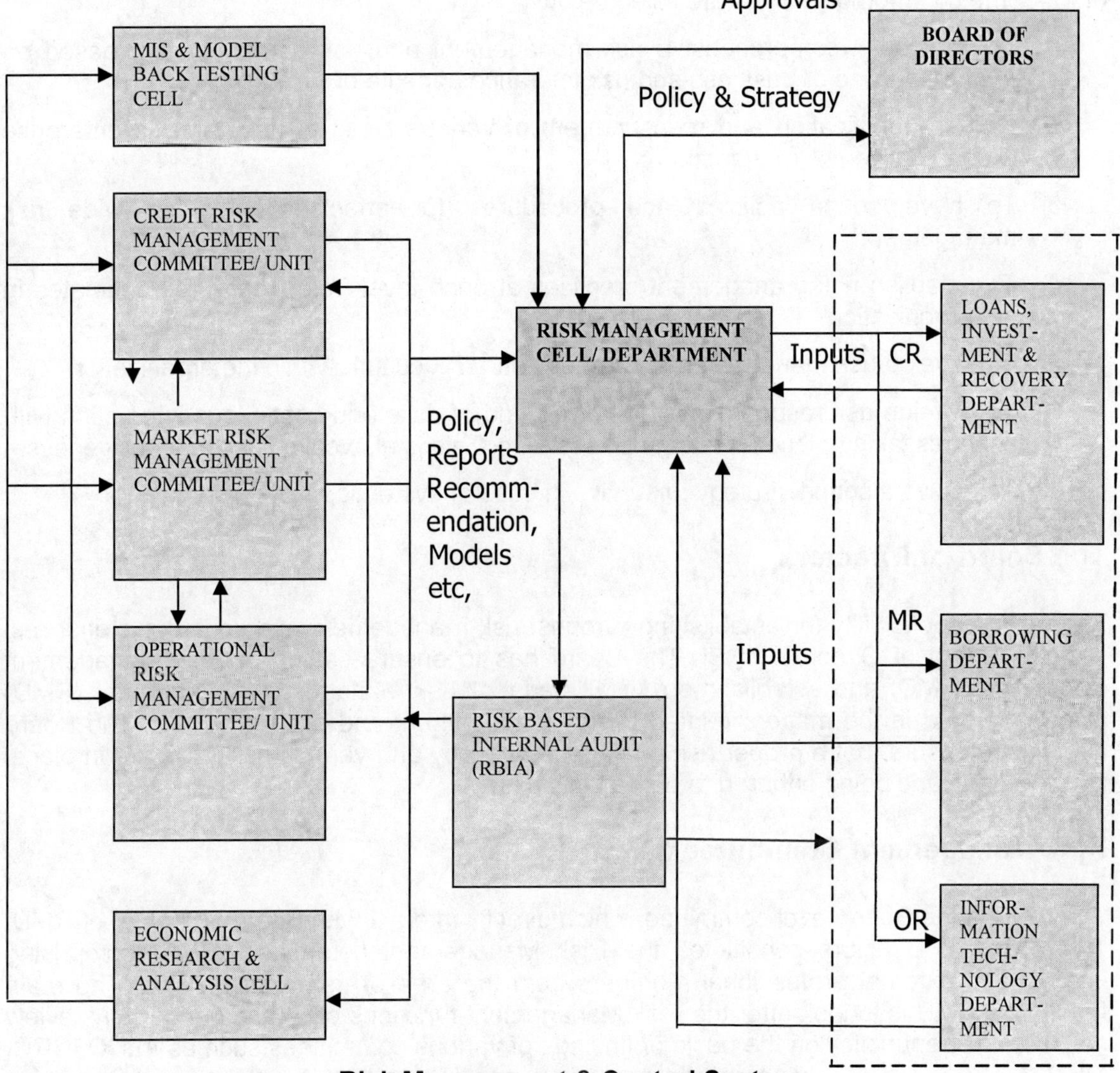

Risk Management & Control System

The above model was developed during Dr.Vivek's research work in the area of financial risk management. Enterprise Wide Risk Management means in simple terms "integrating all risk of an organization and to manage these risks jointly". The various risks cannot deal in isolation as some of these are inter-related. The above model provides an integrated system of risk management netting all the concerned department. The functions, roles and responsibility of all the divisions of an FI related to risk management are defined one by one. Before going in details of functions of each unit/department, it is necessary to establish a clear-cut objective of risk management policy of FI keeping all the business line in the mind.

Risk Management Policy: Objectives

The objectives of Risk Management policy are defined on the basis of nature and business of FI. Some common objectives are listed below:

1. To develop a comprehensive risk management and risk control system based on nature and size of business and risk tolerance appetite of FI.
2. Proper identification and measurement of various types of risks and its enterprise wide effective risk management.
3. To have sound policies and procedures for effective enterprise wide risk management.
4. To establish risk management practices at each level from where risk originates in the organisation.
5. To develop risk management awareness and risk culture within the organization.
6. To develop risk response system for all kind of risks and continuous interaction with changes taking place affecting risk scenario. This is also called risk responsiveness.
7. To evolve a sound strategy to survive in case of systemic risk.

The Board of Directors

The main responsibility for establishing a robust risk management and control systems rest with the Board of Directors of FI. The Board has to ensure set up of Risk Management Committee (RMC) and establishment of full-fledged Risk Management Department (RMD) assisting Board in the matters related to risk management and assisting RMC. The Board also has to ensure that a proper risk management policy and various risk limits are in place, implemented, and being adhered to on periodic basis.

Risk Management Committee (RMC)

The RMC is the Board level committee, which directly interact with Board on behalf of RMD. The Board of Directors constitutes the Risk Management committee (RMC) comprising internal and external professional members from the area of risk management. The main function of RMC is to look after the Risk Management functions of FI and periodically review risk management policy on the basis of findings of various committees such as ALCO, CRC, MRC, ORC, Economic research and analysis wing , IT & MIS wing, Loans and Borrowing department, and inputs received from Risk based audit cell.

The members of RMC include CEO as Chairman of RMC, Director Finance, Senior Finance Professionals of Risk department, loan department, borrowing department and economic research & analysis department, two or three external risk management professionals.

Roles and Responsibilities of Risk Management Committee

1. Formulate strategies and policies for enterprise wide risk management as per the directions of Basel III and the guidelines & directives of country's financial sector regulators.
2. Periodic review of strategies and risk management policies of FI based on the feed back received from user department and the changes taking place in financial market worldwide. Risk management is a dynamic function of parameters like regulatory changes, new derivative product introduction, BIS guidelines, market shocks and movements, change in portfolio of FI, market concentration, etc. The review of risk management policy should have been on quarterly basis followed by major annual review and its validation from the Board of Directors. Any change in risk management policy may also be notified in annual report of FI.
3. Approval of different risk management techniques, models, risk limits setting, sectoral exposure, risk premium charges, negative list of sectors and borrowers, etc. from BOD.
4. Approval of investment policy, hedging policy, ALM policy, structure of investment and loan portfolio from BOD.
5. Review the performance of various models and techniques adopted for interest rate risk, market risk, credit risk, operational risk and foreign exchange risk.
6. Evaluate and monitor gain and losses arising out risk management practices and capital adequacy requirement and buffer available.
7. Monitoring the working of all related units of risk management such as credit risk management unit, market risk management unit, operational risk management unit, etc.
8. Comprehensive review of various reports such as ALM report and other regulatory compliance. To notify remarks to the BOD along with corrective actions.
9. Besides above, some of the internal members should always be in constant touch with RMD.

Risk Management Department (RMD)

Risk Management Department is responsible for formulation of enterprise wide risk management policy formulation and its successful implementation. The risk management department is independent of any business of an FI and is directly responsible to CEO of the FI. The RMD usually has functions of framing policies for Market Risk, Credit Risk, Foreign Exchange Risk and Operational Risk, and its implementation. Apart from this, RMD also work as main hub for other related departments that come under risk management ambit. All the departments need to give continuous input to RMD in order to make suitable amendment in risk management policy of FI. The input from other departments also helps RMD in risk limit setting.

The roles and responsibilities of RMD are given below:

1. Document the business line of FI and indentifying the various risks.
2. Measurement of interest rate risk, market risk, liquidity risk, credit/default risk, foreign exchange risk and operational risk.
3. Formulation of overall risk management policy including sub policies to manage individual risk and its implementation. The risk management policy is to be approved first by Risk Management committee and by the Board of Directors.
4. Developing model to manage market and credit risk either internally or as per the direction of regulator/Basel and to supervise its implementation by concerned department such as credit risk models will be used and implemented by credit risk management unit.
5. To develop sector wise/category wise credit rating/credit scoring models for borrowers and to define risk charges to be levied over and above the normal interest rate based on credit rating of borrower.
6. To define risk limit (credit exposure) for loans and investments on the basis of sector, size of loan, etc.
7. To develop suitable model to identify operational risk for each business line of FI. Assessing the probability of event occurrence posing operational risk.
8. To prepare market risk matrix or credit matrix to identify the slippage of loans and investment from one rating category to other.
9. Estimation of parameters such as PD, EAD, LGD, etc. in order to assess credit risk.
10. To formulate ALM policy for interest rate risk and liquidity risk and its implementation. Analysis of ALM report for possible risk and informing RMC, Board and other concerned about finding. Suggesting changes required in risk management policy based on findings of ALM report.
11. To ensure the back testing of models and circulation of its findings by Economic Research and Analysis department.
12. To formulate hedging policy for foreign exchange risk, suggesting various strategies and its implementation by market risk management unit.
13. To work in supportive role to Risk Management Committee and Board (for the matters related to risk management).
14. Supervise treasury function as risk limit set in policy. Any breach in risk limits to be informed immediately to CEO and Board.
15. To formulate investment policy and monitoring.

Sub-committees of Risk Management Committee (RMC)

Risk management is a comprehensive and complex exercise and cannot be looked after only by RMC. The RMC needs support of various sub committees formulated for taking care of core risk such as interest rate risk/market risk/foreign exchange risk, credit risk and operational risk. In risk management policy, the roles and responsibilities of various sub committees should be clearly defined. Here we discuss three main sub committees that should definitely be in place in all FI. Based on nature and size of business of FI, some other committees may be formulated to take care of liquidity risk, sovereign risk, etc.

Market Risk Management Committee (MRMC)

For management of market risk such as interest rate risk, foreign exchange risk and liquidity risk, a sub-committee of RMC for market risk management is constituted. Indian FIs name this committee as Asset-Liability Management Committee (ALCO) as also prescribed by RBI. This is the one of the important committee that looks after the functions of Market Risk Management Unit (MRMU). The functions of MRMU involve preparation of ALM policy and report, investment policy, hedging policy, ALM report, liquidity statement, foreign exchange exposure report, etc to support MRMC. The role and responsibility of MRMU may be widened by MRMC/ALCO based on need of FI. MRMU will not be the part of actual business of FI. All these units and committees related to risk management are independent of the business of FI and are under the chairmanship of CEO of FI. MRMU will not look after the functions of resource mobilization including external commercial borrowings or borrowings in foreign currency, treasury functions or hedging deals done for interest rate risk or foreign exchange risk.

The members of MRMC/ALCO include CEO as Chairman of MRMC/ALCO, Director Finance, Senior Finance Professionals of Risk management department, loans and recovery department, borrowing department, economic research & analysis department and IT & MIS department. The committee will be supported by MRMU. The inputs for all the roles and responsibilities of MRMC will be provided by MRMU. The MRMC may meet once in a month or on major policy change by the government of banking regulator such as credit policy etc.

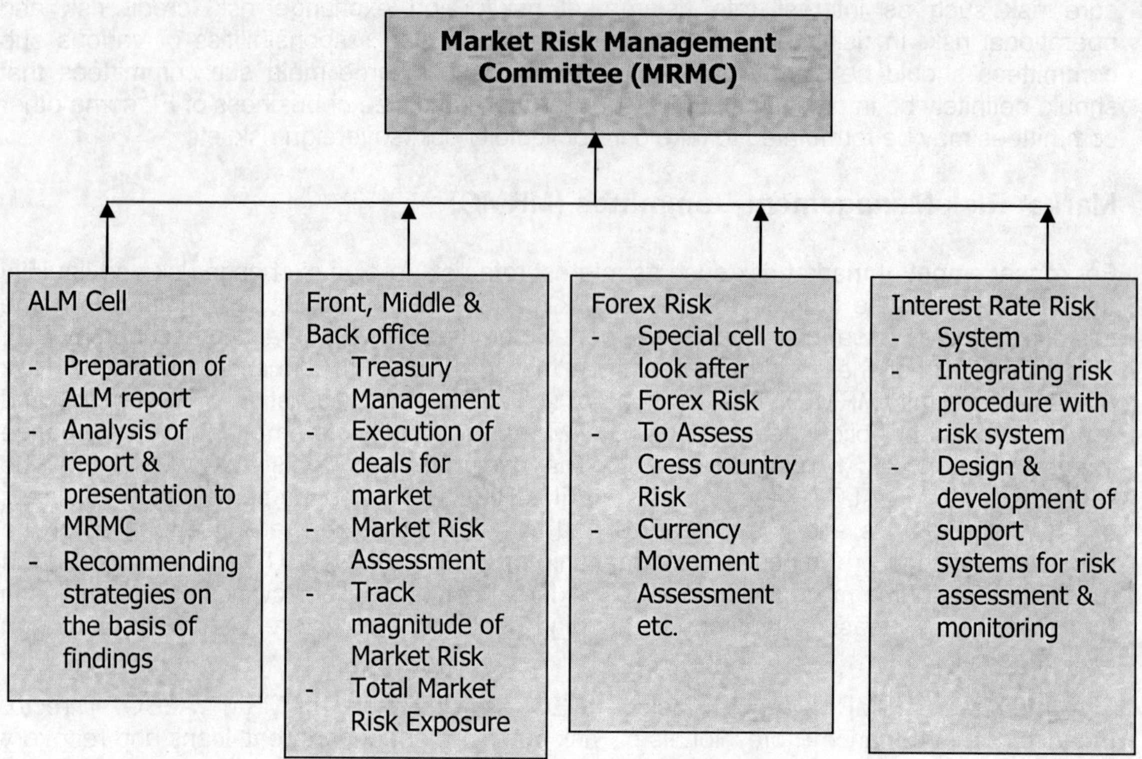

MARKET RISK MANAGEMENT UNIT

The roles & responsibilities of MRMC/ALCO are given below:

1. Formulation of ALM policy, investment policy and hedging policy, its review and recommendation to RMC. Submission of various policy issues to RMC for BOD approvals.
2. Review of models developed to manage market risk and to review the investment decision for calculated VaR.
3. Periodic review of ALM report, report on interest rate sensitivity, duration gap analysis, structural and dynamic liquidity statements, statement of foreign risk exposure etc. and submission of various reports along with remarks to RMC.
4. To review the impact of interest rate changes and foreign exchange changes on Net Interest Income (NII) and Market Value of Equity (MVE) of FI.
5. Incorporating new investment avenues in investment policy and new derivative products in hedging policy.
6. To evaluate the cost effectiveness of hedging tools and retruns from forex assets and investments.

7. To recommend changes in strategies for forex and interest rate risk management and in investment mix.
8. To review resource raising plan of FI and cost of fund of FI. Recommending cost effective borrowing mix for FI.
9. To review the risk arising out of Off-Balance-Sheet items and its impact on earnings.
10. Estimation of regulatory capital required for market risk as per Basel III/RBI directives.

Functions of Market Risk Management Unit (MRMU)

The MRMU will prepare all policy and report to be submitted to MRMC based on inputs received from loans & recovery department, borrowing department, economic research & analysis cell. The main function involves preparation of ALM reports, i.e. liquidity statements, gap analysis and interest rate sensitivity statement. MRMU will also develop models for market risk management and calculate VaR for investments made in various securities. The impact of various OBS items posing OBS risk will be evaluated and the statement to be submitted to MRMC. MRMU will be responsible for holding periodic meeting of MRMC, preparation of agendas, etc.

Credit Risk Management Committee (CRMC)

It is a sub-committee of the RMC to supervise the functions related to mainly credit/ default risk, prepayment risk, and loan portfolio and concentration risk. This committee will formulate credit risk management policy of FI which consists of policies on loan portfolio, sectoral exposure, loan pricing based on borrowers rating and sectoral rating, credit rating model to be used, i.e. internal rating based model, scoring models or external rating agency model, loan appraisal, default monitoring and recovery, etc. The CRMC will also assist RMC in consultation with MRMC for finalising investment policy of FI.

The members of CRMC include CEO as Chairman of CRMC, Director Finance, senior finance professionals of risk management department, loans and recovery department, economic research & analysis department and IT & MIS department. The committee will be supported by CRMU. The inputs for all the roles and responsibilities of CRMC will be provided by CRMU. The CRMC may meet once in the month or on major policy change by the government of banking regulator such as credit policy etc.

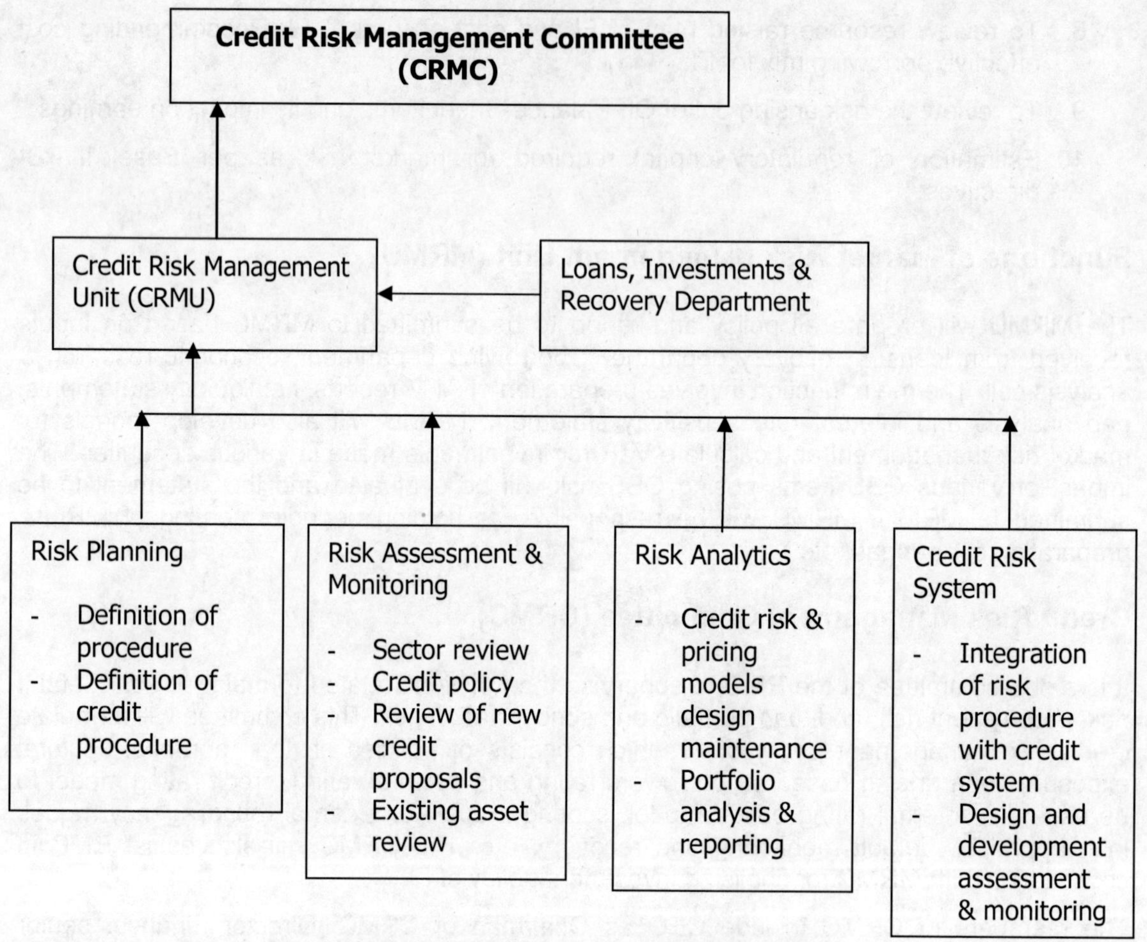

CREDIT RISK MANAGEMENT UNIT

Roles & responsibilities of CRMC

1. Formulation of strategy and policy for credit risk management for FI and place it to RMC for BOD approval. This includes policies on credit exposure, risk pricing, loan sanctioning powers, concentration risk, loan risk, monitoring of defaults, credit scoring models and its usage, rating models, credit review mechanism, loan pricing, loan slippage and monitoring, etc. To set the credit procedures for loan and investment approvals in line with credit risk management policy.

2. Formulation of investment policy jointly with MRMC.

3. Formulation of hedging policy jointly with MRMC.

4. Risk limit setting on credit limit exposure and credit concentration for each type of loans and investments and its monitoring for any possible breach in consultation with RBIA group.
5. To supervise the implementation of credit risk policy.
6. To develop credit risk measurement model, scoring models and to develop a risk pricing model based on rating and score.
7. To develop credit risk matrix to monitor slippage of loan rating and assess probability of default and other parameters such as LGD & EAD.
8. Default analysis for recovery mechanism and to monitor slippage of loan from standard to substandard.
9. Estimation of regulatory capital required for credit risk as per Basel III/RBI directives.

Functions of Credit Risk Management Unit (CRMU)

The CRMU will prepare all policy and report to be submitted to CRMC based on inputs received from loans & recovery department, borrowing department, economic research & analysis cell. The main functions of CRMU involves developing of internal rating based model, credit scoring model, guidelines for loan appraisal, loan pricing, risk pricing and default analysis. Based on default analysis, the parameters such as PD, EAD and LGD will be calculated and a model to watch slippage of loan from standard to sub-standard will be developed. If robust credit risk management system is in place, CRMU will also calculate credit VaR for FI loans. CRMU along with MRMU will formulate investment and hedging policy. CRMU will be responsible for holding periodic meeting of CRMC, preparation of agendas etc.

Operational/Technology Risk Management Committee (ORMC)

It is a sub-committee of the RMC to supervise the functions related to operational risk arising out of internal & external frauds, damage of data or physical assets, suit filed by customers, process failure, etc. The committee formulates operation risk management policy for FI and submits it to RMC for BOD approval. The committee also monitors implementation and compliance of operational risk management policy and submit compliance report to RMC and BOD. The members of ORMC include one Director, Senior Finance Professionals of risk management department, loans and recovery department, borrowing department and IT & MIS department. The committee will be supported by ORMU. The inputs for all the roles and responsibilities of ORMC will be provided by ORMU. The ORMC may meet once in a month or on occurrence of some major event affecting FI on operational front which is likely to be converted in operational risk for FI.

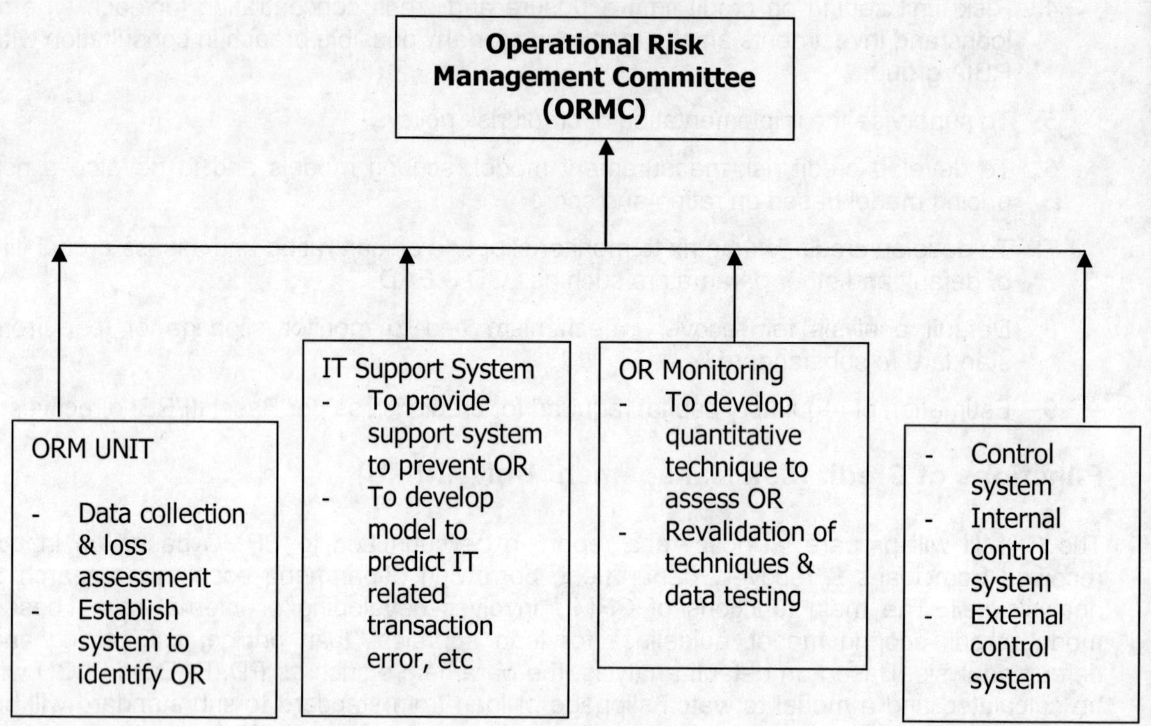

OPERATIONAL RISK MANAGEMENT UNIT

Roles & responsibilities of CRMC

1. Formulate strategy and policy to mitigate operational risk.
2. Identifying various sources of operation risk of the organization based on business line and data available on operational risk for same line of business.
3. To develop robust check and balance system to avoid internal and external frauds.
4. To put disaster management policy in place along with details of exercising power in case of emergency, disaster recovery mechanism and standby systems.
5. Estimation of possible loss of capital in case of operational risk and provision of adequate capital as per Basel approaches such as Basic Indicator Approach, Standardized Approach and Advanced Measurement Approach.
6. Submission of report on operational risk for each business line to RMC and BOD.
7. Review and Revision in policy as per new list of events posing operational risk.

Functions of Operation Risk Management Unit (ORMU)

The ORMU will draft all policies and prepare reports to be submitted to RMC via ORMC. The ORMU will prepare estimates of loss of capital for each business line or event based on internal or external database available. Operational risk management is a continuous process hence ORMU will keep updating the list of likely events and the development in the area of operational risk will be informed to ORMC on regular basis.

Economic Research & Analysis Cell (ERAC)

This cell is the backbone of entire risk management and control system as it provides vital information regarding financial markets to the risk policy makers of FI. The information includes movements in currency prices, interest rate movements, bond yields, credit off take, demand of credit in the market, liquidity position, credit policy, regulators move affecting business, stock market movements, etc. ERAC collects information from the market on continuous basis and informs the various units in usable formats for possible future movements in different markets. ERAC also keep continuous watch on reports published by RBI and research organization and retrieve useful information for further use by risk management department.

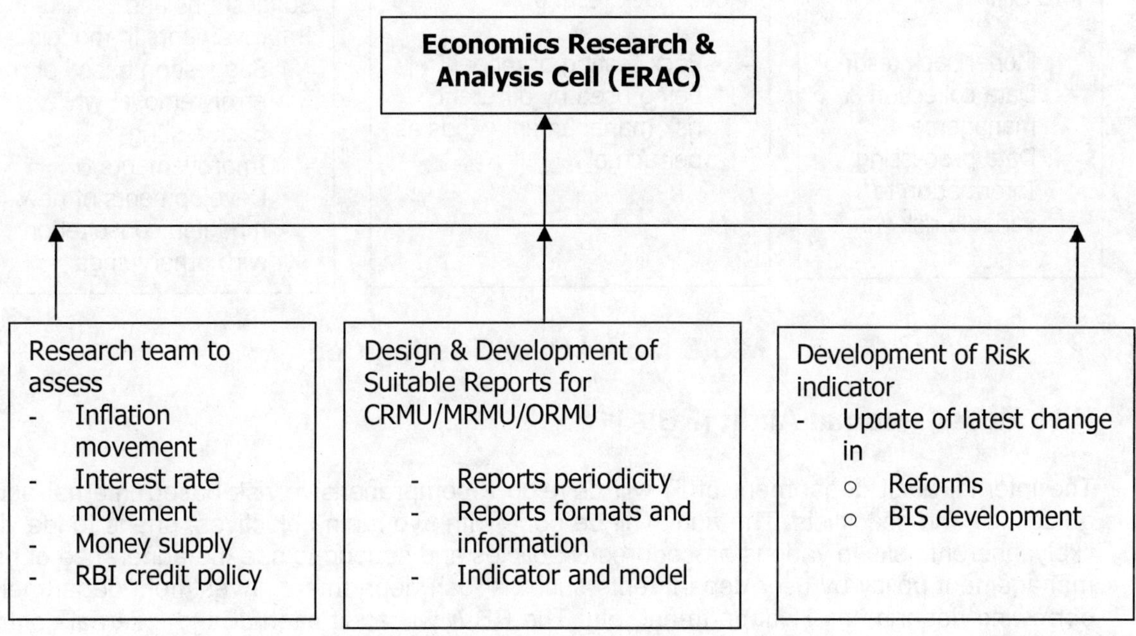

ECONOMIC RESEARCH & ANALYSIS CELL

Management Information System (MIS) & Model Back Testing Cell

This department will maintain all the data related to risk analysis and provide this to MRMU, CRMU, ORMU and ERAC. The department will also do the back testing of various models developed by various units of risk management and submit its findings to RMC and Board for their future reference for policy amendments. The unit who is developing the models cannot be allowed to back test its own developed models due to likelihood of biased result. Hence, this department, independent of these units, will back test the models under intimation to BOD as well the respective units.

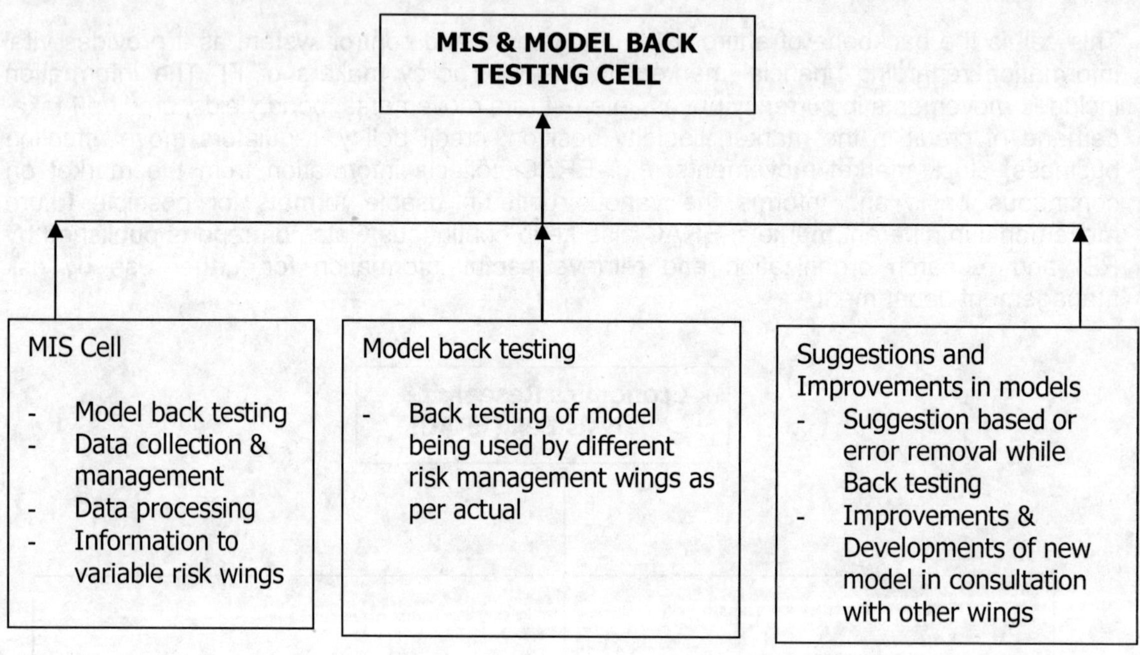

MIS & Model Bank Testing Cell

Risk Based Internal Audit (RBIA)

The internal audit department of FI will develop a comprehensive risk based internal audit guidelines and checklists. The audit will be done with two main objectives, one is to identify likely inherent risks in various procedures & policies and second to see the adherence of risk management policy by user departments such as loan department, investment department, borrowing department, IT department, etc. The RBIA will audit internal and external control systems, compliance of various guidelines on risk management, fulfilling roles and responsibility of various units, compliance of risk limit setting by user department and its breach, quantification of loss due to risk limit breach, authenticity of various reports sent to RMC & BOD, etc. The scope of RBIA may be enhanced based on the progress of setting up of risk management and control system. The periodicity of risk based internal audit may be started on annual basis and reduced on quarterly basis.

Risk Based Internal Audit (RBIA)

- To conduct Risk based audit as per guidelines and risk limits set by different RM committees
- Suggestions to improve interest & External control system

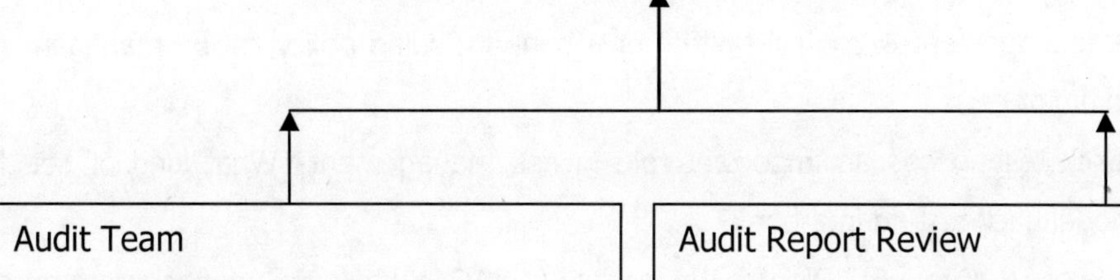

Audit Team

- To conduct Risk Based Audit
- Reporting major–minor shortcomings

Audit Report Review

- To Review Audit Report and recommend improvements
- Final Report to RMC

Risk Based Internal Audit

Summary

The risk management is an integrated and complex task, hence the concept of risk management and control system has been discussed. The concept of EWRM has been detailed. The objectives of risk management policy and roles and responsibility of risk management department have been discussed. Three subcommittees, MRMC, CRMC & ORMC, support the risk management committee. The importance of economic research and analysis and model back testing have been discussed, as many financial crisis are witness to model failure. The set up of ERAC and MIS & Model Back Testing has been detailed. The role of RBIA has been discussed in order to understand the importance of audit in risk management process and to check the adherence of risk limit setting and compliance of guidelines.

KEY CONCEPTS

EWRM	RMC	RMD
MRMC	CRMC	ORMC
ERAC	RBIA	

Review Questions and Problems

1. What is Enterprise Wide Risk Management? Discuss the Risk Management & Control System for an FI.
2. What are the objectives of risk management policy of a bank?
3. What are the various committees set up in bank for risk management? Discuss each committee in detail.
4. Study the risk management & control system of a bank including policy set by management and the various committees.
5. Why model back testing has an important role in risk management? What kind of set do you suggest for model back testing in a bank?
6. What is the role of ERAC in a FI? Discuss the merits of ERAC in whole risk management process.
7. What is RBIA? How does RBIA support risk management control system?

Reference:

1. *http://riskinstitute.ch*

Chapter – 20

Risk Reporting

Chapter Objective

- To understand Accounting, Tax and Legal issues in Risk Management
- To have understanding about International Accounting Standard (IAS)
- To have understanding about International Financial Reporting Standard (IFRS)
- To have understanding about Financial Accounting Standard Board (SFAS)

Introduction

Internal Reporting

The information that the risk management process is required to give to the various levels in the organisation include:

The Board of Directors

- To know about the most significant risks facing the organisation
- To know the possible effects on shareholder value of deviations to expected performance ranges
- To ensure appropriate levels of awareness throughout the organisation
- To know how the organisation will manage a crisis
- To know the importance of stakeholder confidence in the organisation
- To know how to manage communications with the investment community where applicable
- To assure that the risk management process is working effectively
- To publish a clear risk management policy covering risk management philosophy and responsibilities

Business Units

- To be aware of risks which fall into their area of responsibility, the possible impacts these may have on other areas and the consequences other areas may have on them

- To have performance indicators which allow them to monitor the key business and financial activities, progress towards objectives and identify developments which require intervention (e.g. forecasts and budgets)
- To have systems which communicate variances in budgets and forecasts at appropriate frequency to allow action to be taken
- To report systematically and promptly to senior management any perceived new risks or failures of existing control measures

Individuals

- To understand their accountability for individual risks
- To understand how they can enable continuous improvement of risk management response
- To understand that risk management and risk awareness are a key part of the organisation's culture
- To report systematically and promptly to senior management any perceived new risks or failures of existing control measures

External Reporting

A company needs to report to its stakeholders on a regular basis setting out its risk management policies and the effectiveness in achieving its objectives. Increasingly stakeholders look to organisations to provide evidence of effective management of the organisation's non-financial performance in such areas as community affairs, human rights, employment practices, health and safety and the environment. Good corporate governance requires that companies adopt a methodical approach to risk management which:

- Protects the interests of their stakeholders
- Ensures that the Board of Directors discharges its duties to direct strategy, build value and monitor performance of the organisation
- Ensures that management controls are in place and are performing adequately

The arrangements for the formal reporting of risk management should be clearly stated and be available to the stakeholders. The formal reporting should address:

- The control methods - particularly management responsibilities for risk management
- The processes used to identify risks and how they are addressed by the risk management systems
- The primary control systems in place to manage significant risks
- The monitoring and review system in place; any significant deficiencies uncovered by the system, or in the system itself, should be reported together with the steps taken to deal with them.

Accounting, Tax and Legal Issues in Risk Management

One of the main objectives of accounting in risk management is to provide true picture to the management, regulators and the stakeholders. The traditional accounting is done on historical basis whereas risk management emphasizes on real time and futuristic accounting approach covering the events may take place in future. Accounting risk arises when the data is unreliable or manipulated and the decisions based on such data results in unexpected losses. Company's accounts should reflect real market value, not the overestimated or underestimated profit figures. The management and employees main concern is maximizing profit through accounting jugglery as seen in case of Enron and Barring where the performance of employees is linked with profit making.

Risk management approach on accounting on asset valuation is different from traditional method of valuation based on book value or value at cost. Risk management focuses on market value of assets on record date based on various market parameters which influence market value of assets. Under the risk management, accounts are prepared on the basis of market value of assets and liabilities to give true picture of market value of equity of the company. The market value of equity of a company can not be derived from traditional accounting method. Only the market value of assets and liabilities give true input to risk management practices. Incorrect accounting information may lead to wrong decision for hedging and mismatches. Many of the banks and FIs have started preparing their accounts on market value basis by marking all their assets and liabilities to market and where market benchmark is available to value assets and liabilities marking to model approach adopted. The other very important issue in risk management based accounting is accounting of financial instrument i.e. derivative accounting. The ICAI has issued AS 32 and AS 39 on the same regard. AS 32 deals with Financial Instrument Presentation and AS 39 deals with Financial Instrument Recognition and Measurement. Further, any changes in interest rates have an impact of changing the value of fixed rate assets and liabilities. However, accounting does not capture such an impact, but in long run the impact of the same may be seen in declining NII of the bank. Hence, the need of risk based accounting and audit is felt.

Treatment of tax differs from country to country and the changes in tax laws are an ongoing process. Most of the banks and FIs having presence in various countries have to make a smart tax management in order to avoid any unforeseen tax liability or litigation arising out of non compliance of country's tax rules. The product and services in international market are customized on the basis of tax and legal framework prevailing in that country. Sometimes the pricing of products and services are based on country's tax rules and legal environment. A small change in tax rules or laws may impact profitability of banks. The impact of rule changes may be seen in Indian equity market for FII and PE investors. Certain changes have been made in tax treatment for these entities for recognizing capital gain, which has resulted in lower income. The tax implication may also lead to litigation if rule and law of land is not adhered to. Legal risk implies that either the contracts are not documented correctly or that there are difficulties in their legal enforceability. Legal risk often arises when counterparty loses money in a transaction. This may be seen as in the first quarter of 2008, many of the corporates in India booked heavy losses in derivatives position such as ICICI Bank, Haxaware and many of the public sector banks. The derivative products were sold to them by foreign banks and the risk involved was not understood correctly by Indian counterparties. Many of the banks are now facing litigation from corporates. Corporates alleged that the products were not as per Indian market and they were not explained the features of the derivative products. Some of the corporates even alleged that the derivative products were sold to them even when there was no such requirement. There is more inherent risk involved in the counter derivative contracts that are customised to suit the requirements of the counterparty. The exact details of suing parties are not available, as banks are not disclosing the litigation being faced by them out of derivative deals.

Now we will discuss various accounting standards evolved over the years and are related to the accounting and disclosure of derivative products in brief.

The standards discussed below are the brief extract of these standards however for the requirements reference must be made to International Accounting Standards (IAS), International Financial Reporting Standards (IFRS) and Financial Accounting Standard Board (FASB) Statements.

International Accounting Standards

IAS 32 Financial Instruments: Presentation

The objective of this Standard is to establish principles for presenting financial instruments as liabilities or equity and for offsetting financial assets and financial liabilities. It applies to the classification of financial instruments, from the perspective of the issuer, into financial assets, financial liabilities and equity instruments; the classification of related interest, dividends, losses and gains; and the circumstances in which financial assets and financial liabilities should be offset. The principles in this Standard complement the principles for recognising and measuring financial assets and financial liabilities in IFRS 9 Financial Instruments, and for disclosing information about them in IFRS 7 Financial Instruments: Disclosures. The issuer of a financial instrument shall classify the instrument, or its component parts, on initial recognition as a financial liability, a financial asset or an equity instrument in accordance with the substance of the contractual arrangement and the definitions of a financial liability, a financial asset and an equity instrument. The issuer of a non-derivative financial instrument shall evaluate the terms of the financial instrument to determine whether it contains both a liability and an equity component. Such components shall be classified separately as financial liabilities, financial assets or equity instruments.

A financial instrument is any contract that gives rise to a financial asset of one entity and a financial liability or equity instrument of another entity.

A financial asset is any asset that is:

(a) cash;

(b) an equity instrument of another entity;

(c) a contractual right

- to receive cash or another financial asset from another entity; or
- to exchange financial assets or financial liabilities with another entity under conditions that are potentially favourable to the entity

(d) a contract that will or may be settled in the entity's own equity instruments and is:

- a non-derivative for which the entity is or may be obliged to receive a variable number of the entity's own equity instruments; or
- a derivative that will or may be settled other than by the exchange of a fixed amount of cash or another financial asset for a fixed number of the entity's own equity instruments.

A financial liability is any liability that is:

(a) a contractual obligation

- to deliver cash or another financial asset to another entity; or
- to exchange financial assets or financial liabilities with another entity under conditions that are potentially unfavourable to the entity

(b) a contract that will or may be settled in the entity's own equity instruments and is:

- a non-derivative for which the entity is or may be obliged to deliver a variable number of the entity's own equity instruments; or
- a derivative that will or may be settled other than by the exchange of a fixed amount of cash or another financial asset for a fixed number of the entity's own equity instruments.

An equity instrument is any contract that evidences a residual interest in the assets of an entity after deducting all of its liabilities. A financial instrument may require the entity to deliver cash or another financial asset, or otherwise to settle it in such a way that it would be a financial liability in the event of the occurrence or non-occurrence of uncertain future events (or on the outcome of uncertain circumstances) that are beyond the control of both the issuer and the holder of the instrument, such as a change in a stock market index, consumer price index, interest rate or taxation requirements, or the issuer's future revenues, net income or debt-to-equity ratio. The issuer of such an instrument does not have the unconditional right to avoid delivering cash or another financial asset (or otherwise to settle it in such a way that it would be a financial liability).

Therefore, it is a financial liability of the issuer unless:

(a) the part of the contingent settlement provision that could require settlement in cash or another financial asset (or otherwise in such a way that it would be a financial liability) is not genuine;

(b) the issuer can be required to settle the obligation in cash or another financial asset (or otherwise to settle it in such a way that it would be a financial liability) only in the event of liquidation of the issuer; or

(c) the instrument has all the features when a derivative financial instrument gives one party a choice over how it is settled (eg the issuer or the holder can choose settlement net in cash or by exchanging shares for cash), it is a financial asset or a financial liability unless all of the settlement alternatives would result in it being an equity instrument.

If an entity reacquires its own equity instruments, those instruments ('treasury shares') shall be deducted from equity. No gain or loss shall be recognised in profit or loss on the purchase, sale, issue or cancellation of an entity's own equity instruments. Such treasury shares may be acquired and held by the entity or by other members of the consolidated group. Consideration paid or received shall be recognised directly in equity. Interest, dividends, losses and gains relating to a financial instrument or a component that is a financial liability shall be recognised as income or expense in profit or loss. Distributions to holders of an equity instrument shall be debited by the entity directly to equity, net of any related income tax benefit. Transaction costs of an equity transaction shall be accounted for as a deduction from equity, net of any related income tax benefit.

A financial asset and a financial liability shall be offset and the net amount presented in the statement of financial position when, and only when, an entity:

(a) currently has a legally enforceable right to set off the recognised amounts; and

(b) intends either to settle on a net basis, or to realise the asset and settle the liability simultaneously.

IAS 39 Financial Instruments: Recognition and Measurement

The International Accounting Standards Board has decided to replace IAS 39 Financial Instruments: Recognition and Measurement over a period of time. The first instalment, dealing with classification and measurement of financial assets, was issued as IFRS 9 Financial Instruments in November 2009. The requirements for classification and measurement of financial liabilities and derecognition of financial assets and liabilities were added to IFRS 9 in October 2010. As a consequence, parts of IAS 39 are being superseded and will become obsolete for annual periods beginning on or after 1 January 2013 and earlier application was permitted in 2010. The remaining requirements of IAS 39 continue in effect until superseded by future instalments of IFRS 9. The Board expects to replace IAS 39 in its entirety.

Impairment and uncollectibility of financial assets measured at amortised cost

An entity shall assess at the end of each reporting period whether there is any objective evidence that a financial asset or group of financial assets measured at amortised cost is impaired. If there is objective evidence that an impairment loss on financial assets measured at amortised cost has been incurred, the amount of the loss is measured as the difference between the asset's carrying amount and the present value of estimated future cash flows (excluding future credit losses that have not been incurred) discounted at the financial asset's original effective interest rate (ie the effective interest rate computed at initial recognition). The carrying amount of the asset shall be reduced either directly or through use of an allowance account. The amount of the loss shall be recognised in profit or loss.

Hedging

A hedging relationship qualifies for hedge, accounting under paragraphs 89–102, if and only if, all of the following conditions are met.

(a) At the inception of the hedge, there is formal designation and documentation of the hedging relationship and the entity's risk management objective and strategy for undertaking the hedge. That documentation shall include identification of the hedging instrument, the hedged item or transaction, the nature of the risk being hedged and how the entity will assess the hedging instrument's effectiveness in offsetting the exposure to changes in the hedged item's fair value or cash flows attributable to the hedged risk.

(b) The hedge is expected to be highly effective in achieving offsetting changes in fair value or cash flows attributable to the hedged risk, consistently with the originally documented risk management strategy for that particular hedging relationship.

(c) For cash flow hedges, a forecast transaction that is the subject of the hedge must be highly probable and must present an exposure to variations in cash flows that could ultimately affect profit or loss.

(d) The effectiveness of the hedge can be reliably measured, i.e., the fair value or cash flows of the hedged item that are attributable to the hedged risk and the fair value of the hedging instrument can be reliably measured.

(e) The hedge is assessed on an ongoing basis and determined actually to have been highly effective throughout the financial reporting periods for which the hedge was designated.

Hedging relationships are of three types:

(a) ***Fair value hedge:*** A hedge of the exposure to changes in fair value of a recognised asset or liability or an unrecognised firm commitment, or an identified portion of such an asset, liability or firm commitment, that is attributable to a particular risk and could affect profit or loss.

(b) ***Cash flow hedge:*** A hedge of the exposure to variability in cash flows that (i) is attributable to a particular risk associated with a recognised asset or liability (such as all or some future interest payments on variable rate debt) or a highly probable forecast transaction and (ii) could affect profit or loss.

(c) ***Hedge of a net investment*** in a foreign operation as defined in IAS 21.

If a fair value hedge meets the conditions in paragraph 88 during the period, it shall be accounted for as follows:

(a) the gain or loss from remeasuring the hedging instrument at fair value (for a derivative hedging instrument) or the foreign currency component of its carrying amount measured in accordance with IAS 21 (for a nonderivative hedging instrument) shall be recognised in profit or loss; and

(b) the gain or loss on the hedged item attributable to the hedged risk shall adjust the carrying amount of the hedged item and be recognised in profit or loss. This applies if the hedged item is otherwise measured at cost. Recognition of the gain or loss attributable to the hedged risk in profit or loss applies if the hedged item is an available-for-sale financial asset.

If a cash flow hedge meets the conditions in paragraph 88 during the period, it shall be accounted for as follows:

(a) the portion of the gain or loss on the hedging instrument that is determined to be an effective hedge (see paragraph 88) shall be recognised in other comprehensive income; and

(b) the ineffective portion of the gain or loss on the hedging instrument shall be recognised in profit or loss.

Hedges of a net investment in a foreign operation, including a hedge of a monetary item that is accounted for as part of the net investment (see IAS 21), shall be accounted for similarly to cash flow hedges:

(a) the portion of the gain or loss on the hedging instrument that is determined to be an effective hedge (see paragraph 88) shall be recognised in other comprehensive income; and

(b) the ineffective portion shall be recognised in profit or loss.

International Financial Reporting Standards

IFRS 7 Financial Instruments: Disclosures

The objective of this IFRS is to require entities to provide disclosures in their financial statements that enable users to evaluate:

(a) the significance of financial instruments for the entity's financial position and performance; and

(b) the nature and extent of risks arising from financial instruments to which the entity is exposed during the period and at the end of the reporting period, and how the entity manages those risks. The qualitative disclosures describe management's objectives, policies and processes for managing those risks. The quantitative disclosures provide information about the extent to which the entity is exposed to risk, based on information provided internally to the entity's key management personnel. Together, these disclosures provide an overview of the entity's use of financial instruments and the exposures to risks they create.

The IFRS applies to all entities, including entities that have few financial instruments (eg a manufacturer whose only financial instruments are accounts receivable and accounts payable) and those that have many financial instruments (eg a financial institution most of whose assets and liabilities are financial instruments).

When this IFRS requires disclosures by class of financial instrument, an entity shall group financial instruments into classes that are appropriate to the nature of the information disclosed and that take into account the characteristics of those financial instruments. An entity shall provide sufficient information to permit reconciliation to the line items presented in the statement of financial position. The principles in this IFRS complement the principles for recognising, measuring and presenting financial assets and financial liabilities in IAS 32 Financial Instruments: Presentation and IFRS 9 Financial Instruments.

IFRS 9 Financial Instruments

All financial instruments are initially measured at fair value plus or minus, in the case of a financial asset or financial liability not at fair value through profit or loss transaction costs.

Subsequent measurement of financial assets

IFRS 9 divides all financial assets that are currently in the scope of IAS 39 into two classifications – those measured at amortised cost and those measured at fair value. Classification is made at the time the financial asset is initially recognised, namely when the entity becomes a party to the contractual provisions of the instrument.

Debt instruments

A debt instrument that meets the following two conditions can be measured at amortised cost (net of any write-down for impairment):

Business model test: The objective of the entity's business model is to hold the financial asset to collect the contractual cash flows (rather than to sell the instrument prior to its contractual maturity to realise its fair value changes).

Cash flow characteristics test: The contractual terms of the financial asset give rise on specified dates to cash flows that are solely payments of principal and interest on the principal outstanding.

All other debt instruments must be measured at fair value through profit or loss (FVTPL).

Fair value option

Even if an instrument meets the two amortised cost tests, IFRS 9 contains an option to designate a financial asset as measured at FVTPL if doing so eliminates or significantly reduces a measurement or recognition inconsistency (sometimes referred to as an 'accounting mismatch') that would otherwise arise from measuring assets or liabilities or recognising the gains and losses on them on different basis.

IAS 39's AFS and HTM categories are eliminated. The available-for-sale and held-to-maturity categories currently in IAS 39 are not included in IFRS 9.

Equity instruments

All equity investments in scope of IFRS 9 are to be measured at fair value in the statement of financial position, with value changes recognised in profit or loss, except for those equity investments for which the entity has elected to report value changes in 'other comprehensive income'. There is no 'cost exception' for unquoted equities.

'Other comprehensive income' option

If an equity investment is not held for trading, an entity can make an irrevocable election at initial recognition to measure it at fair value through other comprehensive income (FVTOCI) with only dividend income recognised in profit or loss.

Measurement guidance

Despite the fair value requirement for all equity investments, IFRS 9 contains guidance on when cost may be the best estimate of fair value and also when it might not be representative of fair value.

Subsequent measurement of financial liabilities

IFRS 9 does not change the basic accounting model for financial liabilities under IAS 39. Two measurement categories continue to exist: fair value through profit or loss (FVTPL) and amortised cost. Financial liabilities held for trading are measured at FVTPL, and all other financial liabilities are measured at amortised cost unless the fair value option is applied.

Fair value option

IFRS 9 contains an option to designate a financial liability as measured at FVTPL if:

- doing so eliminates or significantly reduces a measurement or recognition inconsistency (sometimes referred to as an 'accounting mismatch') that would otherwise arise from measuring assets or liabilities or recognising the gains and losses on them on different bases, or
- the liability is part or a group of financial liabilities or financial assets and financial liabilities that is managed and its performance is evaluated on a fair value basis, in accordance with a documented risk management or investment strategy, and information about the group is provided internally on that basis to the entity's key management personnel.

A financial liability which does not meet any of these criteria may still be designated as measured at FVTPL when it contains one or more embedded derivatives that would require separation.

IFRS 9 requires gains and losses on financial liabilities designated at fair value through profit or loss to be split into the amount of change in the fair value that is attributable to changes in the credit risk of the liability, which shall be presented in other comprehensive income, and the remaining amount of change in the fair value of the liability which shall be presented in profit or loss. The new guidance allows the recognition of the full amount of change in the fair value in the profit or loss only if the recognition of changes in the liability's credit risk in other comprehensive income would create or enlarge an accounting mismatch in profit or loss. That determination is made at initial recognition and is not reassessed. Amounts presented in other comprehensive income shall not be subsequently transferred to profit or loss, the entity may only transfer the cumulative gain or loss within equity.

Derecognition of financial assets

The basic premise for the derecognition model in IFRS 9 (carried over from IAS 39) is to determine whether the asset under consideration for derecognition is:

- an asset in its entirety, or
- specifically identified cash flows from an asset (or a group of similar financial assets), or
- a fully proportionate (pro rata) share of the cash flows from an asset (or a group of similar financial assets), or
- a fully proportionate (pro rata) share of specifically identified cash flows from a financial asset (or a group of similar financial assets).

Once the asset under consideration for derecognition has been determined, an assessment is made as to whether the asset has been transferred, and if so, whether the transfer of that asset is subsequently eligible for derecognition.

An asset is transferred if either the entity has transferred the contractual rights to receive the cash flows, or the entity has retained the contractual rights to receive the cash flows from the asset, but has assumed a contractual obligation to pass those cash flows under an arrangement that meets the following three conditions:

- the entity has no obligation to pay amounts to the eventual recipient unless it collects equivalent amounts on the original asset
- the entity is prohibited from selling or pledging the original asset (other than as security to the eventual recipient)
- the entity has an obligation to remit those cash flows without material delay

Once an entity has determined that the asset has been transferred, it then determines whether or not it has transferred all the risks substantially and rewards of ownership of the asset. If substantially all the risks and rewards have been transferred, the asset is derecognised. If substantially all the risks and rewards have been retained, derecognition of the asset is precluded.

If the entity has neither retained nor transferred substantially all of the risks and rewards of the asset, then the entity must assess whether it has relinquished control of the asset or not. If the entity does not control the asset then derecognition is appropriate; however if the entity has retained control of the asset, then the entity continues to recognise the asset to the extent to which it has a continuing involvement in the asset.

Derecognition of financial liabilities

A financial liability should be removed from the balance sheet when, and only when, it is extinguished, that is, when the obligation specified in the contract is either discharged or cancelled or expires. Where there has been an exchange between an existing borrower and lender of debt instruments with substantially different terms, or there has been a substantial modification of the terms of an existing financial liability, this transaction is accounted for as an extinguishment of the original financial liability and the recognition of a new financial liability. A gain or loss from extinguishment of the original financial liability is recognised in profit or loss.

Derivatives

All derivatives, including those linked to unquoted equity investments, are measured at fair value. Value changes are recognised in profit or loss unless the entity has elected to treat the derivative as a hedging instrument in accordance with IAS 39, in which case the requirements of IAS 39 apply.

Embedded derivatives

An embedded derivative is a component of a hybrid contract that also includes a non-derivative host, with the effect that some of the cash flows of the combined instrument vary in a way similar to a stand-alone derivative. A derivative that is attached to a financial instrument but is contractually transferable independently of that instrument, or has a different counterparty, is not an embedded derivative, but a separate financial instrument.

The embedded derivative concept of IAS 39 has been included in IFRS 9 to apply only to hosts that are not assets within the scope of the standard. Consequently, embedded derivatives that under IAS 39 would have been separately accounted for at FVTPL because they were not closely related to the financial host asset and will no longer be separated. Instead, the contractual cash flows of the financial asset are assessed in their entirety, and the asset as a whole is measured at FVTPL if any of its cash flows do not represent payments of principal and interest. The embedded derivative concept of IAS 39 is now included in IFRS 9 and continues to apply to financial liabilities and hosts not within the scope of the standard (e.g. leasing contracts, insurance contracts, contracts for the purchase or sale of a non-financial items).

Reclassification

For financial assets, reclassification is required between FVTPL and amortised cost, or vice versa, if and only if the entity's business model objective for its financial assets changes so its previous model assessment would no longer apply. If reclassification is appropriate, it must be done prospectively from the reclassification date. An entity does not restate any previously recognised gains, losses, or interest.

IFRS 9 does not allow reclassification where:

- the 'other comprehensive income' option has been exercised for a financial asset, or
- the fair value option has been exercised in any circumstance for a financial assets or financial liability.

Financial Accounting Standards Board Statements

FAS 133 : Accounting for Derivative Instruments and Hedging Activities

Statement 133 (FAS 133 or SFAS 133) establishes accounting and reporting standards for derivative instruments, including certain derivative instruments embedded in other contracts and for hedging activities. FAS 133 focuses on the hedge tools and not the sort of risk that is being hedged. FAS 133 occupies itself with derivatives, no matter how they are used. FAS 133 is a compromise on fair value accounting. FAS 133 offers hedgers (vs. traders of derivatives) a halfway house in the form of Other Comprehensive Income (OCI). OCI is a place to 'park' gains and losses on hedges until it is time to recognize them in current income. It is part of the income statement, but not current earnings. FAS 133 outlaws some common hedge practices such as marco and portfolio hedging, netting and synthetic accounting in its various incarnation. The result is a much greater chance that hedge mismatch will create volatile earnings' sometimes for 'good' reasons, and often for technical reasons that do not necessarily reflect the economics of the hedging relationship.

For example, time value in options must be marked to market in income in most cases, so even if the option hedge is perfectly effective at limiting the company's downside risk with respect to future cash flows, the cost of the hedge (which used to be amortized in a straight line fashion) can become a source of undue volatility.

Under FAS 133 (in order to qualify for hedge accounting) treasuries can define the relationship between a derivative and an exposure in one of three basic ways:

- Fair value hedges: Hedges of exposures to the changes in value of a recognized asset or liability, or unrecognized firm commitment.
- Cash flow hedges: Hedges of forecasted transactions, or the variability in the cash flow of a recognized asset or liability.
- Net investment hedges: Hedges of the net investment in a foreign operation.

While the accounting for these hedge relationships may vary:

Fair value hedges : The derivatives are marked to market in earnings. The value of the hedge will be offset by changes in the value of the underlying exposure.

Cash flow hedges : The derivatives are marked to market and carried at fair value. The effective portion is recorded in OCI. The ineffective portion goes into current income.

Net investment hedges : The gain/losses in the hedge are recorded in OCI. Consequently, these hedges are inconsistent with much of the new derivatives accounting rule. For example, they allow treasury to hedge the 'net' exposure. They also allow companies to use nonderivatives (e.g. foreign currency borrowing) to cover their investment risk.

FAS 133 defines derivatives as:

A derivative instrument is a financial instrument or other contract with all three of the following characteristics:

(a) It has

- one or more underlying, and
- one or more notional amounts (by any other name) or payment provisions or both. Those terms determine the amount of the settlement or settlements, and, in some cases, whether or not a settlement is required.

(b) It requires no initial net investment or an initial net investment that is smaller than would be required for other types of contracts that would be expected to have a similar response to changes in market factors.

(c) Its terms require or permit net settlement, it can readily be settled net by a means outside the contract, or it provides for delivery of an asset that puts the recipient in a position not substantially different from net settlement.

SFAS 138: An amendment to SFAS 133

SFAS 138 includes the following four major amendments:

- The normal purchases and normal sales exception is expanded to certain commodity contracts.
- The risk that can be hedged in an interest rate hedge is redefined.
- Recognized foreign currency-denominated assets and liabilities may be hedged with a single cross-currency compound hedge.
- Net hedging of certain intercompany derivatives may be designated as cash flow hedges of foreign currency risk.

Normal Purchases and Normal Sales Excel

In their normal course of business, companies that consume or produce commodities often enter contracts to physically deliver nonfinancial assets, such as electricity, natural gas, oil, aluminum, wheat, or corn. Although these physical contracts are typically settled by the delivery of the commodity, they often include cash settlement provisions in case one party does not deliver or accept delivery of the goods, although these provisions are not intended as derivatives. Historically, the accounting principles for executory contracts applied to physical contracts.

FASB decided contracts that permit but do not require settlement by delivery of a commodity are often used interchangeably with other derivatives and present similar risks; therefore, they should be considered derivatives.

Interest Rate

SFAS 138 sought to reduce the implementation confusion caused by the definition of interest rate risk used in SFAS 133. The new standard combines all components of risk into interest rate risk and credit risk, and broadens the concept of interest rate risk to include the interest rate benchmarked in the hedged item's index, including the popular LIBOR (London Interbank Offer Rate) hedging rate that, strictly speaking, also captures risk movements beyond the risk-free rate. In the SFAS 138 amendments, credit risk consists of all elements of interest rate risk other than the benchmark interest rate.

Under certain conditions, SFAS 133 allows interest rate swaps to use a shortcut method that assumes no ineffectiveness. The shortcut method does not apply, however, to a hedging strategy that designates the benchmark interest rate as the hedged risk when the hedged item is stated at a different index, such as the prime rate. The basic difference between those indices would affect the assessment and measurement of hedge ineffectiveness and possibly force more items into quarterly hedge effectiveness testing.

SFAS 138 has broadened the scope of qualifying hedges. It allows companies to hedge interest rates with available derivatives products based on LIBOR Hedge effectiveness will increase because changes in credit spreads will not be considered a source of ineffectiveness if hedging with a benchmark interest rate. It has also complicated the accounting, however, forcing more frequent effectiveness testing. Entities should evaluate how they hedge interest rate risk and determine whether new polities are required.

Hedging of Foreign Currency Denominated Items

One important provision of SFAS 138 is that it allows joint hedging of interest rate risk and foreign exchange (FX risk in one compound hedge). SFAS 138 widens the net of qualified FX hedges to include the following:

- Foreign currency-denominated (FD) assets or liabilities can be hedged in fair value or cash flow hedges. However, cash flow hedges of recognized FCD assets or liabilities are permitted only when all the variability in the hedged items' functional currency equivalent cash flows is reduced to zero.
- Unrecognized FCD firm commitments can be hedged in fair value or cash flow hedges.

Prior to SFAS 138, hedge accounting for foreign currency risk exposures was limited to fair value hedges of unrecognized FCD firm commitments, cash flow hedges of forecasted FCD transactions, and net investments in FCD foreign operations.

FCD items (e.g., a fixed-rate bond in deutsche marks) are subject to two underlying risks: fair value risk in terms of changes in German interest rates, and changes in the FX rates (between the deutsche mark and the U.S. dollar). Before SFAS 138, the debtor would first hedge the interest rate risk by locking in the combined value of the bond and swap at a fixed amount in marks with a swap in which variable interest was received and fixed interest was paid. Then another derivative contract, such as a forward contract to hedge against the possible fall of the mark against the dollar, would hedge the combined FCD value for FX risk. Under SFAS 133, the FCD debt was remeasured (via the income statement) based on the prevailing spot rate of exchange and the derives five was marked to market (also via the income statement). However, these two adjustments rarely match, creating unintended earnings volatility.

Under the SFAS 138 amendments, it is now possible to acquire a single compound derivative to hedge the joint fair value risk of interest rate and FX movements. One such derivative is a crosscurrency interest swap, which would receive a fixed interest rate in foreign currency and pay a variable interest rate in domestic currency. SFAS 138 permits these recognized FCD assets and liabilities to be designated as the hedged items in fair value or cash flow hedges.

Incompany Exposures

Multinational corporations enter into many transactions with FX risk exposure. A centralized treasury center that assesses corporate-wide FX exposure and hedges the net exposure with a single derivative offers significant cost savings over subsidiaries acquiring their own third-party hedges.

For example: A German subsidiary forecasts sales of DM 5 million from a Japanese purchaser in the next three months, and a Japanese subsidiary expects to purchase DM 3 million worth of inventory from a German supplier in the same period. The net exposure would be a long position of DM 2 million and the parent company could hedge its risk by selling a forward contract or buying a put option for DM 2 million.

SFAS 133 discouraged hedge accounting by treasury centers because it required individual members of a consolidated group to enter individual offsetting derivative contracts with third parties, which nullifies the cost savings benefits. The SFAS 138 amendments allow certain intercompany derivatives that are offset by unrelated third-party contracts to be designated as the hedging instrument in cash flow hedges of foreign currency risk in the consolidated financial statements.

Amendments to DIG Guidance

SFAS 138 also amends related interpretations issued by the Derivatives Implementation Group (DIG). Issue G3: Discontinuation of a cash flow hedge. SFAS 138 amends the accounting for discontinued cash flow hedges by requiring that the net derivative gain or loss from a discontinued cash flow hedge be reported in accumulated other comprehensive income, unless it is probable that the forecasted transaction will not occur by the end of the originally specified time period or within an additional two months.

Summary

There are various accounting issues are involved in accounting of derivative products. IAS 32 talks about financial instrument presentation and IAS 39 talks about financial instrument recognition and measurement. The process of replacing IAS 39 by IFRS 9 is in consideration. IFRS 7 has detailed directions on financial instrument disclosure. Statement 133 (FAS 133 or SFAS 133) establishes accounting and reporting standards for derivative instruments, including certain derivative instruments embedded in other contracts and for hedging activities. Certain provisions of SFAS 133 were amended and new SFAS 138 was introduced.

KEY CONCEPTS

BIS	RBI	ICAAP
BASEL II	SEBI	ALM
OTC	EWRM	Derivative Accounting

Review Questions

1. What do you understand by internal and external risk reporting?
2. Write a short note on IAS 32 and IAS 39.
3. What are the various accounting, tax and legal issues involved in risk management?

4. What are the financial assets and liabilities as defined in IAS 32?
5. Define hedging as per IAS39.
6. How many hedging relationships have been defined in IAS 39? Discuss.
7. Write a short note on IFRS 7 and IFRS 9.
8. Write a short note on SFAS 133 and SFAS 138.
9. What are the amendments carried out in SFAS 133 to bring SFAS 138?

References:

1. *www.ifrs.org*
2. *http://www.iasplus.com*

PART D

Regulatory and Other Issues in Risk Management

21. Regulatory Issues in Risk Management

22. Bank for International Settlement, Basel I, II & III

Chapter – 21

Regulatory Issues in Risk Management

Chapter Objective

- Discuss Regulatory Framework for Banks
- Discuss organisation structure for Risk Management
- Know RBI and SEBI norms for Risk Management
- Discuss NHB guidelines for ALM
- Discuss Best Practice Report of Group of Thirty (G-30)
- To know about Exchange Traded Interest Rate Futures (IRF)
- To study guidelines on Credit Default Swaps (CDS) for Corporate Bonds
- To study RBI guidelines on derivatives

Introduction

There is a set regulatory framework for banks and financial institutions in their own countries and worldwide. All the banks and financial institutions having a worldwide presence have to follow certain regulations framed by Bank for International Settlement (BIS) in order to protect depositor's and investor's money. Any internationally active bank must comply with the internationally agreed capital and risk-related framework. Country specific regulations must also be complied with and various accounting standards must also be adhered to. Every business of the company has certain kind of risk exposure. Hence, the risk management approach should be such covering whole organisation and is known as Enterprise Wide Risk Management (EWRM).

Regulatory Framework

Reserve Bank of India (RBI)

Since the year 1998, RBI has been giving serious efforts and attention towards evolving suitable and comprehensive models for risk management by the banks and to integrate this new discipline in the working systems of the banks.

RBI has defined that the broad parameters of risk management function should encompass:

1. Organisational structure
2. Comprehensive risk measurement approach

3. Risk management policies approved by the Board which should be consistent with the broader business strategies, capital strength, management expertise and overall willingness to assume risk
4. Guidelines and other parameters used to govern risk taking including detailed structure of prudential limits
5. Strong MIS for reporting, monitoring and controlling risks
6. Well laid out procedures, effective control and comprehensive risk reporting framework
7. Separate risk management framework independent of operational departments and with clear delineation of levels of responsibility for management of risk, and
8. Periodical review and evaluation

In terms of this objective to provide risk-management tools and strategies to the commercial banks, RBI has been formulating number guidelines since 1998, to cover each type of risk, like asset liability risk, credit risk, market risk, country risk, etc. In the year 1999, as a further measure, RBI circulated guidelines to evolve a comprehensive risk management approach. These guidelines, together with the guidelines on asset-liability management, were purported to serve as benchmark to those banks, which have not established integrated risk management systems. RBI has since evolved separate guidelines for each broad segment of risk, viz. credit risk, market risk and country risk.

Revised RBI Risk Management Norms to Banks

The Reserve Bank of India (RBI) has issued new risk management norms as a part of efforts to prepare Indian banks for compliance with Basel II norms for risk management.

Under the revised guidelines, the Central Bank has raised the capital adequacy level for banks to cover extended areas of risks, including those that could damage the reputation of banks. The new guidelines, issued under the RBI's 'Supervisory Review Process', make it obligatory for banks to make provision for risks relating to credit concentration, liquidity, settlement risk, reputation, strategy, and under-estimation of credit risk that were not specified earlier. Banks will now have to keep additional capital to cover possible risks which are underestimated as also to ensure quality of risk management.

Already, the Reserve Bank (RBI) has issued two guidelines on minimum capital ratio and market disciplines for Basel II norms, called Pillar I and Pillar III. The RBI now issued guidelines for an Internal Capital Adequacy Assessment Process (ICAAP), which forms the second pillar of the Basel-II capital adequacy framework. While the existing Basel II guidelines recognise three risks - credit, market and operational risks - the guidelines issued today specified new risks as well. Banks will now be insulated against the risks that are not completely captured by the minimum capital adequacy ratio and caused by external factors, according to the new guidelines.[1]

The guidelines also aim at encouraging banks to develop and use better techniques for monitoring and managing their risks. Banks would be required to have a well-defined internal assessment process to assure RBI that adequate capital is held toward various risks they are exposed to. However, these norms provide only broad principles to help banks in developing their Internal Capital Adequacy Assessment Process. Basel II norms required banks to make provisioning for wider range of risks than under the earlier norms that talked about credit risks alone. Now in Basel III norms new features such as buffer capital etc has been introduced.

Foreign banks and those Indian banks that have operations outside the country had to implement the Basel II norms from 31st March 2008, while for all other commercial banks, excluding the local area banks and regional rural banks implementation was to be done by 31st March 2009. The banks are advised to develop and put in place, with the approval of their boards, an ICAAP commensurate with their size, level of complexity, risk profile and scope of operations. At present, there is no common approach for conducting ICAAP. These guidelines, therefore, attempt to provide only broad principles for banks to develop their ICAAP. (Guidelines are available at www.rbi.org) The new Basel III compliance will start from 1st January'2013 and the full compliance will be done by 1st Januray'2019.

TYPICAL ORGANISTATIONAL STRUCTURE FOR RISK MANAGEMENT
(Market Risk)

BOARD OF DIRECTORS
(Decide overall risk management policy and strategy)

RISK MANAGEMENT COMMITTEE
Board Subcommittee including CEO and Head of Credit, Market and Operational Risk Management Committee
(Policy and Strategy for Integrated Risk Management)

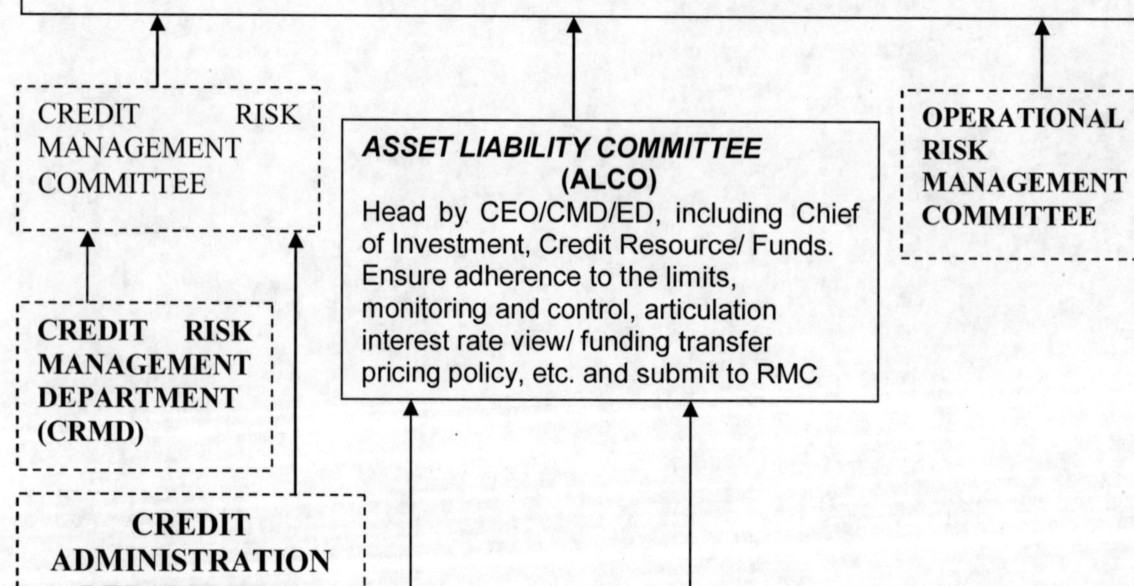

ALM SUPPORT GROUP/RISK MANAGEMENT GROUP
Consisting of operating staff. Responsible for analyzing, monitoring and reporting the risk profiles to ALCO, prepare forecasts /simulations on possible change in market conditions and recommend action on bank's limits

MIDDLE OFFICE
Consisting of experts in market risk management, economists, statisticians and general bankers. Responsible for independent risk assessment, which is critical to ALCO's key-function of controlling and managing market risks in accordance with the mandate established by the Board/ Risk Management Committee Track the magnitude of market risk on a real time basis, aggregate total market risk exposure assumed by bank at any point of time.

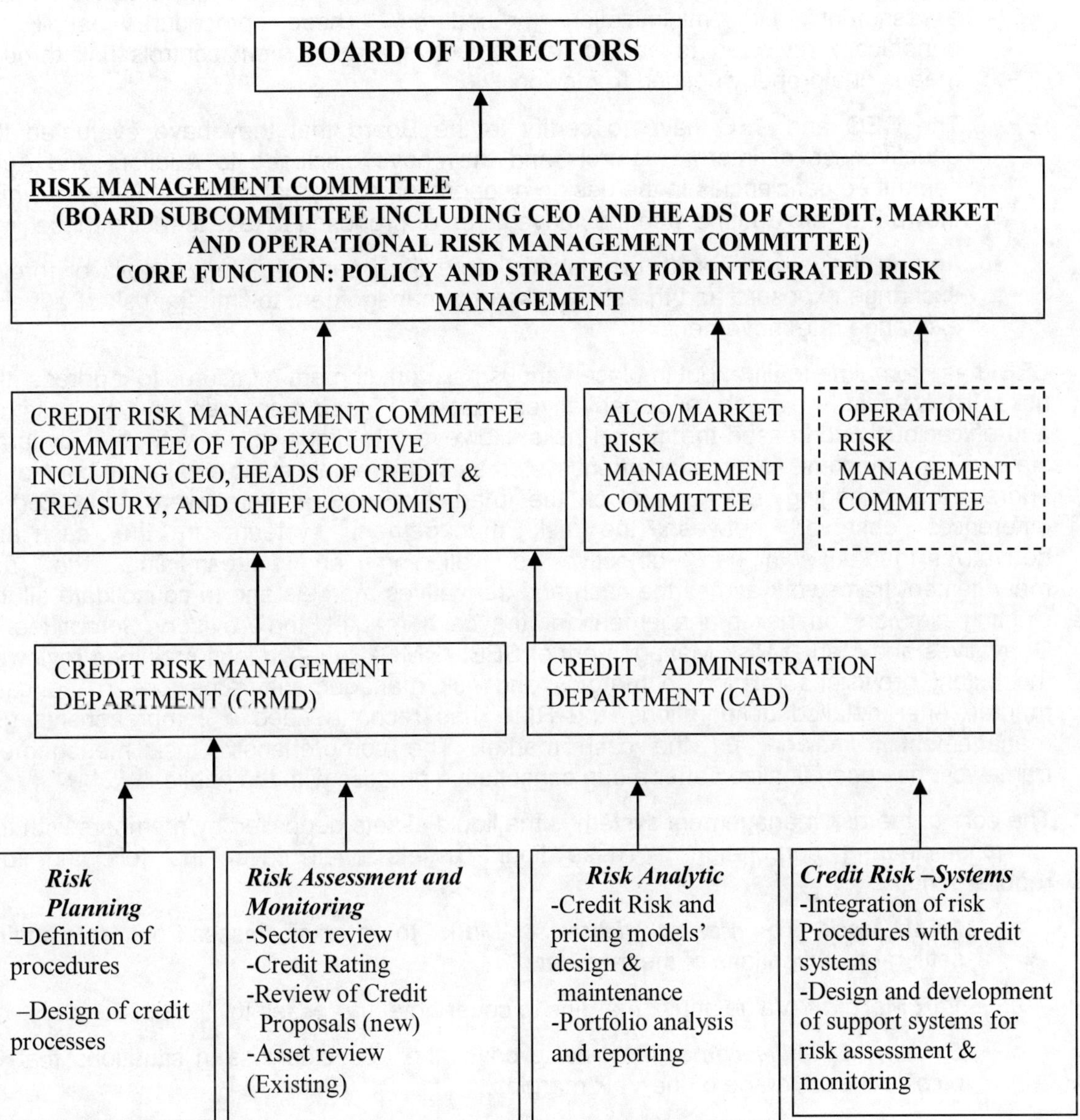

Securities and Exchange Board of India (SEBI)

According to Clause 49 – IV (C) of the listing agreement of SEBI, the company agrees to comply with the following provisions:[3]

Board Disclosures – Risk Management

- The company shall lay down procedures to inform Board members about the risk assessment and minimization procedures. These procedures shall be periodically reviewed to ensure that executive management controls risk through means of a properly defined framework.
- The CEO and CFO have to certify to the Board that they have evaluated the effectiveness of internal controls and they have disclosed to Auditors and Audit committee deficiencies in the design or operation of internal controls, if any, of which they are aware and the step they have taken or proposed to take to rectify these.
- Among the information to be placed before the board, quarterly details of foreign exchange exposure and the steps taken by management to limit the risk of adverse exchange rate movement.

SEBI has, from time to time, put in place various risk containment measures to address the risks involved in the cash and derivatives market. These measures have successfully and efficaciously addressed the market risks. However, to keep pace with the dynamic state of the markets, risk management systems cannot remain static and has to constantly address the changing risk profile of the market. Further, there were also certain differences observed between the risk management systems in the cash and derivatives market. With an objective of aligning and streamlining the risk management framework across the cash and derivatives markets and to consolidate all the existing circulars on risk management for the cash market, the Advisory Committee of Derivatives and Market Risk Management of SEBI (RMG), in its various meetings reviewed the extant provisions relating to margins and risk management framework in the cash market. After detailed deliberations, the RMG has recommended a comprehensive risk management framework for the cash market. The comprehensive risk management framework has been finalized after a due consultative process with the public.

The core of the risk management system is the liquid assets deposited by members with the exchange/clearing corporation. These liquid assets shall cover the following four requirements:

a. ***MTM (Mark To Market) Losses:*** Mark to market losses on outstanding settlement obligations of the member.

b. ***VaR Margins:*** Value at risk margins to cover potential losses for 99% of the days.

c. ***Extreme Loss Margins:*** Margins to cover the expected loss in situations that lie outside the coverage of the VaR margins.

d. ***Base Minimum Capital:*** Capital required for all risks other than market risk (For example, operational risk and client claims).

At all points of time, the liquid assets of the member shall be adequate to cover all the above four requirements. There are no other margins in the risk management system.

National Housing Bank (NHB)

Guidelines for Asset Liability Management system in Housing Finance Companies[4]

In the normal course, Housing Finance Companies (HFCs) are exposed to credit and market risks in view of the asset-liability transformation. With liberalisation in Indian financial markets over the last few years and growing integration of the domestic markets with external markets, the risks associated with the operations of an HFC have become complex and large, requiring strategic management. HFCs are operating in a fairly deregulated environment and are required to determine on their own, interest rates on advances and deposits, subject to the ceiling on maximum rate of interest they can offer on deposits, on a dynamic basis. The interest rates on investments of HFCs in government and other securities are also now market related. Intense competition for business involving both the assets and liabilities has brought pressure on the managements of HFCs to maintain a good balance amongst spreads, profitability and long-term viability. These pressures call for structured and comprehensive measures and not just ad hoc action. The managements of HFCs have to base their business decisions on a dynamic and integrated risk management system and process driven by corporate strategy. HFCs are exposed to several major risks in the course of their business - credit risk, interest rate risk, equity/commodity price risk, liquidity risk and operational risk. It is, therefore, important that HFCs introduce effective risk management systems that address the issues relating to interest rate and liquidity risks.

HFCs need to address these risks in a structured manner by upgrading their risk management and adopting more comprehensive Asset-Liability Management (ALM) practices than has been done hitherto. ALM, among other functions, is also concerned with management of risks and provides a comprehensive and dynamic framework for measuring, monitoring and managing liquidity and interest rate risks of an HFC that need to be closely integrated with the HFC's business strategy. It involves assessment of various types of risks and altering the asset-liability portfolio in a dynamic way in order to manage risks.

The initial focus of the ALM function is to enforce the discipline of market risk management viz. managing business after assessing the market risks involved. The objective of a good risk management system should be to evolve into a strategic tool for effective management of HFCs.

The ALM process rests on three pillars:

a. ALM Information System

- Management Information Systems
- Information availability, accuracy, adequacy and expediency

b. ALM Organisation

- Structure and responsibilities
- Level of top management involvement

c. ALM Process

- Risk parameters
- Risk identification
- Risk measurement
- Risk management
- Risk policies and tolerance levels

The Basel Committee

The Basel Committee was established in 1974 by the central bank Governors of the Group of Ten countries. The Committee's members are Belgium, Canada, France, Germany, Italy, Japan, Luxembourg, the Netherlands, Spain, Sweden, Switzerland, United Kingdom and United States. Member countries are represented by their central bank or the authority responsible for the prudential supervision of banking business. The Basel committee has its Secretariat in Basel provided by Bank for International Settlements (BIS). The Secretariat is managed by professional supervisors from member institutions. The committee formulates supervisory standards and guidelines and recommends best practices.

In 1988, the Basel Committee of G-10 countries issued comprehensive guidelines for capital adequacy with reference to risk-weighted assets. Though these guidelines did not have any legal status in other countries, most other regulators have adopted them. A set of agreements set by the Basel Committee on Bank Supervision (BCBS), which provides recommendations on banking regulations in regards to capital risk, market risk and operational risk. The purpose of the accords is to ensure that financial institutions have enough capital on account to meet obligations and absorb unexpected losses. The first Basel Accord, known as Basel I, was issued in 1988 and focuses on the capital adequacy of financial institutions. The capital adequacy risk, (the risk that a financial institution will be hurt by an unexpected loss), categorizes the assets of financial institution into five risk categories (0%, 10%, 20%, 50%, 100%). Banks that operate internationally are required to have a risk weight of 8% or less.

In June 1999, the Basel Committee proposed a New Capital Adequacy Framework to replace the 1988 Accord. In 2004, the committee came up with a document called "International Convergence of Capital Measurement and Capital Standards", more popularly known as Basel II.

Best Practices Report Group of Thirty (G-30)[5]

Introduction

Derivatives have fundamentally changed financial management by providing new tools to manage risk. As the use of derivatives has grown rapidly in the past 15 years, they have moved into the mainstream of finance. Yet many, both inside and outside of the financial industry, remain uncomfortable with derivatives activity. They see it as complex and obscure, potentially subject to abuse that might lead to the failure of individual firms or even to a crisis in the financial system. This study recognizes and addresses these concerns by explaining derivatives and their uses and by formulating and disseminating recommendations about their management. The distinguishing feature of this study is the practical character of its contents. Other studies of derivatives have been conducted by academics or supervisors; this study was conducted largely by market participants.

Why Derivatives Matter

In general terms, a derivatives transaction is a contract whose value depends on (or "derives" from) the value of an underlying asset, reference rate, or index. This study focuses on global "over-the-counter" (OTC) derivatives--those privately negotiated contracts provided directly by dealers to end-users, as opposed to the standardized contracts (such as futures) sold on exchanges. The main over-the-counter derivatives include swaps, forwards, and options, based upon interest rates, currencies, equities, and commodities.

By any measure, derivatives are a major financial activity. Some have even portrayed it as a multi-trillion dollar business dwarfing activity in other financial markets. But a more careful comparison reveals that, while derivatives activity is growing rapidly, its size remains modest in relation to foreign exchange, bonds, or equities. What makes derivatives important is not so much the size of the activity, as the role it plays in fostering new ways to understand, measure, and manage financial risk. Through derivatives, the complex risks that are bound together in traditional instruments can be teased apart and managed independently, and often more efficiently.

The results can benefit a wide variety of institutions. For many that issue securities, and for many that invest, derivatives can save costs and increase returns while broadening the range of funding and investment alternatives. For them and others, derivatives can reduce the risk of loss. And for financial institutions, derivatives can be a source of strength because they reinforce existing activities with clients, and help to build diversified credit portfolios.

Derivatives and Risk

Derivatives help to manage risk in new ways an important economic function. Yet the risks involved in derivatives activities are neither new nor unique. They are the same kinds of risks found in traditional financial products: market, credit, legal, and operational risks.

Because over-the-counter derivatives are customized transactions, they often assemble risks in complex ways. This can make the measurement and control of these risks more difficult and create the possibility of unexpected loss. Banking supervisors have conducted several studies into the implications of derivatives for the financial system. These studies neither concluded that derivatives significantly increase systemic risk nor did they find cause for complacency.

For derivatives activity to grow and prosper, those who take part in it whether as dealers, end-users, or both should continue laying a strong foundation of good management practice. They also should provide the public with information that will allay unjustified fears by demystifying this activity. And participants should discuss openly with legislators, supervisors, and regulators, ways to further strengthen the current institutional framework.

These steps are both appropriate and sufficient to address the systemic and other concerns about derivatives activity. Without minimizing the significance of these concerns, this study does not conclude that any fundamental changes in the current regulatory framework, such as separate regulation of this activity, are needed. Separate regulation of global derivatives would be at cross-purposes with the existing framework of supervision, with its focus on the common risks contained in derivatives and traditional instruments. There is also a danger in imposing regulatory formulas that inhibit new product innovation or discourage firms from developing the individualized, robust risk management systems on which they should rely.

The Global Derivatives Study

This Study consists of the Recommendations, an Overview of Derivatives Activity, and three sections. The study offers 20 recommendations to help dealers and end-users manage derivatives activity and continue to benefit from its use. The study also recommends four ways that supervisors and regulators, for their part, can help the financial infrastructure keep up with derivatives activity. The Overview section of this study explains in relatively plain language what derivatives are, the needs they serve, their risks, and their relationship to traditional financial instruments. The overview is intended to promote understanding and discussion among the growing number of people--in financial institutions, other corporations, and official bodies--that have an interest in the subject.

Three separately bound volumes of section contain the study's detailed background material, which should be of special interest to professionals involved in various aspects of derivatives.

- Section I contains the six working papers that form the basis of the study and whose analysis supports the recommendations. Each covers one of the main areas studied by the Working Group: valuation and market risk; credit risk; enforceability; systems, operations, and controls; accounting and reporting; and systemic issues.
- Section II is a compilation of legal memoranda discussing issues of enforceability in nine jurisdictions: Australia, Brazil, Canada, England, France, Germany, Japan, Singapore, and the United States.
- Section III summarizes the findings of the Survey of Industry Practice conducted for this study. A representative group of 80 dealers and 72 end-users responded to a detailed questionnaire.

By contributing to the public understanding of the nature and potential of derivatives and by providing guidance on principles of good management, the authors of this study hope to add to the soundness and utility of these instruments.

The best practice report has 24 recommendations covering General Policies, Credit Risk Measurement and Management, Enforceability, and Accounting and Disclosure.

The Recommendations

Global over-the-counter derivatives activity is relatively new, and until now there has been no thorough study of its management. Dealers and end-users, being aware of the broader challenges, have focused their discussions on specific issues and have addressed these with a variety of practices, some more effective than others. This study presents the first comprehensive effort to take stock of what the industry has learned, and to broaden awareness of the more successful management approaches. It provides practical guidance in the form of 20 recommendations addressed to dealers and end-users alike (some firms perform both functions). These recommendations can help them to manage derivatives activity, to respond to its growth and complexity, and to continue to benefit from its use.

The recommendations, which the Steering Committee has endorsed unanimously, were formulated by the Working Group--a diverse cross-section of end-users, dealers, academics, accountants, and lawyers involved in derivatives. Input also came from a detailed survey of Industry Practice among 80 dealers and 72 end-users worldwide, involving both questionnaires and in-depth interviews. Some of the recommendations reflect a strong consensus among participants, and are already in widespread use; others represent the Working Group's choice among alternative practices. Still others point to emerging practices currently followed by a handful of participants. These 20 recommendations are not necessarily the only means to good management. What they do offer is a benchmark against which participants can measure their own practices.

To summarize, the recommendations suggest that each dealer and end-user of derivatives should:

- *Determine at the highest level* of policy and decision making the scope of its involvement in derivatives activities and policies to be applied.
- *Value derivatives positions at market*, at least for risk management purposes.
- *Quantify its market risk* under adverse market conditions against limits, perform stress simulations, and forecast cash investing and funding needs.
- *Assess the credit risk* arising from derivatives activities based on frequent measures of current and potential exposure against credit limits.
- *Reduce credit risk by broadening* the use of multi-product master agreements with close-out netting provisions, and by working with other participants to ensure legal enforceability of derivatives transactions within and across jurisdictions.
- *Establish market and credit risk management functions* with clear authority independent of the dealing function.
- *Authorize only professionals* with the requisite skills and experience to transact and manage the risks, as well as to process, report, control, and audit derivatives activities.
- *Establish management information systems* sophisticated enough to measure, manage, and report the risks of derivatives activities in a timely and precise manner.
- *Voluntarily adopt accounting and disclosure practices* for international harmonization and greater transparency, pending the arrival of international standards.

In addition, there are four recommendations for legislators, regulators, and supervisors. To help strengthen the financial infrastructure for derivatives activities, officials are called upon to:

- *Recognize close-out netting arrangements* and amend the Basel Accord to reflect their benefits in bank capital regulations.

- *Work with market participants to remove legal and regulatory uncertainties* regarding derivatives.
- *Amend tax regulations* that disadvantage the economic use of derivatives.
- *Provide comprehensive and consistent guidance* on accounting and reporting of derivatives and other financial instruments.

The recommendations are generally grouped below according to specific areas of study. Six subcommittees of the Working Group addressed these areas in detail.

Recommendations for Dealers and End-Users

These recommendations are addressed to participants in derivatives activity, both dealers and end-users. The terms "dealer" and "end-user" do not refer to particular types of institution, but rather to the nature of their derivatives activity. A bank, for instance, may participate both as a dealer and as an end-user. Likewise, some corporate end-users of derivatives may also be involved as dealers.

Recommendation 1: The Role of Senior Management

Dealers and end-users should use derivatives in a manner consistent with the overall risk management and capital policies approved by their boards of directors. These policies should be reviewed as business and market circumstances change. Policies governing derivatives use should be clearly defined, including the purposes for which these transactions are to be undertaken. Senior management should approve procedures and controls to implement these policies, and management at all levels should enforce them.

Derivatives activities merit senior management attention because they can generate significant benefits or costs for any firm. A firm's policies for derivatives should be an integral part of its overall policies for risk taking and management, either in its underlying business (if it is an end-user) or in its other lines of business (if it is a dealer). Periodic reviews will help ensure that these policies reflect changing circumstances and innovations.

Recommendation 2: Marking to Market

Dealers should mark their derivatives positions to market, on at least a daily basis, for risk management purposes.

Marking to market is the only valuation technique that correctly reflects the current value of derivatives cash flows to be managed and provides information about market risk and appropriate hedging actions. Lower-of-cost-or-market accounting, and accruals accounting, are not appropriate for risk management.

The Survey of Industry Practice shows that the practice of marking to market daily is widespread among dealers, reflecting the importance of the information it provides to risk managers. Intraday or even real time valuation can help greatly, especially in managing the market risk of some option portfolios.

Recommendation 3: Market Valuation Methods

Derivatives portfolios of dealers should be valued based on mid-market levels less specific adjustments, or on appropriate bid or offer levels. Mid-market valuation adjustments should allow for expected future costs such as unearned credit spread, close-out costs, investing and funding costs, and administrative costs.

Marking to mid-market less adjustments specifically defines and quantifies adjustments that are implicitly assumed in the bid or offer method. Using the mid-market valuation method without adjustment would overstate the value of a portfolio by not deferring income to meet future costs and to provide a credit spread.

Two adjustments to mid-market are necessary even for a perfectly matched portfolio: the "unearned credit spread adjustment" to reflect the credit risk in the portfolio and the "administrative costs adjustment" for costs that will be incurred to administer the portfolio. The unearned credit spread adjustment represents amounts set aside to cover expected credit losses and to provide compensation for credit exposure. Expected credit losses should be based upon expected exposure to counterparties (taking into account netting arrangements), expected default experience, and overall portfolio diversification. The unearned credit spread should preferably be adjusted dynamically as these factors change. It can be calculated on a transaction basis, on a portfolio basis, or across all activities with a given client.

Two additional adjustments are necessary for portfolios that are not perfectly matched: the "close-out costs adjustment" which factors in the cost of eliminating their market risk and the "investing and funding costs adjustment" relating to the cost of funding and investing cash flow mismatches at rates different from the LIBOR rate which models typically assume.

The survey reveals a wide range of practice concerning the mark-to-market method and the use of adjustments to mid-market value. The most commonly used adjustments are for credit and administrative costs.

Recommendation 4: Identifying Revenue Sources

Dealers should measure the components of revenue regularly and in sufficient detail to understand the sources of risk.

By identifying and isolating individual sources of revenue, dealers develop a more refined understanding of the risks and returns of derivatives activities. Components of revenue generally include origination revenue, credit spread revenue, if applicable, and other trading revenue. It is useful, though complex, to split other trading revenue among components of market risk.

The Survey of Industry Practice indicates that few dealers identify individual sources of revenue. This should become a more common practice.

Recommendation 5: Measuring Market Risk

Dealers should use a consistent measure to calculate daily the market risk of their derivatives positions and compare it to market risk limits.

- Market risk is best measured as "value at risk" using probability analysis based upon a common confidence interval (e.g., two standard deviations) and time horizon (e.g., a one-day exposure).
- Components of market risk that should be considered across the term structure include: absolute price or rate change (delta), convexity (gamma), volatility (vega), time decay (theta), basis or correlation, and discount rate (rho).

Reducing market risks across derivatives to a single common denominator makes aggregation, comparison, and risk control easier. "Value at risk" is the expected loss from an adverse market movement with a specified probability over a particular period of time. For example, with 97.5% probability (that is, a "confidence interval" of 97.5%), corresponding to calculations using about two standard deviations, it can be determined that any change in portfolio value over one day resulting from an adverse market movement will not exceed a specific amount. Conversely, there is a 2.5% probability of experiencing an adverse change in excess of the calculated amount.

Value at risk should encompass changes in all major market risk components listed in the recommendation. The difficulty in applying the technique of value at risk increases with the complexity of the risks being managed. For comparability, value at risk should be calculated to a common confidence interval and time horizon. For most portfolios without options, once the expected loss is known for events with a given probability, the loss for a more likely or less likely scenario can easily be deduced. Therefore, for such portfolios, the choice of confidence interval is of no great significance. For option-based portfolios, however, this does not hold true. In their case, it would also be useful to calculate the loss from more or less likely scenarios.

A time horizon of one day is consistent with Recommendation 2 for daily marking to market, which allows management to know and decide daily any change of the risk profile.

Once a method of risk measurement is in place, market risk limits must be decided based on factors such as: management tolerance for low probability extreme losses versus higher probability modest losses, capital resources, market liquidity, expected profitability, trader experience, and business strategy. The survey suggests that most dealers know and consider some or all of the components of market risk. However, the use of one consistent measure of market risk, such as value at risk, is more prevalent among large dealers.

Recommendation 6: Stress Simulations

Dealers should regularly perform simulations to determine how their portfolios would perform under stress conditions.

Simulations of improbable market environments are important in risk analysis because many assumptions that are valid for normal markets may no longer hold true in abnormal markets.

These simulations should reflect both historical events and future possibilities. Stress scenarios should include not only abnormally large market swings but also periods of prolonged inactivity. The tests should consider the effect of price changes on the mid-market value of the portfolio, as well as changes in the assumptions about the adjustments to mid-market (such as the impact that decreased liquidity would have on close-out costs). Dealers should evaluate the results of stress tests and develop contingency plans accordingly.

The survey indicates that some stress testing is being conducted, mainly by large dealers, and that broader usage is planned.

Recommendation 7: Investing and Funding Forecasts

Dealers should periodically forecast the cash investing and funding requirements arising from their derivatives portfolios.

The frequency and precision of forecasts should be determined by the size and nature of mismatches. A detailed forecast should determine surpluses and funding needs, by currency, over time. It also should examine the potential impact of contractual unwind provisions or other credit provisions that produce cash or collateral receipts or payments.

The survey indicates that at present, half of responding dealers are conducting forecasts of cash investing and funding requirements. This type of forecast should become a more common practice.

Recommendation 8: Independent Market Risk Management

Dealers should have a market risk management function, with clear independence and authority, to ensure that the following responsibilities are carried out:

- The development of risk limit policies and the monitoring of transactions and positions for adherence to these policies. (See Recommendation 5)
- The design of stress scenarios to measure the impact of market conditions, however improbable, that might cause market gaps, volatility swings, or disruptions of major relationships, or might reduce liquidity in the face of unfavorable market linkages, concentrated market making, or credit exhaustion. (See Recommendation 6)
- The design of revenue reports quantifying the contribution of various risk components, and of market risk measures such as value at risk. (See Recommendations 4 and 5)
- The monitoring of variance between the actual volatility of portfolio value and that predicted by the measure of market risk.
- The review and approval of pricing models and valuation systems used by front- and back-office personnel, and the development of reconciliation procedures if different systems are used.

The growth of activities in derivatives and other financial instruments has led many firms to establish market (and credit) risk management functions to assist senior management in establishing consistent policies and procedures applicable to various activities. Market risk management is typically headed by a board level or near board level executive.

The market risk management function acts as a catalyst for the development of sound market risk management systems, models, and procedures. Its review of trading performance typically answers the question: Are results consistent with those suggested by analysis of value at risk? The risk management function is rarely involved in actual risk-taking decisions.

According to the survey, a large majority of dealers already have such a function in place and over 50% of those that do not plan to establish one in the near future.

Recommendation 9: Practices by End-Users

As appropriate to the nature, size, and complexity of their derivatives activities, end-users should adopt the same valuation and market risk management practices that are recommended for dealers. Specifically, they should consider: regularly marking to market their derivatives transactions for risk management purposes; periodically forecasting the cash investing and funding requirements arising from their derivatives transactions; and establishing a clearly independent and authoritative function to design and assure adherence to prudent risk limits.

While many end-users do not expect significant change in the combined value of their derivatives positions and the underlying positions, others do. Derivatives are customer-specific transactions, often designed to offset precisely the market risk of an end-user's business position (e.g., buying a commodity as a raw material). End-users should establish the performance assessment and control procedures that are appropriate for their derivatives activities.

Less than half of those end-users surveyed currently mark their derivatives hedges to market for risk management purposes. About half plan to do so.

Credit Risk Measurement and Management

Recommendation 10: Measuring Credit Exposure

Dealers and end-users should measure credit exposure on derivatives in two ways:

- Current exposure, which is the replacement cost of derivatives transactions, that is, their market value.
- Potential exposure, which is an estimate of the future replacement cost of derivatives transactions. It should be calculated using probability analysis based upon broad confidence intervals (e.g., two standard deviations) over the remaining terms of the transactions.

To assess credit risk, a dealer or end-user should ask two questions. If a counterparty was to default today, what would it cost to replace the derivatives transaction? If a counterparty defaults in the future, what is a reasonable estimate of the future replacement cost?

Current exposure is an accurate measure of credit risk that addresses the first question. It simply evaluates the replacement cost of outstanding derivatives commitments. The result can be positive or negative. It is an important measure of credit risk as it represents the actual risk to a counterparty at any point in time. The regular calculation of current exposure is a broadly accepted practice today.

Potential exposure is more difficult to assess, and the methods used to determine it vary. The most rigorous methods use either simulation analysis or option valuation models. The analysis generally involves a statistical modeling of the effects on the value of the derivatives of movement in the prices of the underlying variables (such as interest rates, exchange rates, equity prices, or commodity prices). These techniques are often used to generate two measures of potential exposure: expected exposure; and maximum or "worst case" exposure.

Dealers and end-users that cannot justify the simulation and statistical systems needed to perform such potential exposure calculations should use tables of factors developed under the same principles. The factors used should differentiate appropriately by type and maturity of transaction and be adjusted periodically for changes in market conditions.

The survey shows that dealers use several different methods for calculating credit exposures. These include: the BIS original and current exposure methods, used by one-third of all dealers; methods based on worst-case scenarios applied to each transaction, used by about a quarter of dealers and expected to become the most common in the future; and methods that rely upon tables of factors, used by almost 40% of dealers. End-users tend to rely on simpler methods primarily based on notional amounts.

Recommendation 11: Aggregating Credit Exposures

Credit exposures on derivatives, and all other credit exposures to a counterparty, should be aggregated taking into consideration enforceable netting arrangements. Credit exposures should be calculated regularly and compared to credit limits.

In calculating the current credit exposure for a portfolio of transactions with a counterparty, the first question is whether netting applies. If it does, the current exposure is simply the sum of positive and negative exposures on transactions in the portfolio. The calculation of potential exposure is more complicated. Simply summing the potential exposures of all transactions will in most cases dramatically overstate the actual exposure, even if netting does not apply. This is because a straight summation fails to take into account transactions in the portfolio that offset each other or that have peak potential exposures at different times. The most accurate calculation of potential exposure simulates the entire portfolio. Although portfolio-level simulation is not commonly used by dealers at present, they should pursue it more widely to avoid overstating aggregate exposure.

Credit exposures should be calculated regularly. In particular, dealers should monitor current exposures daily; they can generally measure potential exposures less frequently. End-users with derivative portfolios should also periodically assess credit exposures. For them, the appropriate frequency will depend upon how material their credit exposures are.

Credit exposures should also be regularly compared to credit limits, and systems should be in place to monitor when limits are approached or exceeded, so that management can take appropriate actions. By aggregating credit exposures on derivatives as described above, participants will have a consistent basis for comparison with other credit exposures including those resulting from on-balance-sheet activity. This would permit a more effective evaluation of the adequacy of credit reserves relative to overall credit exposure.

The Survey suggests that most dealers monitor gross credit use against limits. Aggregating current and potential exposures by counterparty on a net basis is not common among dealers, although some who do not net at present plan to in the future. Frequent monitoring of credit exposure is widespread among dealers, with three-quarters of respondents doing it either intraday or overnight. The majority of end-users monitor credit exposures at least once a month.

Recommendation 12: Independent Credit Risk Management

Dealers and end-users should have a credit risk management function with clear independence and authority, and with analytical capabilities in derivatives, responsible for:

- Approving credit exposure measurement standards
- Setting credit limits and monitoring their use
- Reviewing credits and concentrations of credit risk
- Reviewing and monitoring risk reduction arrangements

For dealers, credit exposures should be monitored by an independent credit risk management group. According to the survey, most dealers and some end-users have such a group. For end-users, this role may not necessarily be performed by a separate group; however, the credit risk should be managed independently from dealing personnel. This separation of responsibility is intended to prevent conflicts of interest and to ensure that credit exposure is assessed objectively. The credit risk management function should approve exposure management standards, and should establish credit limits for counterparties consistent with these standards. Specifically, it should conduct an internal credit review before engaging in transactions with a counterparty, and should guide the use of documentation and credit support tools. Credit limits and guidelines should ensure that only those potential counterparties that meet the appropriate credit standards, with or without credit support, become actual counterparties.

The credit risk management function should continually review the creditworthiness of counterparties and their credit limits.

Recommendation 13: Master Agreements

Dealers and end-users are encouraged to use one master agreement as widely as possible with each counterparty to document existing and future derivatives transactions, including foreign exchange forwards and options. Master agreements should provide for payments netting and close-out netting, using a full two-way payments approach.

Participants should use one master agreement with each counterparty. That agreement should provide for close-out and settlement netting as widely as possible to document derivatives transactions. In particular, there is substantial scope for reducing credit risk by including foreign exchange forwards and options under master agreements along with other derivatives transactions.

A single master agreement that documents transactions between two parties creates the greatest legal certainty that credit exposure will be netted. The use of multiple master agreements between two parties introduces the risk of "cherry-picking" among master agreements (rather than among individual transactions); and the risk that the right to set off amounts due under different master agreements might be delayed. Dealers and end-users will be well served by using a single master agreement with counterparties to document as many derivatives transactions as law or regulation permit. The practices of using separate agreements for each transaction between two parties, or standard terms that do not constitute a master agreement, are not good practices and should be discontinued. According to the survey, two-fifths of all dealers now document derivatives transactions under a multi-product master, and more plan to do so in the future.

Full two-way payments, as opposed to limited two-way payments, is now the preferred payments approach in master agreements. Under full two-way payments, the net amount calculated through the netting provisions in a bilateral master agreement is due regardless of whether it is to, or from, the defaulting party. Under limited two-way payments, the defaulting party is not entitled to receive anything, even if the net amount is in its favor. This discourages default and enhances cross-product and cross-affiliate set-off. However, when master agreements cover a wide range of derivatives transactions, the benefits created by increasing the certainty about the value of a net position under full two-way payments outweigh any possible benefits under limited two-way payments.

Recommendation 14: Credit Enhancement

Dealers and end-users should assess both the benefits and costs of credit enhancement and related risk-reduction arrangements. Where it is proposed that credit downgrades would trigger early termination or collateral requirements, participants should carefully consider their own capacity and that of their counterparties to meet the potentially substantial funding needs that might result.

Credit risk reduction arrangements can be useful in the management of counterparty credit risk. These include collateral and margin arrangements; third-party credit enhancement such as guarantees or letters of credit; and structural credit enhancement through the establishment of special-purpose vehicles to conduct derivatives business.

The survey indicates that about two-thirds of dealers are prepared to accept credit enhancement with cash or securities as collateral, and over three-quarters accept a third party guarantee or enhancement. Reflecting strong dealer credit ratings, only one-third are prepared to provide cash or securities collateral and only 10% or so will offer a third party guarantee.

Enforceability

Recommendation 15: Promoting Enforceability

Dealers and end-users should work together on a continuing basis to identify and recommend solutions for issues of legal enforceability, both within and across jurisdictions, as activities evolve and new types of transactions are developed.

Dealers regularly develop new types of transactions, and new technologies are developed to confirm them. These developments may not fit clearly within the current legal framework in the jurisdictions where transactions occur. Therefore, dealers and end-users should continue to work together to evaluate developments in light of existing laws to assess what legal issues may arise. They should take the initiative to ensure that risks arising from these developments can be properly handled through analysis, market practices, documentation and, when necessary, legislation.

Enforceability of netting provisions is considered a serious concern by 43% of dealer senior management responding to the survey, and another 45% consider it to be of some concern. It also is considered a serious issue by management of many end-users.

Recommendation 16: Professional Expertise

Dealers and end-users must ensure that their derivatives activities are undertaken by professionals in sufficient number and with the appropriate experience, skill levels, and degrees of specialization. These professionals include specialists who transact and manage the risks involved, their supervisors, and those responsible for processing, reporting, controlling, and auditing the activities.

To establish good management, derivatives activities must be staffed by talented, well-trained, and responsible professionals. There is a danger, however, in relying on a few specialists, and it is essential that their managers understand not only derivatives but also the broader business context.

Derivatives support functions are technical and generally require a level of expertise higher than for other financial instruments or activities. Respondents to the survey expressed concern that, while they are satisfied with the quality of staff in line derivatives activities, the quality of support staff lags. Developing expertise through training programs and appropriate standards of professionalism is encouraged.

The Survey indicates that, for the majority of respondent dealers, senior management is confident about the general quality of its derivatives professionals. To the extent it is concerned about issues of professionalism, it is more worried about its own lack of understanding, about insufficient understanding of derivatives by other functions, and about overreliance on a few specialists.

Recommendation 17: Systems

Dealers and end-users must ensure that adequate systems for data capture, processing, settlement, and management reporting are in place so that derivatives transactions are conducted in an orderly and efficient manner in compliance with management policies. Dealers should have risk management systems that measure the risks incurred in their derivatives activities including market and credit risks. End-users should have risk management systems that measure the risks incurred in their derivatives activities based upon their nature, size, and complexity.

The size and scope of the required systems will depend upon the nature and scale of an organization's derivatives transactions.

For dealers, operating efficiency and reliability are enhanced through the development of systems that minimize manual intervention. Those benefits are particularly significant for dealers with a large volume of activity and a high degree of customization of transactions. At the moment, confirmations of transactions, for example, are automated for about 40% of dealers, some 10% are partially automated, and another 45% rely on manual systems. Eighty percent plan to automate their confirmations completely. In addition, large dealers have made significant investments to integrate back- and front-office systems for derivatives with their firms' other management information systems. Dealers that have done so have found that the integration further enhances operating efficiency and reliability.

While end-users may invest less extensively in their systems than dealers do, these should still be sufficient to group exposures and analyze aggregated risk in a meaningful and useful way.

Recommendation 18: Authority

Management of dealers and end-users should designate who is authorized to commit their institutions to derivatives transactions.

Authority may be delegated to certain individuals or to persons holding certain positions within the firm. Management may choose to limit authority to certain types of transactions, for example to certain maturities, amounts, or types of underlying risks. It is essential that this information be understood within the firm.

Participants should communicate information on which individuals have the authority to commit to counterparties. They should recognize, however, that the legal doctrine of "apparent authority" may govern the transactions they enter into, and that there is no substitute for appropriate internal controls.

Two-thirds of dealers responding to the survey involve senior management in authorizing traders to commit the firm.

Accounting and Disclosure

Recommendation 19: Accounting Practices

International harmonization of accounting standards for derivatives is desirable. Pending the adoption of harmonized standards, the following accounting practices are recommended:

- Dealers should account for derivatives transactions by marking them to market, taking changes in value to income each period.
- End-users should account for derivatives used to manage risks so as to achieve a consistency of income recognition treatment between those instruments and the risks being managed. Thus, if the risk being managed is accounted for at cost (or, in the case of an anticipatory hedge, not yet recognized), changes in the value of a qualifying risk management instrument should be deferred until a gain or loss is recognized on the risk being managed. Or, if the risk being managed is marked to market with changes in value being taken to income, a qualifying risk management instrument should be treated in a comparable fashion.
- End-users should account for derivatives not qualifying for risk management treatment on a mark-to-market basis.
- Amounts due to and from counterparties should only be offset when there is a legal right to set off or when enforceable netting arrangements are in place.

Where local regulations prevent adoption of these practices, disclosure along these lines is nevertheless recommended.

Accounting policies for derivatives vary widely around the world. In some countries there are local accounting standards that address accounting for derivatives; in other countries there are no specific standards and a variety of customs and practices has developed. In view of the global nature of derivatives, it is desirable to achieve some harmonization of accounting treatment to assist in clarifying the financial statements of dealers and end-users.

The recommendation for dealers to account for changes in the value of their derivatives positions in income during each period has become standard in many, although not all, countries. It provides a better representation of the economic effects of such positions than other methods.

The recommended accounting treatment for end-users using derivatives to manage risks, referred to as "risk management accounting," is also a standard treatment. It has evolved in many countries, at least in a modified form, as a response to anomalies in the existing accounting framework. Traditionally in some countries, this accounting treatment has been applied solely to transactions undertaken to reduce risks, usually referred to as "hedges".

Policies must define when financial instruments are eligible for risk management accounting to ensure that the method is not abused. Among a majority of dealers who responded to the Survey, senior management thought inconsistency of accounting standards with the economics of the business were either of serious or some concern.

Recommendation 20: Disclosures

Financial statements of dealers and end-users should contain sufficient information about their use of derivatives to provide an understanding of the purposes for which transactions are undertaken, the extent of the transactions, the degree of risk involved, and how the transactions have been accounted for. Pending the adoption of harmonized accounting standards, the following disclosures are recommended:

- Information about management's attitude to financial risks, how instruments are used, and how risks are monitored and controlled.
- Accounting policies.
- Analysis of positions at the balance sheet date.
- Analysis of the credit risk inherent in those positions.
- For dealers only, additional information about the extent of their activities in financial instruments.

The survey shows that the quality of financial statement disclosure about derivatives transactions varies even more widely than the accounting policies that are applied. Until local standards-setting bodies can adopt harmonized standards, there is a need to improve the quality of financial statement disclosure concerning transactions in both derivatives and cash market instruments. Its qualitative nature dictates that information about management's attitude to financial risks, how instruments are used, and how risks are monitored and controlled, should appear in the management analysis section of the annual report. The remaining information should appear in the footnotes to the financial statements and be commented on as appropriate in the management analysis.

This recommendation is not apparently precluded by accounting regulations in any country and its early adoption is encouraged. Inadequate public disclosure of exposures of counterparties is of some concern, or of serious concern, to about three-fifths of senior management among dealers responding to the survey.

Recommendations for Legislators, Regulators, and Supervisors

Recommendation 21: Recognizing Netting

Regulators and supervisors should recognize the benefits of netting arrangements where and to the full extent that they are enforceable, and encourage their use by reflecting these arrangements in capital adequacy standards. Specifically, they should promptly implement the recognition of the effectiveness of bilateral close-out netting in bank capital regulations.

The bilateral or multilateral netting of contractual payments due on settlement dates, and of unrealized losses against unrealized gains in the event of a counterparty's default, is the most important means of mitigating credit risk. By reducing settlement risk as well as credit exposures, netting contributes to the reduction of systemic risk. Significant efforts have been made to develop standard master agreements that effect netting across the full range of derivatives products. Nonetheless, the enforceability of such netting provisions remains among the highest concerns of senior management of derivatives dealers, according to the survey.

Regulators and supervisors should officially recognize netting where and to the full extent it is enforceable, and reflect these arrangements in the capital standards. In this way, regulators and supervisors will stimulate efforts to resolve uncertainties where they exist and will create tangible incentives for using this most important method of reducing counterparty risk. An important step in implementing this recommendation was taken in April of this year when the Basel Committee released a Consultative Paper that included a proposal for recognizing the effectiveness of close-out netting. This is an amendment to the agreed framework for measuring bank capital adequacy (the "Basel Accord") published by the Basel Committee in July 1988. When the consultation period for this proposal has ended, the national supervisory authorities represented on the Basel Committee should recognize and implement bilateral close-out netting for capital purposes.

Recommendation 22: Legal and Regulatory Uncertainties

Legislators, regulators, and supervisors, including central banks, should work in concert with dealers and end-users to identify and remove any remaining legal and regulatory uncertainties with respect to:

- The form of documentation required to create legally enforceable agreements (statute of frauds).
- The capacity of parties, such as government entities, insurance companies, pension funds, and building societies, to enter into transactions (ultra vires).
- The enforceability of bilateral close-out netting and collateral arrangements in bankruptcy.
- The enforceability of multibranch netting arrangements in bankruptcy.
- The legality/enforceability of derivatives transactions.

These five main enforceability risks are analyzed for nine major jurisdictions in Appendix II (bound separately). Regulators and legislators in these jurisdictions should remove the remaining uncertainties that have been identified. In other countries, market participants, regulators, and legislators should work to identify and resolve any similar legal risks. These efforts should be conducted on a continuing basis, to account for new types of derivatives transactions and new technologies. It is important to approach these issues aggressively so that the largest risks faced by dealers and end-users are not legal risks from legal systems that have not kept pace with financial developments.

Further work on the enforceability in bankruptcy or insolvency of bilateral netting and collateral arrangements is particularly important if the credit risk reduction techniques for derivatives are to evolve. These techniques are essential building blocks for enforceable multilateral netting arrangements, if that is a direction participants choose to take.

Recommendation 23: Tax Treatment

Legislators and tax authorities are encouraged to review and, where appropriate, amend tax laws and regulations that disadvantage the use of derivatives in risk management strategies. Tax impediments include the inconsistent or uncertain tax treatment of gains and losses on the derivatives, in comparison with the gains and losses that arise from the risks being managed.

In most, if not all jurisdictions, the tax treatment being applied to derivatives transactions dates back to before they came into general use. This can lead to considerable uncertainty in determining how gains and losses associated with these instruments should be taxed depending upon their use. These uncertainties and inconsistencies present real difficulties to organizations that seek to use derivatives to manage risks in their businesses. Confusion can discourage them from pursuing commercially sensible risk management strategies.

Recommendation 24: Accounting Standards

Accounting standards-setting bodies in each country should, as a matter of priority, provide comprehensive guidance on accounting and reporting of transactions in financial instruments, including derivatives, and should work towards international harmonization of standards on this subject. Also, the International Accounting Standards Committee should finalize its accounting standard on Financial Instruments.

At present no country has accounting and reporting standards that comprehensively address all financial instruments, including derivatives. Even in those countries where development of accounting standards is considered far advanced, there are gaps or inconsistencies between different standards. This is an area where action needs to be taken as a matter of priority.

In a number of countries, accounting standards-setters have recognized the need to improve accounting standards in this area and some have commenced work. Furthermore, the International Accounting Standards Committee (IASC) has issued an exposure draft on Financial Instruments (E40) and presently intends to finalize an accounting standard by the end of 1993.

In addressing the accounting and disclosure requirements for financial instruments, the IASC and national accounting standards-setters are encouraged to address the problems of accounting for risk management activities. Most existing accounting regulations were formulated before recent advances in risk management strategies. This poses considerable practical problems, both to end-users and dealers. Developments in accounting regulations have not kept pace with changes in the way risk is managed. In some countries, the accounting standards that govern the eligibility for hedge accounting treatment of hedges of anticipated transactions may be too restrictive: some relaxation should be permitted, subject to safeguards to prevent abuse.

Similarly, accounting standards should deal with risk management in a broad sense and not deal just with risk reduction (hedging) which is only one aspect of risk management. Risk management strategies are increasingly being used by both financial and nonfinancial institutions to achieve an acceptable risk profile, but not necessarily a reduced level of risk. Concern over current accounting regulations is deterring some organizations from pursuing commercially sensible risk management strategies. While standards are necessary to ensure that risk management accounting is not abused, it is essential that accounting standards respond to modern risk management techniques.

Exchange traded Interest Rate Futures (IRF)

RBI had allowed Interest Rate Futures on a notional coupon bearing 10-year Government of India security in August'2009 and Interest Rate Futures on 91-Day Treasury Bills issued by Government of India in March'2011. The brief features of RBI directions are summarized below:

1. Interest Rate Futures means a standardised interest rate derivative contract traded on a recognized stock exchange to buy or sell a notional security or any other interest bearing instrument or an index of such instruments or interest rates at a specified future date, at a price determined at the time of the contract.
2. Interest Rate Futures are permitted on 10-year notional coupon bearing Government of India security / 91-Day Treasury Bills issued by the Government of India or any other product, as may be approved by the Reserve Bank from time to time.
3. Persons resident in India may purchase or sell Interest Rate Futures to hedge an exposure to interest rate risk or otherwise. Foreign Institutional Investors, registered with Securities and Exchange Board of India, may purchase or sell Interest Rate Futures subject to the condition that the total gross long (bought) position in cash and Interest Rate Futures markets taken together does not exceed their individual permissible limit for investment in government securities and the total gross short (sold) position, for the purpose of hedging only, does not exceed their long position in the government securities and in Interest Rate Futures at any point in time.
4. The contract shall be cash settled in Indian Rupees.

Guidelines on Credit Default Swaps (CDS) for Corporate Bonds

Reserve Bank of India (RBI) in May'2011 issued guidelines for Credit Default Swaps (CDS). These guidelines would become effective from October 24, 2011. The brief features of these guidelines are summarized as follows:

1. The objective of introducing Credit Default Swaps (CDS) on corporate bonds is to provide market participants a tool to transfer and manage credit risk in an effective manner through redistribution of risk. CDS as a risk management product offers the participants the opportunity to hive off credit risk and also to assume credit risk which otherwise may not be possible. Since CDS have benefits like enhancing

investment and borrowing opportunities and reducing transaction costs while allowing risk-transfers, such products would increase investors' interest in corporate bonds and would be beneficial to the development of the corporate bond market in India.

2. Users permitted to buy credit protection (buy CDS contracts) only to hedge their underlying credit risk on corporate bonds. Such entities are not permitted to hold credit protection without having eligible underlying as a hedged item. Users are also not permitted to sell protection and are not permitted to hold short positions in the CDS contracts. However, they are permitted to exit their bought CDS positions by unwinding them with the original counterparty or by assigning them in favour of buyer of the underlying bond. Theses entities are Commercial Banks, PDs, NBFCs, Mutual Funds, Insurance Companies, Housing Finance Companies, Provident Funds, Listed Corporates, Foreign Institutional Investors (FIIs) and any other institution.

3. Market-makers permitted to quote both buy and/or sell CDS spreads. They would be permitted to buy protection without having the underlying bond. These entities are Commercial Banks, stand alone Primary Dealers (PDs), Non-Banking Financial Companies (NBFCs).

4. CDS will be allowed only on listed corporate bonds as reference obligations. CDS can also be written on unlisted but rated bonds of infrastructure companies.

5. The credit events specified in the CDS contract may cover: Bankruptcy, Failure to pay, Repudiation/moratorium, Obligation acceleration, Obligation default, Restructuring approved under Board for Industrial and Financial Reconstruction (BIFR) and Corporate Debt Restructuring (CDR) mechanism and corporate bond restructuring. The contracting parties to a CDS may include all or any of the approved credit events.

6. The accounting norms applicable to CDS contracts shall be on the lines indicated in the 'Accounting Standard AS-30 – Financial Instruments: Recognition and Measurement', 'AS-31, Financial Instruments: Presentation' and 'AS-32 on Disclosures' as approved by the Institute of Chartered Accountants of India (ICAI).

7. Market participants shall use FIMMDA published daily CDS curve to value their CDS positions.

8. Proper assessment and management of various risks such as sudden increase in credit spreads resulting in mark-to-market losses, high incidence of credit events, Jump-to-Default Risk, basis risk, counterparty risk, etc., is essential. It needs to be ensured that CDS are not used to build up excessive leveraged exposures. The market participants need to take various risks associated with CDS into account and build robust risk management architecture to manage the same.

9. Market-makers shall report their CDS trades with both users and other market-makerson the reporting platform of CDS trade repository within 30 minutes from the deal time. The users would be required to affirm or reject their trade already reported by the market-maker by the end of the day.

Comprehensive RBI Guidelines on Derivatives

The modified guidelines on derivatives are issued by RBI in August'2011 taking a lesson from financial losses faced by corporates and banks on derivatives product buying and selling. The losses were mainly due to reasons that there were various hidden clauses in the derivative agreement, which exposed buyer to upside risk. The brief guidelines are given below:

The objective of the policy is prudential in nature to protect the market-maker against the credit, reputation and litigation risks that may arise from a user's inadequate understanding of the nature and risks of the derivatives transaction. In general, market-makers should not undertake derivative transactions with or sell structured products to users that do not have properly documented policies regarding management of risks that include among other things, guidelines on risk identification, management and control. Furthermore, structured products should be sold only to those users, which follow prudent accounting and disclosure norms and are capable of ascertaining the mark to market position of these products on an on-going basis. While selling structured products, the selling banks should make available a calculator or at least access to a calculator (say on the market maker's website) which will enable the users to mark to market these structured products on an ongoing basis. Before offering derivative products to clients, banks should obtain resolution of the Board of the corporate authorizing the concerned official of the company to undertake derivative transactions on behalf of the company. The Board resolution being submitted by the company should:

- be signed by a person other than the persons authorized to undertake the transactions;
- be specific and should articulate specific products that can be transacted;
- also mention the person(s) authorised to sign the ISDA and similar agreements;
- explicitly mention the limits assigned to a particular person; and
- specify the names of the people to whom transactions should be reported by the bank. These personnel should be distinct from those authorized to undertake the transactions.

No bank can be a market maker in a product it cannot price independently. This will also be applicable to deals undertaken on back-to-back basis. Similarly, foreign banks operating in India can be market makers for specific products only if they have the ability to price the products locally in India. The pricing of such products should be locally demonstrable at all times, particularly whenever RBI needs such evidence.

Banks are required to obtain Board resolution from the corporate that states the following:

i) The corporate has in place a Risk Management Policy approved by its Board which contains the following:

- Guidelines on risk identification, measurement and control
- Guidelines and procedures to be followed with respect to revaluation and monitoring of positions
- Names and designation of officials authorized to undertake transactions and limits

assigned to them

- A requirement that the assignment of limits to an official would be specific and in case the limits assigned are not quantified, then the bank should offer derivative products to that client only after getting appropriate documents certifying assignment of specific limits
- Accounting policy and disclosure norms to be followed in respect of derivative transactions
- A requirement to disclose the MTM valuations appropriately
- A requirement to ensure separation of duties between front, middle and back office
- Mechanism regarding reporting of data to the Board including financial position of transaction etc

ii) The corporate has laid down clear guidelines for conducting the transactions and institutionalized the arrangements for a periodical review of operations and annual audit of transactions to verify compliance with the regulations.

Summary

The regulators such as BIS have taken all important steps to establish proper risk management environment globally to shield investor's interest/lender interest in Financial Institutions and also to safeguard finance industry from adverse movements in the market. On the basis of BIS Basel Capital Accord I, RBI in India has also initiated steps to create risk awareness and management system in Indian financial institutions. On the same line, NHB also issued the guideline for ALM for Housing Finance Companies. SEBI has also made a cursory clause for listed companies regarding risk management. All these initiatives do not seem to be enough in need a detailed analysis of regulator's steps and implication of these steps in financial systems. Recently RBI has issued guidelines for exchange traded IRFs and for credit default swaps (CDS) for corporate bond. By using theses two derivative products/hedging tools, FIs will have a better risk management in the area of credit risk and interest rate risk. RBI has also issued revised comprehensive guidelines on derivative.

KEY CONCEPTS

BIS	RBI	ICAAP
BASEL II	SEBI	ALM
OTC	EWRM	Derivative Accounting

References:

1. *www.rbi.org.in*
2. *www.rbi.org.in*
3. *www.sebi.gov.in*
4. *www.nhb.org.in*
5. *www.bis.org*

Chapter – 22

Bank for International Settlement, Basel I, II & III

Chapter Objective

- Understand working of Bank for International Settlement (BIS)
- Discuss Basel I Norms
- Discuss Basel II Norms in detail
- Discuss three pillars of Basel II
- Compare Basel I and Basel II
- Development in Basel III

Introduction

The Bank for International Settlements (BIS)

The Bank for International Settlements (BIS) was established in 1930. It is the world's oldest international financial institution and remains the principal centre for international central bank cooperation. The BIS was established in the context of the Young Plan (1930), which dealt with the issue of the reparation payments imposed on Germany by the Treaty of Versailles following the First World War. The new bank was to take over the functions previously performed by the Agent General for Reparations in Berlin collection, administration and distribution of the annuities payable as reparations. The Bank's name is derived from this original role. The BIS was also created to act as a trustee for the Dawes and Young Loans (international loans issued to finance reparations) and to promote central bank cooperation in general. The reparations issue quickly faded, focusing the Bank's activities entirely on cooperation among central banks and, increasingly, other agencies in pursuit of monetary and financial stability.

In the monetary policy field, cooperation at the BIS in the immediate aftermath of the Second World War and until the early 1970s focused on implementing and defending the Bretton Woods system. In the 1970s and 1980s, the focus was on managing cross-border capital flows following the oil crises and the international debt crisis. The 1970s crisis also brought the issue of regulatory supervision of internationally active banks to the fore, resulting in the 1988 Basel Capital Accord and its "Basel II " revision of 2001-06. More recently, the issue of financial stability in the wake of economic integration and globalisation, as highlighted by the 1997 Asian crisis, has received a lot of attention.

Apart from fostering monetary policy cooperation, the BIS has always performed "traditional" banking functions for the central bank community (eg., gold and foreign exchange transactions), as well as trustee and agency functions. The BIS was the agent for the

European Payments Union (EPU, 1950-58), helping the European currencies restore convertibility after the Second World War. Similarly, the BIS had acted as the agent for various European exchange rate arrangements, including the European Monetary System (EMS, 1979-94), which preceded the move to a single currency. Finally, the BIS has also provided or organised emergency financing to support the international monetary system when needed. During the 1931-33 financial crisis, the BIS organised support credits for both the Austrian and German central banks. In the 1960s, the BIS arranged special support credits for the French franc (1968), and two so-called Group Arrangements (1966 and 1968) to support sterling. More recently, the BIS has provided finance in the context of IMF-led stabilisation programmes (eg., for Mexico in 1982 and Brazil in 1998).

The Bank for International Settlements (BIS) is an international organisation which fosters international monetary and financial cooperation and serves as a bank for central banks.

The BIS fulfils this mandate by acting as:

- a forum to promote discussion and policy analysis among central banks and within the international financial community
- a centre for economic and monetary research
- a prime counterparty for central banks in their financial transactions
- agent or trustee in connection with international financial operations

The head office is in Basel, Switzerland and there are two representative offices, one in the Hong Kong Special Administrative Region of the People's Republic of China and the other in Mexico City. Established on 17 May 1930, the BIS is the world's oldest international financial organisation.

As its customers are central banks and international organisations, the BIS does not accept deposits from, or provide financial services to, private individuals or corporate entities. The BIS strongly advises caution against fraudulent schemes. The BIS currently employs around 550 staff from 50 countries.

The Bank's most important decision-making bodies are:

- the General Meeting of member central banks;
- the Board of Directors; and
- the Executive Committee.

Besides the AGM, regular bimonthly meetings bring together the Governors of BIS member central banks, permitting them to monitor global economic and financial developments and to discuss specific policy issues relating to monetary and financial stability. Other meetings of senior central bank officials focus on the conduct of monetary policy, the surveillance of international financial markets and central bank governance issues. In addition, the BIS organises frequent meetings of experts on more technical issues such as reserve management, legal matters, IT systems and internal audit. Though targeted mostly at central banks, BIS meetings also involve senior officials and experts from other financial market authorities, the academic community and market participants.

The economic, monetary, financial and legal research of the BIS supports its meetings and the activities of the Basel-based committees. The BIS is also a hub for sharing statistical information amongst central banks and for publishing statistics on global banking, securities, foreign exchange and derivatives markets. Through its seminars, conferences, web-based information resource tool (FSI Connect) and other activities, the FSI promotes the dissemination and implementation of sound supervisory standards.

Bank for Central Banks

The BIS offers a wide range of financial services specifically designed to assist central banks and other monetary authorities in the management of their foreign exchange reserves. As of 31 March 2007, some 130 such authorities, as well as a number of international institutions made use of BIS financial services. Total currency deposits amounted to nearly SDR 222 billion, representing around 6% of world foreign exchange reserves. BIS financial services are provided out of two linked trading rooms: one at its Basel head office and one at its Representative Office for Asia and the Pacific in Hong Kong SAR.The BIS does not accept deposits from, or provide financial services to, private individuals or corporate entities, nor is it permitted to make advances to governments or open current accounts in their name.

The BIS continually adapts its product range to respond to the evolving needs of central banks. Besides standard services such as sight/notice accounts and fixed-term deposits, the Bank has developed a range of financial products which central banks can actively trade with the BIS to increase the return on their foreign assets. The BIS offers asset management services in sovereign securities or high-grade assets. These may be either a specific portfolio mandate negotiated between the BIS and a central bank or an open-end fund structure, the BIS Investment Pool (BISIP) allowing customers to invest in a common pool of assets. The BIS sometimes grants short-term credits to central banks, usually on a collateralised basis. It also acts as a trustee for a number of international government loans and performs collateral agent functions. Several committees and organisations focusing on monetary and financial stability and the international financial system have secretariats at the BIS and interact closely with the Bank. Those which were set up by the Group of Ten central bank Governors are the Basel Committee on Banking Supervision, the Committee on Payment and Settlement Systems, the Committee on the Global Financial System and the Markets Committee. Four other secretariats operate out of the BIS: those of the Financial Stability Forum, the International Association of Deposit Insurers, the International Association of Insurance Supervisors, and the Irving Fisher Committee on Central Bank Statistics.[1]

BASEL I

Basel Committee on Banking Supervision: International Convergence of Capital Measurement and Capital Standards[2]

In this report, the outcome of the Committee's work over several years to secure international convergence of supervisory regulations governing the capital adequacy of international banks was presented. The framework and standard had been endorsed by the Group of Ten central-bank Governors. Two fundamental objectives lay at the heart of the Committee's work on regulatory convergence. These were, firstly, that the new framework should serve to strengthen the soundness and stability of the international banking system and secondly that the framework should be in fair and have a high degree of consistency in its application to banks in different countries with a view to diminishing an existing source of competitive inequality among international banks. The Basel Committee on Banking Supervision comprises representatives of the central banks and supervisory authorities of the Group of Ten countries (Belgium, Canada, France, Germany, Italy, Japan, Netherlands, Sweden, Switzerland, United Kingdom, United States) and Luxembourg. In developing the framework described in this document, the Committee had sought to arrive at a set of principles which are conceptually sound and at the same time pay due regard to particular features of the present supervisory and accounting systems in individual member countries.

It emphasised that capital adequacy as measured by the present framework, though important, is one of a number of factors to be taken into account when assessing the strength of banks. The framework in this document was mainly directed towards assessing capital in relation to credit risk (the risk of counterparty failure) but other risks, notably interest rate risk and the investment risk on securities, need to be taken into account by supervisors in assessing overall capital adequacy. This agreement was intended to be applied to banks on a consolidated basis, including subsidiaries undertaking banking and financial business.

This document was divided into four sections. The first two described the framework: Section I the constituents of capital and Section II the risk weighting system. Section III dealt with the target standard ratio and Section IV with transitional and implementing arrangements.

I. The constituents of capital

(a) Core capital (basic equity)

The Committee considers that the key element of capital on which the main emphasis should be placed is equity capital and disclosed reserves. The Committee had concluded that capital, for supervisory purposes, should be defined in two tiers in a way which will have the effect of requiring at least 50% of a bank's capital base to consist of a core element comprised of equity capital and published reserves from post-tax retained earnings (tier 1). The other elements of capital supplementary capital) will be admitted into tier 2 up to an amount equal to that of the core capital.

(b) Supplementary capital

(i) ***Undisclosed reserves:*** Unpublished or hidden reserves may be constituted in various ways according to differing legal and accounting regimes in member countries.

(ii) ***Revaluation reserves:*** Some countries, under their national regulatory or accounting arrangements, allow certain assets to be revalued to reflect their current value, or something closer to their current value than historic cost, and the resultant revaluation reserves to be included in the capital base. Such reserves may be included within supplementary capital provided that the assets are considered by the supervisory authority to be prudently valued, fully reflecting the possibility of price fluctuations and forced sale.

(iii) ***General provisions/general loan-loss reserves:*** General provisions or general loan-loss reserves are created against the possibility of future losses, where they are not ascribed to particular assets and do not reflect a reduction in the valuation of particular assets, these reserves qualify for inclusion in capital and it has been agreed that they should be counted within tier 2.

(iv) ***Hybrid debt capital instruments***: In this category, a number of capital instruments fall which combine certain characteristics of equity and certain characteristics of debt.

(v) ***Subordinated term debt:*** Subordinated term debt instruments have significant deficiencies as constituents of capital in view of their fixed maturity and inability to absorb losses except in a liquidation. These deficiencies justify an additional restriction on the amount of such debt capital which is eligible for inclusion within the capital base. Consequently, it was concluded that subordinated term debt instruments with a minimum original term to maturity of over five years may be included within the supplementary elements of capital, but only to a maximum of 50% of the core capital element and subject to adequate amortisation arrangements.

(c) Deductions from capital

It was concluded that the following deductions should be made from the capital base for the purpose of calculating the risk-weighted capital ratio. The deductions will consist of:

(i) goodwill, as a deduction from tier 1 capital elements;

(ii) investments in subsidiaries engaged in banking and financial activities which are not consolidated in national systems. The deduction for such investments will be made against the total capital base.

II. The risk weights

The Committee considered that a weighted risk ratio in which capital is related to different categories of asset or off-balance-sheet exposure, weighted according to broad categories of relative riskiness, was the preferred method for assessing the capital adequacy of banks. The framework of weights was kept as simple as possible and only five weights were used – 0%, 10%, 20%, 50% and 100%.

(i) Categories of risk captured in the framework

There were many different kinds of risks against which banks' managements need to guard. For most banks, the major risk is *credit risk*, that is to say the risk of counterparty failure, but there are many other kinds of risk - for example, investment risk, interest rate risk, exchange rate risk, and concentration risk. The central focus of this framework was credit risk and, as a further aspect of credit risk, country transfer risk. It was concluded that individual supervisory authorities should be free to apply either a zero *or* a low weight to claims on governments (e.g. 10% for all securities or 10% for those maturing in under one year and 20% for one year and over).

(ii) Country transfer risk

In addressing country transfer risk, the Committee was very conscious of the difficulty of devising a satisfactory method for incorporating country transfer risk into the framework of measurement. In its earlier consultative paper, two alternative approaches were put forward for consideration and comment. These were, firstly, a simple differentiation between claims on domestic institutions (central government, official sector and banks) and claims on all foreign countries and secondly, differentiation on the basis of an approach involving the selection of a defined grouping of countries considered to be of high credit standing.

(iii) Claims on non-central-government, public-sector entities (PSEs)

The Committee concluded that it was not possible to settle on a single common weight that can be applied to all claims on domestic public-sector entities below the level of central government (e.g. states. local authorities, etc.) in view of the special character and varying creditworthiness of these entities in different member countries. The Committee therefore opted to allow discretion to each national supervisory authority to determine the appropriate weighting factors for the PSEs within that country. In order to preserve a degree of convergence in the application of such discretion, the Committee agreed that the weights ascribed in this way should be 0%, 10%, 20%, or 50% for domestic PSEs, but that PSEs in foreign countries within the OECD should attract a standard 20% weight. Commercial companies owned by the public sector will attract a uniform weight of 100% inter alia in order to avoid competitive inequality vis-à-vis similar private-sector commercial enterprises.

(iv) Collateral and guarantees

The framework recognised the importance of collateral in reducing credit risk, but only to a limited extent. In view of the varying practices among banks in different countries for taking collateral and different experiences of the stability of physical or financial collateral values, it was not found possible to develop a basis for recognising collateral generally in the weighting system. The more limited recognition of collateral will apply only to loans secured against cash or against securities issued by OECD central governments and specified multilateral development banks. These will attract the weight given to the collateral (i.e. a zero or low weight).

(v) Loans secured on residential property

Loans fully secured by mortgage on occupied residential property have a very low record of loss in most countries. The framework recognised this by assigning a 50% weight to loans fully secured by mortgage on residential property which was rented or is (or is intended to be) occupied by the borrower.

(vi) Off-balance-sheet engagements

The Committee believed that it was of great importance that all off-balance-sheet activity should be caught within the capital adequacy framework. The different instruments and techniques are divided into five broad categories:

(a) those which substitute for loans (e.g. general guarantees of indebtedness, bank acceptance guarantees and standby letters of credit serving as financial guarantees for loans and securities) - these will carry a 100% credit risk conversion factor;

(b) certain transaction-related contingencies (e.g. performance bonds, bid bonds, warranties and standby letters of credit related to particular transactions) - a 50% credit risk conversion factor;

(c) short-term, self-liquidating trade-related contingent liabilities arising from the movement of goods (e.g. documentary credits collateralised by the underlying shipments) - a 20% credit risk conversion factor;

(d) commitments with an original maturity exceeding one year (the longer maturity serving broadly as a proxy for higher risk facilities) and all NIFs and RUFs - a 50% credit risk conversion factor. Shorter-term commitments or commitments which can be unconditionally cancelled at any time, it was agreed, generally carry only low risk and a nil weight for these was considered to be justified on deminimis grounds;

(e) interest and exchange rate related items (e.g. swaps, options, futures) - the credit risk equivalent amount for these contracts will be calculated saperately.

III. A target standard ratio

The Committee decided that the target standard ratio of capital to weighted risk assets should be set at 8% (of which the core capital element will be at least 4%).

Definition of capital included in the capital base (Applied at end-1992)

A. Capital elements

Tier 1 (a) Paid-up share capital/common stock

(b) Disclosed reserves

Tier 2 (a) Undisclosed reserves

(b) Asset revaluation reserves

(c) General provisions/general loan-loss reserves

(d) Hybrid (debt/equity) capital instruments

(e) Subordinated debt

The sum of tier 1 and tier 2 elements will be eligible for inclusion in the capital base, subject to the following limits.

B. Limits and restrictions

(i) The total of tier 2 (supplementary) elements will be limited to a maximum of 100% of the total of tier 1 elements;

(ii) Subordinated term debt will be limited to a maximum of 50% of tier 1 elements;

(iii) Where general provisions/general loan-loss reserves include amounts reflecting lower valuations of asset or latent but unidentified losses present in the balance sheet, the amount of such provisions or reserves will be limited to a maximum of 1.25 percentage points, or exceptionally and temporarily up to 2.0 percentage points, of risk assets;

(iv) Asset revaluation reserves which take the form of latent gains on unrealised securities will be subject to a discount of 55%.

C. Deductions from the capital base

From tier 1: Goodwill

From total capital:

(i) Investments in unconsolidated banking and financial subsidiary companies.

(ii) Investments in the capital of other banks and financial institutions (at the discretion of national authorities).

D. Definition of capital elements

(i) **Tier 1**: includes only *permanent shareholders' equity* (issued and fully paid ordinary shares/common stock and perpetual non-cumulative preference shares) and *disclosed reserves* (created or increased by appropriations of retained earnings or other surplus, e.g. share premiums, retained profit, general reserves and legal reserves). In the case of consolidated accounts, this also includes minority interests in the equity of subsidiaries which are less than wholly owned. This basic definition of capital excludes revaluation reserves and cumulative preference shares.

(ii) **Tier 2:**

(a) Undisclosed reserves

(b) Revaluation reserves

(c) General provisions/general loan-loss reserves

(d) Hybrid (debt/equity) capital instruments

(e) Subordinated term debt

Risk weights by category of on-balance-sheet asset

0%	(a)	Cash
	(b)	Claims on central governments and central banks denominated in national currency and funded in that currency
0, 10, 20 or 50% (at national discretion)	(a)	Claims on domestic public-sector entities, excluding central government, and loans guaranteed by such entities
20%	(a)	Claims on multilateral development banks (IBRD, IADB, AsDB, AfDB, EIB) and claims guaranteed by, or collateralised by securities issued by such banks
	(b)	Claims on banks incorporated in the OECD and loans guaranteed by OECD incorporated banks
	(c)	Claims on banks incorporated in countries outside the OECD with a residual maturity of up to one year and loans with a residual maturity of up to one year guaranteed by banks incorporated in countries outside the OECD
	(d)	Claims on non-domestic OECD public-sector entities, excluding central government, and loans guaranteed by such entities
	(e)	Cash items in process of collection
50%	(a)	Loans fully secured by mortgage on residential property that is or will be occupied by the borrower or that is rented
100%	(a)	Claims on the private sector
	(b)	Claims on banks incorporated outside the OECD with a residual maturity of over one year
	(c)	Claims on central governments outside the OECD
	(d)	Claims on commercial companies owned by the public sector
	(e)	Premises, plant and equipment and other fixed assets
	(f)	Real estate and other investments (including non-consolidated investment participations in other companies)
	(g)	Capital instruments issued by other banks (unless deducted from capital)
	(h)	All other assets

Credit conversion factors for off-balance-sheet items

The framework takes account of the credit risk on off-balance-sheet exposures by applying credit conversion factors to the different types of off-balance-sheet instrument or transaction. With the exception of foreign exchange and interest rate related contingencies, the credit conversion factors are given below:

	Instruments	Credit conversion factors
1.	Direct credit substitutes, e.g. general guarantees of indebtedness (including standby letters of credit serving as financial guarantees for loans and securities) and acceptances (including endorsements with the character of acceptances)	100%
2.	Certain transaction-related contingent items (e.g. performance bonds, bid bonds, warranties and standby letters of credit related to particular transactions)	50%
3.	Short-term self-liquidating trade-related contingencies (such as documentary credits collateralised by the underlying shipments)	20%
4.	Sale and repurchase agreements and asset sales with recourse, where the credit risk remains with the bank	100%
5.	Forward asset purchases, forward forward deposits and partly-paid shares and securities,which represent commitments with certain drawdown	100%
6.	Note issuance facilities and revolving underwriting facilities	50%
7.	Other commitments (e.g. formal standby facilities and credit lines) with an original maturity of over one year	50%
8.	Similar commitments with an original maturity of up to one year, or which can be unconditionally cancelled at any time	0%

BASEL II

International Convergence of Capital Measurement and Capital Standards: A Revised Framework[3]

Introduction

This report presents the outcome of the Basel Committee on Banking Supervision's work over recent years to secure international convergence on revisions to supervisory regulations governing the capital adequacy of internationally active banks. This Framework and the standard it contains have been endorsed by the Central Bank Governors and Heads of Banking Supervision of the Group of Ten countries. The Framework is available for implementation from the year-end 2006. This document has been circulated to supervisory authorities worldwide with a view to encouraging them to consider adopting this revised Framework at such time as they believe is consistent with their broader supervisory priorities.

The Committee has also retaining key elements of the 1988 capital adequacy framework, including the general requirement for banks to hold total capital equivalent to at least 8% of their risk-weighted assets; the basic structure of the 1996 Market Risk Amendment regarding the treatment of market risk; and the definition of eligible capital. A significant innovation of the revised Framework is the greater use of assessments of risk provided by banks' internal systems as inputs to capital calculations. The revised Framework provides a range of options for determining the capital requirements for credit risk and operational risk to allow banks and supervisors to select approaches that are most appropriate for their operations and their financial market infrastructure.

The revised Framework is more risk sensitive than the 1988 Accord. In this report the need for banks and supervisors to give appropriate attention to the second (supervisory review) and third (market discipline) pillars of the revised Framework has been stressed upon. It is critical that the minimum capital requirements of the first pillar be accompanied by a robust implementation of the second, including efforts by banks to assess their capital adequacy and by supervisors to review such assessments. In addition, the disclosures provided under the third pillar of this Framework will be essential in ensuring that market discipline is an effective complement to the other two pillars.

Scope of Application

This Framework will be applied on a consolidated basis to internationally active banks. The scope of application of the Framework will include, on a fully consolidated basis, any holding company that is the parent entity within a banking group to ensure that it captures the risk of the whole banking group. The Framework will also apply to all internationally active banks at every tier within a banking group. A three-year transitional period for applying full sub-consolidation will be provided for those countries where this is not currently a requirement. The Basel II is also to be implemented in Indian banks by 31st March, 2008 for those banks who has international presence and for other banks they have to adopt Basel II by 31st March, 2009.

Basel II and its Basic Architecture

Even though India has one of the strongest banking systems compared to many peer group countries, our credit, market and operational risk measurement and management system is lagging behind the banks of many developed countries. Basel II implementation will certainly improve the working efficiency and competitiveness of Indian banks. Basel II provides a more comprehensive and flexible approach for measuring and managing risk. It adds a new dimension called operational risk and encourages the bank's internal risk management methodologies. The new accord is based on three pillars:

a. Pillar 1: Minimum Capital Requirement

The minimum capital requirement is still kept at 8% of risk weighted assets. This lays emphasis on regulatory requirement for credit, market and operational risk.

$$\text{Capital adequacy ratio} = \frac{\text{Total Regulatory capital Tier I + Tier II + Tier III}}{\text{Risk weighted assets (Credit + Market + Operational)}}$$

To deal with the credit risk, Basel II suggests the following approaches:

- Standardized approach
- Foundation Internal Rating Based (IRB) approach
- Advanced Internal Rating Based (IRB) approach

The first approach requires allocation of risk weight to each of the assets. Bank may use external credit assessment institutions for determining risk weights. The latter two approaches require assessment by banks internally using sophisticated models.

b. Pillar 2: Supervisory Review

The supervisory review process needs to ensure that each financial institution adopts effective internal processes for risk management. The supervisory process is based on the following principles. Banks should have:

- A process for assessing the capital adequacy based on the risk profile
- Strategy for maintaining the capital levels
- A system to evaluate and monitor the capital requirement and ensure compliance
- Mechanism to intervene, prevent at early stage, the capital from falling below the minimum levels.

c. Pillar 3: Market Discipline

This pillar emphasises the basic need of corporate governance and effective use of market discipline by enhanced disclosure. The comparison of Basel I with the enhanced Basel II standard is given in the following table.

Basel I	Basel II
Focused on single risk measure	More emphasis on bank's own internal risk management methodologies, supervisory review and market discipline
One-size-fits- all	Flexibility; menu of approaches; capital incentive for better risk management; granularity in the valuation of assets and type of business and in the risk profile of their systems and operations
Broad brush structure	More risk sensitive; multi-dimensional; focus on all operationa components of banks

Table : Comparison of Basel I and Basel II standards

The key difference of the new accord is the introduction of operational risk. This is not a new practice. However, the growing number of operational loss events worldwide has forced the management of the banks to look into this aspect more critically to prevent any frauds, reduce errors by implementing controls as a part of operating process. Evolving banking practices suggest that the risk other than credit and market risks can be substantial. The importance of operational risk has increased due to the following changes in operation and introduction of sophisticated methods and technology:

a. Highly automated technology, if uncontrolled, can cause system failure. The loss may be much more as compared to manual system.

b. Emergence of e-banking and e-commerce has potential for internal, external fraud and system securities issues. This needs sound internal controls and back up systems.

c. Large-scale acquisitions, mergers and consolidations test the viability of integrated system and HR practices.

Basel committee has identified the following types of operational risks:

- People Risk – connected with placement, competency, work environment and motivation
- Process Risk – connected with errors in processing, complexity of process, documentation and contract, violation of controls, money laundering, frauds, model and methodology errors
- Regulatory risk – connected with failing to comply with laws
- Technology risk – connected with sys- tem and technology failure
- Event Risk – unanticipated changes in external environment
- Reputation Risk

The First Pillar – Minimum Capital Requirements

Calculation of minimum capital requirements

Regulatory capital

Under the first pillar, the calculation of the total minimum capital requirements for credit, market and operational risk has been detailed. The capital ratio is calculated using the definition of regulatory capital and risk-weighted assets. The total capital ratio must be no lower than 8%. Tier 2 capital is limited to 100% of Tier 1 capital. Total risk-weighted assets are determined by multiplying the capital requirements for market risk and operational risk by 12.5 (i.e. the reciprocal of the minimum capital ratio of 8%) and adding the resulting figures to the sum of risk-weighted assets for credit risk.

The Constituents of Capital

Core capital (basic equity or Tier 1)

The key element of capital on which the main emphasis should be placed is equity capital and disclosed reserves. The capital, for supervisory purposes, should be defined in two tiers in a way which will have the effect of requiring at least 50% of a bank's capital base to consist of a core element comprised of equity capital and published reserves from post-tax retained earnings (Tier 1). The other elements of capital (supplementary capital) will be admitted into Tier 2 limited to 100% of Tier 1.

Supplementary capital (Tier 2)

Undisclosed reserves

Unpublished or hidden reserves may be constituted in various ways according to differing legal and accounting regimes in member countries. Under this heading are included only reserves which, though unpublished, have been passed through the profit and loss account and which are accepted by the bank's supervisory authorities.

Revaluation reserves

Some countries, under their national regulatory or accounting arrangements, allow certain assets to be revalued to reflect their current value, or something closer to their current value than historic cost, and the resultant revaluation reserves to be included in the capital base.

General provisions/general loan-loss reserves

General provisions or general loan-loss reserves are created against the possibility of losses not yet identified. Where they do not reflect a known deterioration in the valuation of particular assets, these reserves qualify for inclusion in Tier 2 capital.

Hybrid debt capital instruments

In this category fall a number of capital instruments which combine certain characteristics of equity and certain characteristics of debt.

Subordinated term debt

Subordinated term debt instruments with a minimum original term to maturity of over five years may be included within the supplementary elements of capital, but only to a maximum of 50% of the core capital element and subject to adequate amortisation arrangements.

Short-term subordinated debt covering market risk (Tier 3)

Banks may also, at the discretion of their national authority, employ a third tier of capital ("Tier 3"), consisting of short-term subordinated debt for the *sole* purpose of meeting a proportion of the capital requirements for market risks. Tier 3 capital will be limited to 250% of a bank's Tier 1 capital that is required to support market risks. This means that a minimum of about 28½% of market risks needs to be supported by Tier 1 capital. Tier 2 elements may be substituted for Tier 3 up to the same limit of 250% in so far as the overall limits are not breached, that is to say eligible Tier 2 capital may not exceed total Tier 1 capital, and long-term subordinated debt may not exceed 50% of Tier 1 capital.

Deductions from capital

The following deductions should be made from the capital base for the purpose of calculating the risk-weighted capital ratio. The deductions will consist of:

(i) Goodwill as a deduction from Tier 1 capital elements

(ii) Increase in equity capital resulting from a securitisation exposure, as a deduction from Tier 1 capital elements,

(iii) Investments in subsidiaries engaged in banking and financial activities which are not consolidated in national systems. The assets representing the investments in subsidiary companies whose capital had been deducted from that of the parent would not be included in total assets for the purposes of computing the ratio.

Credit Risk – The Standardised Approach

The Basel II permits banks a choice between two broad methodologies for calculating their capital requirements for credit risk. One alternative, the Standardised Approach, will be to measure credit risk in a standardised manner, supported by external credit assessments. The other alternative, the Internal Ratings-based Approach, which is subject to the explicit approval of the bank's supervisor, would allow banks to use their internal rating systems for credit risk.

The various risk weight assigned to different exposure are as follows:

A. Individual claims

1. Claims on sovereigns

Claims on sovereigns and their central banks will be risk weighted as follows:

Credit Assessment	AAA to AA-	A+ to A-	BBB+ to BBB-	BB+ to B-	Below B-	Unrated
Risk Weight	0%	20%	50%	100%	150%	100%

2. *Claims on non-central government public sector entities (PSEs)*

Claims on PSEs will be risk-weighted at national discretion, according to either option 1 or option domestic 2 for claims on banks. When option 2 is selected, it is to be applied without the use of the preferential treatment for short-term claims.

3. *Claims on multilateral development banks (MDBs)*

The risk weights applied to claims on MDBs will generally be based on external credit assessments as set out under option 2 for claims on banks but without the possibility of using the preferential treatment for short-term claims. A 0% risk weight will be applied to claims on highly rated MDBs.

4. *Claims on banks*

There are two options for claims on banks. National supervisors will apply one option to all banks in their jurisdiction. No claim on an unrated bank may receive a risk weight lower than that applied to claims on its sovereign of incorporation.

Under the first option, all banks incorporated in a given country will be assigned a risk weight one category less favourable than that assigned to claims on the sovereign of that country. However, for claims on banks in countries with sovereigns rated BB+ to B- and on banks in unrated countries the risk weight will be capped at 100%.

The second option bases the risk weighting on the external credit assessment of the bank itself with claims on unrated banks being risk-weighted at 50%. Under this option, a preferential risk weight that is one category more favourable may be applied to claims with an original maturity of three months or less, subject to a floor of 20%. This treatment will be available to both rated and unrated banks, but not to banks risk weighted at 150%.

The two options are summarised in the tables below.

Option 1

Credit assessment of Sovereign	**AAA to AA-**	**A+ to A-**	**BBB+ to BBB-**	**BB+ to B-**	**Below B-**	**Unrated**
Risk weight under Option 1	20%	50%	100%	100%	150%	100%

Option 2

Credit assessment of Banks	**AAA to AA-**	**A+ to A-**	**BBB+ to BBB-**	**BB+ to B-**	**Below B-**	**Unrated**
Risk weight under Option 2	20%	50%	50%	100%	150%	50%
Risk weight for short-term claims under Option 2	20%	20%	20%	50%	150%	20%

5. *Claims on corporates*

The table provided below illustrates the risk weighting of rated corporate claims, including claims on insurance companies. The standard risk weight for unrated claims on corporates will be 100%. No claim on an unrated corporate may be given a risk weight preferential to that assigned to its sovereign of incorporation.

Credit assessment	AAA to AA-	A+ to A-	BBB+ to BB-	Below BB-	Unrated
Risk weight	20%	50%	100%	150%	100%

6. *Claims included in the regulatory retail portfolios*

Claims on retail portfolio may be risk-weighted at 75%, Claim secured by residential property may be risk weigthed at 35%. Claim secured by commercial real estate may be risk weighted by 100%.

The standardised approach credit risk mitigation

Banks use a number of techniques to mitigate the credit risks to which they are exposed. For example, exposures may be collateralised by first priority claims, in whole or in part with cash or securities, a loan exposure may be guaranteed by a third party, or a bank may buy a credit derivative to offset various forms of credit risk. Additionally banks may agree to net loans owed to them against deposits from the same counterparty.

III. Credit Risk – The Internal Ratings-Based Approach

A. Overview

The Framework describes the IRB approach to credit risk. Subject to certain minimum conditions and disclosure requirements, banks that have received supervisory approval to use the IRB approach may rely on their own internal estimates of risk components in determining the capital requirement for a given exposure. The risk components include measures of the probability of default (PD), loss given default (LGD), the exposure at default (EAD), and effective maturity (M). In some cases, banks may be required to use a supervisory value as opposed to an internal estimate for one or more of the risk components. The IRB approach is based on measures of unexpected losses (UL) and expected losses (EL). The risk-weight functions produce capital requirements for the UL portion. Under the IRB approach, banks must categorise banking-book exposures into broad classes of assets with different underlying risk characteristics, subject to the definitions set out below. The classes of assets are (a) corporate, (b) sovereign, (c) bank, (d) retail, and (e) equity.

Foundation and advanced approaches

For each of the asset classes covered under the IRB framework, there are three key elements:

- Risk components — estimates of risk parameters provided by banks some of which are supervisory estimates.
- Risk-weight functions — the means by which risk components are transformed into risk-weighted assets and therefore capital requirements.
- Minimum requirements — the minimum standards that must be met in order for a bank to use the IRB approach for a given asset class.

Under the foundation approach, banks must provide their own estimates of PD associated with each of their borrower grades, but must use supervisory estimates for the other relevant risk components. The other risk components are LGD, EAD and M. Under the advanced approach, banks must calculate the effective maturity (M) and provide their own estimates of PD, LGD and EAD.

Credit Risk — Securitisation Framework

Banks must apply the securitisation framework for determining regulatory capital requirements on exposures arising from traditional and synthetic securitisations or similar structures that contain features common to both. Since securitisations may be structured in many different ways, the capital treatment of a securitisation exposure must be determined on the basis of its economic substance rather than its legal form. Similarly, supervisors will look to the economic substance of a transaction to determine whether it should be subject to the securitisation framework for purposes of determining regulatory capital. Banks are encouraged to consult with their national supervisors when there is uncertainty about whether a given transaction should be considered a securitisation. For example, transactions involving cash flows from real estate (e.g. rents) may be considered specialised lending exposures, if warranted.

A *traditional securitisation* is a structure where the cash flow from an underlying pool of exposures is used to service at least two different stratified risk positions or tranches reflecting different degrees of credit risk. Payments to the investors depend upon the performance of the specified underlying exposures, as opposed to being derived from an obligation of the entity originating those exposures. The stratified/tranched structures that characterise securitisations differ from ordinary senior/subordinated debt instruments in that junior securitisation tranches can absorb losses without interrupting contractual payments to more senior tranches, whereas subordination in a senior/subordinated debt structure is a matter of priority of rights to the proceeds of liquidation.

A *synthetic securitisation* is a structure with at least two different stratified risk positions or tranches that reflect different degrees of credit risk where credit risk of an underlying pool of exposures is transferred, in whole or in part, through the use of funded (e.g. credit-linked notes) or unfunded (e.g. credit default swaps) credit derivatives or guarantees that serve to hedge the credit risk of the portfolio. Accordingly, the investors' potential risk is dependent upon the performance of the underlying pool.

Banks' Securitisation exposures can include but are not restricted to the following: asset-backed securities, mortgage-backed securities, credit enhancements, liquidity facilities, interest rate or currency swaps, credit derivatives and tranched. Reserve accounts, such as cash collateral accounts, recorded as an asset by the originating bank must also be treated as securitisation exposures.

Operational requirements for the recognition of risk transference

The following operational requirements are applicable to both the standardised and IRB approaches of the securitisation framework.

1. Operational requirements for traditional securitisations

An originating bank may exclude securitised exposures from the calculation of risk- weighted assets only if all of the following conditions have been met. Banks meeting these conditions must still hold regulatory capital against any securitisation exposures they retain.

(a) Significant credit risk associated with the securitised exposures has been transferred to third parties.

(b) The transferor does not maintain effective or indirect control over the transferred exposures. The assets are legally isolated from the transferor in such a way (e.g. through the sale of assets or through subparticipation) that the exposures are put beyond the reach of the transferor and its creditors, even in bankruptcy or receivership.

(c) The securities issued are not obligations of the transferor. Thus, investors who purchase the securities only have claim to the underlying pool of exposures.

(d) The transferee is an SPV and the holders of the beneficial interests in that entity have the right to pledge or exchange them without restriction.

2. Operational requirements for synthetic securitisations

For synthetic securitisations, the use of CRM techniques (i.e. collateral, guarantees and credit derivatives) for hedging the underlying exposure may be recognised for risk-based capital purposes only if the conditions outlined below are satisfied:

(a) Credit risk mitigants must comply with the requirements.

(b) Eligible collateral pledged by SPVs may be recognised.

(c) Banks may not recognise SPVs as eligible guarantors in the securitisation framework.

(d) Banks must transfer significant credit risk associated with the underlying exposure to third parties.

(e) The instruments used to transfer credit risk may not contain terms or conditions that limit the amount of credit risk transferred.

Treatment of securitisation exposures

Calculation of capital requirements

Banks are required to hold regulatory capital against all of their securitisation exposures, including those arising from the provision of credit risk mitigants to a securitisation transaction, investments in asset-backed securities, retention of a subordinated tranche, and extension of a liquidity facility or credit enhancement, as set forth in the following sections. Repurchased securitisation exposures must be treated as retained securitisation exposures.

Deduction

Then a bank is required to deduct a securitisation exposure from regulatory capital, the deduction must be taken 50% from Tier 1 and 50% from Tier 2. Credit enhancing I/Os (net of the amount that must be deducted from Tier 1) are deducted 50% from Tier 1 and 50% from Tier 2. Deductions from capital may be calculated net of any specific provisions taken against the relevant securitisation exposures. Banks must deduct from Tier 1 any increase in equity capital resulting from a securitisation transaction, such as that associated with expected future margin income (FMI) resulting in a gain-on-sale that is recognised in regulatory capital. Such an increase in capital is referred to as a "gain-on-sale" for the purposes of the securitisation framework.

The risk-weighted asset amount of a securitisation exposure is computed by multiplying the amount of the position by the appropriate risk weight determined in accordance with the following tables. For off-balance sheet exposures, banks must apply a CCF and then risk weight the resultant credit equivalent amount. If such an exposure is rated, a CCF of 100% must be applied.

Long-term rating category

External Credit Assessment	AAA to AA-	A+ to A-	BBB+ to BBB-	BB+ to BB-	B+ and below or unrated
Risk Weight	20%	50%	100%	350%	Deduction

Short-term rating category

External Credit Assessment	A-1/P-1	A-2/P-2	A-3/P-3	All other ratings or unrated
Risk Weight	20%	50%	100%	Deduction

V. Operational Risk

Operational risk is defined as the risk of loss resulting from inadequate or failed internal processes, people and systems or from external events. This definition includes legal risk, but excludes strategic and reputational risk.

The measurement methodologies

The framework presents three methods for calculating operational risk capital charges in a continuum of increasing sophistication and risk sensitivity: (i) the Basic Indicator Approach; (ii) the Standardised Approach; and (iii) Advanced Measurement Approaches (AMA). Banks are encouraged to move along the spectrum of available approaches as they develop more sophisticated operational risk measurement systems and practices. Internationally active banks and banks with significant operational risk exposures (for example, specialised processing banks) are expected to use an approach that is more sophisticated than the Basic Indicator Approach and that is appropriate for the risk profile of the institution. A bank will not be allowed to choose to revert to a simpler approach once it has been approved for a more advanced approach without supervisory approval.

1. The Basic Indicator Approach

Banks using the Basic Indicator Approach must hold capital for operational risk equal to the average over the previous three years of a fixed percentage (denoted alpha) of positive annual gross income. Figures for any year in which annual gross income is negative or zero should be excluded from both the numerator and denominator when calculating the average. The charge may be expressed as follows:

$$K_{BIA} = [\Sigma (GI_{1.....n} \times \alpha)] / n$$

where:

K_{BIA}	=	the capital charge under the Basic Indicator Approach
GI	=	annual gross income, where positive, over the previous three years
n	=	number of the previous three years for which gross income is positive
α	=	15%, which is set by the Committee, relating the industry wide level of required capital to the industry wide level of the indicator

Gross income is defined as net interest income plus net non-interest income.

2. The Standardised Approach

In the Standardised Approach, banks activities are divided into eight business lines: corporate finance, trading & sales, retail banking, commercial banking, payment & settlement, agency services, asset management, and retail brokerage. The business lines are defined in detail below:

Business Lines

Level 1	Level 2	Activity Groups
Corporate Finance	Corporate Finance	Mergers and acquisitions, underwriting, privatisations, securitisation, research, debt (government, high yield), equity, syndications, IPO, secondary private placements
	Municipal/ Government Finance	
	Merchant Banking	
	Advisory Services	
Trading & Sales	Sales	Fixed income, equity, foreign exchanges, commodities, credit, funding, own position securities, lending and repos, brokerage, debt, prime brokerage
	Market Making	
	Proprietary Positions	
	Treasury	
Retail Banking	Retail Banking	Retail lending and deposits, banking services, trust
	Private Banking	Private lending and deposits, banking services, trust and estates, investment advice
	Card Services	Merchant/commercial/corporate cards, private labels and retail
Commercial Banking	Commercial Banking	Project finance, real estate, export finance, trade finance, factoring, leasing, lending, guarantees, bills of exchange
Payment and Settlement	External Clients	Payments and collections, funds transfer, clearing and settlement
Agency Services	Custody	Escrow, depository receipts, securities lending (customers) corporate actions
	Corporate Agency	Issuer and paying agents
	Corporate Trust	
Asset Management	Discretionary Fund Management	Pooled, segregated, retail, institutional, closed, open, private equity
	Non-Discretionary Fund Management	Pooled, segregated, retail, institutional, closed, open
Retail Brokerage	Retail Brokerage	Execution and full service

Within each business line, gross income is a broad indicator that serves as a proxy for the scale of business operations and thus the likely scale of operational risk exposure within each of these business lines. The capital charge for each business line is calculated by multiplying gross income by a factor (denoted beta) assigned to that business line. Beta serves as a proxy for the industry-wide relationship between the operational risk loss experience for a given business line and the aggregate level of gross income for that business line. It should be noted that in the Standardised Approach gross income is measured for each business line, not the whole institution, i.e. in corporate finance, the indicator is the gross income generated in the corporate finance business line. The total capital charge is calculated as the three-year average of the simple summation of the regulatory capital charges across each of the business lines in each year. In any given year, negative capital charges (resulting from negative gross income) in any business line may offset positive capital charges in other business lines without limit.

However, where the aggregate capital charge across all business lines within a given year is negative, then the input to the numerator for that year will be zero. The total capital charge may be expressed as:

$$K_{TSA} = \{\Sigma_{\text{years } 1\text{-}3} \max[\Sigma (GI_{1\text{-}8} \times \beta_{1\text{-}8}), 0]\} / 3$$

where:

K_{TSA} = the capital charge under the Standardised Approach

$GI_{1\text{-}8}$ = annual gross income in a given year, as defined above in the Basic Indicator Approach, for each of the eight business lines

$\beta_{1\text{-}8}$ = a fixed percentage, set by the Committee, relating the level of required capital to the level of the gross income for each of the eight business lines. The values of the betas are detailed below.

Business Lines	Beta Factors
Corporate finance (β_1)	18%
Trading and sales (β_2)	18%
Retail banking (β_3)	12%
Commercial banking (β_4)	15%
Payment and settlement (β_5)	18%
Agency services (β_6)	15%
Asset management (β_7)	12%
Retail brokerage (β_8)	12%

The Alternative Standardised Approach

At national supervisory discretion, a supervisor can choose to allow a bank to use the Alternative Standardised Approach (ASA) provided the bank is able to satisfy its supervisor that this alternative approach provides an improved basis by, for example, avoiding double counting of risks. Once a bank has been allowed to use the ASA, it will not be allowed to revert to use of the Standardised Approach without the permission of its supervisor. It is not envisaged that large diversified banks in major markets would use the ASA.

Under the ASA, the operational risk capital charge/methodology is the same as for the Standardised Approach except for two business lines — retail banking and commercial banking. For these business lines, loans and advances — multiplied by a fixed factor 'm' — replaces gross income as the exposure indicator. The betas for retail and commercial banking are unchanged from the Standardised Approach. The ASA operational risk capital charge for retail banking (with the same basic formula for commercial banking) can be expressed as:

$$K_{RB} = \beta_{RB} \times m \times LA_{RB}$$

Where,

K_{RB} = capital charge for the retail banking business line

β_{RB} = beta for the retail banking business line

LA_{RB} = total outstanding retail loans and advances (non-risk weighted and gross of provisions), averaged over the past three years

$m = 0.035$

3. *Advanced Measurement Approaches (AMA)*

Under the advanced management approach, the regulatory capital requirement will depend on the risk measure generated by the bank's internal operational risk management system. Banks should classify their business unit along the lines of the standardized approach. Thereafter banks should measure, based on their own internal data, the probability of a loss event (PE) and the loss given event (LGE) for each of their business lines and income generated in business line (EI). The expected loss (EL) can then be calculated as:

$$EL = EI * PE * LGE.$$

The capital charge for operational risk can then be computed as follows:

$$ORC = \Sigma (EI * PE * LGE)$$

Banks using AMA are permitted to recognise the risk mitigating impact of insurance, provided that amount does not exceed 20% of its operational risk capital requirement.

VI. Market Risk

The risk measurement framework

Market risk is defined as the risk of losses in on and off-balance-sheet positions arising from movements in market prices. The risks subject to this requirement are:

(a) The risks pertaining to interest rate related instruments and equities in the trading book;

(b) Foreign exchange risk and commodities risk throughout the bank.

Scope and coverage of the capital charges

The capital charges for interest rate related instruments and equities will apply to the current trading book items prudently valued by banks. The capital charges for foreign exchange risk and for commodities risk will apply to banks total currency and commodity positions, subject to some discretion to exclude structural foreign exchange positions. A trading book consists of positions in financial instruments and commodities held either with trading intent or in order to hedge other elements of the trading book. A financial instrument is any contract that gives rise to both a financial asset of one entity and a financial liability or equity instrument of another entity. Financial instruments include both primary financial instruments (or cash instruments) and derivative financial instruments. A financial asset is any asset that is cash, the right to receive cash or another financial asset; or the contractual right to exchange financial assets on potentially favourable terms, or an equity instrument. A financial liability is the contractual obligation to deliver cash or another financial asset or to exchange financial liabilities under conditions that are potentially unfavourable.

Marking-to-market is at least the daily valuation of positions at readily available close out prices that are sourced independently. Examples of readily available close out prices include exchange prices, screen prices, or quotes from several independent reputable brokers.Banks must mark-to-market as much as possible. The more prudent side of bid/offer must be used unless the institution is a significant market maker in a particular position type and it can close out at mid-market.

Where marking-to-market is not possible, banks may mark-to-model, where this can be demonstrated to be prudent. Marking-to-model is defined as any valuation which has to be benchmarked, extrapolated or otherwise calculated from a market input. When marking to model, an extra degree of conservatism is appropriate.

The capital requirement

In calculating eligible capital for market risk, it will be necessary first to calculate the bank's minimum capital requirement for credit and operational risks, and only afterwards its market risk requirement, to establish how much Tier 1 and Tier 2 capital is available to support market risk. Eligible capital will be the sum of the whole of the bank's Tier 1 capital, plus all of its Tier 2 capital . Tier 3 capital will be regarded as eligible only if it can be used to support market risks.

Market risk – The standardised measurement method

The instruments covered include all fixed-rate and floating-rate debt securities and instruments that behave like them, including non-convertible preference shares. Convertible bonds, i.e. debt issues or preference shares that are convertible at a stated price into common shares of the issuer, will be treated as debt securities if they trade like debt securities and as equities if they trade like equities. The minimum capital requirement is expressed in terms of two separately calculated charges, one applying to the *"specific risk"* of each security, whether it is a short or a long position, and the other to the interest rate risk in the portfolio (termed *"general market risk"*) where long and short positions in different securities or instruments can be offset.

Market Risk – The Internal Models Approach

The use of an internal model will be conditional upon the explicit approval of the bank's supervisory authority. Home and host country supervisory authorities of banks that carry out material trading activities in multiple jurisdictions intend to work co-operatively to ensure an efficient approval process. Banks that use the internal models approach for meeting market risk capital requirements must have in place a rigorous and comprehensive stress testing program. Stress testing to identify events or influences that could greatly impact banks is a key component of a bank's assessment of its capital position. Banks' stress scenarios need to cover a range of factors that can create extraordinary losses or gains in trading portfolios, or make the control of risk in those portfolios very difficult. These factors include low-probability events in all major types of risks, including the various components of market, credit, and operational risks.

The Second Pillar – Supervisory Review Process

Under this process, the key principles of supervisory review, risk management guidance and supervisory transparency and accountability with respect to banking risks, including guidance relating to, among other things, the treatment of interest rate risk in the banking book, credit risk (stress testing, definition of default, residual risk, and credit concentration risk), operational risk, enhanced cross-border communication and cooperation, and securitization have been detailed. The supervisory review process of the Framework is intended not only to ensure that banks have adequate capital to support all the risks in their business, but also to encourage banks to develop and use better risk management techniques in monitoring and managing their risks. The supervisory review process recognises the responsibility of bank management in developing an internal capital assessment process and setting capital targets that are commensurate with the bank's risk profile and control environment. There are three main areas that might be particularly suited to treatment under Pillar 2: risks considered under Pillar 1 that are not fully captured by the Pillar 1 process (e.g. credit concentration risk); those factors not taken into account by the Pillar 1 process (e.g. interest rate risk in the banking book, business and strategic risk); and factors external to the bank (e.g. business cycle effects). A further important aspect of Pillar 2 is the assessment of compliance with the minimum standards and disclosure requirements of the more advanced methods in Pillar 1, in particular the IRB framework for credit risk and the Advanced Measurement Approaches for operational risk. Supervisors must ensure that these requirements are being met, both as qualifying criteria and on a continuing basis.

Four key principles of supervisory review

The Committee has identified four key principles of supervisory review, which complement those outlined in the extensive supervisory guidance that has been developed by the Committee, the keystone of which is the Core Principles for Effective Banking Supervision and the Core Principles Methodology.

Principle 1: Banks should have a process for assessing their overall capital adequacy in relation to their risk profile and a strategy for maintaining their capital levels.

Banks must be able to demonstrate that chosen internal capital targets are well founded and that these targets are consistent with their overall risk profile and current operating environment. In assessing capital adequacy, bank management needs to be mindful of the particular stage of the business cycle in which the bank is operating. Rigorous, forward-looking stress testing that identifies possible events or changes in market conditions that could adversely impact the bank should be performed. Bank management clearly bears primary responsibility for ensuring that the bank has adequate capital to support its risks.

The five main features of a rigorous process are as follows:

a) Board and senior management oversight;
b) Sound capital assessment;
c) Comprehensive assessment of risks;
d) Monitoring and reporting; and
e) Internal control review.

Principle 2: Supervisors should review and evaluate banks' internal capital adequacy assessments and strategies, as well as their ability to monitor and ensure their compliance with regulatory capital ratios. Supervisors should take appropriate supervisory action if they are not satisfied with the result of this process.

The supervisory authorities should regularly review the process by which a bank assesses its capital adequacy, risk position, resulting capital levels, and quality of capital held. Supervisors should also evaluate the degree to which a bank has in place a sound internal process to assess capital adequacy. The emphasis of the review should be on the quality of the bank's risk management and controls and should not result in supervisors functioning as bank management. The periodic review can involve some combination of:

a) On-site examinations or inspections;
b) Off-site review;
c) Discussions with bank management;
d) Review of work done by external auditors (provided it is adequately focused on the necessary capital issues); and
e) Periodic reporting.

The substantial impact that errors in the methodology or assumptions of formal analyses can have on resulting capital requirements requires a detailed review by supervisors of each bank's internal analysis in the following areas:

1. **Review of adequacy of risk assessment**
2. **Assessment of capital adequacy**

3. **Assessment of the control environment**
4. **Supervisory review of compliance with minimum standards**
5. **Supervisory response**

Principle 3: Supervisors should expect banks to operate above the minimum regulatory capital ratios and should have the ability to require banks to hold capital in excess of the minimum.

Pillar 1 minimums are anticipated to be set to achieve a level of bank creditworthiness in markets that is below the level of creditworthiness sought by many banks for their own reasons. In the normal course of business, the type and volume of activities will change, as will the different risk exposures, causing fluctuations in the overall capital ratio. It may be costly for banks to raise additional capital, especially if this needs to be done quickly or at a time when market conditions are unfavourable. For banks to fall below minimum regulatory capital requirements is a serious matter. It may place banks in breach of the relevant law and/or prompt non-discretionary corrective action on the part of supervisors. There may be risks, either specific to individual banks, or more generally to an economy at large, that are not taken into account in Pillar 1. Hence, supervisor should ensure that the banks are maintaining capital above the minimum specified in order to cope with adversities.

Principle 4: Supervisors should seek to intervene at an early stage to prevent capital from falling below the minimum levels required to support the risk characteristics of a particular bank and should require rapid remedial action if capital is not maintained or restored.

Supervisors should consider a range of options if they become concerned that a bank is not meeting the requirements embodied in the supervisory principles outlined above. These actions may include intensifying the monitoring of the bank, restricting the payment of dividends, requiring the bank to prepare and implement a satisfactory capital adequacy restoration plan, and requiring the bank to raise additional capital immediately. Supervisors should have the discretion to use the tools best suited to the circumstances of the bank and its operating environment.

Part 4: The Third Pillar – Market Discipline

General considerations and Disclosure requirements

The rationale for Pillar 3 is sufficiently strong to warrant the introduction of disclosure requirements for banks using the Framework. The purpose of Pillar 3 is to complement the minimum capital requirements (Pillar 1) and the supervisory review process (Pillar 2). The Pillar 3 aims to encourage market discipline by developing a set of disclosure requirements which will allow market participants to assess key pieces of information on the scope of application, capital, risk exposures, risk assessment processes, and hence the capital adequacy of the institution. In principle, banks' disclosures should be consistent with how senior management and the board of directors assess and manage the risks of the bank.

A bank should decide which disclosures are relevant for it based on the materiality concept. Information would be regarded as material if its omission or misstatement could change or influence the assessment or decision of a user relying on that information for the purpose of making economic decisions. The disclosures set out in Pillar 3 should be made on a semi-annual basis. Qualitative disclosures that provide a general summary of a bank's risk management objectives and policies, reporting system and definitions may be published on an annual basis. Proprietary information encompasses information (for example on products or systems), which if shared with competitors would render a bank's investment in these products/systems less valuable, and hence would undermine its competitive position. Information about customers is often confidential, in that it is provided under the terms of a legal agreement or counterparty relationship. This has an impact on what banks should reveal in terms of information about their customer base, as well as details on their internal arrangements, for instance methodologies used, parameter estimates, data, etc. The Committee believes that the requirements set out below strike an appropriate balance between the need for meaningful disclosure and the protection of proprietary and confidential information. In exceptional cases, disclosure of certain items of information required by Pillar 3 may prejudice seriously the position of the bank by making public information that is either proprietary or confidential in nature. In such cases, a bank need not disclose those specific items, but must disclose more general information about the subject matter of the requirement, together with the fact that, and the reason why, the specific items of information have not been disclosed. This limited exemption is not intended to conflict with the disclosure requirements under the accounting standards.

The disclosure requirements

General disclosure principle

Banks should have a formal disclosure policy approved by the board of directors that addresses the bank's approach for determining what disclosures it will make and the internal controls over the disclosure process. In addition, banks should implement a process for assessing the appropriateness of their disclosures, including validation and frequency of them.

Scope of application

Disclosures related to individual banks within the groups would not generally be required to fulfil the disclosure requirements. An exception to this arises in the disclosure of Total and Tier 1 Capital Ratios by the top consolidated entity where an analysis of significant bank subsidiaries within the group is appropriate, in order to recognise the need for these subsidiaries to comply with this Framework and other applicable limitations on the transfer of funds or capital within the group.

Risk exposure and assessment

The risks to which banks are exposed and the techniques that banks use to identify, measure, monitor and control those risks are important factors market participants consider in their assessment of an institution. Several key banking risks are considered: credit risk, market risk, interest rate risk and equity risk in the banking book and operational risk. For each separate risk area (e.g. credit, market, operational, banking book interest rate risk, equity) banks must describe their risk management objectives and policies, including:

a) strategies and processes;

b) the structure and organisation of the relevant risk management function;

c) the scope and nature of risk reporting and/or measurement systems;

d) policies for hedging and/or mitigating risk and strategies and processes for monitoring the continuing effectiveness of hedges/mitigants.

Definition of Capital Included in the Capital Base

A. Capital elements

Tier 1 (a) Paid-up share capital/common stock

(b) Disclosed reserves

Tier 2 (a) Undisclosed reserves

(b) Asset revaluation reserves

(c) General provisions/general loan-loss reserves

(d) Hybrid (debt/equity) capital instruments

(e) Subordinated debt

Tier 3 At the discretion of their national authority, banks may also use a third tier of capital (Tier 3), consisting of short-term subordinated debt for the sole purpose of meeting a proportion of the capital requirements for market risks.

The sum of Tier 1, Tier 2, and Tier 3 elements will be eligible for inclusion in the capital base, subject to the following limits.

B. Limits and restrictions

(i) The total of Tier 2 (supplementary) elements will be limited to a maximum of 100% of the total of Tier 1 elements;

(ii) Subordinated term debt will be limited to a maximum of 50% of Tier 1 elements;

(iii) Tier 3 capital will be limited to 250% of a bank's Tier 1 capital that is required to support market risks;

(iv) Where general provisions/general loan-loss reserves include amounts reflecting lower valuations of asset or latent but unidentified losses present in the balance sheet, the amount of such provisions or reserves will be limited to a maximum of 1.25 percentage points;

(v) Asset revaluation reserves which take the form of latent gains on unrealised securities will be subject to a discount of 55%.

C. Deductions from the capital base

From Tier 1: Goodwill and increase in equity capital resulting from a securitisation exposure.

50% from Tier 1 and 50% from Tier 2 capital:

(i) Investments in unconsolidated banking and financial subsidiary companies

(ii) Investments in the capital of other banks and financial institutions (at the discretion of national authorities)

(iii) Significant minority investments in other financial entities.

D. Definition of capital elements

(i) **Tier 1**: includes only **permanent shareholders' equity** (issued and fully paid ordinary shares/common stock and perpetual non-cumulative preference shares) and **disclosed reserves** (created or increased by appropriations of retained earnings or other surplus, e.g. share premiums, retained profit, general reserves and legal reserves). Disclosed reserves also include general funds (such as fund for general banking risk in certain EC countries) of the same quality that meet the following criteria:

a) Allocations to the funds must be made out of post-tax retained earnings or out of pre-tax earnings adjusted for all potential tax liabilities;

b) The funds and movements into or out of them must be disclosed separately in the bank's published accounts;

c) The funds must be available to a bank to meet losses for unrestricted and immediate use as soon as they occur;

d) Losses cannot be charged directly to the funds but must be taken through the profit and loss account.

In the case of consolidated accounts, this also includes minority interests in the equity of subsidiaries, which are less than wholly owned. This basic definition of capital excludes revaluation reserves and cumulative preference shares.

(ii) **Tier 2**

(a) Undisclosed reserves are eligible for inclusion within supplementary elements provided these reserves are accepted by the supervisor. Such reserves consist of that part of the accumulated after-tax surplus of retained profits which banks in some countries may be permitted to maintain as an undisclosed reserve. Apart from the fact that the reserve is not identified in the published balance sheet, it should have the same high quality and character as a disclosed capital reserve; as such, it should not be encumbered by any provision or other known liability but should be freely and immediately available to meet unforeseen future losses. This definition of undisclosed reserves excludes hidden values arising from holdings of securities in the balance sheet at below current market prices.

(b) **Revaluation** reserves arise in two ways. Firstly, in some countries, banks (and other commercial companies) are permitted to revalue fixed assets, normally their own premises, from time to time in line with the change in market values. In some of these countries the amount of such revaluations is determined by law. Revaluations of this kind are reflected on the face of the balance sheet as a revaluation reserve.

Secondly, hidden values of "latent" revaluation reserves may be present as a result of long-term holdings of equity securities valued in the balance sheet at the historic cost of acquisition.

Both types of revaluation reserve may be included in Tier 2 provided that the assets are prudently valued, fully reflecting the possibility of price fluctuation and forced sale. In the case of "latent" revaluation reserves a discount of 55% will be applied to the difference between historic cost book value and market value to reflect the potential volatility of this form of unrealised capital and the notional tax charge on it.

(c) **General provisions/general loan-loss reserves** (for banks using the Standardised Approach for credit risk): provisions or loan-loss reserves held against future, presently unidentified losses are freely available to meet losses which subsequently materialise and therefore qualify for inclusion within supplementary elements. Provisions ascribed to identified deterioration of particular assets or known liabilities, whether individual or grouped, should be excluded. Furthermore, general provisions/general loan-loss reserves eligible for inclusion in Tier 2 will be limited to a maximum of 1.25 percentage points of weighted risk assets

(d) **Hybrid (debt/equity) capital instruments**. This heading includes a range of instruments which combine characteristics of equity capital and of debt. Their precise specifications differ from country to country, but they should meet the following requirements:

- they are *unsecured, subordinated* and *fully paid-up*;
- they are *not redeemable* at the initiative of the holder or without the prior consent of the supervisory authority;
- they are *available to participate in losses* without the bank being obliged to cease trading (unlike conventional subordinated debt);
- although the capital instrument may carry an obligation to pay interest that cannot permanently be reduced or waived (unlike dividends on ordinary shareholders' equity), *it should allow service obligations to be deferred* (as with cumulative preference shares) where the profitability of the bank would not support payment.

Cumulative preference shares, having these characteristics, would be eligible for inclusion in this category. In addition, the following are examples of instruments that may be eligible for inclusion: long-term preferred shares in Canada, titres participatifs and titres subordonnés à durée indéterminée in France, Genusscheine in Germany, perpetual subordinated debt and preference shares in the United Kingdom and mandatory convertible debt instruments in the United States. Debt capital instruments which do not meet these criteria may be eligible for inclusion in item (e).

(e) Subordinated term debt: includes conventional unsecured subordinated debt capital instruments with a minimum original fixed term to maturity of over five years and limited life redeemable preference shares. During the last five years to maturity, a cumulative discount (or amortisation) factor of 20% per year will be applied to reflect the diminishing value of these instruments as a continuing source of strength. Unlike instruments included in item (d), these instruments are not normally available to participate in the losses of a bank which continues trading. For this reason these instruments will be limited to a maximum of 50% of Tier 1.

Basel III: A global regulatory framework for banks and banking systems

(Extract from Bank for International Settlements regulation on Basel III. For reference purpose, consult original document of BIS on Basel III)

Introduction

Basel III regulations have been evolved by Bank of International Settlement to further strengthen global capital and liquidity rules with the goal of promoting a more resilient banking sector. The objective of the reforms is to improve the banking sector's ability to absorb shocks arising from financial and economic stress, whatever the source, thus reducing the risk of spillover from the financial sector to the real economy. A strong and resilient banking system is the foundation for sustainable economic growth, as banks are at the centre of the credit intermediation process between savers and investors. Moreover, banks provide critical services to consumers, small and medium-sized enterprises, large corporate firms and governments who rely on them to conduct their daily business, both at a domestic and international level. One of the main reasons the economic and financial crisis, which began in 2007, became so severe was that the banking sectors of many countries had built up excessive on and off-balance sheet leverage. This was accompanied by a gradual erosion of the level and quality of the capital base. At the same time, many banks were holding insufficient liquidity buffers. The banking system therefore was not able to absorb the resulting systemic trading and credit losses nor could it cope with the reintermediation of large off-balance sheet exposures that had built up in the shadow banking system. The crisis was further amplified by a procyclical deleveraging process and by the interconnectedness of systemic institutions through an array of complex transactions. During the most severe episode of the crisis, the market lost confidence in the solvency and liquidity of many banking institutions. The weaknesses in the banking sector were rapidly transmitted to the rest of the financial system and the real economy, resulting in a massive contraction of liquidity and credit availability. Ultimately the public sector had to step in with unprecedented injections of liquidity, capital support and guarantees, exposing taxpayers to large losses.

The effect on banks, financial systems and economies at the epicentre of the crisis was immediate. However, the crisis also spread to a wider circle of countries around the globe. For these countries the transmission channels were less direct, resulting from a severe contraction in global liquidity, cross-border credit availability and demand for exports. Given the scope and speed with which the recent and previous crises have been transmitted around the globe as well as the unpredictable nature of future crises, it is critical that all countries raise the resilience of their banking sectors to both internal and external shocks. To address the market failures revealed by the crisis, BIS has introduced a number of fundamental reforms to the international regulatory framework. The reforms strengthen bank-level, or microprudential, regulation, which will help raise the resilience of individual banking institutions to periods of stress. The reforms also have a macroprudential focus, addressing system-wide risks that can build up across the banking sector as well as the procyclical amplification of these risks over time. Clearly these micro and macroprudential approaches to supervision are interrelated, as greater resilience at the individual bank level reduces the risk of system-wide shocks.

Strengthening the global capital framework

The Basel Committee is raising the resilience of the banking sector by strengthening the regulatory capital framework, building on the three pillars of the Basel II framework. The reforms raise both the quality and quantity of the regulatory capital base and enhance the risk coverage of the capital framework. They are underpinned by a leverage ratio that serves as a backstop to the risk-based capital measures, is intended to constrain excess leverage in the banking system and provide an extra layer of protection against model risk and measurement error. Finally, the Committee is introducing a number of macroprudential elements into the capital framework to help contain systemic risks arising from procyclicality and from the interconnectedness of financial institutions.

Raising the quality, consistency and transparency of the capital base

The predominant form of Tier 1 capital must be common shares and retained earnings. The remainder of the Tier 1 capital base must be comprised of instruments that are subordinated, have fully discretionary non-cumulative dividends or coupons and have neither a maturity date nor an incentive to redeem. Tier 2 capital instruments will be harmonised and so-called Tier 3 capital instruments, which were only available to cover market risks, eliminated.

Enhancing risk coverage

Failure to capture major on- and off-balance sheet risks, as well as derivative related exposures, was a key destabilising factor during the crisis. The reforms will raise capital requirements for the trading book and complex securitisation exposures, a major source of losses for many internationally active banks. The enhanced treatment introduces a stressed value-at-risk (VaR) capital requirement based on a continuous 12-month period of significant financial stress. The Committee has introduced higher capital requirements for so-called resecuritisations in both the banking and the trading book and also raised the standards of the Pillar 2 supervisory review process and strengthen Pillar 3 disclosures. The Pillar 1 and Pillar 3 enhancements must be implemented by the end of 2011; the Pillar 2 standards became effective when they were introduced in July 2009.

The Committee has introduces measures to strengthen the capital requirements for counterparty credit exposures arising from banks' derivatives, repo and securities financing activities. These reforms will raise the capital buffers backing these exposures, reduce procyclicality and provide additional incentives to move OTC derivative contracts to central counterparties, thus helping reduce systemic risk across the financial system. Banks must determine their capital requirement for counterparty credit risk using stressed inputs. Banks will be subject to a capital charge for potential mark-to-market losses (i.e. credit valuation adjustment – CVA – risk) associated with a deterioration in the credit worthiness of a counterparty. Banks with large and illiquid derivative exposures to a counterparty will have to apply longer margining periods as a basis for determining the regulatory capital requirement. Additional standards have been adopted to strengthen collateral risk management practices. To address the systemic risk arising from the interconnectedness of banks and other financial institutions through the derivatives markets, bank's collateral and mark-to-market exposures to central counterparties (CCPs) will be subject to a low risk weight, proposed at 2%; and default fund exposures to CCPs will be subject to risk-sensitive capital requirements. The Committee is raising counterparty credit risk management standards in a number of areas, including for the treatment of so-called wrong-way risk, i.e. cases where the exposure increases when the credit quality of the counterparty deteriorates. Finally, the Committee assessed a number of measures to mitigate the reliance on external ratings of the Basel II framework. The measures include requirements for banks to perform their own internal assessments of externally rated securitisation exposures, the elimination of certain "cliff effects" associated with credit risk mitigation practices, and the incorporation of key elements of the IOSCO Code of Conduct Fundamentals for Credit Rating Agencies into the Committee's eligibility criteria for the use of external ratings in the capital framework.

Supplementing the risk-based capital requirement with a leverage ratio

One of the underlying features of the crisis was the build up of excessive on and off-balance sheet leverage in the banking system. The Committee therefore is introducing a leverage ratio requirement that is intended to achieve constrain leverage in the banking sector, thus helping to mitigate the risk of the destabilising deleveraging processes which can damage the financial system and the economy; and introduce additional safeguards against model risk and measurement error by supplementing the risk-based measure with a simple, transparent, independent measure of risk. The leverage ratio is calculated in a comparable manner across jurisdictions, adjusting for any differences in accounting standards. The Committee has designed the leverage ratio to be a credible supplementary measure to the risk-based requirement with a view to migrating to a Pillar 1 treatment based on appropriate review and calibration.

Reducing procyclicality and promoting countercyclical buffers

One of the most destabilising elements of the crisis has been the procyclical amplification of financial shocks throughout the banking system, financial markets and the broader economy. The tendency of market participants to behave in a procyclical manner has been amplified through a variety of channels, including through accounting standards for both mark-to-market assets and held-to-maturity loans, margining practices, and through the build up and release of leverage among financial institutions, firms, and consumers. The Basel Committee is introducing a number of measures to make banks more resilient to such procyclical dynamics. These measures will help ensure that the banking sector serves as a shock absorber, instead of a transmitter of risk to the financial system and broader economy. In addition to the leverage ratio, the Committee is introducing a series of measures to address procyclicality and raise the resilience of the banking sector in good times. These measures will dampen any excess cyclicality of the minimum capital requirement, promote more forward looking provisions, conserve capital to build buffers at individual banks and the banking sector that can be used in stress and achieve the broader macroprudential goal of protecting the banking sector from periods of excess credit growth.

Cyclicality of the minimum requirement

It is not possible to achieve greater risk sensitivity across institutions at a given point in time without introducing a certain degree of cyclicality in minimum capital requirements over time. The Committee introduced a number of safeguards to address excess cyclicality of the minimum requirement. They include the requirement to use long term data horizons to estimate probabilities of default, the introduction of so called downturn loss-given-default (LGD) estimates and the appropriate calibration of the risk functions, which convert loss estimates into regulatory capital requirements. The Committee also required that banks conduct stress tests that consider the downward migration of their credit portfolios in a recession.

Forward looking provisioning

The Committee supports an expected loss (EL) approach that captures actual losses more transparently and is also less procyclical than the current "incurred loss" approach.

Capital conservation

The Committee is introducing a framework to promote the conservation of capital and the build-up of adequate buffers above the minimum that can be drawn down in periods of stress. At the onset of the financial crisis, a number of banks continued to make large distributions in the form of dividends, share buy backs and generous compensation payments even though their individual financial condition and the outlook for the sector were deteriorating. Much of this activity was driven by a collective action problem, where reductions in distributions were perceived as sending a signal of weakness. However, these actions made individual banks and the sector as a whole less resilient. Many banks soon returned to profitability but did not do enough to rebuild their capital buffers to support new lending activity. Taken together, this dynamic has increased the procyclicality of the system.

Excess credit growth

As witnessed during the financial crisis, losses incurred in the banking sector during a downturn preceded by a period of excess credit growth can be extremely large. Such losses can destabilise the banking sector, which can bring about or exacerbate a downturn in the real economy. The Basel Committee is introducing a regime which will adjust the capital buffer range, established through the capital conservation mechanism when there are signs that credit has grown to excessive levels. The purpose of the countercyclical buffer is to achieve the broader macroprudential goal of protecting the banking sector in periods of excess aggregate credit growth.

Addressing systemic risk and interconnectedness

While procyclicality amplified shocks over the time dimension, excessive interconnectedness among systemically important banks also transmitted shocks across the financial system and economy. Several of the capital requirements introduced by the Committee to mitigate the risks arising from firm-level exposures among global financial institutions will also help to address systemic risk and interconnectedness. These include capital incentives for banks to use central counterparties for over-the-counter derivatives, higher capital requirements for trading and derivative activities, as well as complex securitisations and off-balance sheet exposures (eg structured investment vehicles), higher capital requirements for inter-financial sector exposures; and the introduction of liquidity requirements that penalise excessive reliance on short term, interbank funding to support longer dated assets.

Introducing a global liquidity standard

A strong liquidity base reinforced through robust supervisory standards is of equal importance. The Basel Committee is introducing internationally harmonised global liquidity standards. The difficulties experienced by some banks were due to lapses in basic principles of liquidity risk management. The Committee developed the Liquidity Coverage Ratio (LCR) to achieve this objective. The second objective is to promote resilience over a longer time horizon by creating additional incentives for a bank to fund its activities with more stable sources of funding on an ongoing structural basis. The Net Stable Funding Ratio (NSFR) has a time horizon of one year and has been developed to provide a sustainable maturity structure of assets and liabilities.

Liquidity Coverage Ratio

The LCR is intended to promote resilience to potential liquidity disruptions over a thirty day horizon. High-quality liquid assets held in the stock should be unencumbered, liquid in markets during a time of stress and, ideally, be central bank eligible.

Net Stable Funding Ratio

The NSFR requires a minimum amount of stable sources of funding at a bank relative to the liquidity profiles of the assets, as well as the potential for contingent liquidity needs arising from off-balance sheet commitments, over a one-year horizon. The NSFR aims to limit over-reliance on short-term wholesale funding during times of buoyant market liquidity and encourage better assessment of liquidity risk across all on- and off-balance sheet items.

Liquidity Monitoring tools

A survey of Basel Committee members conducted in early 2009 identified that more than 25 different measures and concepts are used globally by supervisors. To introduce more consistency internationally, the Committee has developed a set of common metrics that should be considered as the minimum types of information which supervisors should use.

(a) Contractual maturity mismatch

(b) Concentration of funding

(c) Available unencumbered assets

(d) LCR by currency

(e) Market-related monitoring tools

Part 1: Minimum capital requirements and buffers

The global banking system entered the crisis with an insufficient level of high quality capital. The crisis also revealed the inconsistency in the definition of capital across jurisdictions and the lack of disclosure that would have enabled the market to fully assess and compare the quality of capital across jurisdictions. A key element of the new definition of capital is the greater focus on common equity, the highest quality component of a bank's capital.

I. Definition of capital

A. Components of capital

Elements of capital

Total regulatory capital will consist of the sum of the following elements:

1. Tier 1 Capital (going-concern capital)
    a. Common Equity Tier 1
    b. Additional Tier 1
2. Tier 2 Capital (gone-concern capital)

Limits and minima

All elements above are net of the associated regulatory adjustments and are subject to the following restrictions:

- Common Equity Tier 1 must be at least 4.5% of risk-weighted assets at all times
- Tier 1 Capital must be at least 6.0% of risk-weighted assets at all times
- Total Capital (Tier 1 Capital plus Tier 2 Capital) must be at least 8.0% of risk-weighted assets at all times.

Common Equity Tier 1

Common Equity Tier 1 capital consists of the sum of the following elements:

Common shares issued by the bank that meet the criteria for classification as common shares for regulatory purposes (or the equivalent for non-joint stock companies), Stock surplus (share premium) resulting from the issue of instruments included Common Equity Tier 1, Retained earnings, Accumulated other comprehensive income and other disclosed reserves, Common shares issued by consolidated subsidiaries of the bank and held by third parties (ie minority interest) that meet the criteria for inclusion in Common Equity Tier 1 capital, and Regulatory adjustments applied in the calculation of Common Equity Tier 1

Additional Tier 1 capital

Additional Tier 1 capital consists of the sum of the following elements:

Instruments issued by the bank that meet the criteria for inclusion in Additional Tier 1 capital (and are not included in Common Equity Tier 1), Stock surplus (share premium) resulting from the issue of instruments included in Additional Tier 1 capital, Instruments issued by consolidated subsidiaries of the bank and held by third parties that meet the criteria for inclusion in Additional Tier 1 capital and are not included in Common Equity Tier 1 and Regulatory adjustments applied in the calculation of Additional Tier 1 Capital.

Tier 2 capital

Tier 2 capital consists of the sum of the following elements:

Instruments issued by the bank that meet the criteria for inclusion in Tier 2 capital (and are not included in Tier 1 capital), Stock surplus (share premium) resulting from the issue of instruments included in Tier 2 capital, Instruments issued by consolidated subsidiaries of the bank and held by third parties that meet the criteria for inclusion in Tier 2 capital and are not included in Tier 1 capital, certain loan loss provisions, and Regulatory adjustments applied in the calculation of Tier 2 Capital.

Regulatory adjustments

This section sets out the regulatory adjustments to be applied to regulatory capital. In most cases these adjustments are applied in the calculation of Common Equity Tier 1. Goodwill and all other intangibles must be deducted in the calculation of Common Equity Tier 1, including any goodwill included in the valuation of significant investments in the capital of banking, financial and insurance entities that are outside the scope of regulatory consolidation. Deferred tax assets (DTAs) that rely on future profitability of the bank to be realised are to be deducted in the calculation of Common Equity Tier 1. Deferred tax assets may be netted with associated deferred tax liabilities (DTLs) only if the DTAs and DTLs relate to taxes levied by the same taxation authority and offsetting is permitted by the relevant taxation authority. The amount of the cash flow hedge reserve that relates to the hedging of items that are not fair valued on the balance sheet (including projected cash flows) should be derecognised in the calculation of Common Equity Tier 1. This means that positive amounts should be deducted and negative amounts should be added back. The deduction from capital in respect of a shortfall of the stock of provisions to expected losses under the IRB approach should be made in the calculation of Common Equity Tier 1. The full amount is to be deducted and should not be reduced by any tax effects that could be expected to occur if provisions were to rise to the level of expected losses. Gain on sale related to securitisation transactions are derecognised in the calculation of Common Equity Tier 1 any increase in equity capital resulting from a securitisation transaction, such as that associated with expected future margin income (FMI) resulting in a gain-on-sale. Cumulative gains and losses due to changes in own credit risk on fair valued financial liabilities are derecognised in the calculation of Common Equity Tier 1, all unrealised gains and losses that have resulted from changes in the fair value of liabilities that are due to changes in the bank's own credit risk. Defined benefit pension fund liabilities, as included on the balance sheet, must be fully recognised in the calculation of Common Equity Tier 1 (ie Common Equity Tier 1 cannot be increased through derecognising these liabilities). All of a bank's investments in its own common shares, whether held directly or indirectly, will be deducted in the calculation of Common Equity Tier 1. Reciprocal cross holdings of capital that are designed to artificially inflate the capital position of banks will be deducted in full. The regulatory adjustment described above applies to investments in the capital of banking, financial and insurance entities that are outside the scope of regulatory consolidation and where the bank does not own more than 10% of the issued common share capital of the entity.

Transitional arrangements

As of 1 January 2013, banks will be required to meet the following new minimum requirements in relation to risk-weighted assets (RWAs):

- 3.5% Common Equity Tier 1/RWAs;
- 4.5% Tier 1 capital/RWAs; and
- 8.0% total capital/RWAs.

Risk Coverage

Counterparty credit risk

The counterparty credit risk framework will become effective on 1 January 2013. To determine the default risk capital charge for counterparty credit risk, banks must use the greater of the portfolio-level capital charge based on Effective EPE using current market data and the portfolio-level capital charge based on Effective EPE using a stress calibration. The stress calibration should be a single consistent stress calibration for the whole portfolio of counterparties. The greater of Effective EPE using current market data and the stress calibration should not be applied on a counterparty by counterparty basis, but on a total portfolio level.

CVA Risk Capital Charge

In addition to the default risk capital requirements, a bank must add a capital charge to cover the risk of mark-to-market losses on the expected counterparty risk (such losses being known as credit value adjustments, CVA) to OTC derivatives. For the detailed calculation of CVA, the Basel III documents may be referred.

Stress testing

- Banks must have a comprehensive stress testing program for counterparty credit risk. The stress testing program must include the following elements:

- Banks must ensure complete trade capture and exposure aggregation across all forms of counterparty credit risk (not just OTC derivatives) at the counterparty-specific level in a sufficient time frame to conduct regular stress testing.
- For all counterparties, banks should produce, at least monthly, exposure stress testing of principal market risk factors (eg interest rates, FX, equities, credit spreads, and commodity prices) in order to proactively identify, and when necessary, reduce outsized concentrations to specific directional sensitivities.
- Banks should apply multifactor stress testing scenarios and assess material non-directional risks (ie yield curve exposure, basis risks, etc) at least quarterly. Multiple-factor stress tests should, at a minimum, aim to address scenarios in which severe economic or market events have occurred.
- Stressed market movements have an impact not only on counterparty exposures, but also on the credit quality of counterparties. At least quarterly, banks should conduct stress testing applying stressed conditions to the joint movement of exposures and counterparty creditworthiness.
- Exposure stress testing (including single factor, multifactor and material non-directional risks) and joint stressing of exposure and creditworthiness should be performed at the counterparty-specific, counterparty group (eg industry and region), and aggregate bank-wide CCR levels.
- Stress tests results should be integrated into regular reporting to senior management. The analysis should capture the largest counterparty-level impacts across the portfolio, material concentrations within segments of the portfolio (within the same industry or region), and relevant portfolio and counterparty specific trends.
- The severity of factor shocks should be consistent with the purpose of the stress test. When evaluating solvency under stress, factor shocks should be severe enough to capture historical extreme market environments and/or extreme but plausible stressed market conditions. The impact of such shocks on capital resources should be evaluated, as well as the impact on capital requirements and earnings. For the purpose of day-to-day portfolio monitoring, hedging, and management of concentrations, banks should also consider scenarios of lesser severity and higher probability.
- Banks should consider reverse stress tests to identify extreme, but plausible, scenarios that could result in significant adverse outcomes.
- Senior management must take a lead role in the integration of stress testing into the risk management framework and risk culture of the bank and ensure that the results are meaningful and proactively used to manage counterparty credit risk. At a minimum, the results of stress testing for significant exposures should be compared to guidelines that express the bank's risk appetite and elevated for discussion and action when excessive or concentrated risks are present.

Model validation and backtesting

The bank must conduct a regular programme of backtesting, i.e., an ex-post comparison of the risk measures generated by the model against realised risk measures, as well as comparing hypothetical changes based on static positions with realised measures. The bank must carry out an initial validation and an on-going periodic review of its IMM model and the risk measures generated by it. The validation and review must be independent of the model developers. The board of directors and senior management should be actively involved in the risk control process and must regard credit and counterparty credit risk control as an essential aspect of the business to which significant resources need to be devoted. In this regard, the daily reports prepared by the independent risk control unit must be reviewed by a level of management with sufficient seniority and authority to enforce both reductions of positions taken by individual traders and reductions in the bank's overall risk exposure. The bank's internal risk measurement exposure model must be closely integrated into the day-to-day risk management process of the bank. Its output should accordingly be an integral part of the process of planning, monitoring and controlling the bank's counterparty credit risk profile. The risk measurement system should be used in conjunction with internal trading and exposure limits. In this regard, exposure limits should be related to the bank's risk measurement model in a manner that is consistent over time and that is well understood by traders, the credit function and senior management. Banks should have a routine in place for ensuring compliance with a documented set of internal policies, controls and procedures concerning the operation of the risk measurement system. The bank's risk measurement system must be well documented, for example, through a risk management manual that describes the basic principles of the risk management system and that provides an explanation of the empirical techniques used to measure counterparty credit risk. An independent review of the risk measurement system should be carried out regularly in the bank's own internal auditing process. This review should include both the activities of the business trading units and of the independent risk control unit. A review of the overall risk management process should take place at regular intervals (ideally no less than once a year) and should specifically address, at a minimum:

- The adequacy of the documentation of the risk management system and process;
- The organisation of the risk control unit;
- The integration of counterparty credit risk measures into daily risk management;
- The approval process for counterparty credit risk models used in the calculation of counterparty credit risk used by front office and back office personnel;
- The validation of any significant change in the risk measurement process;
- The scope of counterparty credit risks captured by the risk measurement model;
- The integrity of the management information system;
- The accuracy and completeness of position data;
- The verification of the consistency, timeliness and reliability of data sources used to run internal models, including the independence of such data sources;
- The accuracy and appropriateness of volatility and correlation assumptions;
- The accuracy of valuation and risk transformation calculations;

- The verification of the model's accuracy; and
- The on-going validation of counterparty credit risk models, including backtesting, must be reviewed periodically by a level of management with sufficient authority to decide the course of action that will be taken to address weaknesses in the models.

The bank must have an independent risk control unit that is responsible for the design and implementation of the bank's counterparty credit risk management system. The unit should produce and analyse daily reports on the output of the bank's risk measurement model, including an evaluation of the relationship between measures of counterparty credit exposure and trading limits. The unit must be independent from the business trading units and should report directly to senior management of the bank.

Incorporation of IOSCO's Code of Conduct Fundamentals for Credit Rating Agencies

National supervisors are responsible for determining on a continuous basis whether an external credit assessment institution (ECAI) meets the criteria listed in the paragraph below. National supervisors should refer to the IOSCO Code of Conduct Fundamentals for Credit Rating Agencies when determining ECAI eligibility. The assessments of ECAIs may be recognised on a limited basis, e.g. by type of claims or by jurisdiction. The supervisory process for recognising ECAIs should be made public to avoid unnecessary barriers to entry.

Eligibility criteria: An ECAI must satisfy six criteria Objectivity, Independence, International access/Transparency, Disclosure, Resources and Credibility.

Capital conservation buffer

The operation of the capital conservation buffer has been designed to ensure that banks build up capital buffers outside periods of stress which can be drawn down as losses are incurred. The requirement is based on simple capital conservation rules designed to avoid breaches of minimum capital requirements. Outside of periods of stress, banks should hold buffers of capital above the regulatory minimum. When buffers have been drawn down, one way banks should look to rebuild them is through reducing discretionary distributions of earnings. This could include reducing dividend payments, share-backs and staff bonus payments. Banks may also choose to raise new capital from the private sector as an alternative to conserving internally generated capital.

A capital conservation buffer of 2.5%, comprised of Common Equity Tier 1, is established above the regulatory minimum capital requirement. Capital distribution constraints will be imposed on a bank when capital levels fall within this range. Banks will be able to conduct business as normal when their capital levels fall into the conservation range as they experience losses. The constraints imposed only relate to distributions, not the operation of the bank. The distribution constraints imposed on banks when their capital levels fall into the range increase as the banks' capital levels approach the minimum requirements. The table below shows the minimum capital conservation ratios a bank must meet at various levels of the Common Equity Tier 1 (CET1) capital ratios. For example, a bank with a CET1 capital ratio in the range of 5.125% to 5.75% is required to conserve 80% of its earnings in the subsequent financial year (ie payout no more than 20% in terms of dividends, share buybacks and discretionary bonus payments). If the bank wants to make payments in excess of the constraints imposed by this regime, it would have the option of raising capital in the private sector equal to the amount above the constraint which it wishes to distribute. The Common Equity Tier 1 ratio includes amounts used to meet the 4.5% minimum Common Equity Tier 1 requirement, but excludes any additional Common Equity Tier 1 needed to meet the 6% Tier 1 and 8% Total Capital requirements. For example, a bank with 8% CET1 and no Additional Tier 1 or Tier 2 capital would meet all minimum capital requirements, but would have a zero conservation buffer and therefore by subject to the 100% constraint on capital distributions.

Individual bank minimum capital conservation standards

Common Equity Tier 1 Ratio	Minimum Capital Conservation Ratios (expressed as a percentage of earnings)
4.5% - 5.125%	100%
>5.125% - 5.75%	80%
>5.75% - 6.375%	60%
>6.375% - 7.0%	40%
> 7.0%	0%

Transitional arrangements

The capital conservation buffer will be phased in between 1 January 2016 and year end 2018 becoming fully effective on 1 January 2019. It will begin at 0.625% of RWAs on 1 January 2016 and increase each subsequent year by an additional 0.625 percentage points, to reach its final level of 2.5% of RWAs on 1 January 2019. Countries that experience excessive credit growth should consider accelerating the build up of the capital conservation buffer and the countercyclical buffer. National authorities have the discretion to impose shorter transition periods and should do so where appropriate. Banks that already meet the minimum ratio requirement during the transition period but remain below the 7% Common Equity Tier 1 target (minimum plus conservation buffer) should maintain prudent earnings retention policies with a view to meeting the conservation buffer as soon as reasonably possible.

Countercyclical buffer

Losses incurred in the banking sector can be extremely large when a downturn is preceded by a period of excess credit growth. These losses can destabilise the banking sector and spark a vicious circle, whereby problems in the financial system can contribute to a downturn in the real economy that then feeds back on to the banking sector. These interactions highlight the particular importance of the banking sector building up additional capital defences in periods where the risks of system-wide stress are growing markedly. The countercyclical buffer aims to ensure that banking sector capital requirements take account of the macro-financial environment in which banks operate. It will be deployed by national jurisdictions when excess aggregate credit growth is judged to be associated with a build-up of system-wide risk to ensure the banking system has a buffer of capital to protect it against future potential losses. This focus on excess aggregate credit growth means that jurisdictions are likely to only need to deploy the buffer on an infrequent basis. The buffer for internationally-active banks will be a weighted average of the buffers deployed across all the jurisdictions to which it has credit exposures. This means that they will likely find themselves subject to a small buffer on a more frequent basis, since credit cycles are not always highly correlated across jurisdictions.

National authorities will monitor credit growth and other indicators that may signal a build up of system-wide risk and make assessments of whether credit growth is excessive and is leading to the build up of system-wide risk. Based on this assessment, they will put in place a countercyclical buffer requirement when circumstances warrant. This requirement will be released when system-wide risk crystallises or dissipates.

National countercyclical buffer requirements

Each Basel Committee member jurisdiction will identify an authority with the responsibility to make decisions on the size of the countercyclical capital buffer. If the relevant national authority judges a period of excess credit growth to be leading to the build up of system-wide risk, they will consider, together with any other macroprudential tools at their disposal, putting in place a countercyclical buffer requirement. This will vary between zero and 2.5% of risk weighted assets, depending on their judgement as to the extent of the build up of system-wide risk.

Bank specific countercyclical buffer

Banks will be subject to a countercyclical buffer that varies between zero and 2.5% to total risk weighted assets. The buffer that will apply to each bank will reflect the geographic composition of its portfolio of credit exposures. Banks must meet this buffer with Common Equity Tier 1 or other fully loss absorbing capital.

The following table sets out the conservation ratios a bank must meet at various levels of Common Equity Tier 1 capital if the bank is subject to a 2.5% countercyclical buffer requirement.

Individual bank minimum capital conservation standards, when a bank is subject to a 2.5% countercyclical requirement

Common Equity Tier 1 Ratio (including other fully loss absorbing capital)	Minimum Capital Conservation Ratios (expressed as a percentage of earnings)
4.5% - 5.75%	100%
>5.75% - 7.0%	80%
>7.0% - 8.25%	60%
>8.25% - 9.5%	40%
> 9.5%	0%

Leverage ratio

One of the underlying features of the crisis was the build-up of excessive on- and off-balance sheet leverage in the banking system. In many cases, banks built up excessive leverage while still showing strong risk based capital ratios. During the most severe part of the crisis, the banking sector was forced by the market to reduce its leverage in a manner that amplified downward pressure on asset prices, further exacerbating the positive feedback loop between losses, declines in bank capital, and contraction in credit availability. Therefore, the Committee agreed to introduce a simple, transparent, non-risk based leverage ratio that is calibrated to act as a credible supplementary measure to the risk based capital requirements. The Committee will test a minimum Tier 1 leverage ratio of 3% during the parallel run period from 1 January 2013 to 1 January 2017. The capital measure for the leverage ratio should be based on the new definition of Tier 1 capital.

Calibration of the capital framework

Capital requirements and buffers (all numbers in percent)

	Common Equity Tier 1	Tier 1 Capital	Total Capital
Minimum	4.5	6.0	8.0
Conservation buffer	2.5		
Minimum plus conservation buffer	7.0	8.5	10.5
Countercyclical buffer Range	0 – 2.5		

Phase-in arrangements

(shading indicates transition periods - all dates are as of 1 January)

	2011	2012	2013	2014	2015	2016	2017	2018	As of 1 January 2019
Leverage Ratio	Supervisory monitoring		Parallel run 1 Jan 2013 - 1 Jan 2017 Disclosure starts 1 Jan 2015					Migration to Pillar 1	
Minimum Common Equity Capital Ratio			3.5%	4.0%	4.5%	4.5%	4.5%	4.5%	4.5%
Capital Conservation Buffer						0.625%	1.25%	1.875%	2.50%

Minimum common equity plus capital conservation buffer			3.5%	4.0%	4.5%	5.125%	5.75%	6.375%	7.0%
Phase-in of deductions from CET1 (including amounts exceeding the limit for DTAs, MSRs & financials)				20%	40%	60%	80%	100%	100%
Minimum Tier 1 Capital			4.5%	5.5%	6.0%	6.0%	6.0%	6.0%	6.0%
Minimum Total Capital			8.0%	8.0%	8.0%	8.0%	8.0%	8.0%	8.0%
Minimum Total Capital plus conservation buffer			8.0%	8.0%	8.0%	8.625%	9.25%	9.875%	10.5%
Capital instruments that no longer qualify as non-core Tier 1 capital or Tier 2 capital			Phased out over 10 year horizon beginning 2013						
Liquidity coverage ratio	Observation period begins				Introduce minimum standard				
Net stable funding ratio	Observation period begins							Intro-duce minimum standard	

Summary

In this chapter, role of BIS has been discussed on international convergence of Capital Measurement and Capital Standards. The Basel I framework has also been discussed in order to know the changes made in Basel I to Basel II. Basel II guidelines have been discussed in detail covering scope of framework, architecture of framework and all three pillar of Basel II guidelines. The constituents of all Tier I, Tier II and Tier III capital have been discussed in detail. BIS has introduced Basel III, implementation of which will start from 1st January'2013 and will be completed by 1st January'2019. The new concepts such as Leverage Ratio, Capital Conservation Buffer, Liquidity coverage ratio and Net stable funding ratio have been introduced in order to have better capital adequacy in turbulence time.

KEY CONCEPTS

Core capital	Supplementary capital	Country transfer risk
Tier I	Tier II and Tier III capital	Capital conversion factor
Basel II Pillar I	Pillar II and Pillar III	People risk
Process risk	Basel III Leverage Ratio	Capital conservation buffer
Liquidity coverage ratio	Net stable funding ratio	

References:

1. *www.bis.org:*
2. *www.bis.org:* Extract from report of Basel Committee on Banking Supervision: International Convergence of Capital Measurement and Capital Standards, Basel I (1988)
3. *www.bis.org:* Extract from report of Basel Committee on Banking Supervision: International Convergence of Capital Measurement and Capital Standards, Basel II (Nov'2006)
4. *www.bis.org*: Extract from Basel III: A global regulatory framework for more resilient banks and banking systems December 2010.

PART E

Case Studies

23. Cases on Failure of Risk Management

    - Barings Bank Collapses
    - Bank of Credit and Commerce International (BCCI)
    - First National Bank of Keystone
    - Lloyd's, a British Insurance Market
    - Long-Term Capital Management
    - Orange County
    - Bankers Trust (BT)
    - Enron
    - Sub-Prime Lending Debacle in US Mortgage Market
    - Wall Street & The Financial Crisis: Anatomy of a Financial Collapse
    - CRB Capital Market
    - Global Trust Bank (GTB)
    - The US-64 Controversy
    - The JVG Scandal
    - Co-operative Bank Scams in India
    - The Ketan Parekh Scam
    - Life Insurance Corporation's Future Prospects

Chapter – 23

Case on Failure of Risk Management

Chapter Objective

- Understand mistakes in following Risk Management Practices
- Understand right use of Derivatives to Hedge Risk
- Understand implication of Market Changes on Banks Financials
- Know the right way of Risk Management

Introduction

The recent growth of the risk management industry can be traced directly to the increased volatility of financial market since early 1970s. Some of the instances of volatility in financial markets are given below in chronological order[1]:-

1. The fixed exchange rate system broke down in 1971, leading to flexible and volatile exchange rates.
2. The oil price shock starting in 1973 were accompanied by high inflation and wild swings in interest rates.
3. On Black Monday, October 19, 1987, U.S. stocks collapsed by 23 percent, wiping out Rs.1 trillion in capital.
4. The Japanese stock price bubble finally deflated at the end of 1989, sending the Nikkei index from 39000 to 17000 3 years later. A total of Rs.2.7 trillion in the capital was lost, leading to an unprecedented financial crisis in Japan.
5. In the bond debacle of 1994, the Federal Reserve Bank, after having kept interest rates low for 3 years, started a series of six consecutive interest rate hikes that erased Rs.1.5 trillion in global capital.
6. On February 26, 1995 the Barings PLC, a venerable 233-year old bank, had gone bankrupt. The loss of Rs.1.3 billion was caused by a large exposure to the Japanese stock market, which was achieved through the futures market. This loss wiped out the firm's entire equity capital. The Barings PLC was acquired by ING for the grand total of £ 1 (about Rs.1.50).
7. The Asian turmoil of 1997 wiped off about three-fourth of the dollar capitalization of equities in Indonesia, Korea, Malaysia and Thailand.

8. The Russian default in August 1998 sparked a global financial crisis that culminated in the near failure of a big hedge fund, Long Term Capital Management (LTCM).

9. Various ups and downs in Indian stock market have been seen in last 10 years resulting in erosion of thousand crores of market capitalization. The call money market touched the mark of 150% p.a. rate in 1996.

10. The failure of UTI, one of the biggest mutual funds of the world, had shaken south Asian economy. Government of India had to come forward to bail out UTI by pumping crores of rupees. The problem was tackled temporarily after disintegration of UTI in UTI-I and UTI-II. Now Government is planning to sell UTI.

11. LIC, IDBI, etc. had to take back their various schemes of guaranteed returns because of sudden fall in interest rate world wide and its follow up impact in India.

12. Sub Prime lending issue of US mortgage market in mid 2007 is the latest example of sheer ignorance of credit, market, and liquidity risk.

Some important cases of international financial market have been detailed out:-[2]

BARINGS BANK

Introduction and Case Details:

The governor of the Bank of England dubbed him a "rogue dealer," and his former boss accused him of "sabotage". The British tabloids portrayed Nicholas Leeson as a working-class villain who single-handedly brought down Barings PLC, a 233-year-old London merchant bank that helped finance the Napoleonic wars, the Louisiana Purchase and the Canadian Pacific Railway, and which counts Queen Elizabeth II among its wealthy clients. By week's end, Leeson, the 28-year-old trader who had been a supervisor at Barings' Singapore office until he disappeared with his wife, Lisa, was in a German jail. Leeson's complicated trading scheme had gone badly astray, causing Barings to collapse under losses that could exceed $1 billion. The Barings debacle was just the latest and most dramatic event in a string of huge trading losses over the past year based on the sale of derivatives, a range of sophisticated and complex financial products that, depending on how they are used, can either reduce or greatly magnify risk.

As the saga of Barings' collapse unfolded, it became apparent that executives of Britain's oldest merchant bank had failed to manage the risks. And yet, Barings was no newcomer to the complexities of international markets, where it has been active since its founding by Francis Baring in 1762. Indeed, in 1890 it came close to folding when big investments in Argentina soured. That time, the British government helped bail out the blue-blood company. He had bought derivatives that would make money only if Japan's Nikkei stock index rose and if Japanese and European interest rates rose. In fact, Leeson may even have considered those positions to be hedged because stock prices usually rise when interest rates fall and vice versa. (In other words, the Japanese stock market will usually not gain when Japanese interest rates are rising.) The Kobe earthquake in Japan, however, may have thrown off Leeson's initial trading strategy on January 17, which caused enormous turmoil in the country's financial markets.

Indeed, concern about the activities of the firm's Singapore office dates back at least to 1992. In March of that year, a Barings director wrote a memo in which he warned that the company was "in danger of setting up a structure which will subsequently prove disastrous". And in August 1994, according to an investigation by the Singapore International Monetary Exchange (SIMEX), an internal audit of the Singapore office warned that Leeson had "excessive" power.

Leeson, for his part, was both a trader and the trading supervisor in the Singapore office. He also supervised the back office, where his wife worked which processes and monitors all trading positions. That overlap may have helped him hide his trading gamble from Barings senior managers.

In 1993, Nick Leeson became general manager of Barings Futures (Singapore), running the bank's SIMEX (Singapore International Monetary Exchange) activities. Leeson started selling put and call options on the Nikkei 225 equity index, placing the premiums earned into an error account number 88888. This strategy, known as a straddle, is essentially a bet on the stability of market prices. James Baker, an internal auditor, spends two weeks in Singapore investigating the immense profits being made there. Baker identified the weakness of internal controls and recommends that the general manager should no longer be responsible for the back office. In response, a separate financial manager in Hong Kong was given part-time responsibility for watching over the back office. In an attempt to better evaluate its overall risk, Barings set up an integrated Group Treasury and Risk function, reporting to a new asset and liability committee (Alco). A later Barings investigation revealed that, for unknown reasons, Leeson had ran up an accrued loss amounting to Y7.7 billion on the account by the end of 1994. In January 1995, the Nikkei 225 crashed by 1000 points after an earthquake hits Japan's industrial heartland. Leeson began purchasing March and June 1995 futures contracts on the Nikkei. The London futures team gave Barings' Alco Committee a presentation on the Baring Futures (Singapore) operation, which stated that Leeson was operating a perfectly matched book - long in Osaka, but short to the same amount on Simex. Coopers & Lybrand decided to hold off signing off on Barings' accounts until it became possible to clear up a few points with Leeson. At close of trading, the error account contained 55,399 Nikkei contracts expiring in March and 5640 expiring in June. As of February 25 1995, this totalled a loss of 59 billion yen on Simex. The Barings Board met to discuss a hastily prepared analysis of the transactions in Account 88888. The Dutch Bank ING agreed to purchase Barings for 1 pound and assumed all of its liabilities.

Lessons learned:

- Even when segregation of duties was suggested by internal audit, the concentration of power in the Leeson's hands was scarcely diluted. This clearly shows Lack of internal checks and balances.
- If Barings' auditors and top management had understood the trading business, they would have realised that it was not possible for Leeson to be making the profits that he was reporting without taking on undue risk, and they might have questioned where the money was coming from. Arbitrage is supposed to be a low risk, and hence low profit,

business, so Leeson's large profits should have inspired alarm rather than praise. Given that arbitrage should be cash-neutral or cash-rich, additional alarms should have gone off as the Bank wired hundreds of millions of dollars to Singapore. This clearly shows lack of understanding of the business by the top management.

- Although Leeson had never held a trading license prior to his arrival in Singapore, there was little oversight of his activities and no individual was directly responsible for monitoring his trading strategies. This is poor supervision of employees.

- Leeson's fraud may have been facilitated by the confusion caused by two reporting lines: one to London, for proprietary trading, and another to Tokyo for trading on behalf of customers. Lack of a clear reporting line is simply visible in whole system.

BANK OF CREDIT AND COMMERCE INTERNATIONAL (BCCI)

Introduction and Case Details:

On July 5, 1991, an incident that has been described as the biggest bank fraud in history came to a head when regulators in seven countries raided and took control of branch offices of the Bank of Credit and Commerce International (BCCI). Monetary losses from the scandal were huge, with estimates ranging from \$10 billion to \$17 billion though many billions have since been recovered for creditors by the banks liquidators, Deloitte & Touche. The scandal had been developing for nearly two decades and encompassed an intricate international web of financial institutions and shell companies that had escaped full regulation. BCCIs activities, and those of some of its officers, included dubious lending, fraudulent record-keeping, rogue trading, flouting of bank ownership regulations and money laundering in addition to legitimate banking activities. The banks structure and deal making was so complex that, a decade after the institution was liquidated, its activities are still not completely understood.

One way to think of the BCCI saga is as an attempt to create the polar opposite of a firm with integrated risk management practices. In this case, certain senior bank personnel and interested parties did not simply overlook risks, but manipulated gaps in the banks risk management structure and between its subsidiaries, to serve various purposes. This put at a disadvantage other stakeholders, such as the million or so small depositors around the world and certain institutional depositors attracted by BCCIs relatively high rates, who provided much of the banks funding. Meanwhile, other bank officers had little understanding of the banks structure and overall financial position, and were encouraged not to question bank practices, or the reason for the flow of funds between bank entities.

Agha Hasan Abedi, a Pakistani banker with Arab backing, founded the Bank of Credit and Commerce International in 1972. The institution was chartered in Luxembourg, but its treasury and other key functions were based in the Cayman Islands and in London before decamping to Abu Dhabi in 1990. Its branches and subsidiaries in 70 countries were held together by a complex structure of holding companies, cross-holdings and nominee owners. BCCIs international nature helped the company avoid a large amount of regulation because for most of its history no single regulator or audit team had full jurisdiction over it.

The bank's involvement in money laundering and financing of arms trafficking: BCCIs presence in the Cayman Islands, and its many offices all around the world, made it a useful route for tainted funds. Clients included such figures as former Panamanian dictator Manuel Noriega, as well as individuals who were involved in various drug and crime cartels. American enforcement officials had uncovered evidence of these transactions by 1983, but did not act on them until 1988. At that point, the US Customs Service completed an undercover operation that led to the arrest of several BCCI figures, who were convicted of money laundering on July 29, 1990. The bank itself pleaded guilty to the laundering charge and was fined $14 million.

In June, Price Waterhouse, a principal BCCI auditor, informed the Bank of England that it had found evidence of widespread fraud and account juggling in BCCIs operations. The auditors came to believe that, despite its pace of growth, the bank might never have made a genuine profit in the whole of its 19-year existence. Throughout its history, BCCI had made large loans to companies and individuals without properly securing them. The loans represented massive concentrations of credit risk, but were often not properly documented or monitored. When these loans went bad, the bank had no legal recourse, and was forced to absorb the losses. This strategy, which ran counter to common sense and all principles of good lending, racked up huge losses for BCCI. It covered up this problem by taking in new deposits and not recording these straightforwardly on its books, and by otherwise creating a matrix of false accounts that hid the losses for years.

Another way BCCI lost money was through huge losses incurred by its treasury department, particularly in the early 1980s though these losses may themselves have been a way of disguising other losses and misdoings. BCCI also reportedly lost hundreds of millions of dollars through a financial services trading company that it set up. Ironically, BCCI itself lost huge amounts of money in the series of illegal US bank acquisitions and from the improperly secured loans underpinning them that led to its investigation and closure in 1991.

When BCCIs problems were uncovered in the 1991 probe, regulators in seven countries moved quickly to take over the banks branches. On July 5, offices in the UK, US, France, Spain, Switzerland, Luxembourg and the Cayman Islands were seized, and the banks business activities were frozen. BCCIs assets were ultimately liquidated, and a pool was established to reimburse depositors who had lost their funds when the bank shut down.

Despite various investigations and reports since 1991, it is difficult to sum up the cause of the BCCI scandal in any simple way. Lax corporate governance, manipulation by backers and bank officers with their own personal agendas, general fraud and failure of fundamental risk management structures at the highest level of the bank can be considered the primary engines driving the losses to the banks stakeholders. More specifically, the banks untenable loan and acquisitions strategies, poor treasury and record-keeping practices, and its habit of hiding the massive losses that resulted, led to its downfall. BCCIs numerous regulatory violations and legal liabilities, and its negligence in protecting the interests of depositors who were not wealthy or well connected, hardly need pointing out.

On a brighter note, the bank officers and liquidators appointed by the courts after the scandal have used settlements, forfeitures and fines to recover significant monies for stakeholders, particularly small depositors, damaged by the banks failure. In December 1991, BCCI made the first of many large contributions to the depositor's restitution pool, when it pleaded guilty to criminal charges and agreed to forfeit $550 million. In 1994, the government of Abu Dhabi, which took over BCCI after the scandal broke, agreed to pay $1.9 billion to the depositor's pool. Meanwhile, from 1995, several of BCCIs wealthy Middle Eastern backers who had been sued or fined for their involvement in the scandal began to reach settlements worth hundreds of millions of dollars. In March 2001, BCCIs liquidators were granted leave by the House of Lords to sue one of BCCIs principal regulators, the Bank of England, for up to 1 billion for failing to monitor BCCI properly.

Lessons Learned:

- The critical role of senior management and key investors in establishing an honest, open and prudent bank culture.
- The need for powerful executives and backers of institutions to be controlled within a secure enterprise-wide corporate governance structure, if the interests of other stakeholders, such as deposit holders, are to be safeguarded.
- The need for independent and unified regulation and auditing of complex financial conglomerates.
- The danger that attempts to preserve confidence in a bank, even when well-intentioned, will lead to further cover-ups inside and outside the bank.
- The oldest lesson of all: the ease with which massive bad loans and trading losses can be covered up in banks by extending further credit, failing to record deposits, and juggling accounts.

FIRST NATIONAL BANK OF KEYSTONE

Introduction and Case Details:

On the 1 September 1999 the US Office of the Comptroller of the Currency (OCC) closed the First National Bank of Keystone, saying investigators were unable to account for some $515 million of the $1.1 billion assets recorded on the books of the 85-year old mortgage bank.

The bank had long been the economic mainstay of Keystone, a small town in a depressed coal-mining region of West Virginia. But it soon became clear that bank officer fraud, risky bank strategies and poor oversight had turned Keystone's only financial institution into one of the costliest failures for the Federal Deposit Insurance Corporation (FDIC) since the Great Depression. Losses to the FDIC (which compensates depositors for insured deposits when a bank fails) rose from that early estimate of $515 million to estimates in spring 2002 of $780-$820 million.

Keystone's failure at the height of the late 1990s economic boom sent shock waves through the regulatory and banking community. It concentrated attention on bank exposure to subprime loans and securitisation risks, and on the need for regulatory bodies to act decisively when they suspect that management might be obstructing regulatory scrutiny. By the late 1990s, Keystone's business centred on providing high-loan-to-value home equity loans, including home improvement and debt consolidation loans. It was feted as one of the most profitable small banks in the country and in 1999 it reported assets of $1.1 billion.

Keystone was also precocious on the liability side of its balance sheet, where it took advantage of the emerging wholesale deposit market to an unusual degree. This market allowed banks to collect deposits in chunks of millions of dollars from brokers, as opposed to the traditional route of gaining new funds by attracting larger numbers of individual, local depositors. But if Keystone had turned itself into a credit pipeline to channel asset-backed risk into the investment markets, the pipeline was poorly engineered in terms of board oversight, accounting, documentation and risk management. Indeed, regulators later wondered whether the complex risky loan investment programme had been set up primarily as a 'front' so that certain bank executives could disguise irregular payments to themselves and businesses that they owned.

The irregular payments only became apparent after the bank's collapse, but Keystone's risky business strategy attracted regulatory interest through the 1990s. A subsequent report on the regulatory examinations of the bank found that regulators had, since 1992, routinely identified unsafe and unsound practices, regulatory violations and questionable management activities. By 1997, the OCC had transferred responsibility for reviewing Keystone to a unit that focused on problem banks, and in 1998 the bank was banned from accepting any further brokered deposits. But its relatively complex transactions, and protests from its management, meant that bank examiners never seemed to push quite hard enough to reveal Keystone's true condition until the summer of 1999. (Ironically, bank executives were later to argue that regulatory prejudice was a contributing factor to the bank's failure.)

Investigators also came to believe that the bank recklessly accepted very poor quality loan assets and inflated the value of assets to mend gaps in its balance sheet. In part, Keystone's business strategy had left it open to attempts to fudge the books. Credit risky 'residual assets' are an inevitable side-effect of bank securitisation programmes. But their value can be very volatile and uncertain, because it depends upon default and prepayment rates that are hard to forecast at the time of the securitisation. At an industry level, the collapse revealed the level of losses that can be incurred when a small bank begins to take advantage of innovations in banking and financial markets such as wholesale brokerages and securitisation. The failure of the bank proved deeply embarrassing to the OCC and other regulators, and expensive for the FDIC

Lessons learned:

- Nothing is too strange to be true when bank fraud by top executives is suspected.
- Bank boards and others charged with oversight must understand a bank's business and maintain checks that are independent of any dominating group of bank executives.
- New bank markets and products offer opportunities for fraud because they tend to speed up the rate and scale of potential risk-taking while deterring and confusing investigators.
- Fraud is a special risk: any suspicion of fraud should prompt deeper, wider investigations (rather than a request to resolve the immediate problem).

LLOYD'S, A BRITISH INSURANCE MARKET

Introduction and Case details:

From the 1930s through to the 1950s, Lloyd's, a British insurance market, attempted to establish a strong foothold in the U.S market. It did so by using broadly worded policies without monetary limits that gave it a competitive advantage. Unfortunately, during this time period, exposure to asbestos and other pollutants and health hazards was causing health problems that would later lead to an avalanche of claims and lawsuits. The losses began to surface in 1991. The losses announced in 1991 for the 1988 syndicates were 509 million pounds sterling, the largest single-year loss in Lloyd's history. Once the premium reserves were paid out, Lloyd's began demanding cash from Names in the affected syndicates. Some of the Names objected to this and began filing lawsuits against Lloyd's, and, in some cases, against their members' agents. The story of Lloyd's is a tale in which a misunderstanding of the relevant business resulted in the near-downfall of an old and venerable institution - Lloyd's had been in business for 300 years before scandal hit - as well as immeasurable personal heartache.

The market's general business strategy was to sell insurance policies backed by the personal wealth of investors, known as "Names", since their signatures once appeared on the face of each of Lloyd's insurance policies. Names signed up through managers of syndicates, known as "working Names", and pledged their entire personal wealth, to cover any insurance losses the syndicate must pay out. In exchange, the Names could expect to share in any profits the syndicate made. The Names signed on to a one-year syndicate to insure risks; two additional years were allotted for settling claims. If all claims were not settled at that point, the remaining risks (incurred but not reported "IBNR" liabilities) were insured with a syndicate from the next year, so that the Names from the prior syndicate could receive their share of the profits (or pay their share of the losses).

Of course, this practice required that the risks associated with future claims be calculated accurately, so that the new syndicate could be paid a fair premium for taking on the risks of the old one. At the time that this practice was developed, only about 100 of the Names (the working Names) were actually involved in the Lloyd's business. The other Names, known as "external Names", relied on their syndicate managing agents to protect their interests by ensuring that the IBNR liabilities were accurately calculated. Companies who wished to purchase insurance policies from Lloyd's went to brokers who handled Lloyd's business exclusively. Lloyd's was able to write many large policies, some of an innovative nature, because the risks of the policies could then be divided among many different syndicates.

During the 1980s, Lloyd's took steps to shore up its legal position. In 1982, the UK Parliament passed the Lloyd's act, granting Lloyd's immunity from most lawsuits and giving the Council of Lloyd's the authority to unilaterally and retroactively change Lloyd's by-laws, which had previously required a majority vote of Names at a General Meeting. In 1986, for the 1987 year of account, Lloyd's required members to sign a new General Undertaking in which Names agreed that any legal disputes with Lloyd's would be brought in English courts and under English law. Major losses began to surface in 1991. The losses announced that year, for the 1988 syndicate, were 509 million pounds sterling, the largest single-year loss in Lloyd's history. Once the premium reserves were paid out, Lloyd's began demanding cash from Names in the affected syndicates, both to cover outstanding claims and to amass reserves against future IBNR claims.

Lloyd's had returned to profit: in 1998, the company reported a record profit of 1.149 billion pounds sterling for the 1995 calendar year. Its unique and historic structure, however, has changed significantly. It has been forced to allow corporations in as investors, so that the Names are now a minority. The market also suffered substantial reputational damage - the fact that Names refused to pay up was especially damaging, since Lloyd's was structured on the guarantee that these investors gave to pay all claims. Since the scandal, Lloyd's has lost considerable amounts of business to U.S. insurers and insurers in new markets such as Bermuda. These competitors have stolen a large share of segments such as property reinsurance that were once dominated by Lloyd's.

As in the case of many fiascos, Lloyd's woes arose from an intermingling of two factors. First, there was the imprudence of writing of broadly-worded policies, which opened Lloyd's up to the vagaries of unknown risks such as asbestos as well as to American litigiousness. The second component of the problem stemmed from the poor relationship between the external Names and the working Names. Many of the working Names knew nothing about insurance and were relying on the working Names to inform them of the risks. It was when the working Names felt that this relationship of trust had been violated that they refused to pay up, compounding the reputational damage to Lloyd's.

Lessons learned:

- When Lloyd's began issuing the broadly-worded insurance policies, the resulting gain in market share apparently overshadowed the grim possibility of being held liable for immense losses. It was purely a business strategy's large upside blind you to its downside.
- Although there was no way that Lloyd's could have specifically predicted the massive losses from asbestos-related claims, the very fact that insurance claims are unpredictable should have dictated caution in issuing broadly-worded policies.
- The entire Lloyd's structure was predicated upon the Names, it was essential that they should feel completely informed. While it could not be known exactly what the working Names told external Names, they should have been sure to explicitly warn the Names, many of whom likely knew little about insurance, of the possibility of large losses, and of the existence of broadly-worded policies that could incur losses at any time. If the external Names had felt more involved and informed, it was possible that few of them would have refused to pay up and/or filed lawsuits, resulting in a less damaging scandal.
- Even if Lloyd's did not inform investors of the existence of the broadly-worded policies, savvy investors might have been able to unearth these facts. Likewise, if investors had made themselves aware of the Lloyd's Act of 1982, they might have realised that they might have little recourse in court.
- Risk managers and auditors tend to focus on the business activities associated with high losses. However, business activities that generate high growth or profitability should also be scrutinized. In Lloyd's case, success in gaining market share through lenient policy terms created significant "tail risk" in the insurance portfolio.

LONG-TERM CAPITAL MANAGEMENT

Introduction and Case Details:

In 1994, John Meriwether, the famed Salomon Brothers bond trader, founded a hedge fund called Long-Term Capital Management. Meriwether assembled an all-star team of traders and academics in an attempt to create a fund that would profit from the combination of the academics' quantitative models and the traders' market judgement and execution capabilities. Sophisticated investors, including many large investment banks, flocked to the fund, investing $1.3 billion at inception. But four years later, at the end of September 1998, the fund had lost substantial amounts of the investors' equity capital and was teetering on the brink of default. To avoid the threat of a systemic crisis in the world financial system, the Federal Reserve orchestrated a $3.5 billion rescue package from leading U.S. investment and commercial banks. In exchange the participants received 90% of LTCM's equity. LTCM's main strategy was to make convergence trades. These trades involved finding securities that were mispriced relative to one another, taking long positions in the cheap ones and short positions in the rich ones. There were four main types of trade:

- Convergence among U.S., Japan, and European sovereign bonds;
- Convergence among European sovereign bonds;
- Convergence between on-the-run and off-the-run U.S. government bonds;
- Long positions in emerging markets sovereigns, hedged back to dollars.

Because these differences in values were tiny, the fund needed to take large and highly leveraged positions in order to make a significant profit. At the beginning of 1998, the fund had equity of $5 billion and had borrowed over $125 billion — a leverage factor of roughly thirty to one. LTCM's partners believed, on the basis of their complex computer models, that the long and short positions were highly correlated and so the net risk was small.

In 1994, Long-Term Capital Management was founded by John Meriwether and accepted investments from 80 investors who put up a minimum of $10 million each. The initial equity capitalisation of the firm was $1.3 billion. By the end of 1997, after two years of returns running close to 40%, the fund had some $7 billion under management and was achieving only a 27% return — comparable with the return on US equities that year. Meriwether returns about $2.7 billion of the fund's capital back to investors because "investment opportunities were not large and attractive enough". In the year 1998, the portfolio under LTCM's control amounts to well over $100 billion, while net asset value stands at some $4 billion; its swaps position was valued at some $1.25 trillion notional, equal to 5% of the entire global market. It had become a major supplier of index volatility to investment banks, was active in mortgage-backed securities and was dabbling in emerging markets such as Russia. Meanwhile, Russia devalued the rouble and declares a moratorium on 281 billion roubles ($13.5 billion) of its Treasury debt. The result was a massive "flight to quality", with investors flooding out of any remotely risky market and into the most secure instruments within the already "risk-free" government bond market. Ultimately, this results in a liquidity crisis of enormous proportions, dealing a severe blow to LTCM's portfolio. LTCM's equity had dropped to $2.3 billion. John Meriwether circulated a letter which disclosed the massive loss and offered the chance to invest in the fund "on special terms". Existing investors were told that they would not be allowed to withdraw more than 12% of their investment. LTCM's equity had dropped to $600 million. The portfolio had not shrunk significantly, and so its leverage was even higher. Banks began to doubt the fund's ability to meet its margin calls but could not move to liquidate for fear that it would precipitate a crisis that would cause huge losses among the fund's counterparties and potentially lead to a systemic crisis. Goldman Sachs, AIG and Warren Buffett offered to buy out LTCM's partners for $250 million, to inject $4 billion into the ailing fund and ran it as part of Goldman's proprietary trading operation. The offer was not accepted. The Federal Reserve Bank of New York, acting to prevent a potential systemic meltdown, organised a rescue package under which a consortium of leading investment and commercial banks, including LTCM's major creditors, injected $3.5-billion into the fund and took over its management, in exchange for 90% of LTCM's equity.

The damage from LTCM's near-demise was widespread. Many banks took a substantial write-off as a result of losses on their investments. UBS took a third-quarter charge in 1998 of $700 million, Dresdner Bank AG a $145 million charge, and Credit Suisse $55 million. Additionally, UBS chairman Mathis Cabiallavetta and three top executives resigned in the wake of the bank's losses and Merrill Lynch's global head of risk and credit management likewise left the firm. Initially, LTCM posted strong growth figures, capital grew from $1 bn to more than $2.7 bn by 1997. LTCM also charged higher fees as compared to its peer funds. In 1997, for example, it charged around $1.5 bn as fees. The total asset size of the fund had grown to around $125 bn by the year 1997 with around 60,000 trades on its books. This, when compared to its equity of $5 bn revealed a leverage ratio of around 25:1. Even more surprising, though, was the off-balance sheet portfolio of the fund. LTCM had entered into swaps and other derivative transactions whose notional principal amount added to $1.25 trillion. The "relative-value" arbitrage strategy worked well for LTCM till 1997. This was as a result of yield spreads narrowing till 1997, when it reached 20 year lows. Thus LTCM was able to make profits through its strategy. In 1997, however, yield spreads began to widen. As a result of this LTCM began losing money on its strategy. The fund's returns fell to around 17% from around 40%. To maintain the earlier returns, the fund decided to reduce its capital base. It returned $2.7 bn to investors while maintaining an asset base of $130 bn. This raised the leverage to around 28. The critical event, however, was the default by Russia on international debt. This single event sent bond yield spreads soaring. LTCM lost heavily in its strategy, posting a loss of $550 m in a single day. The event wiped out half of the capital base of LTCM. The leverage of the fund increased from 28 to 55.

Lesson learned:

- The proximate cause for LTCM's debacle was Russia's default on its government obligations (GKOs). LTCM believed it had somewhat hedged its GKO position by selling rubles. In theory, if Russia defaulted on its bonds, then the value of its currency would collapse and a profit could be made in the foreign exchange market that would offset the loss on the bonds. Unfortunately, the banks guaranteeing the ruble hedge shut down when the Russian ruble collapsed, and the Russian government prevented further trading in its currency. While this caused significant losses for LTCM, these losses were not even close to being large enough to bring the hedge fund down. Rather, the ultimate cause of its demise was the ensuing flight to liquidity.
- The ultimate cause of the LTCM debacle was the "flight to liquidity" across the global fixed income markets. As Russia's troubles became deeper and deeper, fixed-income portfolio managers began to shift their assets to more liquid assets. In particular, many investors shifted their investments into the U.S. Treasury market. In fact, so great was the panic that investors moved money not just into Treasuries, but into the most liquid part of the U.S. Treasury market "on-the-run" Treasuries. While the U.S. Treasury market is relatively liquid in normal market conditions, this global flight to liquidity hit the on-the-run Treasuries like a freight train. The spread between the yields on on-the-run Treasuries and off-the-run Treasuries widened dramatically, even though the off-the-run bonds were theoretically cheap relative to the on-the-run bonds. What LTCM had failed

to account for is that a substantial portion of its balance sheet was exposed to a general change in the "price" of liquidity. If liquidity became more valuable (as it did following the crisis) its short positions would increase in price relative to its long positions. This was essentially a massive, unhedged exposure to a single risk factor. As an aside, this situation was made worse by the fact that the size of the new issuance of U.S. Treasury bonds has declined over the past several years. This has effectively reduced the liquidity of the Treasury market, making it more likely that a flight to liquidity could dislocate this market.

- The preceding analysis explains why LTCM almost failed. However, it does not explain why this near-failure should threaten the stability of the global financial markets. The reason was that virtually all of the leveraged Treasury bond investors had similar positions, Salomon Brothers, Merrill Lynch, the III Fund (a fixed-income hedge fund that also failed as a result of the crisis) and likely others. There were two reasons for the lack of diversity of opinion in the market. The first is that virtually all of the sophisticated models being run by the leveraged players said the same thing that off-the-run treasury were significantly cheap compared with the on-the-run treasuries. The second is that many of the investment banks obtained order flow information through their dealings with LTCM. They therefore would have known many of the actual positions and would have taken up similar positions alongside their client. Indeed, one industry participant suggested that the Russian crisis was the crowning blow on a domino effect that had started months before. In early 1998, Sandy Weill, as co-head of Citigroup, decided to shut down the famous Salomon Brothers Treasury bond arbitrage desk. Salomon, one of the largest players in the on-the-run/off-the-run trade, had to begin liquidating its positions. As it did so, these trades became cheaper and cheaper, putting pressure on all of the other leveraged players.

- LTCM was perhaps the biggest disaster of its kind, but it was not the first. It had been preceded by a number of other cases of highly-leveraged quantitative firms that went under in similar circumstances. One of them was Franklin Savings and Loan, a hedge fund dressed down as a savings and loan. Franklin's management had figured out that many of the riskier pieces of mortgage derivatives were undervalued because the market could not understand the risk on the risky pieces and the market overvalued those pieces with well-behaved accounting results. Franklin decided it was willing to suffer volatile accounting results in exchange for good economics.

  The Granite funds, which specialised in mortgage-backed securities trading, suffered as the result of similar trading strategies. The funds took advantage of the fact that "toxic waste" (risky tranches) from the mortgage derivatives market were good economic value. However, when the Fed raised interest rates in February 1994, Wall Street firms rushed to liquidate mortgage-backed securities, often at huge discounts. Both of these firms claimed to have been hedged, but both went under when they were "margin-called". In Franklin's case, the caller was the Office of Thrift Supervision; in the Granite Fund's, the margin lenders. What is the common theme among Franklin, the Granite Funds and LTCM? All three depended on exploiting deviations in market value from fair value. And all three depended on "patient capital", shareholders and lenders who believed that what mattered was fair value and not market value. That is, these fund managers convinced their stakeholders that because the fair values were hedged, it didn't matter what happened to market values in the short run — they would converge to fair value over time. That was the reason for the "Long Term" part of LTCM's name.

The problem with this logic is that capital is only as patient as its least patient provider. The fact is that lenders generally lose their patience precisely when the funds need them to keep it in times of market crisis. As all three cases demonstrate, the lenders are the first to get nervous when an external shock hits. At that point, they begin to ask the fund manager for market valuations, not models-based fair valuations. This starts the fund along the downward spiral, illiquid securities are marked-to-market, margin calls are made, the illiquid securities must be sold, more margin calls are made, and so on. In general, shareholders may provide patient capital; but debt-holders do not. The lesson learned from these case studies spoils some of the supposed "free lunch" features of taking liquidity risk. These plays can indeed generate excellent risk-adjusted returns, but only if held for a long time. Unfortunately the only real source of capital that is patient enough to take fluctuations in market values, especially through crises, is equity capital.

- LTCM fell victim to a flight to liquidity. This phenomenon is common enough in capital markets crises that it should be built into risk models, either by introducing a new risk factor, liquidity or by including a flight to liquidity in the stress testing. This could be accomplished crudely by classifying securities as either liquid or illiquid. Liquid securities are assigned a positive exposure to the liquidity factor; illiquid securities are assigned a negative exposure to the liquidity factor. The size of the factor movement (measured in terms of the movement of the spread between liquid and illiquid securities) can be estimated either statistically or heuristically (perhaps using the LTCM crisis as a "worst case" scenario). Using this approach, LTCM might have classified most of its long positions as illiquid and most of its short positions as liquid, thus having a notional exposure to the liquidity factor equal to twice its total balance sheet. A more refined model would account for a spectrum of possible liquidity across securities; at a minimum, however, the general concept of exposure to a liquidity risk factor should be incorporated in to any leveraged portfolio.

- Another key lesson to be learnt from the LTCM debacle is that even (or especially) the most sophisticated financial models are subject to model risk and parameter risk, and should therefore be stress-tested and tempered with judgement. According to the complex mathematical models used by LTCM, the positions were low risk. Judgement tells that the key assumption that the models depended on was the high correlation between the long and short positions. Certainly, recent history suggested that correlations between corporate bonds of different credit quality would move together (a correlation of between 90-95% over a 2-year horizon). During LTCM's crisis, however, this correlation dropped to 80%. Stress-testing against this lower correlation might have led LTCM to assume less leverage in taking this bet. However, if LTCM had thought to stress test this correlation, given that it was such an important assumption, it would not even have had to make up a stress scenario. Simply including this stress scenario in the risk management of the fund might have led LTCM to assume less leverage in taking this bet.

- One of the other lessons to be learned by other financial institutions is that it is important to aggregate risk exposures across businesses. Many of the large dealer banks exposed to a Russian crisis across many different businesses only became aware of the commonality of these exposures after the LTCM crisis. For example, these banks owned Russian GKOs on their arbitrage desks, made commercial loans to Russian corporates in their lending businesses, and had indirect exposure to a Russian crisis through their prime brokerage lending to LTCM. A systematic risk management process should have discovered these common linkages *ex ante* and reported or reduced the risk concentration.

ORANGE COUNTY

Introduction and Case details:

On December 6 1994, Orange County, a prosperous district in California, declared bankruptcy after suffering losses of around $1.6 billion from a wrong-way bet on interest rates in one of its principal investment pools. The pool was intended to be a conservative but profitable way of managing the county's cash flows, and those of 241 associated local government entities. Instead, it triggered the largest financial failure of a local government in US history. Robert Citron, the hitherto widely respected Orange County treasurer who controlled the $7.5 billion pool, had riskily invested the pools funds in a leveraged portfolio of mainly interest-linked securities. His strategy depended on short-term interest rates remaining relatively low when compared with medium-term interest rates. But from February 1994, the Federal Reserve Bank began to raise US interest rates, causing many securities in Orange County's investment pool to fall in value.

During much of 1994, Citron ignored the shift in the interest rate environment and the mounting paper losses in his portfolio. But by the end of 1994, demands for billions of dollars of collateral from Citrons Wall Street counterparties, and the threat of a run on deposits from spooked local government investors, created a liquidity trap that he could not escape. Citron could not have undertaken such a risky investment strategy if his actions had been subject to informed and independent risk oversight, and detailed risk-averse investment guidelines. Following the debacle, Orange County revised many aspects of its control procedures and its financial governance, and established a stricter set of investment policies.

One thing is certain while the pool offered greater returns than those of similar cash management pools, it did so only by taking on more risk. In particular, Citron gambled that medium-term interest-bearing securities would maintain or increase their value. He used various techniques to leverage his $7.5 billion of funds into more than $20 billion of investments so that both the returns and the risks were multiplied. One way he did this was to enter into contracts known as reverse repurchase agreements, which allowed him to use securities the pool had already purchased as collateral on further borrowings, and further cycles of investing. But these agreements left him vulnerable to calls for more collateral if the market value of the original collateral fell.

Citron also used around $2.8 billion of structured notes, or derivatives, to increase his bet on the structure of the interest rate yield curve. These included many inverse floaters notes whose coupon falls as interest rates rise as well as index amortising notes and collateralised mortgage obligations. The relative complexity of the instruments, the daisy-chain structure of the portfolio and Citrons limited financial reporting made it difficult for independent critics to understand or prove how risky the strategy really was. But the end result is clear the pool transformed short-term funds intended for vital public services into a risky and leveraged investment in medium-term financial instruments. As long as short-term interest rates remained low, as they did in the early 1990s, Citrons bet on the relative value of medium-term interest rate-linked securities paid off and all concerned prospered. The strategy soured with a shift in policy by the Federal Reserve in February 1994. That month saw the first of a succession of hikes in interest rates that ultimately saw the Fed raise rates by some 2.25 per cent over the course of 1994. By November, the investment pool was in crisis as the value of its interest rate-sensitive medium-term investments sank, and calls for more collateral arrived from Wall Street.

Citrons counterparties prepared to seize and liquidate billions of dollars of the investment pools collateral, while the government entities that had invested in the fund, lacking credible reassurances, looked to withdraw their money. Wall Street institutions began to sell off the securities they held as collateral against their agreements with Orange County. The Orange County Board of Supervisors took legal advice and declared bankruptcy, a move that prevented investors withdrawing any more of their funds. But this makes little difference to the fundamental lessons to be learned from the debacle. Citron exposed a set of conservative investors with specific funding needs to a risky portfolio. He failed to communicate the extent of the market risk, or liquidity risk, to either the investors or to his supervisory board though he did not try to hide the fundamentals of his strategy. (Had he properly assessed and communicated the level of risk, the pool would not have attracted risk-averse funds in the first place).

In February 1994, Fed made the first of a series of interest rate hikes, and so threatened the directional bet on interest rates built into the Orange County investment pool. Orange County treasurer Robert Citron tried to calm growing fears among investors. Auditors found that the pool has massively lost value and Citron confirmed that the pool faces $1.5 billion loss and subsequently Citron resigned. By the end of 1994, Orange Country filed for protection prompted by due date of certain repo transactions. In 1995, US Bankruptcy Court endorsed settlement of what is left in the investment pool. Some 241 participants got 77 cents in each dollar of their investment balance as a cash distribution. By 1997, Moodys Investors Service rewarded the county's recovery and new investment policies with an investment grade rating for key county borrowings. In 2000, some 200 municipal and governmental agencies finally made good in a disbursement of $864 million. But Orange County continued to pay off the recovery bonds it issued in 1995/1996 to fund the bulk of the pools losses.

Lessons Learned:

- Beware the unconstrained star performer, even when he or she has a long track record. Where there is excess reward, there is risk, though it might take time to surface.
- If the organisational structure, planning and risk oversight mechanisms of an institution are fractured, it is easy for powerful individuals to hide risk in the gaps.
- Borrowing short and investing long means liquidity risk, as every bank knows.
- Risk-averse investors must tie investment objectives to investment actions by means of a strict framework of investment policies, guidelines, risk reporting and independent and expert oversight.

- Risk reporting should be complete, and easily comprehensible to independent professionals. Strategies that are not possible to explain to third parties should not be employed by the risk averse.

BANKERS TRUST (BT)

Introduction and Case Details:

Bankers Trust (BT) was sued by four of its major clients - Federal Paper Board Company, Gibson Greetings, Air Products and Chemical, and Procter & Gamble, who asserted that Bankers Trust had misled them with respect to the riskiness and value of derivatives that they had purchased from the bank. The first three cases were settled out of court for a total of $93 million. The $195 million Procter & Gamble suit was settled at a net gain to P&G of $78 million. The most lasting damage, however, was to BT's reputation. In the mid-1990s, Bankers Trust (now part of Deutsche Bank) was one of the leading bank in the marketing of innovative financial products. The bank prided itself on its superior financial abilities and on its leading edge risk management with respect to its derivatives trading. Yet Bankers Trust's reputation took a pounding after the bank was sued by several customers alleging various forms of fraud and racketeering with respect to derivatives transactions they had entered into with the bank. Several of these suits have since been settled both in and out of court, costing the company millions of dollars in settlement and possibly much more in damage to its reputation. The root cause of these problems appears to have been that BT's clients felt that BT had unfairly exploited their comparative lack of sophistication in handling these sophisticated derivative products. For example, Procter & Gamble (P&G), the client whose case received the most publicity, had entered into complex interest-rate derivatives transactions with the bank. These transactions represented a bet on P&G's part that US interest rates would remain stable, or decline, over the transaction period. If interest rates rose, however, P&G would lose a substantial amount of money. In addition, P&G made its bets more aggressive by leveraging its positions twenty-to-one.

The transactions lost a substantial amount after the US Federal Reserve Board raised interest rates repeatedly in 1994. P&G subsequently sued BT for $195 million, claiming that the bank had failed to fully inform it with respect to the risk involved in the transactions. BT countered that it was not acting in an advisory (or "fudiciary") role to P&G, since the firm had retained its own outside experts to create interest rate forecasts. It also claimed that P&G's reputation for using cutting-edge financing techniques cast doubt on its claims to be nave in this matter. This appears to be an example of poor stakeholder management. In focusing on increasing profits, Bankers Trust didn't pay adequate attention to the fact that its clients were vital to its business. Even if it did nothing dishonest, it failed to serve its clients in terms of making them feel informed and at ease with their deals.

In 1994, Procter and Gamble Co. sued Bankers Trust for $195 million (the company recorded a $102 million charge against fiscal 1994 earnings to cover losses from derivatives transactions), alleging that BT misled it with regard to the value and risks of its derivatives positions. BT signed consent decrees with federal securities regulators and agreed to pay a $10 million fine over allegations that it wilfully gave Gibson Greetings inaccurate values for its derivatives portfolio, causing Gibson to violate SEC laws. BT neither admited nor denies guilt. In 1995, US District Judge John Feikens allowed P&G to add civil racketeering charges to its suit, which would allow the company to seek treble damages. In early 1996, Bankers

Trust settled with Air Products and Chemicals, Inc. for $67 million, 63% of the $107 in losses in fiscal 1994 that Air Products wrote off in connection with interest-rate swaps the company entered into with Bankers Trust. Bankers Trust and Procter & Gamble reached an out-of-court settlement in which P&G agrees to pay $35 million of the $195 million it owed BT and forgo between $5 and $14 million in gains on a separate contract. P&G reported a net gain of $78 million with respect to the issue in its quarterly reports.

Lessons Learned:

- An enterprise risk management program must balance the "hard side" of risk management (including policies, limits and systems) and the soft side (including people, culture and incentives). It is ironic that BT, a company that was considered by many to be a leader in risk management and in innovative derivative products, lost so much of its reputation as a result of operational risk (in this case, sales practices).
- Reputational risk management suggests that in a time of crisis, management should focus on integrity and openness in dealing with customer complaints and public perception, if the allegations brought by P&G had any basis in reality, Bankers Trust did an inadequate job in resolving them.
- Performance pressure may encourage participation in deals that ultimately backfire, especially if incentives and oversight are not aligned properly. Despite the urgency of the rush to sell a deal or gain a client, proper thought needs to be given to the long-term wisdom of all aspects of the deal.
- Clients are stakeholders, too! In the rush to create profits for shareholders, attention must still be given to the clients who are integral to the business.

ENRON

Introduction and Case Details:

Enron was formed by merger of Houston Natural Gas and InterNorth in 1985. The company adopted the name Enron in 1986. Enron, a natural gas pipeline company of $2 billion grown to a global energy giant with total revenues of more than $100 billion by year 2000. During its transition from a simple pipeline company to global energy company, Enron took heavy positions in off-balance sheet financial instruments for buying assets and to hedge its investment. In the year 1998, Enron launched EnronOnline trading company and became one of the world largest trader. Enron took exposure in all segments of derivative trade such as commodity, financial, weather etc. using exotic derivatives. In year 2001, Enron filed for bankruptcy.

In fact, it was through the unscrupulous acts of some of the top management people that the downfall of Enron occurred. Enron Development Corporation was formed in 1991 with Rebecca Mark as the CEO. In 1993, EDC became Enron International and in 1998, Enron purchased Sao Paulo and Wessex Water for $1.3 billion and $2.4 billion respectively. In November 1999, UK regulators ordered a 12% cut in the prices Wessex could charge customers, with operating expense going through the roof, problems were accentuated. In 2002, Wessex Water was sold to a Malaysian company for a fraction of the price paid. Enron's India business in Dabhol (Maharashtra) which involved an investment of $900 million also went sour. Enron had to shut down the plant in the end. This project was also met wrong end because of Mark. At least 25 banks and financial institutions worldwide were having gross exposure of $10 billion to Enron. None of the major bank in the world was left who had not given money to Enron and most of the loans were unsecured. Energy companies were also having Enron relative derivative positions of $6 billion.

In the year 2000, the price of Enron share soared by 87%. In March 2001, California officials began investigation into alleged price gouging by Enron as well as other power marketers. In the mid of 2001, Enron executives started selling shares which led to 39% fall in stock price. By the end of year 2001, Enron started reporting loss.

Lessons Learned:

- Enron was under debt trap and its credit rating was of investment grade. Still company spent lavishly on corporate offices and entertaining clients and counterparties. Not only this Enron purchased a fleet and a $41.6 million Gulfstream V for personal use of management. Enron's staff strength also got doubled, going from 7,456 employees to 15,555 during 1996 and 1997. This shows unrelated business expenses without any revenue generation which led to uncontrolled expenditure.
- In 1998, Enron invested $10 million in an Internet company and the time of listing Enron investment grown by 3 folds. By May 1999, the value of Enron's investment was over $ 300 million but it could not sell because of a six-month lockout provision. Enron was also having large unrealized gain on a forward contract it had purchases from Union Bank of Switzerland (UBS) against its own stock. The income from this could not be booked because accounting rules prohibited firms from including the gains on their own stock in their income. To protect these gains and recognize them as income, Enron floated four Special Purpose Vehicle (SPV). The net effect was to transfer the forward contracts on Enron stock to SPVs. The accounting was dubious for many reasons. This way Enron booked income resulting from rises in its own stock price. If an asset changed hands at an inflated price, it would be market-to-market at that new price, and the selling party would recognize income. Enron realised millions of dollars in market value gains from SPVs. At the same time, SPV was earning high returns for its investors. Larger and increasingly dubious SPVs followed and the SPVs also generated extraordinary returns for investors. Some of the senior management was the investors in these SPVs and having conflict of interest.
- The SPV deal caused serious problems both within Enron and in its accounting firm, Arthur Andersen. Still, the deal moved forward and Enron was a very big client of Andersen and the latter was determined to keep Enorn happy. It signed off on the deal. In June 2002, Arthur Andersen was convicted of obstruction of justice for its destruction of Enron documents Andersen, once the largest accounting firm in the United States was barred from auditing clients.
- In 1993, Enorn had formed a limited partnership (Joint Venture) with pension fund to invest in natural gas projects. Enron earned profits from the partnership but JV debts were not appearing on Enron's balance sheet. In 1997, Enron formed a new venture to take earlier partners place as an investor in JV. By replacing earlier partner Enron

kept JV debt off its balance sheet. This led to an elaborate scheme involving multiple Special Purpose Entities. All of new venture Funding originated either from Enron or as loans guaranteed by Enron. Enron treated new venture as an independent entity for accounting purposes, but this was not correct. Later this was treated as inadequate disclosure by Enron in its accounts and Enron hide chanelising of its own fund into JVs without taking effects in own book.

- In 1991, Enron's Audit Committee allowed to apply mark-to-market accounting to Enron Capital's trading books. For liquid trading activities, mark-to-market accounting is used and gives better picture about investment in comparison to accrual accounting. It is used in the capital markets but Enron Capital was trading mostly in illiquid markets such as long-dated gas and power deals for which no liquid markets existed. In this context, mark-to-market accounting was not appropriate. Traders manipulated prices as their bonuses were depending upon the profitability of deals. There was a hidden conflict of interest. In October 2001, Enron reported third quarter earnings including one-time charge of $1 billion for writing down bad investments. In November 2001, Enron filed restated financial results with the SEC, consolidating the financials of its JVs with Enron's for the period 1997-2002. The consolidation of accounts of partnership companies reduced Enron's earnings for the period and increased Enron's debt by $2.6 billion.

SUB-PRIME LENDING DEBACLE IN US MORTGAGE MARKET[3]

Introduction and Case Details:

The subprime mortgage financial crisis refers to the sharp rise in foreclosures in the subprime mortgage market that began in the United States in 2006 and became a global financial crisis in July 2007. Rising interest rates increased newly-popular adjustable rate mortgages and property values suffered declines from the demise of the housing bubble, leaving home owners unable to meet financial commitments and lenders without a means to recoup their losses. The sharp rise in foreclosures after the housing bubble caused several major subprime mortgage lenders, such as New Century Financial Corporation, to shut down or file for bankruptcy, with some accused of actively encouraging fraudulent income inflation on loan applications, leading to the collapse of stock prices for many in the subprime mortgage industry, and drops in stock prices of some large lenders like Countrywide Financial.

This has been associated with declines in stock markets worldwide, several hedge funds becoming worthless, coordinated national bank interventions, contractions of retail profits, and bankruptcy of several mortgage lenders. Observers of the meltdown have cast blame widely. Some, like Senate Banking, Housing, and Urban Affairs Committee Chairman Chris Dodd of Connecticut, have highlighted the predatory lending practices of subprime lenders and the lack of effective government oversight. Others have charged mortgage brokers with steering borrowers to unaffordable loans, appraisers with inflating housing values, and Wall Street investors with backing subprime mortgage securities without verifying the strength of the portfolios. Borrowers have also been criticized for over-stating their incomes on loan applications and entering into loan agreements they could not meet. The effects of the meltdown spread beyond housing and disrupted global financial markets as investors, largely deregulated foreign and domestic hedge funds, were forced to re-evaluate the risks they were taking and consumers lost the ability to finance further consumer spending, causing increased volatility in the fixed income, equity, and derivative markets.

Subprime lending is a general term that refers to the practice of making loans to borrowers who do not qualify for market interest rates because of problems with their credit history or the ability to prove that they have enough income to support the monthly payment on the loan for which they are applying. Subprime loans or mortgages are risky for both creditors and debtors because of the combination of high interest rates, bad credit history, and murky financial situations often associated with subprime applicants. A subprime loan is one that is offered at a rate higher than A-paper loans due to the increased risk. Subprime, therefore, is not the same as "Alt-A", because Alt-A loans qualify for the "A-rating" by Moody's or other rating firms, albeit for an "alternative" means.

In the 20th century, collateralized debt obligations became popular investment vehicles, in use world-wide. Traditionally, when payments on a mortgage were late, the personal relationship between debtor and creditor allowed some leeway when paying off a mortgage. But when subprime mortgage-backed securities were collateralized, the traditional links between lenders and their creditors were severed. This created a vicious circle when subprime loan payers defaulted on their obligation, leaving foreclosure of their mortgages as the only perceived recourse for investors in the loan. When other homeowners with mortgages also attempt to meet their financial obligations, some of them put their homes up for sale, which drags down the price of other houses in their neighborhood, not merely those houses with subprime mortgages.

In 2006, substantial market correction was seen in US housing market. U.S. Home Construction Index was down over 40% as of mid-August 2006 compared to a year earlier. At the same time about $400 billion of ARMs were reset according to a NY Times report. In 2007, home sales and prices both continued to fall. The plunge in existing-home sales was the steepest since 1989. The subprime mortgage industry collapsed, and a surge of foreclosure activity (twice as bad as 2006) and rising interest rates threatened to depress prices further as problems in the subprime markets spreaded to the near-prime and prime mortgage markets. About $1 trillion of ARMs were to reset in 2007. Investors lost billions of dollars in securities tied to subprime mortgage assets, triggering turmoils in global financial markets. Many of the banks and financial institutions in US are still reporting losses in billion of dollars every day and the analysts feels that the problem of subprime is still not over. The size of losses may be even bigger than what has been disclosed so far.

Lesson Learned:

- There was an economic bubble in many parts of the U.S. housing market from 2001 to 2005, especially in populous areas such as California, Florida, New York, the BosWash megalopolis, and the Southwest markets. The real estate bubble in these and other parts of the U.S. was caused by historically low interest rates (meant to soften the blow of the massive collapse of the dot-com bubble), poor lending standards, and a mania for purchasing houses. This bubble is related to the stock market or dot-com bubble of the 1990s. A housing bubble is characterized by rapid increases in the valuations of real property such as housing until unsustainable levels are reached relative to incomes, price-to-rent ratios, and other economic indicators of affordability. This in turn is followed by decreases in home prices that can result in many owners holding negative equity, a mortgage debt higher than the value of the property.

- Bubbles may be definitively identified only in hindsight, after a market correction, which began for the U.S. housing market in 2005–2006. In the wake of the subprime mortgage crisis in 2007, which was caused by a large number of home owners unable to pay the mortgage as their home values declined, Freddie Mac CEO Richard Syron concluded, "We had a bubble," and concurred with Yale economist Robert Shiller's warning that home prices appear overvalued and that the correction could last years with trillions of dollars of home value being lost. Problems for home owners with good credit surfaced in mid-2007, causing the U.S.'s largest mortgage lender Countrywide Financial to warn that a recovery in the housing sector is not expected to occur at least until 2009 because home prices are falling "almost like never before, with the exception of the Great Depression". The impact of booming home valuations on the U.S. economy since the 2001–2002 recession was an important factor in the recovery because a large component of consumer spending came from the related refinancing boom, which simultaneously allowed people to reduce their monthly mortgage payments with lower interest rates and withdraw equity from their homes as values increased. The collapse of the U.S. Housing Bubble has a direct impact not only on home valuations, but the nation's mortgage markets, home builders, home supply retail outlets, and Wall Street hedge funds held by large institutional investors, increasing the risk of a nationwide recession.
- Homeowners had been using the increased property value experienced in the housing bubble to refinance their homes with lower interest rates and take out second mortgages against the added value to use the funds for consumer spending. In the early 2000s recession that began in early 2001 and was exacerbated by the September 11, 2001 terrorist attacks, Americans were asked to go "shopping because President Bush asked us to and for personal patriotism" and spend their way out of economic decline with "consumerism... cast as the new patriotism". The call linking patriotism to shopping was bipartisan with former President Bill Clinton urging his countrymen to "get out and shop", and corporations like General Motors producing commercials with the same theme. The housing bubble was largely fed by the lowering of interest rates to record low levels to diminish the blow of the massive collapse of the dot-com bubble. The collapse of the housing bubble, and resultant decline in property values, and increase in defaults has left lenders unable to recover losses.
- Other central banks around the world have begun coordinated efforts of their own to increase liquidity in their own currencies to stabilize foreign exchange rates (thus stemming a further fall in the American dollar and diminishing any incentive to sell them off) and prevent the probable significant global consequences a run on the American dollar would cause. It marks the first time the American, European, and Japanese central banks have taken such actions together since the aftermath of the September 11, 2001 terrorist attacks. Mortgage lenders and home builders fared terribly, but losses cut across sectors, with some of the worst-hit industries, such as metals & mining companies, having only the vaguest connection with lending or mortgages.

- Wall Street investment banks and other financial institutions around the world have also been affected. On June 20, 2007, Merrill Lynch seized $800 million in assets from two Bear Stearns hedge funds that were involved in securities backed by subprime loans. The two funds are now essentially worthless. American Home Mortgage Investment Corporation (AHMI, Melville, New York) filed bankruptcy after a layoff of its employees. Accredited Home Lenders reported that company expected to see up to a $60 million loss for the first quarter 2007. On 8 August 2007, Mortgage Guaranty Insurance Corporation (MGIC, Milwaukee, Wisconsin) announced it would discontinue its purchase of Radian Group (Philadelphia, Pennsylvania) after suffering a billion-dollar loss of its investment in Credit-Based Asset Servicing and Securitization (C-BASS, New York City). C-BASS is seeking to restructure its financing. The MGIC-Radian transaction would have been a $4.9 billion deal. Later, on August 9, French bank BNP Paribas stopped valuing three of its funds and suspended all withdrawals by investors after United States subprime mortgage woes had caused "a complete evaporation of liquidity". Goldman Sachs' $8 billion Global Alpha hedge fund, its largest, reportedly lost 26% in 2007. Later, on August 13, the company announced that a group of investors bailed out its Global Equity Opportunities fund by infusing $3 billion after it lost 28% of its total value in one week. Also, Citigroup has reported taking $700 million in losses in its credit business in July and August 2007.
- On August 15 2007, the stock of Countrywide Financial, which is the largest mortgage lender in the United States, fell around 13% on the New York Stock Exchange, its largest one-day decline since the 1987 stock market crash, on fears that the company could face bankruptcy. This comes a day after Countrywide said foreclosures and mortgage delinquencies had risen to their highest levels since early 2002. Home Depot announced on August 14, 2007, that second quarter profits fell 15% and are expected to drop another 18% by the end of the year citing the "U.S. housing market". On the same day, Wal-Mart, which is considered "a barometer of the health of the U.S. retail sector", reported that it had a lower than expected second quarter profit and cut its projected full-year earning forecast saying its "customers remain under economic pressure" and that those pressures are now being felt in "Mexico and Canada", adding that it planned to discount heavily on "thousands of items by as much as 50 percent to boost sales" in the months ahead, which would "hurt margins" further.
- Subprime woes have been blamed for causing the U.S. dollar to continue its decline. The Associated Press described the current climate of the market on August 13, 2007, as one where investors were waiting for "the next shoe to drop" as problems from "an overheated housing market and an overextended consumer" are "just beginning to emerge." MarketWatch has cited several economic analysts with Stifel Nicolaus claiming that the problem mortgages are not limited to the subprime niche saying "the rapidly increasing scope and depth of the problems in the mortgage market suggest that the entire sector has plunged into a downward spiral similar to the subprime woes whereby each negative development feeds further deterioration", calling it a "vicious cycle" and adding that they "continue to believe conditions will get worse". The lesson learned from the above financial crises in US and world wide

could not be established because till the time of finalising the thesis the outcome of the crises was not fully established and the revelation was continue.

Wall Street and The Financial Crisis: Anatomy of a Financial Collapse

(EXTRACT FROM MAJORITY AND MINORITY STAFF REPORT, PERMANENT SUBCOMMITTEE ON INVESTIGATIONS, UNITED STATES SENATE APRIL, 2011)

In the fall of 2008, America suffered a devastating economic collapse. Once valuable securities lost most or all of their value, debt markets froze, stock markets plunged, and storied financial firms went under. Millions of Americans lost their jobs; millions of families lost their homes; and good businesses shut down. These events cast the United States into an economic recession so deep that the country has yet to fully recover. The crisis was not a natural disaster, but the result of high risk, complex financial products; undisclosed conflicts of interest; and the failure of regulators, the credit rating agencies, and the market itself to rein in the excesses of Wall Street. The reasons for massive financial disasters were high risk lending by U.S. financial institutions; regulatory failures; inflated credit ratings; and high risk, poor quality financial products designed and sold by some investment banks.

High Risk Lending: Case Study of Washington Mutual Bank (WaMu)

At the time of its failure, WaMu was the nation's largest thrift and sixth largest bank, with $300 billion in assets, $188 billion in deposits, 2,300 branches in 15 states, and over 43,000 employees. Beginning in 2004, it embarked upon a lending strategy to pursue higher profits by emphasizing high risk loans. By 2006, WaMu's high risk loans began incurring high rates of delinquency and default, and in 2007, its mortgage backed securities began incurring ratings downgrades and losses. Also in 2007, the bank itself began incurring losses due to a portfolio that contained poor quality and fraudulent loans and securities. Its stock price dropped as shareholders lost confidence, and depositors began withdrawing funds, eventually causing a liquidity crisis at the bank. On September 25, 2008, WaMu was seized by its regulator, the Office of Thrift Supervision, placed in receivership with the Federal Deposit Insurance Corporation (FDIC), and sold to JPMorgan Chase for $1.9 billion. Had the sale not gone through, WaMu's failure might have exhausted the entire $45 billion Deposit Insurance Fund.

This case study focuses on how one bank's search for increased growth and profit led to the origination and securitization of hundreds of billions of dollars in high risk, poor quality mortgages that ultimately plummeted in value, hurting investors, the bank, and the U.S. financial system. WaMu had held itself out as a prudent lender, but in reality, the bank turned increasingly to higher risk loans. Over a four-year period, those higher risk loans grew from 19% of WaMu's loan originations in 2003, to 55% in 2006, while its lower risk, fixed rate loans fell from 64% to 25% of its originations. At the same time, WaMu increased its securitization of subprime loans sixfold, primarily through its subprime lender, Long Beach Mortgage Corporation, increasing such loans from nearly $4.5 billion in 2003, to $29 billion in 2006. From 2000 to 2007, WaMu and Long Beach together securitized at least $77 billion in subprime loans. WaMu also originated an increasing number of its flagship product, Option Adjustable Rate Mortgages (Option ARMs), which created high risk, negatively amortizing mortgages and, from 2003 to 2007, represented as much as half of all of WaMu's loan originations. In 2006 alone, Washington Mutual originated more than $42.6 billion in Option ARM loans and sold or securitized at least $115 billion to investors, including sales to the Federal National Mortgage Association (Fannie Mae) and Federal Home Loan Mortgage Corporation (Freddie Mac). In addition, WaMu greatly increased its origination and securitization of high risk home equity loan products. By 2007, home equity loans made up $63.5 billion or 27% of its home loan portfolio, a 130% increase from 2003. At the same time that WaMu was implementing its high risk lending strategy, WaMu and Long Beach engaged in a host of shoddy lending practices that produced billions of dollars in high risk, poor quality mortgages and mortgage backed securities. Those practices included qualifying high risk borrowers for larger loans than they could afford; steering borrowers from conventional mortgages to higher risk loan products; accepting loan applications without verifying the borrower's income; using loans with low, short term "teaser" rates that could lead to payment shock when higher interest rates took effect later on; promoting negatively amortizing loans in which many borrowers increased rather than paid down their debt; and authorizing loans with multiple layers of risk. In addition, WaMu and Long Beach failed to enforce compliance with their own lending standards; allowed excessive loan error and exception rates; exercised weak oversight over the third party mortgage brokers who supplied half or more of their loans; and tolerated the issuance of loans with fraudulent or erroneous borrower information. They also designed compensation incentives that rewarded loan personnel for issuing a large volume of higher risk loans, valuing speed and volume over loan quality. As a result, WaMu, and particularly its Long Beach subsidiary, became known by industry insiders for its failed mortgages and poorly performing residential mortgage backed securities (RMBS). Among sophisticated investors, its securitizations were understood to be some of the worst performing in the marketplace.

WaMu management was provided with compelling evidence of deficient lending practices in internal emails, audit reports, and reviews. Internal reviews of two high volume WaMu loan centers, for example, described "extensive fraud" by employees who "willfully" circumvented bank policies. A WaMu review of internal controls to stop fraudulent loans from being sold to investors described them as "ineffective". On at least one occasion, senior managers knowingly sold delinquency-prone loans to investors. WaMu launched its high risk lending strategy primarily because higher risk loans and mortgage backed securities could be sold for higher prices on Wall Street. They garnered higher prices because higher risk meant the securities paid a higher coupon rate than other comparably rated securities, and investors paid a higher price to buy them. Selling or securitizing the loans also removed them from WaMu's books and appeared to insulate the bank from risk. Unacceptable lending and securitization practices were not restricted to Washington Mutual, but were present at a host of financial institutions that originated, sold, and securitized billions of dollars in high risk, poor quality home loans that inundated U.S. financial markets. Many of the resulting securities ultimately plummeted in value, leaving banks and investors with huge losses that helped send the economy into a downward spiral. These lenders were not the victims of the financial crisis; the high risk loans they issued were the fuel that ignited the financial crisis.

Regulatory Failure: Case Study of the Office of Thrift Supervision (OTS)

This case study focuses on the failure of the Office of Thrift Supervision (OTS) to stop the unsafe and unsound practices that led to the demise of Washington Mutual, one of the nation's largest banks. Over a five year period from 2004 to 2008, OTS identified over 500 serious deficiencies at WaMu, yet failed to take action to force the bank to improve its lending operations and even impeded oversight by the bank's backup regulator, the FDIC. Washington Mutual Bank was the largest thrift under the supervision of OTS and was among the eight largest financial institutions insured by the FDIC.

OTS records show that, during the five years prior to WaMu's collapse, OTS examiners repeatedly identified significant problems with Washington Mutual's lending practices, risk management, asset quality, and appraisal practices, and requested corrective action. Year after year, WaMu promised to correct the identified problems, but never did. OTS failed to respond with meaningful enforcement action, such as by downgrading WaMu's rating for safety and soundness, requiring a public plan with deadlines for corrective actions, or imposing civil fines for inaction. To the contrary, until shortly before the thrift's failure in 2008, OTS continually rated WaMu as financially sound. The agency's failure to restrain WaMu's unsafe lending practices stemmed in part from an OTS regulatory culture that viewed its thrifts as "constituents," relied on bank management to correct identified problems with minimal regulatory intervention, and expressed reluctance to interfere with even unsound lending and securitization practices. OTS displayed an unusual amount of deference to WaMu's management, choosing to rely on the bank to police itself in its use of safe and sound practices. The reasoning appeared to be that if OTS examiners simply identified the problems at the bank, OTS could then rely on WaMu's assurances that problems would be corrected, with little need for tough enforcement actions. It was a regulatory approach with disastrous results. Despite identifying over 500 serious deficiencies in five years, OTS did not once, from 2004 to 2008, take a public enforcement action against Washington Mutual to correct its lending practices, nor did it lower the bank's rating for safety and soundness.

Only in 2008, as the bank incurred mounting losses, did OTS finally take two informal, nonpublic enforcement actions, requiring WaMu to agree to a "Board Resolution" in March and a "Memorandum of Understanding" in September, neither of which imposed sufficient changes to prevent the bank's failure. OTS officials resisted calls by the FDIC, the bank's backup regulator, for stronger measures and even impeded FDIC oversight efforts by at times denying FDIC examiners office space and access to bank records. Tensions between the two agencies remained high until the end. Two weeks before the bank was seized, the FDIC Chairman contacted WaMu directly to inform it that the FDIC was likely to have a ratings disagreement with OTS and downgrade the bank's safety and soundness rating, and informed the OTS Director about that communication, prompting him to complain about the FDIC Chairman's "audacity". Hindered by a culture of deference to management, demoralized examiners, and agency infighting, OTS officials allowed the bank's short term profits to excuse its risky practices and failed to evaluate the bank's actions in the context of the U.S. financial system as a whole. Its narrow regulatory focus prevented OTS from analyzing or acknowledging until it was too late that WaMu's practices could harm the broader economy. OTS' failure to restrain Washington Mutual's unsafe lending practices allowed high risk loans at the bank to proliferate, negatively impacting investors across the United States and around the world. Similar regulatory failings by other agencies involving other lenders repeated the problem on a broad scale. The result was a mortgage market saturated with risky loans, and financial institutions that were supposed to hold predominantly safe investments but instead held portfolios rife with high risk, poor quality mortgages. When those loans began defaulting in record numbers and mortgage related securities plummeted in value, financial institutions around the globe suffered hundreds of billions of dollars in losses, triggering an economic disaster. The regulatory failures that set the stage for those losses were a proximate cause of the financial crisis.

Inflated Credit Ratings: Case Study of Moody's and Standard & Poor's

This case study is about how inflated credit ratings contributed to the financial crisis by masking the true risk of many mortgage related securities. Using case studies involving Moody's Investors Service, Inc. (Moody's) and Standard & Poor's Financial Services LLC (S&P), the nation's two largest credit rating agencies responsible for the inaccurate ratings, including conflicts of interest that placed achieving market share and increased revenues ahead of ensuring accurate ratings.

Between 2004 and 2007, Moody's and S&P issued credit ratings for tens of thousands of U.S. residential mortgage backed securities (RMBS) and collateralized debt obligations (CDO). Taking in increasing revenue from Wall Street firms, Moody's and S&P issued AAA and other investment grade credit ratings for the vast majority of those RMBS and CDO securities, deeming them safe investments even though many relied on high risk home loans. In late 2006, high risk mortgages began incurring delinquencies and defaults at an alarming rate. Despite signs of a deteriorating mortgage market, Moody's and S&P continued for six months to issue investment grade ratings for numerous RMBS and CDO securities. Then, in July 2007, as mortgage delinquencies intensified and RMBS and CDO securities began incurring losses, both companies abruptly reversed course and began downgrading at record numbers hundreds and then thousands of their RMBS and CDO ratings, some less than a year old. Investors like banks, pension funds, and insurance companies, who are by rule barred from owning low rated securities, were forced to sell off their downgraded RMBS and CDO holdings, because they had lost their investment grade status. RMBS and CDO securities held by financial firms lost much of their value, and new securitizations were unable to find investors. The subprime RMBS market initially froze and then collapsed, leaving investors and financial firms around the world holding unmarketable subprime RMBS securities that were plummeting in value. A few months later, the CDO market collapsed as well.

Traditionally, investments holding AAA ratings have had a less than 1% probability of incurring defaults. But in 2007, the vast majority of RMBS and CDO securities with AAA ratings incurred substantial losses; some failed outright. Analysts have determined that over 90% of the AAA ratings given to subprime RMBS securities originated in 2006 and 2007 were later downgraded by the credit rating agencies to junk status. In the case of Long Beach, 75 out of 75 AAA rated Long Beach securities issued in 2006, were later downgraded to junk status, defaulted, or withdrawn. Investors and financial institutions holding the AAA rated securities lost significant value. Those widespread losses led, in turn, to a loss of investor confidence in the value of the AAA rating, in the holdings of major U.S. financial institutions, and even in the viability of U.S. financial markets. Inaccurate AAA credit ratings introduced risk into the U.S. financial system and constituted a key cause of the financial crisis. In addition, the July mass downgrades, which were unprecedented in number and scope, precipitated the collapse of the RMBS and CDO secondary markets, and perhaps more than any other single event triggered the beginning of the financial crisis.

A host of factors were responsible for the inaccurate credit ratings issued by Moody's and S&P. One significant cause was the inherent conflict of interest arising from the system used to pay for credit ratings. Credit rating agencies were paid by the Wall Street firms that sought their ratings and profited from the financial products being rated. Under this "issuer pays" model, the rating agencies were dependent upon those Wall Street firms to bring them business, and were vulnerable to threats that the firms would take their business elsewhere if they did not get the ratings they wanted. The rating agencies weakened their standards as each competed to provide the most favorable rating to win business and greater market share. The result was a race to the bottom. Additional factors responsible for the inaccurate ratings include rating models that failed to include relevant mortgage performance data; unclear and subjective criteria used to produce ratings; a failure to apply updated rating models to existing rated transactions; and a failure to provide adequate staffing to perform rating and surveillance services, despite record revenues.

Compounding these problems were federal regulations that required the purchase of investment grade securities by banks and others, which created pressure on the credit rating agencies to issue investment grade ratings. While these federal regulations were intended to help investors stay away from unsafe securities, they had the opposite effect when the AAA ratings proved inaccurate. The credit rating agencies were aware of problems in the mortgage market, including an unsustainable rise in housing prices, the high risk nature of the loans being issued, lax lending standards, and rampant mortgage fraud. Instead of using this information to temper their ratings, the firms continued to issue a high volume of investment grade ratings for mortgage backed securities. If the credit rating agencies had issued ratings that accurately reflected the increasing risk in the RMBS and CDO markets and appropriately adjusted existing ratings in those markets, they might have discouraged investors from purchasing high risk RMBS and CDO securities, and slowed the pace of securitizations. It was not in the short term economic interest of either Moody's or S&P, however, to provide accurate credit ratings for high risk RMBS and CDO securities, because doing so would have hurt their own revenues. Instead, the credit rating agencies' profits became increasingly reliant on the fees generated by issuing a large volume of structured finance ratings. In the end, Moody's and S&P provided AAA ratings to tens of thousands of high risk RMBS and CDO securities and then, when those products began to incur losses, issued mass downgrades that shocked the financial markets, hammered the value of the mortgage related securities, and helped trigger the financial crisis.

Investment Bank Abuses: Case Study of Goldman Sachs & Deutsche Bank

This case study examines how investment banks contributed to the financial crisis, using as case studies Goldman Sachs and Deutsche Bank, two leading participants in the U.S. mortgage market.

Investment banks can play an important role in the U.S. economy, helping to channel the nation's wealth into productive activities that create jobs and increase economic growth. But in the years leading up to the financial crisis, large investment banks designed and promoted complex financial instruments, often referred to as structured finance products, that were at the heart of the crisis. They included RMBS and CDO securities, credit default swaps (CDS), and CDS contracts linked to the ABX Index. These complex, high risk financial products were engineered, sold, and traded by the major U.S. investment banks.

From 2004 to 2008, U.S. financial institutions issued nearly $2.5 trillion in RMBS and over $1.4 trillion in CDO securities, backed primarily by mortgage related products. Investment banks typically charged fees of $1 to $8 million to act as the underwriter of an RMBS securitization, and $5 to $10 million to act as the placement agent for a CDO securitization. Those fees contributed substantial revenues to the investment banks, which established internal structured finance groups, as well as a variety of RMBS and CDO origination and trading desks within those groups, to handle mortgage related securitizations. Investment banks sold RMBS and CDO securities to investors around the world, and helped develop a secondary market where RMBS and CDO securities could be traded. The investment banks' trading desks participated in those secondary markets, buying and selling RMBS and CDO securities either on behalf of their clients or in connection with their own proprietary transactions.

The financial products developed by investment banks allowed investors to profit, not only from the success of an RMBS or CDO securitization, but also from its failure. CDS contracts, for example, allowed counterparties to wager on the rise or fall in the value of a specific RMBS security or on a collection of RMBS and other assets contained or referenced in a CDO. Major investment banks developed standardized CDS contracts that could also be traded on a secondary market. In addition, they established the ABX Index which allowed counterparties to wager on the rise or fall in the value of a basket of subprime RMBS securities, which could be used to reflect the status of the subprime mortgage market as a whole. The investment banks sometimes matched up parties who wanted to take opposite sides in a transaction and other times took one or the other side of the transaction to accommodate a client. At still other times, investment banks used these financial instruments to make their own proprietary wagers. In extreme cases, some investment banks set up structured finance transactions which enabled them to profit at the expense of their clients.

Two case studies, involving Goldman Sachs and Deutsche Bank, illustrate a variety of troubling practices that raise conflicts of interest and other concerns involving RMBS, CDO, CDS, and ABX related financial instruments that contributed to the financial crisis.

The Goldman Sachs case study focuses on how it used net short positions to benefit from the downturn in the mortgage market, and designed, marketed, and sold CDOs in ways that created conflicts of interest with the firm's clients and at times led to the bank profiting from the same products that caused substantial losses for its clients. From 2004 to 2008, Goldman was a major player in the U.S. mortgage market. In 2006 and 2007 alone, it designed and underwrote 93 RMBS and 27 mortgage related CDO securitizations totaling about $100 billion, bought and sold RMBS and CDO securities on behalf of its clients, and amassed its own multi-billion-dollar proprietary mortgage related holdings. In December 2006, however, when it saw evidence that the high risk mortgages underlying many RMBS and CDO securities were incurring accelerated rates of delinquency and default, Goldman quietly and abruptly reversed course. Over the next two months, it rapidly sold off or wrote down the bulk of its existing subprime RMBS and CDO inventory, and began building a short position that would allow it to profit from the decline of the mortgage market. Throughout 2007, Goldman twice built up and cashed in sizeable mortgage related short positions. At its peak, Goldman's net short position totaled $13.9 billion. Overall in 2007, its net short position produced record profits totaling $3.7 billion for Goldman's Structured Products Group, which when combined with other mortgage losses, produced record net revenues of $1.1 billion for the Mortgage Department as a whole. Throughout 2007, Goldman sold RMBS and CDO securities to its clients without disclosing its own net short position against the subprime market or its purchase of CDS contracts to gain from the loss in value of some of the very securities it was selling to its clients.

The case study examines in detail four CDOs that Goldman constructed and sold called Hudson 1, Anderson, Timberwolf, and Abacus 2007-AC1. In some cases, Goldman transferred risky assets from its own inventory into these CDOs; in others, it included poor quality assets that were likely to lose value or not perform. In three of the CDOs, Hudson, Anderson and Timberwolf, Goldman took a substantial portion of the short side of the CDO, essentially betting that the assets within the CDO would fall in value or not perform. Goldman's short position was in direct opposition to the clients to whom it was selling the CDO securities, yet it failed to disclose the size and nature of its short position while marketing the securities. While Goldman sometimes included obscure language in its marketing materials about the possibility of its taking a short position on the CDO securities it was selling, Goldman did not disclose to potential investors when it had already determined to take or had already taken short investments that would pay off if the particular security it was selling, or RMBS and CDO securities in general, performed poorly. In the case of Hudson 1, for example, Goldman took 100% of the short side of the $2 billion CDO, betting against the assets referenced in the CDO, and sold the Hudson securities to investors without disclosing its short position. When the securities lost value, Goldman made a $1.7 billion gain at the direct expense of the clients to whom it had sold the securities. In the case of Anderson, Goldman selected a large number of poorly performing assets for the CDO, took 40% of the short position, and then marketed Anderson securities to its clients. When a client asked how Goldman "got comfortable" with the New Century loans in the CDO, Goldman personnel tried to dispel concerns about the loans, and did not disclose the firm's own negative view of them or its short position in the CDO. In the case of Timberwolf, Goldman sold the securities to its clients even as it knew the securities were falling in value. In some cases, Goldman knowingly sold Timberwolf securities to clients at prices above its own book values and, within days or weeks of the sale, marked down the value of the sold securities, causing its clients to incur quick losses and requiring some to post higher margin or cash collateral. Timberwolf securities lost 80% of their value within five months of being issued and today are worthless. Goldman took 36% of the short position in the CDO and made money from that investment, but ultimately lost money when it could not sell all of the Timberwolf securities. In the case of Abacus, Goldman did not take the short position, but allowed a hedge fund, Paulson & Co. Inc., that planned on shorting the CDO to play a major but hidden role in selecting its assets. Goldman marketed Abacus securities to its clients, knowing the CDO was designed to lose value and without disclosing the hedge fund's asset selection role or investment objective to potential investors. Three long investors together lost about $1 billion from their Abacus investments, while the Paulson hedge fund profited by about the same amount. Today, the Abacus securities are worthless. In the Hudson and Timberwolf CDOs, Goldman also used its role as the collateral put provider or liquidation agent to advance its financial interest to the detriment of the clients to whom it sold the CDO securities.

The Deutsche Bank case study describes how the bank's top global CDO trader, Greg Lippmann, repeatedly warned and advised his Deutsche Bank colleagues and some of his clients seeking to buy short positions about the poor quality of the RMBS securities underlying many CDOs. He described some of those securities as "crap" and "pigs", and predicted the assets and the CDO securities would lose value. At one point, Mr. Lippmann was asked to buy a specific CDO security and responded that it "rarely trades", but he "would take it and try to dupe someone" into buying it. He also at times referred to the industry's ongoing CDO marketing efforts as a "CDO machine" or "ponzi scheme". Deutsche Bank's senior management disagreed with his negative views, and used the bank's own funds to make large proprietary investments in mortgage related securities that, in 2007, had a notional or face value of $128 billion and a market value of more than $25 billion. Despite its positive view of the housing market, the bank allowed Mr. Lippmann to develop a large proprietary short position for the bank in the RMBS market, which from 2005 to 2007, totaled $5 billion. The bank cashed in the short position from 2007 to 2008, generating a profit of $1.5 billion, which Mr. Lippmann claims is more money on a single position than any other trade had ever made for Deutsche Bank in its history. Despite that gain, due to its large long holdings, Deutsche Bank lost nearly $4.5 billion from its mortgage related proprietary investments.

A $1.1 billion CDO underwritten by Deutsche Bank known as Gemstone CDO VII Ltd. (Gemstone 7), which issued securities in March 2007. It was one of 47 CDOs totaling $32 billion that Deutsche Bank underwrote from 2004 to 2008. Deutsche Bank made $4.7 million in fees from Gemstone 7, while the collateral manager, a hedge fund called HBK Capital Management, was slated to receive $3.3 million. Gemstone 7 concentrated risk by including within a single financial instrument 115 RMBS securities whose financial success depended upon thousands of high risk, poor quality subprime loans. Many of those RMBS securities carried BBB, BBB-, or even BB credit ratings, making them among the highest risk RMBS securities sold to the public. Nearly a third of the RMBS securities contained subprime loans originated by Fremont, Long Beach, and New Century, lenders well known within the industry for issuing poor quality loans. Deutsche Bank also sold securities directly from its own inventory to the CDO. Deutsche Bank's CDO trading desk knew that many of these RMBS securities were likely to lose value, but did not object to their inclusion in Gemstone 7, even securities which Mr. Lippmann was calling "crap" or "pigs". Despite the poor quality of the underlying assets, Gemstone's top three tranches received AAA ratings. Deutsche Bank ultimately sold about $700 million in Gemstone securities, without disclosing to potential investors that its global head trader of CDOs had extremely negative views of a third of the assets in the CDO or that the bank's internal valuations showed that the assets had lost over $19 million in value since their purchase. Within months of being issued, the Gemstone 7 securities lost value; by November 2007, they began undergoing credit rating downgrades; and by July 2008, they became nearly worthless.

Both Goldman Sachs and Deutsche Bank underwrote securities using loans from subprime lenders known for issuing high risk, poor quality mortgages, and sold risky securities to investors across the United States and around the world. They also enabled the lenders to acquire new funds to originate still more high risk, poor quality loans. Both sold CDO securities without full disclosure of the negative views of some of their employees regarding the underlying assets and, in the case of Goldman, without full disclosure that it was shorting the very CDO securities it was marketing, raising questions about whether Goldman complied with its obligations to issue suitable investment recommendations and disclose material adverse interests.

The case studies also illustrate how these two investment banks continued to market new CDOs in 2007, even as U.S. mortgage delinquencies intensified, RMBS securities lost value, the U.S. mortgage market as a whole deteriorated, and investors lost confidence. Both kept producing and selling high risk, poor quality structured finance products in a negative market, in part because stopping the "CDO machine" would have meant less income for structured finance units, smaller executive bonuses, and even the disappearance of CDO desks and personnel, which is what finally happened. The two case studies also illustrate how certain complex structured finance products, such as synthetic CDOs and naked credit default swaps, amplified market risk by allowing investors with no ownership interest in the reference obligations to place unlimited side bets on their performance. Finally, the two case studies demonstrate how proprietary trading led to dramatic losses in the case of Deutsche Bank and undisclosed conflicts of interest in the case of Goldman Sachs. Investment banks were the driving force behind the structured finance products that provided a steady stream of funding for lenders originating high risk, poor quality loans and that magnified risk throughout the U.S. financial system. The investment banks that engineered, sold, traded, and profited from mortgage related structured finance products were a major cause of the financial crisis.

How the Financial Crises could have been avoided

1. Ensure "Qualified Mortgages" Are Low Risk: Federal regulators should use their regulatory authority to ensure that all mortgages deemed to be "qualified residential mortgages" have a low risk of delinquency or default.

2. Require Meaningful Risk Retention: Federal regulators should issue a strong risk retention requirement by requiring the retention of not less than a 5% credit risk in each, or a representative sample of, an asset backed securitization's tranches, and by barring a hedging offset for a reasonable but limited period of time.

3. Safeguard Against High Risk Products: Federal banking regulators should safeguard taxpayer dollars by requiring banks with high risk structured finance products, including complex products with little or no reliable performance data, to meet conservative loss reserve, liquidity, and capital requirements.

4. Require Greater Reserves for Negative Amortization Loans: Federal banking regulators should use their regulatory authority to require banks issuing negatively amortizing loans that allow borrowers to defer payments of interest and principal, to maintain more conservative loss, liquidity, and capital reserves.

5. Safeguard Bank Investment Portfolios: Federal banking regulators should use the Section 620 banking activities study to identify high risk structured finance products and impose a reasonable limit on the amount of such high risk products that can be included in a bank's investment portfolio.

6. Complete OTS Dismantling: The Office of the Comptroller of the Currency (OCC) should complete the dismantling of the Office of Thrift Supervision (OTS), despite attempts by some OTS officials to preserve the agency's identity and influence within the OCC.

7. Strengthen Enforcement: Federal banking regulators should conduct a review of their major financial institutions to identify those with ongoing, serious deficiencies, and review their enforcement approach to those institutions to eliminate any policy of deference to bank management, inflated CAMELS ratings, or use of short term profits to excuse high risk activities.

***8. Strengthen CAMELS Ratings*:** Federal banking regulators should undertake a comprehensive review of the CAMELS ratings system to produce ratings that signal whether an institution is expected to operate in a safe and sound manner over a specified period of time, asset quality ratings that reflect embedded risks rather than short term profits, management ratings that reflect any ongoing failure to correct identified deficiencies, and composite ratings that discourage systemic risks.

9. Evaluate Impacts of High Risk Lending: The Financial Stability Oversight Council should undertake a study to identify high risk lending practices at financial institutions, and evaluate the nature and significance of the impacts that these practices may have on U.S. financial systems as a whole.

10. Rank Credit Rating Agencies by Accuracy: The SEC should use its regulatory authority to rank the Nationally Recognized Statistical Rating Organizations in terms of performance, in particular the accuracy of their ratings.

11. Help Investors Hold CRAs Accountable: The SEC should use its regulatory authority to facilitate the ability of investors to hold credit rating agencies accountable in civil lawsuits for inflated credit ratings, when a credit rating agency knowingly or recklessly fails to conduct a reasonable investigation of the rated security.

12. Strengthen CRA Operations: The SEC should use its inspection, examination, and regulatory authority to ensure credit rating agencies institute internal controls, credit rating methodologies, and employee conflict of interest safeguards that advance rating accuracy.

13. Ensure CRAs Recognize Risk: The SEC should use its inspection, examination, and regulatory authority to ensure credit rating agencies assign higher risk to financial instruments whose performance cannot be reliably predicted due to their novelty or complexity, or that rely on assets from parties with a record for issuing poor quality assets.

14. Strengthen Disclosure: The SEC should exercise its authority to ensure that the credit rating agencies complete the required new ratings forms by the end of the year and that the new forms provide comprehensible, consistent, and useful ratings information to investors, including by testing the proposed forms with actual investors.

15. Reduce Ratings Reliance: Federal regulators should reduce the federal government's reliance on privately issued credit ratings.

16. Review Structured Finance Transactions: Federal regulators should review the RMBS, CDO, CDS, and ABX activities described in this Report to identify any violations of law and to examine ways to strengthen existing regulatory prohibitions against abusive practices involving structured finance products.

17. Narrow Proprietary Trading Exceptions: To ensure a meaningful ban on proprietary trading, any exceptions to that ban, such as for marketmaking or risk-mitigating hedging activities, should be strictly limited in the implementing regulations to activities that serve clients or reduce risk.

18. Design Strong Conflict of Interest Prohibitions: Regulators implementing the conflict of interest prohibitions should consider the types of conflicts of interest in the Goldman Sachs case study.

19. Study Bank Use of Structured Finance: Regulators conducting the banking activities study should consider the role of federally insured banks in designing, marketing, and investing in structured finance products with risks that cannot be reliably measured and naked credit default swaps or synthetic financial instruments.

Financial Products or Factors responsible for Financial Crisis

Securitization: For years, securitization worked well. Borrowers paid their 30-year, fixed rate mortgages with few defaults, and mortgage backed securities built up a reputation as a safe investment. Lenders earned fees for bundling the home loans into pools and either selling the pools or securitizing them into mortgage backed securities. Investment banks also earned fees from working with the lenders to assemble the pools, design the mortgage backed securities, obtain credit ratings for them, and sell the resulting securities to investors. Investors like pension funds, insurance companies, municipalities, university endowments, and hedge funds earned a reasonable rate of return on the RMBS securities they purchased. Due to the 2002 Treasury rule that reduced capital reserves for securitized mortgages, RMBS holdings also became increasingly attractive to banks, which could determine how much capital they needed to hold based on the credit ratings their RMBS securities received from the credit ratings agencies. According to economist Arnold Kling, among other problems, the 2002 rule “created opportunities for banks to lower their ratio of capital to assets through structured financing” and “created the incentive for rating agencies to provide overly optimistic assessment of the risk in mortgage pools”.

High Risk Mortgages: The resulting increased demand for mortgage backed securities, joined with Wall Street’s growing appetite for securitization fees, prompted lenders to issue mortgages not only to well qualified borrowers, but also higher risk borrowers. Higher risk borrowers were often referred to as “subprime” borrowers to distinguish them from the more creditworthy “prime” borrowers who traditionally qualified for home loans. Some lenders began to specialize in issuing loans to subprime borrowers and became known as subprime lenders. Subprime loans provided new fuel for the securitization engines on Wall Street. Some lenders engaged in a host of risky lending practices that allowed them to quickly generate a large volume of high risk loans to both subprime and prime borrowers. Those practices, for example, required little or no verification of borrower income, required borrowers to provide little or no down payments, and used loans in which the borrower was not required to pay down the loan amount, and instead incurred added debt over time, known as “negative amortization” loans. Some lenders offered a low initial “teaser rate,” followed by a higher interest rate.

Hybrid ARMs: One common high risk loan used by lenders in the years leading up to the financial crisis was the short term hybrid adjustable rate mortgage (Hybrid ARM), which was offered primarily to subprime borrowers. These 30-year mortgages typically had a low fixed teaser rate, which then reset to a higher floating interest rate, after two years for the 2/28, three years for the 3/27, or five years for the 5/25. The initial loan payment was typically calculated by assuming the initial low, fixed interest rate would be used to pay down the loan. In some cases, the loan used payments that initially covered only the interest due on the loan and not any principal; these loans were called “interest only” loans. After the fixed period for the teaser rate expired, the monthly payment was typically recalculated using the higher floating rate to pay off the remaining principal and interest owing over the course of the remaining loan period. The resulting monthly payment was much larger and sometimes caused borrowers to experience "payment shock" and default on their loans.

Pick-A-Payment or Option ARMs: Another common high risk loan, offered to both prime and subprime borrowers during the years leading up to the financial crisis, was known as the "pick-a-payment" or "option adjustable rate mortgage" (Option ARM).

Home Equity Loans: A third type of high risk loan that became popular during the years leading up to the financial crisis was the home equity loan (HEL). HELs provided loans secured by the borrower's equity in his or her home, which served as the loan collateral. HELs typically provided a lump sum loan amount that had to be repaid over a fixed period of time, such as 5, 10, or 30 years, using a fixed interest rate, although adjustable rates could also be used.

Alt A Loans: Another type of common loan during the years leading up to the financial crisis was the "Alt A" loan. Alt A loans were issued to borrowers with relatively good credit histories, but with aggressive underwriting that increased the risk of the loan. The resulting high loan-to-value ratio, and the lack of borrower equity in the home, meant that, if the borrower defaulted and the home had to be sold, the sale proceeds were unlikely to be sufficient to repay both loans.

Stated Income Loans: Stated income loans were a more extreme form of low doc Alt A loans, in that they imposed no documentation requirements and required little effort by the lender to verify the borrower's income. These loans allowed borrowers simply to "state" their income, with no verification by the lender of the borrower's income or assets other than to consider the income's "reasonableness". They were sometimes called "NINA" loans, because "No Income" and "No Assets" of the borrower were verified by the lender. They were also referred to as "liar loans", since borrowers could lie about their incomes, and the lender would make little effort to substantiate the claimed income. Many lenders believed they could simply rely on the other underwriting tools, such as the borrower's credit score and the property appraisal, to ensure the loans would be repaid.

Structured Finance: In recent years, Wall Street firms have devised increasingly complex financial instruments for sale to investors. These instruments are often referred to as structured finance. Because structured finance products are so complicated and opaque, investors often place particular reliance on credit ratings to determine whether they should buy them. Among the oldest types of structured finance products are RMBS securities. To create these securities, issuers – often working with investment banks – bundle large numbers of home loans into a loan pool, and calculate the revenue stream coming into the loan pool from the individual mortgages. They then design a "waterfall" that delivers a stream of revenues in sequential order to specified "tranches". The first tranche is at the top of the waterfall and is typically the first to receive revenues from the mortgage pool. Since that tranche is guaranteed to be paid first, it is the safest investment in the pool. The issuer creates a security, often called a bond, linked to that first tranche. That security typically receives a AAA credit rating since its revenue stream is the most secure. The security created from the next tranche receives the same or a lower credit rating and so on until the waterfall reaches the "equity" tranche at the bottom. The equity tranche typically receives no rating since it is the last to be paid, and therefore the first to incur losses if mortgages in the loan pool default. Since virtually every mortgage pool has at least some mortgages that default, equity tranches are intended to provide loss protection for the tranches above it.

Because equity tranches are riskier, however, they are often assigned and receive a higher rate of interest and can be profitable if losses are minimal. One mortgage pool might produce five to a dozen or more tranches, each of which is used to create a residential mortgage backed security that is rated and then sold to investors.

Cash CDOs: Collateralized debt obligations (CDOs) are another type of structured finance product whose securities receive credit ratings and are sold to investors. CDOs are a more complex financial product that involves the re-securitization of existing income-producing assets. CDOs can also contain other types of assets, such as commercial mortgage backed securities, corporate bonds, or other CDO securities. These CDOs are often called "cash CDOs", because they receive cash revenues from the underlying RMBS bonds and other assets.

Synthetic CDOs: Some investment banks also created "synthetic CDOs" which mimicked cash CDOs, but did not contain actual mortgages or other assets that produced income. Instead, they simply "referenced" existing assets and then allowed investors to use credit default swaps to place bets on the performance of those referenced assets. Investors who bet that the referenced assets would maintain or increase in value bought the CDO's securities and, in exchange, received periodic coupon payments to recoup their principal investment plus interest.

Ratings Used to Market RMBS and CDOs: Wall Street firms helped design RMBS and CDO securities, worked with the credit rating agencies to obtain ratings for the securities, and sold the securities to investors like pension funds, insurance companies, university endowments, municipalities, and hedge funds. Without investment grade ratings, Wall Street firms would have had a more difficult time selling structured finance products to investors, because each investor would have had to perform its own due diligence review of the product.

Conflicts of Interest: Credit rating agencies are paid by the issuers seeking ratings for the products they sell. Issuers and the investment banks want high ratings, whether to help market their products or ensure they comply with federal regulations. Because credit rating agencies issue ratings to issuers and investment banks who bring them business, they are subject to an inherent conflict of interest that can create pressure on the credit rating agencies to issue favorable ratings to attract business. The issuers and investment banks engage in "ratings shopping," choosing the credit rating agency that offers the highest ratings.

Mass Downgrades: From 2004 through the first half of 2007, Moody's and S&P provided AAA ratings to a majority of the RMBS and CDO securities issued in the United States, sometimes providing AAA ratings to as much as 95% of a securitization. Beginning in July 2007, however, Moody's and S&P issued hundreds and then thousands of downgrades of RMBS and CDO ratings, the first mass downgrades in U.S. history. By 2010, analysts had determined that over 90% of the AAA ratings issued to RMBS securities originated in 2006 and 2007 had been downgraded to junk status.

Shorting the Mortgage Market: Prior to the financial crisis, investors commonly purchased RMBS or CDO securities as long-term investments that produced a steady income. In 2006, however, the high risk mortgages underlying these securities began to incur record levels of delinquencies. Investors, worried about the value of their holdings, sought to sell their RMBS or CDO securities, but had a difficult time doing so due to the lack of an active market.

Proprietary Trading: Financial institutions also built increasingly large proprietary holdings of mortgage related assets. Numerous financial firms, including investment banks, bought RMBS and CDO securities, and retained these securities in their investment portfolios.

Market Oversight: U.S. financial regulators failed to stop financial firms from engaging in high risk, conflict-ridden activities. Those regulatory failures arose, in part, from the fragmented nature of U.S. financial oversight as well as statutory barriers to regulating high risk financial products. The regulators also oversight of Lenders and Securities Firms.

Systemic Risk: While bank and securities regulators focused on the safety and soundness of individual financial institutions, no regulator was charged with identifying, preventing, or managing risks that threatened the safety and soundness of the overall U.S. financial system. In the area of high risk mortgage lending, for example, bank regulators allowed banks to issue high risk mortgages as long as it was profitable and the banks quickly sold the high risk loans to get them off their books. Securities regulators allowed investment banks to underwrite, buy, and sell mortgage backed securities relying on high risk mortgages, as long as the securities received high ratings from the credit rating agencies and so were deemed "safe" investments. No regulatory agency focused on what would happen when poor quality mortgages were allowed to saturate U.S. financial markets and contaminate RMBS and CDO securities with high risk loans. In addition, none of the regulators focused on the impact derivatives like credit default swaps might have in exacerbating risk exposures, since they were barred by federal law from regulating or even gathering data about these financial instruments.

***Government Sponsored Enterprises*:** Some federal housing policies encouraged people to purchase homes they were ultimately unable to afford, which helped to inflate the housing bubble.

Fannie Mae and Freddie Mac: Two government sponsored entities (GSE), the Federal National Mortgage Association (Fannie Mae) and the Federal Home Loan Mortgage Corporation (Freddie Mac), were chartered by Congress to encourage homeownership primarily by providing a secondary market for home mortgages. They created that secondary market by purchasing loans from lenders, securitizing them, providing a guarantee that they would make up the cost of other requirements, the rules prohibited lenders "from making loans based on collateral without regard to [the borrower's] repayment ability," required lenders to "verify income and obligations", and imposed "more stringent restrictions on prepayment penalties". Over time, however, Fannie Mae and Freddie Mac began to purchase larger quantities of higher risk loans, providing a secondary market for those loans and encouraging their proliferation. Because of their [Fannie Mae and Freddie Mac] size and interconnectedness with other financial institutions, they posed substantial systemic risk—the risk that their failure could impose very high costs on the financial system and the economy.

Ginnie Mae: Additional housing policies that allowed borrowers with less than adequate credit to obtain traditional mortgages included programs at the Federal Housing Administration (FHA) and the Department of Veterans Affairs (VA). Both agencies provided loan guarantees to lenders that originated loans for borrowers that qualified under the agencies' rules.

CASE STUDIES OF INDIAN FINANCIAL MARKETS[4]

In Indian financial market, many financial disasters were seen in previous years, which taken place for not following risk management practices by Indian FIs. Hence a brief study of these financial debacles also requires attention before designing risk management model for Indian FIs.

CRB CAPITAL MARKET

Introduction and Case Details:

The CRB Capital Market scrip started moving down from October 1996, soon after a downgrade in the company's debt rating. The CRB Corporation scrip started declining sharply from December 1996. During the period September 3, 1996 to April 17, 1997, before the whistle was blown on the group, the value of the CRB Capital Markets scrip declined from Rs. 39.50 to Rs. 10.40, while the value of the CRB Corporation scrip fell from Rs. 24.50 to Rs. 9.80 during the same period. Obviously, the market was not impressed by CRB Capital Market's declared Rs. 5.5 annualised earnings per share based on the first half results of 1996-97.

It can be argued that, if only the investors in the company's fixed deposits had paid more attention to the share price of the company, and taken the trouble to enquire into the reasons for the decline, they could have pulled out earlier from the company. More accurately, if a vibrant debt market existed, and if CRB's bonds were traded, these would have provided reliable benchmarks to fixed deposit investors on the market perception about the company. Contrast the market's lack of interest in the CRB group scrips with the behaviour of the BSE Sensex. During the period September 3, 1996 to April 17, 1994, while the value of the CRB scrips declined so precipitously, the BSE Sensex actually increased, from 3484 to 3696. It is clear that the market knew more than the regulator. The information available to the supervising institution is limited to the knowledge and competence available to their supervisors. Often, the supervisor has no specialisation, and has no in-depth knowledge of any industry. And so far, as the market intelligence gathering activities of supervisors are concerned, the less said the better. Further, bureaucratic supervision has no built-in incentives--a supervisor is not paid extra bonuses if he is able to uncover new information.

Contrast this state of affairs with the information available in the market. Any market player is constantly on the look-out for new information, as he can use it to his advantage. The market pricing mechanism resembles a complex, decentralised computer which receives information through purchases and sales made by investors and speculators, and synthesises all this information into the market price. The advantage of the market is that the source of information is very widespread, consisting of thousands of market players. Even more importantly, market price also reflects privileged information, as company employees and directors seek to profit from their knowledge. This is especially true in markets such as India, where managements easily get away with insider trading.

Regulation therefore is best done by the markets, and the question which remains is how should markets be assisted to become better regulators? The answer is simple--since the market relies on information, more disclosure, greater transparency, and more frequent information about corporates should be supplied to the market. We could, for example, insist on quarterly unaudited accounts, with a corresponding cash flow statement. For financial companies, where asset quality is important, a quarterly revealing of its asset portfolio, perhaps certified by accountants, could be made mandatory. All this would basically amount to a privatisation of regulation. Instead of remaining a secretive bureaucratic method, regulation would be participatory, with each market player contributing to the process.

Furthermore, the costs of regulation would be drastically reduced and the hordes of supervisors engaged in policing the markets could be put to more productive work. Part of the onus of regulation is even today being carried by private parties such as the merchant bankers to an issue. Rating agencies too should be encouraged to take up further responsibilities. But for that to happen, some changes need to be made in the way ratings are given, and unsolicited ratings, which will increase competition between agencies, should be used allowed in order to keep rating agencies on their toes.

No regulatory system in the world can prevent rogue trading, as happened in the Barings and Sumitomo scandals. But the markets are more reliable early warning systems than bureaucracies. In cybernetics, there is a law called the Law of Requisite Variety, which states that the variety of a regulator must equal that of the disturbances whose effects it is to negate.

Translated into finance, this means that a regulator's learning systems must be as complex as the external environment which it seeks to regulate. In an increasingly complex financial world, the capacity of bureaucrats to regulate is under severe strain. In order to be effective, the energies of supervisors should be directed towards improving and developing the markets, in order to make them more efficient regulators.

GLOBAL TRUST BANK (GTB)

Introduction and Case details:

On July 24, 2004, the Government of India imposed a moratorium on Global Trust Bank (GTB), a leading private sector bank, on the grounds of 'wrong financial disclosures'. The moratorium was for three months from close of business on July 24, 2004 till October 23, 2004.

Earlier, the Reserve Bank of India (RBI) had announced that GTB's net worth had turned negative as it had incurred huge losses and accumulated a significant number of non-performing assets (NPAs). RBI stated that the numbers reported in GTB's balance sheet did not match its audited figures. Moreover, GTB failed to provide satisfactory explanations to most of RBI's queries regarding its capital market exposures and why prudent lending norms were not observed in disbursing huge amounts for investments in the stock market. RBI said the moratorium was imposed in public interest and to protect the interests of depositors. All operations of GTB were frozen and it was ordered not to give loans without RBI permission. It was allowed only to make payments for day-to-day operations or for meeting obligations entered into before the order. The liberalization process initiated by the Government of India, during the early 1990's witnessed the entry of several private players in the Indian banking sector. GTB was one of the earliest private sector banks to be incorporated on October 30, 1994, in Hyderabad.

GTB was promoted by Jayant Madhab (Madhab), Ramesh Gelli (Gelli) and Sridhar Subasri (Subasri). Madhab, a development banker, was employed with the Asian Development Bank, Manila. Gelli who was Chairman of Vysya Bank for 10 years had played a major role in transforming that bank into one of India's top private sector banks. Subasri was a former bank executive and a close friend of Gelli. Though the license to GTB was given in the name of Jayant Madhab and Associates, Madhab's involvement with GTB was affected by the loss of his only son. The bank's operations were managed by Gelli. Apart from the three promoters, the International Finance Corporation (IFC) and the Asian Development Bank (ADB) were the bank's major shareholders. It is a clear example of rise and fall story of the growth and collapse of Global Trust Bank, a leading private sector bank in India. Since 2001, GTB's name was associated with scams and controversies, thereby casting shadows over the credibility of the bank and its management. Due to the over exposure to capital markets and huge NPAs, the bank was in a financial mess. When GTB tried to cover up its monumental NPAs through under provisioning, RBI - the Central bank and the regulatory authority for banks in India, appointed an independent team to review the finances of the bank. The review revealed various financial discrepancies kept covered by the bank. RBI imposed a three month moratorium on GTB on the ground of "wrong financial disclosures" and within two days the bank was merged with Oriental Bank of Commerce (OBC), a public sector bank. With the merger becoming effective, GTB's identity came to an end and it became a part of OBC.

THE US-64 CONTROVERSY

Introduction and Case Details:

In 1998, investors of Unit Trust of India's (UTI) Unit Scheme-1964 (US-64) were shaken by media reports claiming that things were seriously wrong with the mutual fund major. For the first time in its 32 years of existence, US-64 faced depleting funds and redemptions exceeding the sales. Between July 1995 and March 1996, funds declined by Rs. 3,104 crore. Analysts remarked that the depleting corpus coupled with the redemptions could soon result in a liquidity crisis.

Soon, reports regarding the lack of proper fund management and internal control systems at UTI added to the growing investor frenzy. By October 1998, US-64's equity component's market value had come down to Rs 4200 crore from its acquisition price of Rs. 8200 crore. The net asset value (NAV) of US-64 also declined significantly during 1993-1996 due to turbulent stock market conditions. A Business Today survey cited US-64's NAV at Rs. 9.68. The US-64 units, which were sold at Rs. 14.55 and repurchased at Rs. 14.25 in October 1998, thus were around 50% and 47%, above their estimated NAV.

Amidst growing concerns over the fate of US-64 investors, it became necessary for UTI to take immediate steps to put rest to the controversy. The case of 'The US-64 Controversy' provides insight into the problems faced by the Indian mutual fund major UTI's flagship scheme US-64. This case intends to highlight the importance of portfolio management and risk management for a mutual fund. The importance of having an adequate regulatory mechanism for the financial institutions is highlighted. This is the fit case of ignoring market and credit risk.

THE JVG SCANDAL

Introduction and Case Details:

In October 1997, the Reserve Bank of India (RBI) banned all Non-Banking Financial Companies (NBFCs) of the JVG Group of companies - JVG Finance, JVG Leasing and JVG Securities - from accepting deposits from the public. This was after an investigation revealed that these companies had been accepting deposits in excess of their stipulated limits. Soon after, JVG downed the shutters of several of its offices in small towns of Maharashtra, Uttar Pradesh and Bihar, claiming it had detected huge irregularities in the operations. The closing of the offices created a panic among the depositors and strong voices were raised against the group in the media.

In November 1997, JVG hurriedly rented an office in Gurgaon (Haryana) to accommodate irate investors. Hundreds of investors and agents camped on the grounds of the office. The agents (or the field-workers), who raised deposits from investors on behalf of JVG, were extremely worried. They said they could not go back to their local offices without collecting the dues fearing the wrath of the investors. More and more depositors and field workers teemed over the next few days with hopes of getting their money back. The situation seemed rather bleak with rumours of the JVG group being in deep financial crisis. At this point, JVG Chairman V.K.Sharma (Sharma) dropped another bombshell on the investors. He claimed that a majority of the certificates were fake and hence they would not be paid back. For many depositors who had invested as little as Rs 500 and who could not even dream of taking the dispute to court, it meant kissing their investments goodbye.

Analysts remarked that the investors and agents had themselves to blame for the loss - because the activities of the JVG Group had always been looked at with suspicion by the industry. From being a small-time contractor earning less than Rs. 2500 a month, Sharma went on to run a group, which on paper had an annual turnover of Rs. 1000 crore, in just seven years. Known for his lavish lifestyle - his farmhouse in Delhi, his fleet of expensive cars and the helicopter he had taken on lease to tap deposits from small towns in north India were talked about quite often.

CO-OPERATIVE BANK SCAMS IN INDIA

Introduction and Case Details:

In the early 20th century, the availability of credit in India, more particularly in rural areas was non existent. There was no organized institutional credit for agricultural and related activities. People in the rural areas largely depended on money lenders who lent money at very high rates of interest. Thus, there was need to create an institution which would cater to the needs of ordinary people and was based on the principles of cooperative organisation and management. In 1904, the first legislation on co-operatives was passed. In 1914, the Maclagen committee suggested a three tier structure for cooperative banking i.e. Primary Agricultural Credit Societies at the grass root level, Central Cooperative Banks at the district level and State Cooperative Banks at the State or apex level. Cooperative banks were expected to serve as substitutes for money lenders, and provide both short-term and long-term institutional credit at reasonable rates of interest.

Cooperative banks were established in India to facilitate rural credit, and to cater to the needs of small farmers and businessmen. They were popular with middle and lower income groups because of the high interest rates they offered as compared to commercial banks. However, with the passage of time, most cooperative banks lost their purpose. Excessive state control and politicisation further led to their deterioration. By the 1990s, none of the public or private sector banks were willing to deal with cooperative banks and thus even otherwise healthy cooperative banks were facing a tough time.

In 2001-2002, many cooperative banks were rocked by scams that exposed the malpractices in these banks. Many of these banks did not adhere to the prudential norms prescribed by the Reserve bank of India (RBI). The Madhavapura Mercantile Cooperative Bank (MMCB) had invested a huge amount in the equity market which was almost equal to its deposit base, thus, violating the RBI norms relating to exposure to the equity market. Another bank, the Krushi Cooperative Urban Bank (KCUB) had issued loans and advances amounting to Rs. 530 million as against its deposit base of Rs. 350 million. Not only that, most of its loans had not been secured. Similarly, the Charminar Cooperative Urban Bank (CCUB) faced liquidity problems due to indiscriminate lending to big borrowers against worthless land. More recently the Nagpur District Central Cooperative Bank (NDCCB) was involved in fraudulent dealings in government securities through brokers.

The case of "Cooperative Bank Scams in India" gives an insight into the various scams and malpractices in cooperative banks in India and their implications on the Indian financial sector. It briefly describes the structure of cooperative banks and their characteristics. The scams surfaced in four cooperative banks, viz., Madhavpura Mercantile Cooperative Bank (MMCB), Krushi Cooperative Urban Bank (KCUB), Charminar Cooperative Urban Bank (CCUB) and Nagpur District Central Cooperative Bank (NDCCB) in 2001-02.

THE KETAN PAREKH SCAM

Introduction and Case Details:

The 176-point Sensex crash on March 1, 2001 came as a major shock for the Government of India, the stock markets and the investors alike. More so, as the Union budget tabled a day earlier had been acclaimed for its growth initiatives and had prompted a 177-point increase in the Sensex. This sudden crash in the stock markets prompted the Securities Exchange Board of India (SEBI) to launch immediate investigations into the volatility of stock markets. SEBI also decided to inspect the books of several brokers who were suspected of triggering the crash.

Meanwhile, the Reserve Bank of India (RBI) ordered some banks to furnish data related to their capital market exposure. This was after media reports appeared regarding a private sector bank having exceeded its prudential norms of capital exposure, thereby contributing to the stock market volatility. The panic run on the bourses continued and the Bombay Stock Exchange (BSE) President Anand Rathi's (Rathi) resignation added to the downfall. Rathi had to resign following allegations that he had used some privileged information, which contributed to the crash. The scam shook the investor's confidence in the overall functioning of the stock markets. By the end of March 2001, at least eight people were reported to have committed suicide and hundreds of investors were driven to the brink of bankruptcy. The scam opened up the debate over banks funding capital market operations and lending funds against collateral security. It also raised questions about the validity of dual control of co-operative banks. (Analysts pointed out that RBI was inspecting the accounts once in two years, which created ample scope for violation of rules.) The first arrest in the scam was of the noted bull, Ketan Parekh (KP), on March 30, 2001, by the Central Bureau of Investigation (CBI). Soon, reports abounded as to how KP had single handedly caused one of the biggest scams in the history of Indian financial markets. He was charged with defrauding Bank of India (BoI) of about Rs.30 million among other charges.

Ketan Parekh's arrest was followed by yet another panic run on the bourses and the Sensex fell by 147 points. By this time, the scam had become the 'talk of the nation,' with intensive media coverage and unprecedented public outcry.

LIFE INSURANCE CORPORATION'S FUTURE PROSPECTS

Introduction and Case Details:

In 1956, there were 154 Indian insurers, 16 foreign insurers and 75 provident societies in the life insurance sector in the country. The life insurance business was concentrated in urban areas and served only the wealthy sections. In January 1956, the management of the 245 Indian and foreign insurers and provident societies was taken over by the Central Government. Life Insurance Corporation was formed as a government regulated monopoly in September 1956 by an Act of Parliament, (LIC Act 1956) with a capital contribution of Rs 50 million. Ravi Bhargava (Bhargava), Assistant Marketing Manager, Life Insurance Corporation of India (LIC) was disconcerted by the full-page advertisement in the newspaper. The advertisement, by an Indian company in alliance with a US insurance company declared, Till now we were all buying insurance blindfolded, wake up. Experience the new phenomenon, one giving shape to all your dreams and driving away all your fears.' On the next page was another advertisement by an Indian bank, inviting applications from agency managers, promising a very good work atmosphere and 'best in the industry' remuneration. Bhargava had been Marketing Manager at LIC for the past eighteen months and eight of his best performing agents had submitted their resignations. He feared more would follow suit. The new players in the life insurance market were already affecting LIC. The Monitor Group, a Boston-based strategy consulting firm, which studied the trends in the Indian insurance market after it was thrown open to private players, predicted that LIC would find the going tough.

But Prakash Sharma, (GM, Marketing Division) was more optimistic: "It is obvious they will look for the best of our people, but we are not unduly worried. LIC offers a commission of 35% of the premiums for the first year and 7.5% for the next two years, and 5% for the rest of the period for which the sum is assured. At the most, the new players will be able to offer 40% - not good enough to attract our people. These are all new players and none can beat our 44 years of experience." But Bhargava and Sharma knew that the issues involved were not that simple.

In 2000, the Insurance Regulatory & Development Authority Bill was passed by the Government of India, throwing open the Indian insurance market to foreign players. The domestic life insurance monopoly, Life Insurance Corporation (LIC) had to take various steps to compete with the new players.

The lesson has been drawn from the detailed study of all the above cases that a proper risk management system and supervision should be in-force in true spirit and not only for some regulatory compliance. The tools and technique available should be used to safeguard FIs risk rather than for speculative purposes to increase profit beyond normalcy. It is also gathered that in risk management practices the top management of any financial institution should be fully involved in managing the risk instead of going through a cursory review of the various reports prepared by employees. The risk management in any financial institution should be discussed very frequently and there should not be any hesitation to bring out any malpractice.

Summary

In this chapter, some case studies illustrate how the absence of formal risk management, when compounded by other problems, can risk the existence of an organisation or result in major losses. The analysis of case has been bifurcated in two areas: Case studies of Global market and Case studies of Indian Market. The case studies of global market includes barring bank collapses which depicts how financial management can go wrong and within a few days bank may go from apparent strength to bankruptcy. It also covers BCCI that describe incidence of biggest bank fraud in history. It also covers the cases of First national Bank of Keystone, Lloyd's, a British Insurance Market and Orange county. The most famous case of LTCM has also been discussed in the chapter. The cases of Indian financial market include cases like CRB capital market, Global Trust Bank failure, US64 controversy, JVG scandal, Co-operative bank scam in India and Ketan Parikh scam. The future prospectus of LIC has also been studied with reference to risk management threats. From all the above cases of global market or domestic market, it is gathered that management of financial institution is very eminent part of overall organisational process and its functioning. Thus an effective and efficient risk management and control system is very integral and important part of a financial institution. Without this, FIs are always do the business in uncertainty, which not only affects its profitability but also put question mark on its survival in case of unexpected adversities in economy or financial market. All the above cases are the perfect examples of loss due to uncertainty and overlooking proper risk management and control system. The cases of Washington Mutual Bank, Moody rating agency, S & P rating agency, Goldman Sachs and Deutsche Bank have been discussed which led to deep financial crises in US and failure of various FIs and Banks in US.

KEY CONCEPTS

SIMEX NIKKEI ALCO FDIC

References:

1 Philippe Jorion, Value at Risk, Second Edition, Pg.5

2 *www.riskglossary.com/articles*: For international financial market cases

3 *http://en.wikipedia.org/wiki/*

4 *www.icfai.org:* For Indian financial market cases

PART F

Other Important Concepts of Risk Management

24. Concepts related to Risk Management

    - Time Value of Money
    - Advance Bond Concepts
    - Calculation of VaR
    - Black–Scholes Model
    - Moody's KMV Portfolio Manager
    - Probability Distribution and Fundamental of Statistics
    - Derivatives Products and its Markets

Time Value of Money[1]

Introduction

Time Value of Money (TVM) is based on the concept that a rupee that you have today is worth more than the promise or expectation that you will receive a rupee in the future. Money that you hold today is worth more because you can invest it and earn interest on it. After all, you should receive some compensation for foregoing spending. For instance, you can invest your rupee for one year at a 6% annual interest rate and accumulate Rs.1.06 at the end of the year. You can say that the future value of the rupee is Rs.1.06 given a 6% interest rate and a one-year period. It follows that the present value of the Rs.1.06 you expect to receive in one year is only Re.1.

Simple Interest

Simple interest is calculated on the original principal only. Accumulated interest from prior periods is not used in calculations for the following periods. Simple interest is normally used for a single period of less than a year, such as 30 or 60 days.

$$\text{Simple Interest} = p * i * n$$

Where

p = principal (original amount borrowed or loaned)

i = interest rate for one period

n = number of periods

Compound Interest

Compound interest is calculated each period on the original principal and all interest accumulated during past periods. Although the interest may be stated as a yearly rate, the compounding periods can be yearly, semiannually, quarterly, or even continuous.

Rate of Return

When we know the Present Value (amount today), Future Value (amount to which the investment will grow), and Number of Periods, we can calculate the rate of return with this formula:

$$i = (FV / PV)^{(1/n)} - 1$$

Effective Rate (Effective Yield)

The effective rate is the actual rate that you earn on an investment or pay on a loan after the effects of compounding frequency are considered. The effective rate of an investment will always be higher than the nominal or stated interest rate when interest is compounded more than once per year. As the number of compounding periods increase, the difference between the nominal and effective rates will also increase.

To convert a nominal rate to an equivalent effective rate, the formula is:

$$\text{Effective Rate} = (1 + (i / n))^n - 1$$

Where

i = Nominal or stated interest rate

n = Number of compounding periods per year

Present Value

Present Value of a Single Amount

Present Value is an amount today that is equivalent to a future payment, or a series of payments, that has been discounted by an appropriate interest rate. Since money has time value, the present value of a promised future amount is worth less the longer you have to wait to receive it. The difference between the two depends on the number of compounding periods involved and the interest (discount) rate. The relationship between the present value and future value can be expressed as:

$$PV = FV\,[\,1 / (1 + i)^n\,]$$

Where:

PV = Present Value

FV = Future Value

i = Interest Rate Per Period

n = Number of Compounding Periods

Present Value of Annuities

An annuity is a series of equal payments or receipts that occur at evenly spaced intervals. Leases and rental payments are examples. The payments or receipts occur at the end of each period for an ordinary annuity while they occur at the beginning of each period for an annuity due.

Present Value of an Ordinary Annuity

The Present Value of an Ordinary Annuity (PVOA) is the value of a stream of expected or promised future payments that have been discounted to a single equivalent value today. The Present Value of an Ordinary Annuity could be solved by calculating the present value of each payment in the series using the present value formula and then summing the results. A more direct formula is:

$$PVOA = PMT\,[(1 - (1 / (1 + i)^n)) / i]$$

Where:

PVOA = Present Value of an Ordinary Annuity

PMT = Amount of each payment

i = Discount Rate Per Period

n = Number of Periods

Present Value of an Annuity Due (PVAD)

The Present Value of an Annuity Due is identical to an ordinary annuity except that each payment occurs at the beginning of a period rather than at the end. Since each payment occurs one period earlier, we can calculate the present value of an ordinary annuity and then multiply the result by (1 + i).

$$PVAD = PVOA\,(1+i)$$

Where:

PVAD = Present Value of an Annuity Due

PVOA = Present Value of an Ordinary Annuity

i = Discount Rate Per Period

Future Value

Future Value of A Single Amount

Future Value is the amount of money that an investment made today (the present value) will grow to by some future date. Since money has time value, we naturally expect the future value to be greater than the present value. The difference between the two depends on the number of compounding periods involved and the going interest rate. The relationship between the future value and present value can be expressed as:

$$FV = PV\,(1 + i)^n$$

Where:

FV = Future Value

PV = Present Value

i = Interest Rate Per Period

n = Number of Compounding Periods

Future Value of Annuities

An annuity is a series of equal payments or receipts that occur at evenly spaced intervals. Leases and rental payments are examples. The payments or receipts occur at the end of each period for an ordinary annuity while they occur at the beginning of each period for an annuity due.

Future Value of an Ordinary Annuity

The Future Value of an Ordinary Annuity (FVOA) is the value that a stream of expected or promised future payments will grow to after a given number of periods at a specific compounded interest. The Future Value of an Ordinary Annuity could be solved by calculating the future value of each individual payment in the series using the future value formula and then summing the results. A more direct formula is:

$$FVOA = PMT\ [((1 + i)^n - 1) / i]$$

Where:

FVOA = Future Value of an Ordinary Annuity

PMT = Amount of each payment

i = Interest Rate Per Period

n = Number of Periods

Future Value of an Annuity Due (FVAD)

The Future Value of an Annuity Due is identical to an ordinary annuity except that each payment occurs at the beginning of a period rather than at the end. Since each payment occurs one period earlier, we can calculate the present value of an ordinary annuity and then multiply the result by (1 + i).

$$FVAD = FVOA\ (1+i)$$

Where:

FVAD = Future Value of an Annuity Due

FVOA = Future Value of an Ordinary Annuity

i = Interest Rate Per Period

The Risk/Return Tradeoff

Low levels of uncertainty (low risk) are associated with low potential returns. High levels of uncertainty (high risk) are associated with high potential returns. The risk/return tradeoff is the balance between the desire for the lowest possible risk and the highest possible return. This is demonstrated graphically in the chart below. A higher standard deviation means a higher risk and higher possible return.

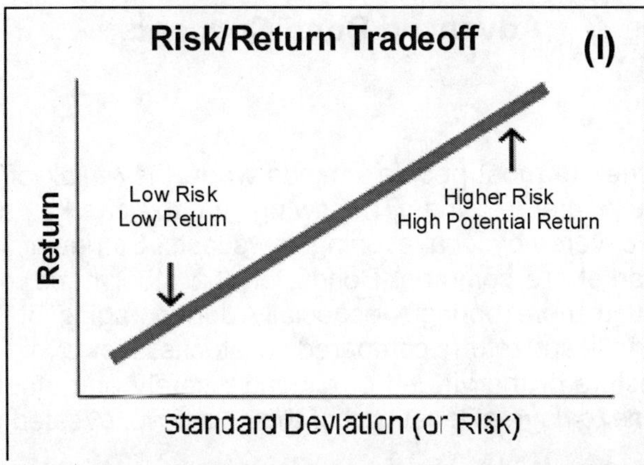

A common misconception is that higher risk equals greater return. The risk/return tradeoff tells us that the higher risk gives us the possibility of higher returns. There are no guarantees. Just as risk means higher potential returns, it also means higher potential losses.

Capital Asset Pricing Model (CAPM)

The Capital Asset Pricing Model (CAPM) describes the relationship between risk and expected return, and it serves as a model for the pricing of risky securities. CAPM says that the expected return of a security or a portfolio equals the rate on a risk-free security plus a risk premium. If this expected return does not meet or beat our required return, the investment should not be undertaken. The commonly used formula to describe the CAPM relationship is as follows:

Required (or expected) Return = RF Rate + (Market Return - RF Rate)*Beta

For example, let's say that the current risk free-rate is 5%, and the S&P 500 is expected to return to 12% next year. You are interested in determining the return that Joe's Oyster Bar Inc (JOB) will have next year. You have determined that its beta value is 1.9. The overall stock market has a beta of 1.0, so JOB's beta of 1.9 tells us that it carries more risk than the overall market; this extra risk means that we should expect a higher potential return than the 12% of the S&P 500. We can calculate this as follows:

Required (or expected) Return = 5% + (12% - 5%)*1.9

Required (or expected) Return = 18.3%

What CAPM tells us is that Joe's Oyster Bar has a required rate of return of 18.3%. So, if you invest in JOB, you should be getting at least 18.3% return on your investment. If you do not think that JOB will produce those kinds of returns for you, then you should consider investing in a different company.

It is important to remember that high-beta shares usually give the highest returns. Over a long period of time, however, high beta shares are the worst performers during market declines (bear markets). While you might receive high returns from high beta shares, there is no guarantee that the CAPM return is realized.

Advanced Bond Concepts[2]

Introduction

The first thing that comes to most people's minds when they think of investing is the stock market. After all, stocks are exciting. The swings in the market are scrutinized in the newspapers and even covered by local evening newscasts. Stories of investors gaining great wealth in the stock market are common. Bonds, on the other hand, do not have the same appeal. Bonds are much more boring - especially during raging bull markets, when they seem to offer an insignificant return compared to stocks. However, all it takes is a bear market to remind investors of the virtues of a bond's safety and stability. In fact, for many investors it makes sense to have at least part of their portfolio invested in bonds.

Just as people need money, so do companies and governments. A company needs funds to expand into new markets, while governments need money for everything from infrastructure to social programs. The problem THAT large organisations run into is that they typically need far more money than the average bank can provide. The solution is to raise money by issuing bonds (or other debt instruments) to a public market. Thousands of investors then each lend a portion of the capital needed. Really, a bond is nothing more than a loan for which you are the lender. The organization that sells a bond is known as the issuer. You can think of a bond as an IOU given by a borrower (the issuer) to a lender (the investor).

Of course, nobody would loan his or her hard-earned money for nothing. The issuer of a bond must pay the investor something extra for the privilege of using his or her money. This "extra" comes in the form of interest payments, which are made at a predetermined rate and schedule. The interest rate is often referred to as the coupon. The date on which the issuer has to repay the amount borrowed (known as face value) is called the maturity date. Bonds are known as fixed-income securities because you know the exact amount of cash you'll get back if you hold the security until maturity is known.

For example, say you buy a bond with a face value of Rs.1,000, a coupon of 8%, and a maturity of 10 years. This means you'll receive a total of Rs. 80 (Rs.1,000*8%) of interest per year for the next 10 years. Actually, because most bonds pay interest semi-annually, you'll receive two payments of Rs. 40 a year for 10 years. When the bond matures after a decade, you'll get your Rs.1,000 back.

Bond Type Specifics

A bond is simply a contract between a lender and a borrower by which the borrower promises to repay a loan with interest. However, bonds can take on many additional features and/or options that can complicate the way in which prices and yields are calculated. The classification of a bond depends on its type of issuer, priority, coupon rate and redemption features. The following chart outlines these categories of bond characteristics:

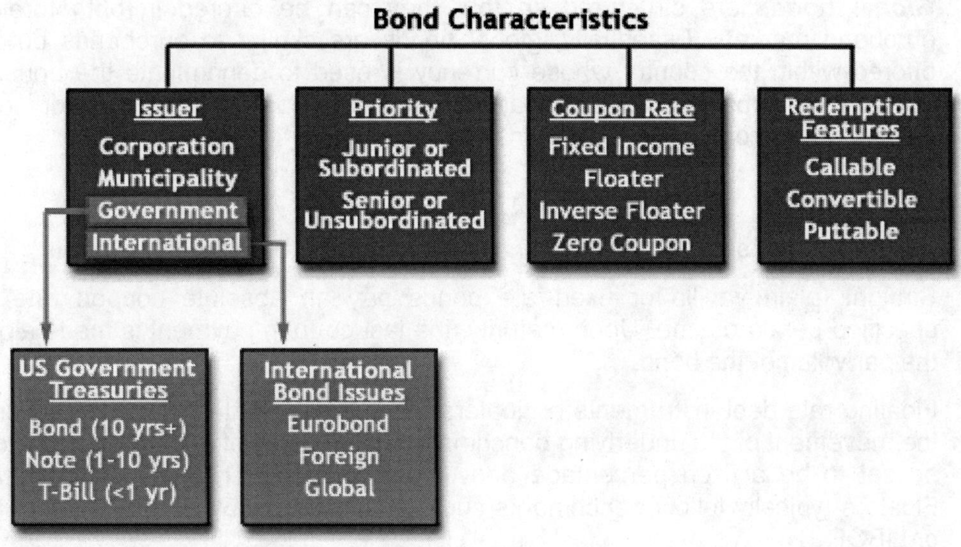

Bond Issuers

As the major determiner of a bond's credit quality, the issuer is one of the most important characteristics of a bond. There are significant differences between bonds issued by corporations and those issued by a state government/municipality or national government. In general, securities issued by the central government have the lowest risk of default while corporate bonds are considered to be riskier ventures. It is important that like corporate bonds, government bonds carry various levels of risk; because all national governments are different, so are the bonds they issue.

International bonds (government or corporate) are complicated by different currencies. That is, these types of bonds are issued within a market that is foreign to the issuer's home market, but some international bonds are issued in the currency of the foreign market and others are denominated in another currency. Here are some types of international bonds:

- The definition of the ***eurobond*** market can be confusing because of its name. Although the euro is the currency used by participating European Union countries, eurobonds refer neither to the European currency nor to a European bond market. A eurobond instead refers to any bond that is denominated in a currency other than that of the country in which it is issued. Bonds in the eurobond market are categorized according to the currency in which they are denominated. As an example, a eurobond denominated in Japanese yen but issued in the U.S. would be classified as a euroyen bond.

- ***Foreign bonds*** are denominated in the currency of the country in which a foreign entity issues the bond. An example of such a bond is the samurai bond, which is a yen-denominated bond issued in Japan by an American company. Other popular foreign bonds include bulldog and yankee bonds.

- ***Global bonds*** are structured so that they can be offered in both foreign and eurobond markets. Essentially, global bonds are similar to eurobonds but can be offered within the country whose currency is used to denominate the bond. As an example, a global bond denominated in yen could be sold to Japan or any other country throughout the Eurobond market.

Coupon Rate

Bond issuers may choose from a variety of types of coupons, or interest payments.

- Straight, plain vanilla or fixed-rate bonds pay an absolute coupon rate over a specified period of time. Upon maturity, the last coupon payment is made along with the par value of the bond.
- Floating rate debt instruments or floaters pay a coupon rate that varies according to the movement of the underlying benchmark. These types of coupons could, however, be set to be a fixed percentage above, below, or equal to the benchmark itself. Floaters typically follow benchmarks such as the three, six or nine-month T-bill rate or LIBOR.
- Inverse floaters pay a variable coupon rate that changes in direction opposite to that of short-term interest rates. An inverse floater subtracts the benchmark from a set coupon rate. For example, an inverse floater that uses LIBOR as the underlying benchmark might pay a coupon rate of a certain percentage, say 6%, minus LIBOR.
- Zero coupon, or accrual bonds do not pay a coupon. Instead, these types of bonds are issued at a deep discount and pay the full face value at maturity.

Redemption Features

Both investors and issuers are exposed to interest rate risk because they are locked into either receiving or paying a set coupon rate over a specified period of time. For this reason, some bonds offer additional benefits to investors or more flexibility for issuers:

- Callable, or a redeemable bond features gives a bond issuer the right, but not the obligation, to redeem his issue of bonds before the bond's maturity. The issuer, however, must pay the bond holders a premium. There are two subcategories of these types of bonds: American callable bonds and European callable bonds. American callable bonds can be called by the issuer any time after the call protection period while European callable bonds can be called by the issuer only on pre-specified dates.
- Convertible bonds give bondholders the right but not the obligation to convert their bonds into a predetermined number of shares at predetermined dates prior to the bond's maturity.
- Puttable bonds give bondholders the right but not the obligation to sell their bonds back to the issuer at a predetermined price and date. These bonds generally protect investors from interest rate risk. If prevailing bond prices are lower than the exercise par of the bond, resulting from interest rates being higher than the bond's coupon rate, it is optimal for investors to sell their bonds back to the issuer and reinvest their money at a higher interest rate.

Bond Pricing

Fundamentally, however, the price of a bond is the sum of the present values of all expected coupon payments plus the present value of the par value at maturity. Calculating bond price is simple: all we are doing is discounting the known future cash flows. Remember that to calculate present value (PV) - which is based on the assumption that each payment is re-invested at some interest rate once it is received--we have to know the interest rate that would earn us a known future value. For bond pricing, this interest rate is the required yield.

Here is the formula for calculating a bond's price, which uses the basic present value (PV) formula:

$$\text{Bond Price} = \frac{C}{(1+i)} + \frac{C}{(1+i)^2} + \ldots\ldots + \frac{C}{(1+i)^n} + \frac{M}{(1+i)^n}$$

C = coupon payment
n = number of payments
i = interest rate, or required yield
M = value at maturity, or par value

The succession of coupon payments to be received in the future is referred to as an ordinary annuity, which is a series of fixed payments at set intervals over a fixed period of time. (Coupons on a straight bond are paid at ordinary annuity.) The first payment of an ordinary annuity occurs one interval from the time at which the debt security is acquired. The calculation assumes this time is the present.

By incorporating the annuity model into the bond pricing formula, which requires us to also include the present value of the par value received at maturity, we arrive at the following formula:

$$\text{Bond Price} = C * \frac{\left[1 - \left[\frac{1}{(1+i)^n}\right]\right]}{i} + \frac{M}{(1+i)^n}$$

If coupons were paid semi-annually, we divided the interest rate and coupon payments in half to represent the two payments per year. A simple modification of the above formula will allow you to adjust interest rates and coupon payments to calculate a bond price for any payment frequency:

$$\text{Bond Price} = \frac{C}{F} * \frac{\left[1 - \left[\frac{1}{(1+\frac{i}{F})^{n*F}}\right]\right]}{\frac{i}{F}} + \frac{M}{(1+\frac{i}{F})^{n*F}}$$

Pricing Zero-Coupon Bonds

In zero-coupon bond, there is no coupon payment until maturity. Because of this, the present value of annuity formula is unnecessary. You simply calculate the present value of the par value at maturity. Here's a simple example:

Example: Let's look at how to calculate the price of a zero-coupon bond that is maturing in five years, has a par value of Rs.1,000 and a required yield of 6%. Interest is compounded semiannually.

$$\text{Zero Coupon Bond Price} = \frac{M}{(1+i)^n}$$

$$= \frac{1000}{(1+0.03)^{10}}$$

$$= \$744.09$$

Yield and Bond Price

The general definition of yield is the return an investor will receive by holding a bond to maturity. So if you want to know what your bond investment will earn, you should know how to calculate yield. Required yield, on the other hand, is the yield or return a bond must offer in order for it to be worthwhile for the investor. The required yield of a bond is usually the yield offered by other plain vanilla bonds that are currently offered in the market and have similar credit quality and maturity.

Calculating Current Yield

A simple yield calculation that is often used to calculate the yield on both bonds and the dividend yield for stocks is the current yield. The current yield calculates the percentage return that the annual coupon payment provides the investor. In other words, this yield calculates what percentage the actual rupee coupon payment is of the price the investor pays for the bond. The multiplication by 100 in the formulas below converts the decimal into a percentage, allowing us to see the percentage return:

$$\text{Current Yield} = \frac{\text{Annual Dollar Interest Paid}}{\text{Market Price}} * 100\%$$

So, if you purchased a bond with a par value of Rs.100 for Rs.95.92 and it paid a coupon rate of 5%, this is how you will calculate its current yield:

$$= \frac{(0.05 * \$100)}{\$95.92} * 100\% = 5.21\%$$

Notice how this calculation does not include any capital gains or losses the investor would make if the bond were bought at a discount or premium. Because the comparison of the bond price to its par value is a factor that affects the actual current yield, the above formula would give a slightly inaccurate answer - unless of course the investor pays par value for the bond. To correct this, investors can modify the current yield formula by adding the result of the current yield to the gain or loss the price gives the investor: [(Par Value – Bond Price)/Years to Maturity]. The modified current yield formula then takes into account the discount or premium at which the investor bought the bond. This is the full calculation:

$$\text{Adjusted Current Yield} = \frac{\text{Annual Coupon}}{\text{Market Price}} * 100\% + \left[\frac{(100 - \text{Market Price})}{\text{Years to Maturity}}\right]$$

Let's re-calculate the yield of the bond in our first example, which matures in 30 months and has a coupon payment of Rs.5:

$$= \frac{\$5}{\$95.92} * 100\% + \frac{(100 - 95.92)}{2.5} = 6.84\%$$

The adjusted current yield of 6.84% is higher than the current yield of 5.21% because the bond's discounted price (Rs.95.92 instead of Rs.100) gives the investor more of a gain on the investment.

Now we must also account for other factors such as the coupon payment for a zero-coupon bond, which has only one coupon payment. For such a bond, the yield calculation would be as follows:

$$\text{Yield} = \left(\frac{\text{Future Value}}{\text{Purchase Price}}\right)^{\frac{1}{n}} - 1$$

n = years left until maturity

If we were considering a zero-coupon bond that has a future value of Rs.1,000 that matures in two years and can be currently purchased for Rs.925, we would calculate its current yield with the following formula:

$$\text{Yield} = \left(\frac{\$1000}{\$925}\right)^{\frac{1}{2}} - 1$$

$$= 0.03975 \text{ or } 3.95\%$$

Calculating Yield to Maturity

The yield to maturity (YTM) is the interest rate by which the present values of all the future cash flows are equal to the bond's price. YTM is the return the investor will receive from his or her entire investment. It is the return that an investor gains by receiving the present values of the coupon payments, the par value and capital gains in relation to the price that is paid.

In general, as a bond's price increases, yield decreases. This relationship is measured using the price value of a basis point (PVBP). By taking into account factors such as the bond's coupon rate and credit rating, the PVBP measures the degree to which a bond's price will change when there is a 0.01% change in interest rates. The charted relationship between bond price and required yield appears as a negative curve:

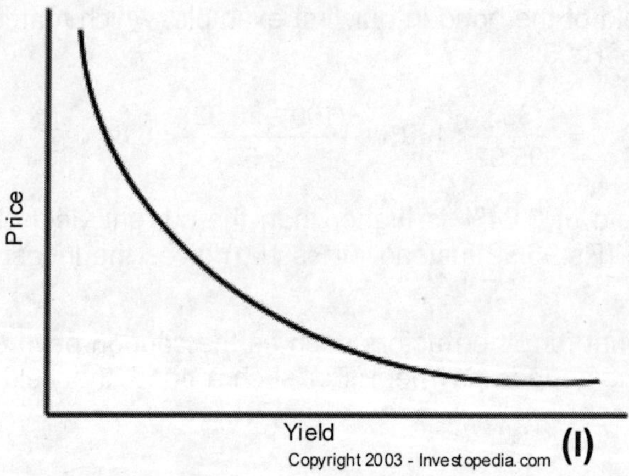

(I)

This is due to the fact that a bond's price will be higher when it pays a coupon that is higher than prevailing interest rates. As market interest rates increase, bond prices decrease.

The calculation can be presented as:

$$\text{Bond Price} = \frac{\text{Cashflow 1}}{(1+\text{yield})^1} + \frac{\text{Cashflow 2}}{(1+\text{yield})^2} + ... + \frac{\text{Last Cashflow}}{(1+\text{yield})^n}$$

OR

$$\text{Bond Price} = \text{Cashflow} * \frac{1 - \left(\frac{1}{(1+\text{interest rate})^n}\right)}{\text{interest rate}} + \left[\text{Maturity Value} * \frac{1}{(1+\text{interest rate})^n}\right]$$

Calculating Yield for Callable and Puttable Bonds

Bonds with callable or puttable redemption features have additional yield calculations. A callable bond's valuations must account for the issuer's ability to call the bond on the call date and the puttable bond's valuation must include the buyer's ability to sell the bond at the pre-specified put date. The yield for callable bonds is referred to as yield-to-call, and the yield for puttable bonds is referred to as yield-to-put. Yield to Call (YTC) is the interest rate that investors would receive if they held the bond until the call date. The period until the first call is referred to as the call protection period. Yield to call is the rate that would make the bond's present value equal to the full price of the bond. Essentially, its calculation requires two simple modifications to the yield-to-maturity formula:

$$\text{Bond Price} = \text{Cashflow} * \frac{1 - \left(\frac{1}{(1+\text{interest rate})^n}\right)}{\text{interest rate}} + \left[\text{Call Value} * \frac{1}{(1+\text{interest rate})^n}\right]$$

Call price replaces maturity value

Time until call date replaces time to maturity

Note that European callable bonds can have multiple call dates and that a yield to call can be calculated for each.

Yield to Put (YTP) is the interest rate that investors would receive if they held the bond until its put date. To calculate yield to put, the same modified equation for yield to call is used except the bond put price replaces the bond call value and the time until put date replaces the time until call date.

Term Structure of Interest Rates

The term structure of interest rates, also known as the yield curve, is a very common bond valuation method. Constructed by graphing the yield to maturities and the respective maturity dates of benchmark fixed-income securities, the yield curve is a measure of the market's expectations of future interest rates given the current market conditions. Treasuries, issued by the central government, are considered risk-free, and as such, their yields are often used as the benchmarks for fixed-income securities with the same maturities. The term structure of interest rates is graphed as though each coupon payment of a noncallable fixed-income security were a zero-coupon bond that "matures" on the coupon payment date. The exact shape of the curve can be different at any point in time. So if the normal yield curve changes shape, it tells investors that they may need to change their outlook on the economy.

There are three main patterns created by the term structure of interest rates:

1) Normal Yield Curve: As its name indicates, this is the yield curve shape that forms during normal market conditions, wherein investors generally believe that there will be no significant changes in the economy, such as in inflation rates, and that the economy will continue to grow at a normal rate. During such conditions, investors expect higher yields for fixed income instruments with long-term maturities that occur farther into the future. In other words, the market expects long-term fixed income securities to offer higher yields than short-term fixed income securities. This is a normal expectation of the market because short-term instruments generally hold less risk than long-term instruments; the farther into the future the bond's maturity, the more time and, therefore, uncertainty the bondholder faces before being paid back the principal. To invest in one instrument for a longer period of time, an investor needs to be compensated for undertaking the additional risk.

Remember that as general current interest rates increase, the price of a bond will decrease and its yield will increase.

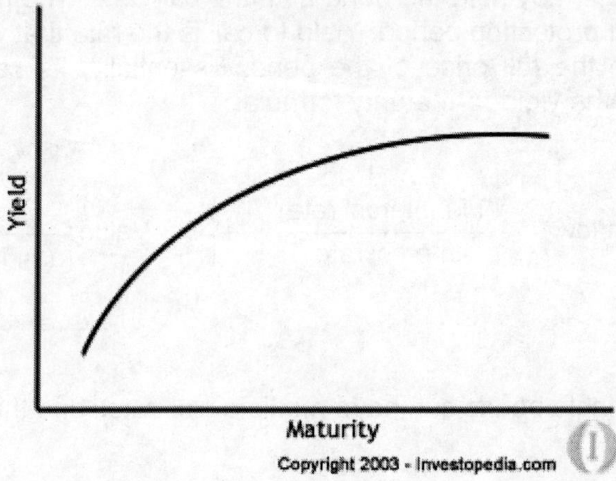

2) Flat Yield Curve: These curves indicate that the market environment is sending mixed signals to investors, who are interpreting interest rate movements in various ways. During such an environment, it is difficult for the market to determine whether interest rates will move significantly in either direction farther into the future. A flat yield curve usually occurs when the market is making a transition that emits different but simultaneous indications of what interest rates will do. In other words, there may be some signals that short-term interest rates will rise and other signals that long-term interest rates will fall. This condition will create a curve that is flatter than its normal positive slope. When the yield curve is flat, investors can maximize their risk/return tradeoff by choosing fixed-income securities with the least risk, or highest credit quality. In the rare instances wherein long-term interest rates decline, a flat curve can sometimes lead to an inverted curve.

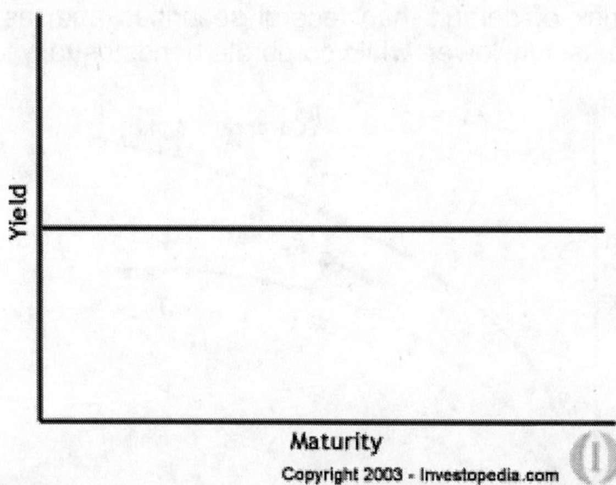

3) Inverted Yield Curve: These yield curves are rare, and they form during extraordinary market conditions wherein the expectations of investors are completely the inverse of those demonstrated by the normal yield curve. In such abnormal market environments, bonds with maturity dates further into the future are expected to offer lower yields than bonds with shorter maturities. The inverted yield curve indicates that the market currently expects interest rates to decline as time moves farther into the future, which in turn means the market expects yields of long-term bonds to decline. Remember, also, that as interest rates decrease, bond prices increase and yields decline.

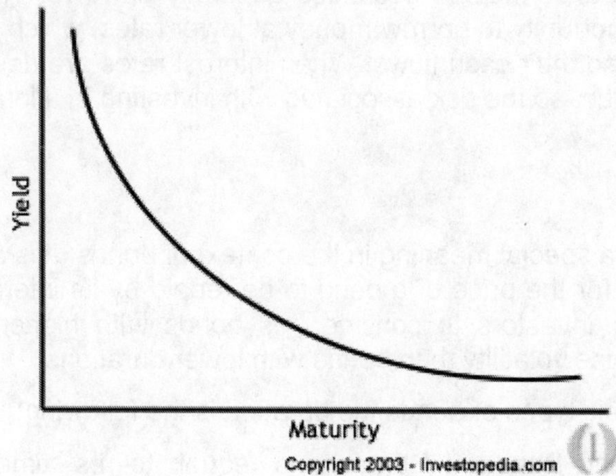

The Credit Spread

The credit spread, or quality spread, is the additional yield an investor receives for acquiring a corporate bond instead of a similar federal instrument. As illustrated in the graph, the spread is demonstrated as the yield curve of the corporate bond and is plotted with the term structure of interest rates. Remember that the term structure of interest rates is a gauge of the direction of interest rates and the general state of the economy. Corporate fixed-income securities have more risk of default than federal securities and, as a result, the prices of corporate securities are usually lower, while corporate bonds usually have a higher yield.

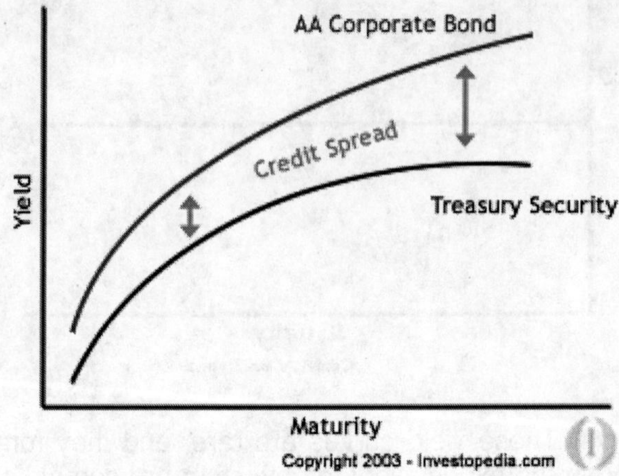

When inflation rates are increasing (or the economy is contracting) the credit spread between corporate and Treasury securities widens. This is because investors must be offered additional compensation (in the form of a higher coupon rate) for acquiring the higher risk associated with corporate bonds.

When interest rates are declining (or the economy is expanding), the credit spread between Federal and corporate fixed-income securities generally narrows. The lower interest rates give companies an opportunity to borrow money at lower rates, which allows them to expand their operations and also their cash flows. When interest rates are declining, the economy is expanding in the long run, so the risk associated with investing in a long-term corporate bond is also generally lower.

Duration

The term duration has a special meaning in the context of bonds. It is a measurement of how long, in years, it takes for the price of a bond to be repaid by its internal cash flows. It is an important measure for investors to consider, as bonds with higher durations carry more risk and have higher price volatility than bonds with lower durations.

For each of the two basic types of bonds the duration is the following:

1. Zero-Coupon Bond – Duration is equal to its time to maturity.
2. Vanilla Bond - Duration will always be less than its time to maturity.

Duration: Other factors

Besides the movement of time and the payment of coupons, there are other factors that affect a bond's duration: the coupon rate and its yield. Bonds with high coupon rates and, in turn, high yields will tend to have lower durations than bonds that pay low coupon rates or offer low yields. This makes empirical sense, because when a bond pays a higher coupon rate or has a high yield, the holder of the security receives repayment for the security at a faster rate. The diagram below summarizes how duration changes with coupon rate and yield.

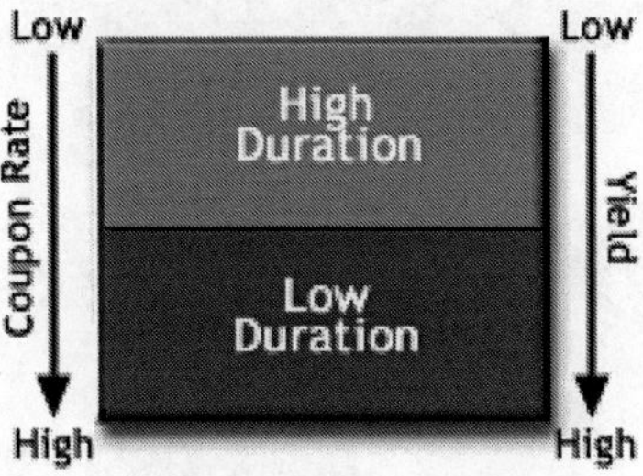

Types of Duration

There are four main types of duration calculations, each of which differ in the way they account for factors such as interest rate changes and the bond's embedded options or redemption features. The four types of durations are Macaulay duration, modified duration, effective duration and key-rate duration.

Macaulay Duration

The formula usually used to calculate a bond's basic duration is the Macaulay duration. Macaulay duration is calculated by adding the results of multiplying the present value of each cash flow by the time it is received and dividing by the total price of the security. The formula for Macaulay duration is as follows:

$$\text{Macaulay Duration} = \frac{\sum_{t=1}^{n} \frac{t * C}{(1+i)^t} + \frac{n * M}{(1+i)^n}}{P}$$

n = number of cash flows

t = time to maturity

C = cash flow

i = required yield

M = maturity (par) value

P = bond price

Remember that bond price equals:

$$C * \frac{\left[1 - \left[\frac{1}{(1+i)^n}\right]\right]}{i} + \frac{M}{(1+i)^n}$$

So the following is an expanded version of Macaulay duration:

$$\text{Macaulay Duration} = \frac{\sum_{t=1}^{n} \frac{t * c}{(1+i)^t} + \frac{n * M}{(1+i)^n}}{C * \left[\frac{1 - \left[\frac{1}{(1+i)^n} \right]}{i} \right] + \frac{M}{(1+i)^n}}$$

Modified Duration

Modified duration is a modified version of the Macaulay model that accounts for changing interest rates. Because they affect yield, fluctuating interest rates will affect duration, so this modified formula shows how much the duration changes for each percentage change in yield. For bonds without any embedded features, bond price and interest rate move in opposite directions, so there is an inverse relationship between modified duration and an approximate 1% change in yield. Because the modified duration formula shows how a bond's duration changes in relation to interest rate movements, the formula is appropriate for investors wishing to measure the volatility of a particular bond. Modified duration is calculated as the following:

$$\text{Macaulay Duration} = \left[\frac{\text{Macaulay Duration}}{\left(1 + \frac{\text{Yield - to - maturity}}{\text{number of coupon periods per year}} \right)} \right]$$

OR

$$\text{Modified Duration} = \left[\frac{\text{Macaulay Duration}}{\left(1 + \frac{\text{YTM}}{n} \right)} \right]$$

Effective Duration

The modified duration formula discussed above assumes that the expected cash flows will remain constant, even if prevailing interest rates change; this is also the case for option-free fixed-income securities. On the other hand, cash flows from securities with embedded options or redemption features will change when interest rates change. For calculating the duration of these types of bonds, effective duration is the most appropriate. Effective duration requires the use of binomial trees to calculate the Option Adjusted Spread (OAS). There are, however, many programs available to investors wishing to calculate effective duration.

Key-Rate Duration

The final duration calculation to learn is key-rate duration, which calculates the spot durations of each of the 11 "key" maturities along a spot rate curve. These 11 key maturities are at the three-month and one, two, three, five, seven, 10, 15, 20, 25, and 30-year portions of the curve. In essence, key-rate duration, while holding the yield for all other maturities constant, allows the duration of a portfolio to be calculated for a one-basis-point change in interest rates. The key-rate method is most often used for portfolios such as the bond ladder, which consists of fixed-income securities with differing maturities. Here is the formula for key-rate duration:

$$\frac{\text{Price of security after a 1\% decrease in yield} - \text{Price of security after a 1\% increase in yield}}{2 * (\text{Initial price of security}) * 1\%}$$

The sum of the key-rate durations along the curve is equal to the effective duration.

Duration and Bond Price Volatility

Generally, bonds with a high duration will have a higher price fluctuation than bonds with a low duration. But it is important to know that there are also three other factors that determine how sensitive a bond's price is to changes in interest rates. These factors are term to maturity, coupon rate and yield to maturity. Knowing what affects a bond's volatility is important to investors who use duration-based immunization strategies, which we discuss below, in their portfolios.

Factors 1 and 2: Coupon rate and Term to Maturity

If term to maturity and a bond's initial price remain constant, the higher the coupon, the lower the volatility, and the lower the coupon, the higher the volatility. If the coupon rate and the bond's initial price are constant, the bond with a longer term to maturity will display higher price volatility and a bond with a shorter term to maturity will display lower price volatility.Therefore, if you would like to invest in a bond with minimal interest rate risk, a bond with high coupon payments and a short term to maturity would be optimal. An investor who predicts that interest rates will decline would best potentially capitalize on a bond with low coupon payments and a long term to maturity, since these factors would magnify a bond's price increase.

Factor 3: Yield to Maturity (YTM)

The sensitivity of a bond's price to changes in interest rates also depends on its yield to maturity. A bond with a high yield to maturity will display lower price volatility than a bond with a lower yield to maturity, but a similar coupon rate and term to maturity. Yield to maturity is affected by the bond's credit rating, so bonds with poor credit ratings will have higher yields than bonds with excellent credit ratings. Therefore, bonds with poor credit ratings typically display lower price volatility than bonds with excellent credit ratings.

All three factors affect the degree to which bond price will change in the face of a change in prevailing interest rates. These factors work together and against each other. Consider the chart below:

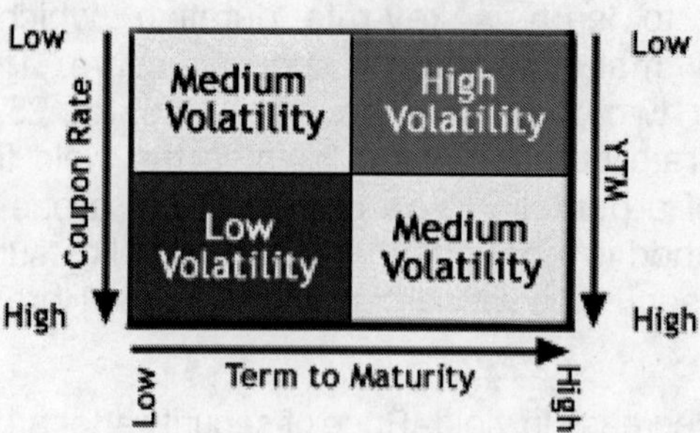

So, if a bond has both a short term to maturity and a low coupon rate, its characteristics have opposite effects on its volatility: the low coupon raises volatility and the short term to maturity lowers volatility. The bond's volatility would then be an average of these two opposite effects.

Convexity

For any given bond, a graph of the relationship between price and yield is convex. This means that the graph forms a curve rather than a straight-line (linear). The degree to which the graph is curved shows how much a bond's yield changes in response to a change in price.

Convexity and Duration

If we graph a tangent at a particular price of the bond (touching a point on the curved price-yield curve), the linear tangent is the bond's duration. The exact point where the two lines touch represents Macaulay duration.

Furthermore, as yield moves further from Y*, the actual bond price and the prices estimated by duration (tangent line) increases. The convexity calculation, therefore, accounts for the inaccuracies of the linear duration line. This calculation that plots the curved line uses a Taylor series, a very complicated calculus theory that we will not be describing here. The main thing for you to remember about convexity is that it shows how much a bond's yield changes in response to changes in price.

Properties of Convexity

Convexity is also useful for comparing bonds. If two bonds offer the same duration and yield but one exhibits greater convexity, changes in interest rates will affect each bond differently. A bond with greater convexity is less affected by interest rates than a bond with less convexity. Also, bonds with greater convexity will have a higher price than bonds with a lower convexity, regardless of whether interest rates rise or fall. This relationship is illustrated in the following diagram:

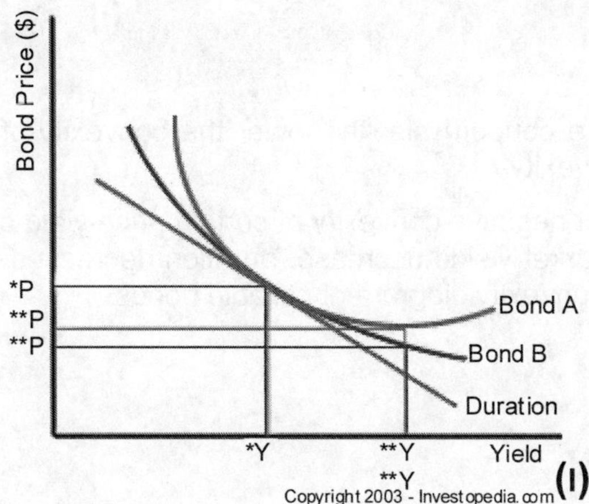

As you can see Bond A has greater convexity than Bond B, but they both have the same price and convexity when price equals *P and yield equals *Y. If interest rates change from this point by a very small amount, then both bonds would have approximately the same price, regardless of the convexity. When yield increases by a large amount, however, the prices of both Bond A and Bond B decrease, but Bond B's price decreases more than Bond A's. Notice how at **Y the price of Bond A remains higher, demonstrating that investors will have to pay more money (accept a lower yield to maturity) for a bond with greater convexity.

Factors Affecting Convexity

Here is a summary of the different kinds of convexities produced by different types of bonds:

1) The graph of the price-yield relationship for a plain vanilla bond exhibits positive convexity. The price-yield curve will increase as yield decreases, and *vice versa*. Therefore, as market yields decrease, the duration increases (and vice versa).

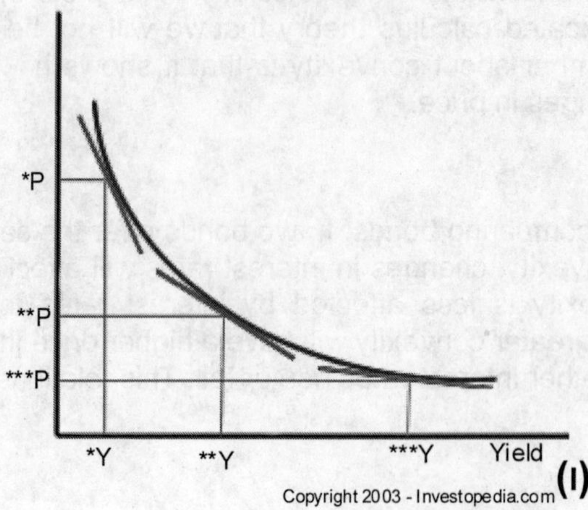

2) In general, the higher the coupon rate, the lower the convexity of a bond. Zero-coupon bonds have the highest convexity.

3) Callable bonds will exhibit negative convexity at certain price-yield combinations. Negative convexity means that as market yields decrease, duration decreases as well. See the chart below for an example of a convexity diagram of callable bonds.

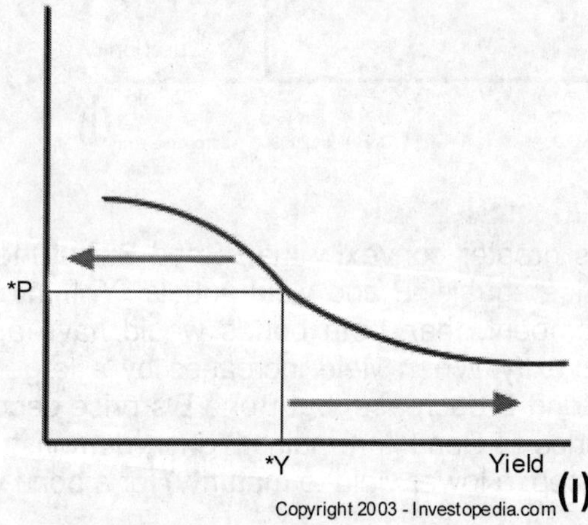

Convexity is the final major concept you need to know for gaining insight into the more technical aspects of the bond market. Understanding even the most basic characteristics of convexity allows the investor to better comprehend the way in which duration is best measured and how changes in interest rates affect the prices of both plain vanilla and callable bonds.

Calculation of Value at Risk (VaR)[3]

Introduction

Value at risk (VaR or sometimes VaR) has been called the "new science of risk management". The most popular and traditional measure of risk is volatility. The main problem with volatility, however, is that it does not care about the direction of an investment's movement: a stock can be volatile because it suddenly jumps higher. For investors, risk is about the odds of losing money, and VaR is based on that common-sense fact. By assuming investors care about the odds of a really big loss, VaR answers the question, "What is my worst-case scenario?" or "How much could I lose in a really bad month?".

A VaR statistic has three components: a time period, a confidence level and a loss amount (or loss percentage). Keep these three parts in mind as we give some examples of variations of the question that VaR answers:

- What is the most I can - with a 95% or 99% level of confidence - expect to lose in rupees over the next month?
- What is the maximum percentage I can - with 95% or 99% confidence - expect to lose over the next year?

You can see how the "VaR question" has three elements: a relatively high level of confidence (typically either 95% or 99%), a time period (a day, a month or a year) and an estimate of investment loss (expressed either in rupee or percentage terms).

Methods of Calculating VaR

Institutional investors use VaR to evaluate portfolio risk, but it may also be used to evaluate the risk of a single index that trades like a stock: the Nasdaq 100 Index, which trades under the ticker QQQQ. The QQQQ is a very popular index of the largest non-financial stocks that trade on the Nasdaq exchange. There are three methods of calculating VaR: the historical method, the variance-covariance method and the Monte Carlo simulation.

1. Historical Method

The historical method simply re-organizes actual historical returns, putting them in order from worst to best. It then assumes that history will repeat itself, from a risk perspective. The QQQ started trading in Mar 1999, and if we calculate each daily return, we produce a rich data set of almost 1,400 points. Let's put them in a histogram that compares the frequency of return "buckets". For example, at the highest point of the histogram (the highest bar), there were more than 250 days when the daily return was between 0% and 1%. At the far right, you can barely see a tiny bar at 13%; it represents the one single day (in Jan 2000) within a period of five-plus years when the daily return for the QQQ was a stunning 12.4%!

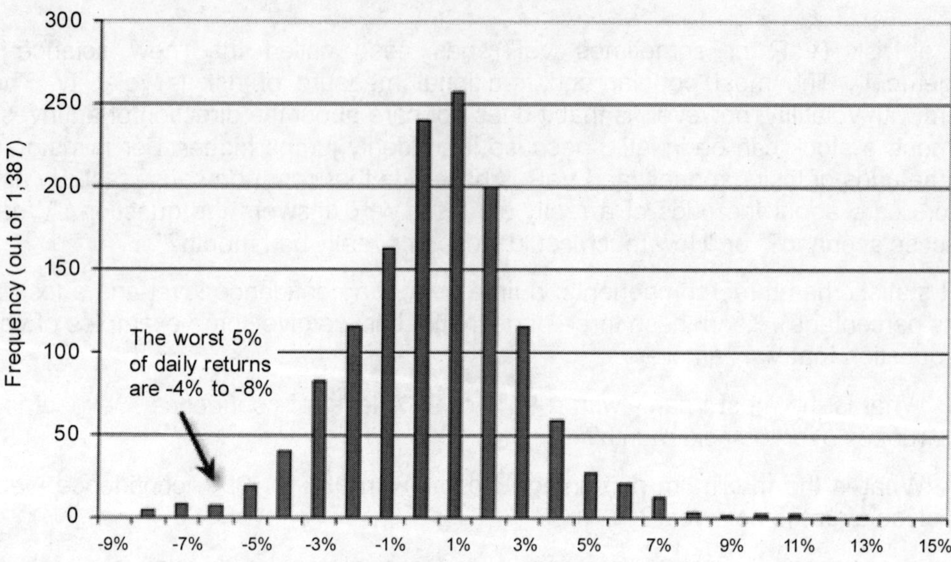

Notice the red bars that compose the "left tail" of the histogram. These are the lowest 5% of daily returns (since the returns are ordered from left to right, the worst are always the "left tail"). The red bars run from daily losses of 4% to 8%. Because these are the worst 5% of all daily returns, we can say with 95% confidence that the worst daily loss will not exceed 4%. Put another way, we expect with 95% confidence that our gain will exceed -4%. That is VaR in a nutshell. Let's re-phrase the statistic into both percentage and rupee terms:

- With 95% confidence, we expect that our worst daily loss will not exceed 4%.
- If we invest Rs.100, we are 95% confident that our worst daily loss will not exceed Rs.4 (Rs.100 x -4%).

You can see that VaR indeed allows for an outcome that is worse than a return of -4%. It does not express absolute certainty but instead makes a probabilistic estimate. If we want to increase our confidence, we need only to "move to the left" on the same histogram, to where the first two red bars, at -8% and -7% represent the worst 1% of daily returns:

- With 99% confidence, we expect that the worst daily loss will not exceed 7%.
- Or, if we invest Rs.100, we are 99% confident that our worst daily loss will not exceed Rs.7.

2. The Variance-Covariance Method

This method assumes that stock returns are normally distributed. In other words, it requires that we estimate only two factors - an expected (or average) return and a standard deviation - which allow us to plot a normal distribution curve. Here we plot the normal curve against the same actual return data:

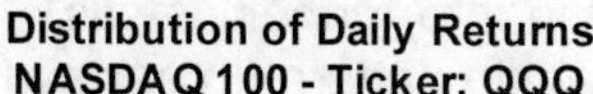

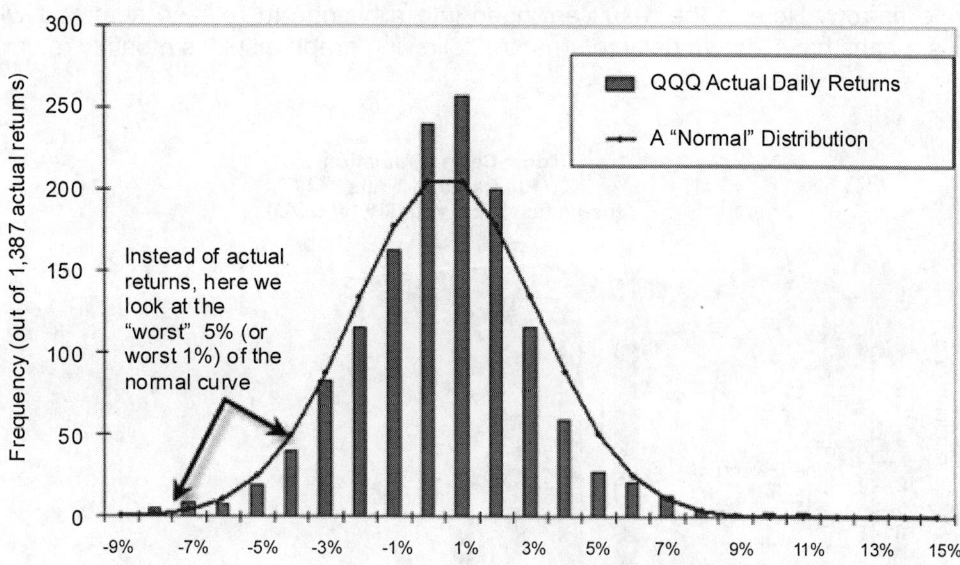

The idea behind the variance-covariance is similar to the ideas behind the historical method - except that we use the familiar curve instead of actual data. The advantage of the normal curve is that we automatically know where the worst 5% and 1% lie on the curve. They are a function of our desired confidence and the standard deviation (σ):

Confidence	# of Standard Deviations (σ)
95% (high)	- 1.65 × σ
95% (really high)	- 2.33 × σ

The blue curve above is based on the actual daily standard deviation of the QQQ, which is 2.64%. The average daily return happened to be fairly close to zero, so we will assume an average return of zero for illustrative purposes. Here are the results of plugging the actual standard deviation into the formulas above:

Confidence	# of σ	Calculation	Equals
95% (high)	-1.65×σ	-1.65×(2.64%)=	-4.36%
99% (really high)	-2.33×σ	-2.33×(2.64%)=	-6.16%

3. Monte Carlo Simulation

The third method involves developing a model for future stock price returns and running multiple hypothetical trials through the model. A Monte Carlo simulation refers to any method that randomly generates trials, but by itself does not tell us anything about the underlying methodology. For most users, a Monte Carlo simulation amounts to a "black box" generator of random outcomes. Without going into further details, if Monte Carlo simulation is run on the QQQ based on its historical trading pattern. In our simulation, 100 trials were conducted. If it is run again, it would give a different result--although it is highly likely that the differences would be narrow. Here is the result arranged into a histogram (please note that while the previous graphs have shown daily returns, the following graph displays monthly returns):

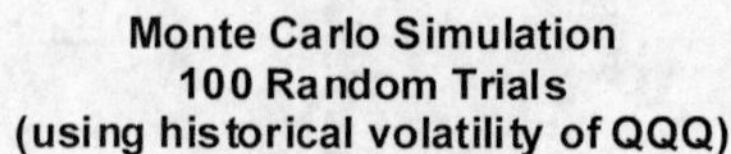

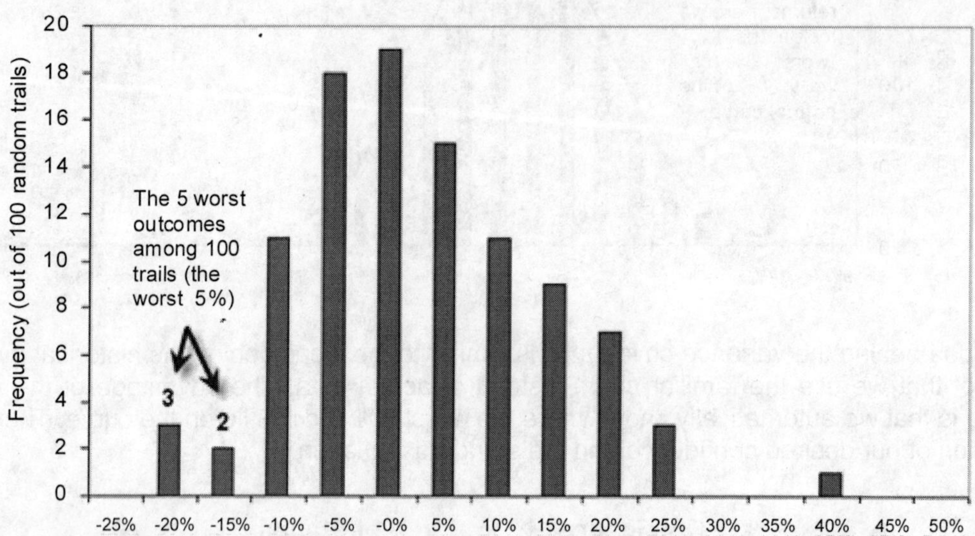

To summarize, we ran 100 hypothetical trials of monthly returns for the QQQ. Among them, two outcomes were between -15% and -20%; and three were between -20% and 25%. That means the worst five outcomes (that is, the worst 5%) were less than -15%. The Monte Carlo simulation therefore leads to the following VaR-type conclusion: with 95% confidence, we do not expect to lose more than 15% during any given month.

Converting One Time Period to Another

Since the time period is a variable, different calculations may specify different time periods - there is no "correct" time period. Commercial banks, for example, typically calculate a daily VaR, asking themselves how much they can lose in a day; pension funds, on the other hand, often calculate a monthly VaR. Because of the time variable, users of VaR need to know how to convert one time period to another, and they can do so by relying on a classic idea in finance: the standard deviation of stock returns tends to increase with the square root of time. If the standard deviation of daily returns is 2.64% and there are 20 trading days in a month (T = 20), then the monthly standard deviation is represented by the following:

$$\sigma_{Monthly} \cong \sigma_{Daily} \times \sqrt{T} \cong 2.64\% \times \sqrt{20}$$

To "scale" the daily standard deviation to a monthly standard deviation, we multiply it not by 20 but by the square root of 20. Similarly, if we want to scale the daily standard deviation to an annual standard deviation, we multiply the daily standard deviation by the square root of 250 (assuming 250 trading days in a year). Had we calculated a monthly standard deviation (which would be done by using month-to-month returns), we could convert to an annual standard deviation by multiplying the monthly standard deviation by the square root of 12.

Below we incorporate the time-conversion element into the variance-covariance method for a single stock (or single investment):

Confindence Level	The Maximum Loss – below the Expected or Average Return – as a Function of Standard Deviation (σ) and Time (T)
95% Confidence	$-1.65 \times \sigma \times \sqrt{T}$
99% Confidence	$-2.33 \times \sigma \times \sqrt{T}$

Now let's apply these formulas to the QQQ. Recall that the daily standard deviation for the QQQ since inception is 2.64%. But we want to calculate a monthly VaR, and assuming 20 trading days in a month, we multiply by the square root of 20:

Confindence Level	Loss below Expected (Average) Return as Function of Standard Deviation (σ) and Time (T)
95% Confidence	$-1.65 \times 2.64\% \times \sqrt{20} = -19.5\%$
99% Confidence	$-2.33 \times 2.64 \times \sqrt{20} = -27.5\%$

* Important Note: These worst losses (-19.5% and -27.5%) are losses below the expected or average return. In this case, we keep it simple by assuming the daily expected return is zero. We rounded down, so the worst loss is also the net loss.

So, with the variance-covariance method, we can say with 95% confidence that we will not lose more than 19.5% in any given month. The QQQ clearly is not the most conservative investment! You may note, however, that the above result is different from the one we got under the Monte Carlo simulation, which said our maximum monthly loss would be 15% (under the same 95% confidence level).

Black–Scholes Model[4]

The term Black–Scholes refers to three closely related concepts:

- The Black–Scholes model is a mathematical model of the market for an equity, in which the equity's price is a stochastic process.
- The Black–Scholes PDE is a partial differential equation which (in the model) must be satisfied by the price of a derivative on the equity.
- The Black–Scholes formula is the result obtained by solving the Black-Scholes PDE for European put and call options.

The model

The key assumptions of the Black–Scholes model are:

- The price of the underlying instrument S_t follows a geometric Brownian motion with constant drift μ and volatility σ, and the prices changes are log-normally distributed:

$$dS_t = \mu S_t dt + \sigma S_t dW_t$$

- It is possible to short sell the underlying stock.
- There are no arbitrage opportunities.
- Trading in the stock is continuous.
- There are no transaction costs or taxes.
- All securities are perfectly divisible (e.g. it is possible to buy any fraction of a share).
- It is possible to borrow and lend cash at a constant risk-free interest rate.
- The stock does not pay a dividend (see below for extensions to handle dividend payments).

The above lead to the following formula for the price *C* of a European call option with exercise price *K* on a stock currently trading at price *S*, *i.e.*, the right to buy a share of the stock at price *K* after *T* years. The constant interest rate is *r*, and the constant stock volatility is σ.

$$C(S,T) = S\Phi(d_1) - Ke^{-rT}\Phi(d_2)$$

Where

$$d_1 = \frac{\ln(S/K) + (r + \sigma^2/2)T}{\sigma\sqrt{T}}$$

$$d_2 = \frac{\ln(S/K) + (r + \sigma^2/2)T}{\sigma\sqrt{T}} = d_1 - \sigma\sqrt{T}$$

Here Φ is the standard normal cumulative distribution function.

Interpretation: $\Phi(d_1)$ and $\Phi(d_2)$ are the probabilities of exercise under the equivalent exponential martingale probability measure and the equivalent martingale probability measure respectively. The equivalent martingale probability measure is also called the risk neutral probability measure. Note that both of these are "probabilities" in a measure theoretic sense, and neither of these is the true probability of exercise under the real probability measure.

The price of a put option may be computed from this by put-call parity and simplifies to:

$$P(S,T) = Ke^{-rT}\Phi(-d_2) - S\Phi(d_1)$$

The Greeks under the Black–Scholes model are calculated below:

	Calls	Puts
delta	$\Phi(d_1)$	$-\Phi(-d_1) = \Phi(d_1) - 1$
gamma	$\frac{\varphi(d_1)}{S\sigma\sqrt{T}}$	
vega	$S\varphi(d_1)\sqrt{T}$	
theta	$-\frac{S\varphi(d_1)\sigma}{2\sqrt{T}} - rKe^{-rT}\Phi(d_2)$	$-\frac{S\varphi(d_1)\sigma}{2\sqrt{T}} + rKe^{-rT}\Phi(d_2)$
rho	$KTe^{-rT}\Phi(d_2)$	$KTe^{-rT}\Phi(-d_2)$

Here, φ is the standard normal probability density function. Note that the gamma and vega formulas are the same for calls and puts. This can be seen directly from put-call parity. In practice, some sensitivities are usually quoted in scaled-down terms, to match the scale of likely changes in the parameters. For example, rho is often reported divided by 10,000 (1bp rate change), vega by 100 (1 vol point change), and theta by 365 or 252 (1 day decay based on either calendar days or trading days per year).

Extensions of the model

The above model can be extended to have non-constant (but deterministic) rates and volatilities. The model may also be used to value European options on instruments paying dividends. In this case, closed-form solutions are available if the dividend is a known proportion of the stock price. American options and options on stocks paying a known cash dividend (in the short term, more realistic than a proportional dividend) are more difficult to value, and a choice of solution techniques is available (for example lattices and grids).

Instruments paying continuous yield dividends

For options on indexes (such as the FTSE where each of 100 constituent companies may pay a dividend twice a year and so there is a payment nearly every business day), it is reasonable to make the simplifying assumption that dividends are paid continuously, and that the dividend amount is proportional to the level of the index.

The dividend payment paid over the time period $[t, t + dt]$ is then modelled as

$$qS_t dt$$

for some constant q (the dividend yield).

Under this formulation the arbitrage-free price implied by the Black–Scholes model could be shown to be:

$$C(S_0,T) = e^{-rT}(F\Phi(d_1) - K\Phi(d_2))$$

Where now

$$F = S_0 e^{(r-q)T}$$

is the modified forward price that occurs in the terms d_1 and d_2:

$$d_1 = \frac{\ln(F/K) + (\sigma^2/2)T}{\sigma\sqrt{T}}$$

$$d_2 = d_1 - \sigma\sqrt{T}$$

Exactly the same formula is used to price options on foreign exchange rates, except that now q plays the role of the foreign risk-free interest rate and S is the spot exchange rate.

Instruments paying discrete proportional dividends

It is also possible to extend the Black–Scholes framework to options on instruments paying discrete proportional dividends. This is useful when the option is struck on a single stock.

A typical model is to assume that a proportion δ of the stock price is paid out at pre-determined times $t_1, t_2, \ldots$. The price of the stock is then modelled as:

$$S_t = S_0(1-\delta)^{n(t)} e^{ut+\sigma W t}$$

where $n(t)$ is the number of dividends that have been paid by time t.

The price of a call option on such a stock is again:

$$C(S_0,T) = e^{-rT}(F\Phi(d_1) - K\Phi(d_2))$$

Where now

$$F = S_0(1-\delta)^{n(T)} e^{rT}$$

is the forward price for the dividend paying stock.

Valuing bond options

Black–Scholes cannot be applied directly to bond securities because of the pull-to-par problem. As the bond reaches its maturity date, all of the prices involved with the bond become known, thereby decreasing its volatility, and the simple Black–Scholes model does not reflect this process. A large number of extensions to Black–Scholes, beginning with the Black model, have been used to deal with this phenomenon.

Interest rate curve

In practice, interest rates are not constant - they vary by tenor, giving an interest rate curve which may be interpolated to pick an appropriate rate to use in the Black-Scholes formula. Another consideration is that interest rates vary over time. This volatility may make a significant contribution to the price, especially of long-dated options.

Short stock rate

It is not free to take a short stock position. Similarly, it may be possible to lend out a long stock position for a small fee. In either case, this can be treated as a continuous dividend for the purposes of a Black-Scholes valuation.

Moody's KMV Portfolio Manager[5]

Moody's KMV Portfolio Manager™ is the credit portfolio management solution used by the world's leading institutions to measure portfolio risk and concentrations, manage economic capital and explore trading opportunities.

Assessing Credit Portfolio Risk and Return

Regulators, investors, and senior management are requiring financial institutions to improve credit portfolio risk management. Measuring and managing portfolio performance requires forward-looking data, leading-edge analytics, and experienced insight. Portfolio Manager provides a methodology for measurement and benchmarking of credit portfolio risk, from credit cards to corporate loans. Portfolio Manager brings a single, cohesive correlation framework to an institution's balance sheet. Only by jointly estimating correlations on actual data across retail, SME and large corporate credit risks, can senior management make the comparisons needed for strategic decisions. Portfolio Manager was used to calibrate the model in the Basel II framework. Regulators and customers value Portfolio Manager's use of empirical credit migration data and validated data on correlations through two business cycles. Portfolio Manager is a transparent solution that includes access to a global expert practitioner base. The product allows users to examine the drivers of portfolio risk and capital, and to gain an intuitive understanding of the impact of rating, recovery, term, industry, size and other drivers of portfolio risk. This clarity is critical as institutions move to allocate economic capital to customers and business units for better decision-making.

Moody's KMV Portfolio Manager offers:

- Risk-return analysis for originations, hedges and trades

- Insight on the contribution of individual positions and customers to portfolio capital risk
- Full portfolio loss and value distributions, both in absolute terms and relative to your benchmark
- Monte Carlo-based risk measures for loss volatility and tail risk
- Performance comparisons to a benchmark portfolio
- Empirically-based calibrations drawn from the world's richest credit data sources
- Leading-edge user base that shares and shapes best practices

Improve Credit Portfolio Performance:

- Make strategic decisions across businesses, industries, geographies and portfolios, based on a unified correlation framework
- Identify outliers and concentrations that impact performance at the exposure, obligor and industry level
- Determine appropriate buy-sell quantities with the Trades Optimizer to enhance performance

Price for Risk:

- Calculate Sharpe ratios and return on risk-adjusted capital (RORAC) for each exposure and the entire portfolio
- Understand how new exposures, or a package of exposures, impacts portfolio risk-return performance on the margin
- Determine the required return or spread on an exposure to match or improve portfolio risk-return performance
- Calculate the shortfall or mispricing in credit revenue for an exposure, given its risk in a portfolio

Understand and Measure Portfolio Credit Risk:

- Quantify and stress-test the probability of portfolio credit losses to examine the adequacy of capital and loss budgets
- Measure risk-return characteristics and the diversification impact of every credit exposure, including aggregates of extremely granular portfolios, such as credit-card lines, HELOCs and mortgages
- Analyze the counterparty credit risk of interest-rate swaps and other trading-desk instruments with highly unusual cash flow properties
- Assess each exposure in terms of stand-alone risk, portfolio risk contribution (taking into account its correlation with all other exposures) and risk-adjusted return
- Create customized graphs with Portfolio Manager's powerful reporting tool, Moody's KMV Portfolio Viewer

Integration with a Suite of Moody's KMV Products

Portfolio Manager can process data from a variety of sources, including public and private-firm EDF™ (Expected Default Frequency) credit measures, internal ratings and LossCalc™. Portfolio Manager also integrates seamlessly with DealAnalyzer® to extend portfolio analytics to the origination and trading desktops.

Portfolio Manager has several modules to help users assess their portfolios:

- GCorr™ provides details on every pair-wise correlation calculation from the Moody's KMV global correlation factor model
- Distributed Monte Carlo speeds processing time by distributing risk calculations across multiple computers or processors
- Modeled R-squared Calculator models the systematic risk of borrowers not covered by the client's Moody's KMV data subscriptions

Probability Distributions[6]

An example will make clear the relationship between random variables and probability distributions. Suppose you flip a coin two times. This simple statistical experiment can have four possible outcomes: HH, HT, TH, and TT. Now, let the variable X represent the number of Heads that result from this experiment. The variable X can take on the values 0, 1, or 2. In this example, X is a random variable because its value is determined by the outcome of a statistical experiment. A probability distribution is a table or an equation that links each outcome of a statistical experiment with its probability of occurence. Consider the coin flip experiment described above. The table below, which associates each outcome with its probability, is an example of a probability distribution.

Number of heads	Probability
0	0.25
1	0.50
2	0.25

The above table represents the probability distribution of the random variable X.

Cumulative Probability Distributions

A cumulative probability refers to the probability that the value of a random variable falls within a specified range. Let us return to the coin flip experiment. If we flip a coin two times, we might ask: What is the probability that the coin flips would result in one or fewer heads? The answer would be a cumulative probability. It would be the probability that the coin flip experiment results in zero heads plus the probability that the experiment results in one head.

$P(X < 1) = P(X = 0) + P(X = 1) = 0.25 + 0.50 = 0.75$

Like a probability distribution, a cumulative probability distribution can be represented by a table or an equation. In the table below, the cumulative probability refers to the probability than the random variable X is less than or equal to x.

Number of heads: x	Probability: $P(X = x)$	Cumulative Probability: $P(X < x)$
0	0.25	0.25
1	0.50	0.75
2	0.25	1.00

Uniform Probability Distribution

The simplest probability distribution occurs when all of the values of a random variable occur with equal probability. This probability distribution is called the uniform distribution.

> Uniform Distribution. Suppose the random variable X can assume k different values. Suppose also that the $P(X = x_k)$ is constant. Then, $P(X = x_k) = 1/k$

Discrete and Continuous Probability Distributions

If a variable can take on any value between two specified values, it is called a continuous variable; otherwise, it is called a discrete variable. Some examples will clarify the difference between discrete and continuous variables.

- Suppose the fire department mandates that all fire fighters must weigh between 150 and 250 pounds. The weight of a fire fighter would be an example of a continuous variable; since a fire fighter's weight could take on any value between 150 and 250 pounds.
- Suppose we flip a coin and count the number of heads. The number of heads could be any integer value between 0 and plus infinity. However, it could not be any number between 0 and plus infinity. We could not, for example, get 2.5 heads. Therefore, the number of heads must be a discrete variable.

Just like variables, probability distributions can be classified as discrete or continuous.

Discrete Probability Distributions

If a random variable is a discrete variable, its probability distribution is called a discrete probability distribution. An example will make this clear. Suppose you flip a coin two times. This simple statistical experiment can have four possible outcomes: HH, HT, TH, and TT. Now, let the random variable X represent the number of Heads that result from this experiment. The random variable X can only take on the values 0, 1, or 2, so it is a discrete random variable.

The probability distribution for this statistical experiment appears below.

Number of heads	Probability
0	0.25
1	0.50
2	0.25

The above table represents a *discrete* probability distribution because it relates each value of a discrete random variable with its probability of occurrence. The following discrete probability distributions are used.

- Binomial probability distribution
- Hypergeometric probability distribution
- Multinomial probability distribution
- Poisson probability distribution

Continuous Probability Distributions

If a random variable is a continuous variable, its probability distribution is called a continuous probability distribution. A continuous probability distribution differs from a discrete probability distribution in several ways.

- The probability that a continuous random variable will assume a particular value is zero.
- As a result, a continuous probability distribution cannot be expressed in tabular form.
- Instead, an equation or formula is used to describe a continuous probability distribution.

Most often, the equation used to describe a continuous probability distribution is called a probability density function. Sometimes, it is referred to as a density function, a PDF, or a pdf. For a continuous probability distribution, the density function has the following properties:

- Since the continuous random variable is defined over a continuous range of values (called the domain of the variable), the graph of the density function will also be continuous over that range.
- The area bounded by the curve of the density function and the x-axis is equal to 1, when computed over the domain of the variable.
- The probability that a random variable assumes a value between *a* and *b* is equal to the area under the density function bounded by *a* and *b*.

For example, consider the probability density function shown in the graph below. Suppose we wanted to know the probability that the random variable *X* was less than or equal to *a*. The probability that *X* is less than or equal to *a* is equal to the area under the curve bounded by *a* and minus infinity - as indicated by the shaded area.

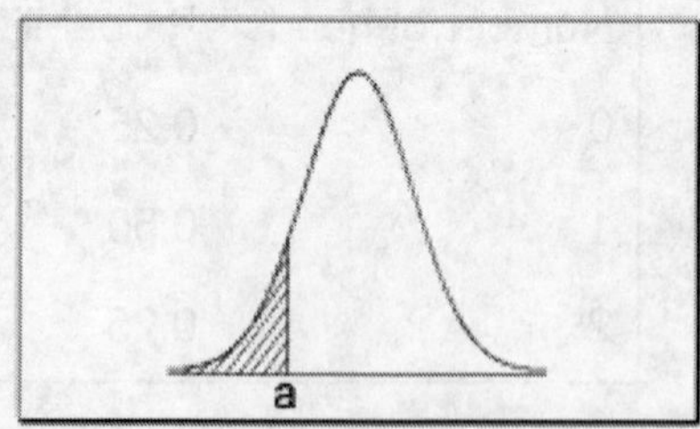

The shaded area in the graph represents the probability that the random variable *X* is less than or equal to *a*. This is a cumulative probability. However, the probability that *X* is *exactly* equal to *a* would be zero. A continuous random variable can take on an infinite number of values. The probability that it will equal a specific value (such as *a*) is always zero. The following continuous probability distributions are used.

- Normal probability distribution
- Student's t distribution
- Chi-square distribution
- F distribution

Binomial Distribution

A binomial random variable is the number of successes *x* in *n* repeated trials of a binomial experiment. The probability distribution of a binomial random variable is called a binomial distribution (also known as a Bernoulli distribution). Suppose we flip a coin two times and count the number of heads (successes). The binomial random variable is the number of heads, which can take on values of 0, 1, or 2. The binomial distribution is presented below.

Number of heads	Probability
0	0.25
1	0.50
2	0.25

The binomial distribution has the following properties:

- The mean of the distribution (μ_x) is equal to $n * P$.
- The variance (σ^2_x) is $n * P * (1 - P)$.
- The standard deviation (σ_x) is sqrt[$n * P * (1 - P)$].

Binomial Probability

The binomial probability refers to the probability that a binomial experiment results in exactly *x* successes. For example, in the above table, we see that the binomial probability of getting exactly one head in two coin flips is 0.50.

Given *x*, *n*, and *P*, we can compute the binomial probability based on the following formula:

Binomial Formula. Suppose a binomial experiment consists of n trials and results in x successes. If the probability of success on an individual trial is P, then the binomial probability is:
$b(x; n, P) = {}_nC_x * P^x * (1 - P)^{n-x}$

Poisson Distribution

A Poisson random variable is the number of successes that result from a Poisson experiment. The probability distribution of a Poisson random variable is called a Poisson distribution. Given the mean number of successes (μ) that occur in a specified region, we can compute the Poisson probability based on the following formula:

Poisson Formula. Suppose we conduct a Poisson experiment, in which the average number of successes within a given region is μ. Then, the Poisson probability is:
$P(x; \mu) = (e^{-\mu}) (\mu^x) / x!$
where x is the actual number of successes that result from the experiment, and e is approximately equal to 2.71828.

The Poisson distribution has the following properties:

- The mean of the distribution is equal to μ
- The variance is also equal to μ

Normal Distribution

The normal distribution refers to a family of continuous probability distributions described by the normal equation. The normal distribution is defined by the following equation:

Normal equation. The value of the random variable Y is:
$Y = [\ 1/\sigma * \text{sqrt}(2\pi)\ ] * e^{(x - \mu)2/2\sigma 2}$
where X is a normal random variable, μ is the mean, σ is the standard deviation, π is approximately 3.14159, and e is approximately 2.71828.

The random variable X in the normal equation is called the normal random variable. The normal equation is the probability density function for the normal distribution.

The Normal Curve

The graph of the normal distribution depends on two factors - the mean and the standard deviation. The mean of the distribution determines the location of the center of the graph, and the standard deviation determines the height and width of the graph. When the standard deviation is large, the curve is short and wide; when the standard deviation is small, the curve is tall and narrow. All normal distributions look like a symmetric, bell-shaped curve, as shown below.

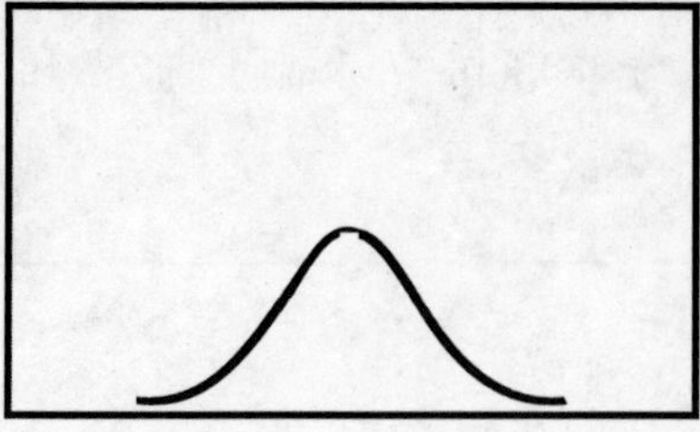

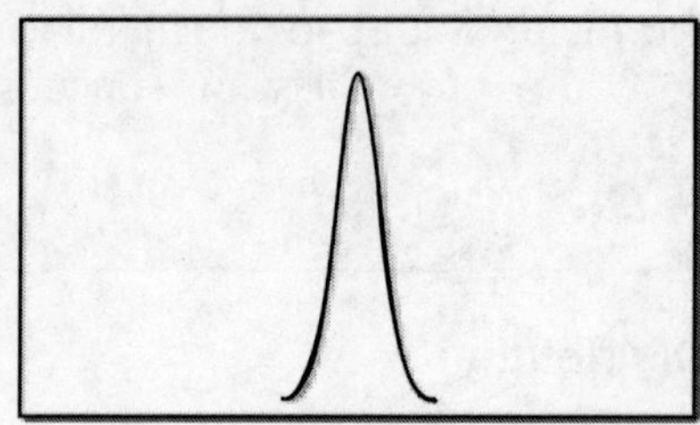

The curve on the left is shorter and wider than the curve on the right, because the curve on the left has a bigger standard deviation.

Probability and the Normal Curve

The normal distribution is a continuous probability distribution. This has several implications for probability.

- The total area under the normal curve is equal to 1.
- The probability that a normal random variable *X* equals any particular value is 0.
- The probability that *X* is greater than *a* equals the area under the normal curve bounded by *a* and plus infinity (as indicated by the *non-shaded* area in the following figure).
- The probability that *X* is less than *a* equals the area under the normal curve bounded by *a* and minus infinity (as indicated by the *shaded* area in the following figure).

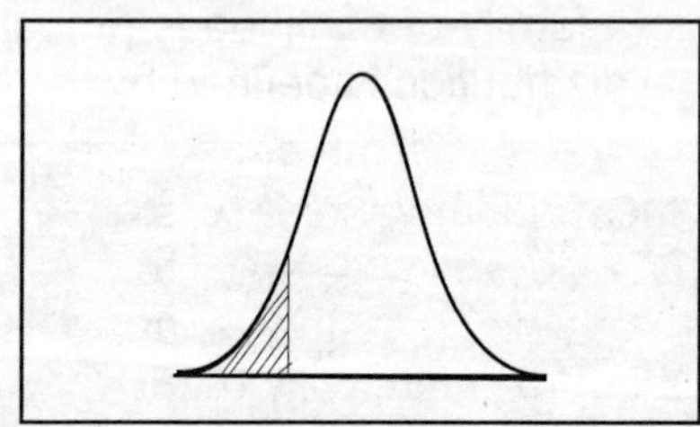

Additionally, every normal curve (regardless of its mean or standard deviation) conforms to the following "rule".

- About 68% of the area under the curve falls within 1 standard deviation of the mean.
- About 95% of the area under the curve falls within 2 standard deviations of the mean.
- About 99.7% of the area under the curve falls within 3 standard deviations of the mean.

Collectively, these points are known as the empirical rule or the 68-95-99.7 rule. Clearly, given a normal distribution, most outcomes will be within 3 standard deviations of the mean.

Standard Normal Distribution

The standard normal distribution is a special case of the normal distribution. It is the distribution that occurs when a normal random variable has a mean of zero and a standard deviation of one. The normal random variable of a standard normal distribution is called a standard score or a z-score. Every normal random variable *X* can be transformed into a *z* score via the following equation:

$z = (X - \mu) / \sigma$

where *X* is a normal random variable, μ is the mean mean of *X*, and σ is the standard deviation of *X*.

Fundamental of Statistics

Measures of Central Tendency

Statisticians use summary measures to describe patterns of data. Measures of central tendency refer to the summary measures used to describe the most "typical" value in a set of values.

The Mean and the Median

The two most common measures of central tendency are the median and the mean, which can be illustrated with an example. Suppose we draw a sample of five women and measure their weights. They weigh 100 pounds, 100 pounds, 130 pounds, 140 pounds, and 150 pounds.

- To find the median, we arrange the observations in order from smallest to largest value. If there is an odd number of observations, the median is the middle value. If there is an even number of observations, the median is the average of the two middle values. Thus, in the sample of five women, the median value would be 130 pounds; since 130 pounds is the middle weight.
- The mean of a sample or a population is computed by adding all of the observations and dividing by the number of observations. Returning to the example of the five women, the mean weight would equal (100 + 100 + 130 + 140 + 150)/5 = 620/5 = 124 pounds. In the general case, the mean can be calculated, using one of the following equations:

  Population mean = $\mu = \Sigma X / N$ OR Sample mean = $x = \Sigma x / n$

  where ΣX is the sum of all the population observations, N is the number of population observations, Σx is the sum of all the sample observations, and n is the number of sample observations.

When statisticians talk about the mean of a population, they use the Greek letter μ to refer to the mean score. When they talk about the mean of a sample, statisticians use the symbol x to refer to the mean score.

The Mean vs the Median

As measures of central tendency, the mean and the median each have advantages and disadvantages. Some pros and cons of each measure are summarized below.

- The median may be a better indicator of the most typical value if a set of scores has an outlier. An outlier is an extreme value that differs greatly from other values.
- However, when the sample size is large and does not include outliers, the mean score usually provides a better measure of central tendency.

To illustrate these points, consider the following example. Suppose we examine a sample of 10 households to estimate the typical family income. Nine of the households have incomes between Rs. 20,000 and Rs. 100,000; but the tenth household has an annual income of Rs. 1,000,000,000. That tenth household is an outlier. If we choose a measure to estimate the income of a typical household, the mean will greatly over-estimate family income (because of the outlier) while the median will not.

Measures of Variability

Statisticians use summary measures to describe the amount of variability or spread in a set of data. The most common measures of variability are the range, the interquartile range (IQR), variance, and standard deviation.

The Range

The range is the difference between the largest and smallest values in a set of values.

For example, consider the following numbers: 1, 3, 4, 5, 5, 6, 7, 11. For this set of numbers, the range would be 11 - 1 or 10.

The Interquartile Range (IQR)

The interquartile range (IQR) is the difference between the largest and smallest values in the middle 50% of a set of data. To compute an interquartile range from a set of data, first remove observations from the lower quartile. Then, remove observations from the upper quartile. Then, from the remaining observations, compute the difference between the largest and smallest values.

For example, consider the following numbers: 1, 3, 4, 5, 5, 6, 7, 11. After we remove observations from the lower and upper quartiles, we are left with: 4, 5, 5, 6. The interquartile range (IQR) would be 6 - 4 = 2.

The Variance

In a population, variance is the average squared deviation from the population mean, as defined by the following formula:

$$\sigma^2 = \Sigma (X_i - \mu)^2 / N$$

where σ^2 is the population variance, μ is the population mean, X_i is the *i*th element from the population, and N is the number of elements in the population.

The variance of a sample, is defined by slightly different formula, and uses a slightly different notation:

$$s^2 = \Sigma (x_i - x)^2 / (n - 1)$$

where s^2 is the sample variance, x is the sample mean, x_i is the *i*th element from the sample, and n is the number of elements in the sample. Using this formula, the sample variance can be considered an unbiased estimate of the true population variance. Therefore, if you need to estimate an unknown population variance, based on data from a sample, this is the formula to use.

The Standard Deviation

The standard deviation is the square root of the variance. Thus, the standard deviation of a population is:

$$\sigma = \text{sqrt} [\sigma^2] = \text{sqrt} [\Sigma (X_i - \mu)^2 / N]$$

where σ is the population standard deviation, σ^2 is the population variance, μ is the population mean, X_i is the *i*th element from the population, and N is the number of elements in the population.

And the standard deviation of a sample is:

$$s = \text{sqrt} [s^2] = \text{sqrt} [\Sigma (x_i - x)^2 / (n - 1)]$$

where *s* is the sample standard deviation, s^2 is the sample variance, x is the sample mean, x_i is the *i*th element from the sample, and n is the number of elements in the sample.

Measures of Position

Statisticians often talk about the position of a value, relative to other values in a set of observations. The most common measures of position are quartiles, percentiles, and standard scores (aka, z-scores).

Percentiles

Assume that the elements in a data set are rank ordered from the smallest to the largest. The values that divide a rank-ordered set of elements into 100 equal parts are called percentiles. An element having a percentile rank of P_i would have a greater value than i percent of all the elements in the set. Thus, the observation at the 50th percentile would be denoted P_{50}, and it would be greater than 50 percent of the observations in the set. An observation at the 50th percentile would correspond to the median value in the set.

Quartiles

Quartiles divide a rank-ordered data set into four equal parts. The values that divide each part are called the first, second, and third quartiles; and they are denoted by Q_1, Q_2, and Q_3, respectively. Note the relationship between quartiles and percentiles. Q_1 corresponds to P_{25}, Q_2 corresponds to P_{50}, Q_3 corresponds to P_{75}. Q_2 is the median value in the set.

Standard Scores (z-Scores)

A standard score (aka, a z-score) indicates how many standard deviations an element is from the mean. A standard score can be calculated from the following formula.

$z = (X - \mu) / \sigma$

where z is the z-score, X is the value of the element, μ is the mean of the population, and σ is the standard deviation.

Here is how to interpret z-scores.

- A z-score less than 0 represents an element less than the mean.
- A z-score greater than 0 represents an element greater than the mean.
- A z-score equal to 0 represents an element equal to the mean.
- A z-score equal to 1 represents an element that is 1 standard deviation greater than the mean; a z-score equal to 2, 2 standard deviations greater than the mean; etc.
- A z-score equal to -1 represents an element that is 1 standard deviation less than the mean; a z-score equal to -2, 2 standard deviations less than the mean; etc.
- If the number of elements in the set is large, about 68% of the elements have a z-score between -1 and 1; about 95% have a z-score between -2 and 2; and about 99% have a z-score between -3 and 3.

Covariance

Covariance provides a measure of the strength of the correlation between two or more sets of random variates. The covariance for two random variates X and Y, each with sample size N, is defined by the expectation value:

$$\mathrm{Cov}(X, Y) = \{(X-\mu X)(Y-\mu Y)\}$$
$$= (X\,Y)-\mu_x \mu_y$$

where $\mu_x = (X)$ and $\mu_y = (Y)$ are the respective means, which can be written out explicitly as

$$\mathrm{cov}(X,Y) = \sum_{i=1}^{N} \frac{(x_i - \bar{x})(y_i - \bar{y})}{N}.$$

For uncorrelated variates,

$\mathrm{Cov}\,(X,Y) = (X,Y) - \mu_x \mu_y = (X)(Y) - \mu_x \mu_y = 0,$

so the covariance is zero. However, if the variables are correlated in some way, then their covariance will be nonzero. In fact, if cov(X,Y) > 0, then *Y* tends to increase as *X* increases, and if cov(X,Y) < 0, then *Y* tends to decrease as *X* increases. Note that while statistically independent variables are always uncorrelated, the converse is not necessarily true.

In the special case of *Y*=*X*,

$$\mathrm{Cov}\,(X, X) = (X^2)-(X)^2$$

$$= \sigma_x^2,$$

so the covariance reduces to the usual variance $\sigma_x^2 = \text{var}(X)$. This motivates the use of the symbol $\sigma_{XY} = \text{cov}(X, Y)$, which then provides a consistent way of denoting the variance as $\sigma_{XX} = \sigma_X^2$, where σ_X is the standard deviation. The derived quantity is called statistical correlation of *X* and *Y*.

$$Cor(X, Y) = \frac{\text{cov}(X, Y)}{\sigma_X \sigma_Y}$$

$$= \frac{\sigma_{XY}}{\sqrt{\sigma_{XX}\sigma_{YY}}},$$

The covariance is especially useful when looking at the variance of the sum of two random variates, since

$$\text{Var}\ (X + Y) = \text{var}\ (X) + \text{var}\ (Y) + 2\ \text{cos}\ (S, Y).$$

The covariance is symmetric by definition since

$$\text{cov}\ (X, Y) = \text{cov}\ (Y, X).$$

Given ^{n} random variates denoted $X_1, \ldots X_n$, the covariance $\sigma_{ij} = \text{cov}(X_i, X_j)$ of X_i and X_j is defined by

$$\text{cov}\ (X_i, X_j) = \langle (X_i - \mu_i)(X_j - \mu_j) \rangle$$

$$= \langle X_i X_i \rangle - \mu_i \mu_j,$$

where $\mu_i = \langle X_i \rangle$ and $\mu_j = \langle X_j \rangle$ are the means of X_i and X_j, respectively. The matrix (V_{ij}) of the quantities $V_{ij} = cov(X_i, X_j)$ is called the covariance matrix.

The covariance obeys the identities

$$\text{cov}\ (X+X, Y) = \langle (X_i - \mu_i)(X_j - \mu_j) \rangle\ \langle (X+Z)\,Y \rangle - \langle X+Z \rangle \langle Y \rangle$$

$$= \langle XY \rangle + \langle ZY \rangle - (\langle X \rangle + \langle Z \rangle)\langle Y \rangle$$

$$= \langle XY \rangle - \langle X \rangle \langle Y \rangle + \langle ZY \rangle - \langle Z \rangle \langle Y \rangle$$

$$= \text{cov}(X, Y) + \text{cov}\ (Z, Y).$$

By induction, it therefore follows that

$$\text{cov}\left(\sum_{i=1}^{n} X_i, Y\right) = \sum_{i=1}^{n} \text{cov}(X_i, Y)$$

$$\operatorname{cov}\left(\sum_{i=1}^{n} X_i, \sum_{j=1}^{m} Y_j\right) = \sum_{i=1}^{n} \operatorname{cov}\left(X_1, \sum_{j=1}^{m} Y_j\right)$$

$$= \sum_{i=1}^{n} \operatorname{cov}\left(\sum_{j=1}^{m} Y_j, X_i\right)$$

$$= \sum_{i=1}^{n}\sum_{j=1}^{m} \operatorname{cov}(Y_j, X_i)$$

$$= \sum_{i=1}^{n}\sum_{j=1}^{m} \operatorname{cov}(X_i, Y_j)$$

Correlation Coefficient, *r*

The quantity *r*, called the *linear correlation coefficient*, measures the strength and the direction of a linear relationship between two variables. The linear correlation coefficient is sometimes referred to as the *Pearson product moment correlation coefficient* in honor of its developer Karl Pearson.

The mathematical formula for computing *r* is:

$$r = \frac{n\sum xy - \left(\sum x\right)\left(\sum y\right)}{\sqrt{n\left(\sum x^2\right) - \left(\sum x\right)^2}\sqrt{n\left(\sum y^2\right) - \left(\sum y\right)^2}}$$

where *n* is the number of pairs of data.

Derivatives Products and its Market[7]

The derivatives markets are the financial markets for derivatives. The market can be divided into two, that for exchange traded derivatives and that for over-the-counter derivatives. The legal nature of these products is very different as well as the way they are traded, though many market participants are active in both.

Futures Markets

Futures Exchange

Futures exchanges, such as Euronext.liffe and the Chicago Mercantile Exchange, trade in standardized derivative contracts. These are options contracts and futures contracts on a whole range of underlying products. The members of the exchange hold positions in these contracts with the exchange, who acts as central counterparty. When one party goes long (buys) a futures contract, another goes short (sells). When a new contract is introduced, the total position in the contract is zero. Therefore, the sum of all the long positions must be equal to the sum of all the short positions. In other words, risk is transferred from one party to another. The total notional amount of all the outstanding positions at the end of June 2004 stood at $53 trillion.

Over-the-counter markets

Tailor-made derivatives traded on a futures exchange, are traded on over-the-counter markets, also known as the OTC market. These consist of investment banks who have traders who make markets in these derivatives, and clients such as hedge funds, commercial banks, government sponsored enterprises, etc. Products that are always traded over-the-counter are swaps, forward rate agreements, forward contracts, credit derivatives, etc. The total notional amount of all the outstanding positions at the end of June 2004 stood at $220 trillion.

Netting

The notional outstanding value of OTC derivatives contracts rose by 36% from $197 trillion at end-2003 to $270 trillion in June 2005. Since end-2000, notional value has increased nearly threefold. Average daily global turnover rose from $764bn to $1508bn between April 2001 and April 2004. The UK reinforced its position as the leading derivatives center with its share of turnover rising from 36% to 43% during this period.

Interest rate instruments remain the key driver of global trading, accounting for 76% of notional value. Derivatives based on foreign exchange contracts also form an important sphere of activity as do equity-linked and commodity contracts. Credit, energy, metal and freight derivatives have grown rapidly in recent years. The euro and the US rupee dominate interest rate derivatives worldwide with 37% and 35% shares respectively based on notional value in June 2005. Turnover data for April 2004 indicated a rather higher share for euro-based derivatives trading. Financial institutions such as hedge funds, mutual funds, insurance companics and smaller banks have become much bigger users of derivatives.

- Total derivatives (notional amount): $96.2 trillion (September, 2005)
    - Interest rate contracts: $82.0 trillion
    - Foreign exchange contracts: $8.6 trillion
- Total number of commercial banks holding derivatives: 769

Commodity markets are markets where raw or primary products are exchanged. These raw commodities are traded on regulated commodities exchanges, in which they are bought and sold in standardized contracts.

Regulation of commodity markets

Cotton, kilowatt-hours of electricity, board feet of wood, long distance minutes, royalty payments due on artists' works, and other products and services have been traded on markets of varying scale, with varying degrees of success. One issue that presents major difficulty for creators of such instruments is the liability accruing to the purchaser: Unless the product or service can be guaranteed or insured to be free of liability based on where it came from and how it got to market, e.g. kilowatts must come to market free from legitimate claims for smog death from coal burning plants, wood must be free from claims that it comes from protected forests, royalty payments must be free of claims of plagiarism or piracy, it becomes impossible for sellers to guarantee a uniform delivery.

Generally, governments must provide a common regulatory or insurance standard and some release of liability, or at least a backing of the insurers, before a commodity market can begin trading. This is a major source of controversy in for instance the energy market, where desirability of different kinds of power generation varies drastically. In some markets, e.g. Toronto, Canada, surveys established that customers would pay 10-15% more for energy that was not from coal or nuclear, but strictly from renewable sources such as wind. In the United States, the principal regulator of commodity and futures markets is the Commodity Futures Trading Commission.

The foreign exchange (currency or forex or FX) market exists wherever one currency is traded for another. It is by far the largest financial market in the world, and includes trading between large banks, central banks, currency speculators, multinational corporations, governments, and other financial markets and institutions. The average daily trade in the global forex and related markets currently is over US $3 trillion.

Market size and liquidity

The foreign exchange market is unique because of

- its trading volumes,
- the extreme liquidity of the market,
- the large number of, and variety of, traders in the market,
- its geographical dispersion,
- its long trading hours: 24 hours a day (except on weekends),
- the variety of factors that affect exchange rates, and
- the low margins of profit compared with other markets of fixed income (but profits can be high due to very large trading volumes).

Market participants

Unlike a stock market, where all participants have access to the same prices, the forex market is divided into levels of access. At the top is the inter-bank market, which is made up of the largest investment banking firms. Within the inter-bank market, spreads, which are the difference between the bid and ask prices, are razor sharp and usually unavailable, and not known to players outside the inner circle. As you descend the levels of access, the difference between the bid and ask prices widens (from 0-1 pip to 1-2 pips for some currencies such as the EUR). This is due to volume. If a trader can guarantee large numbers of transactions for large amounts, they can demand a smaller difference between the bid and ask price, which is referred to as a better spread. The levels of access that make up the forex market are determined by the size of the "line" (the amount of money with which they are trading). The top-tier inter-bank market accounts for 53% of all transactions. After that there are usually smaller investment banks, followed by large multi-national corporations (which need to hedge risk and pay employees in different countries), large hedge funds, and even some of the retail forex market makers. According to Galati and Melvin, "Pension funds, insurance companies, mutual funds, and other institutional investors have played an increasingly important role in financial markets in general, and in FX markets in particular, since the early 2000s." (2004) In addition, he notes, "Hedge funds have grown markedly over the 2001–2004 period in terms of both number and overall size" Central banks also participate in the forex market to align currencies to their economic needs.

Top 10 Currency Traders
% of overall volume, May 2007

Name	Volume
Deutsche Bank	21.70%
UBS AG	14.85%
Citi	9.00%
Royal Bank of Scotland	8.90%
Barclays Capital	8.80%
Bank of America	5.29%
HSBC	4.36%
Goldman Sachs	4.14%
JPMorgan	3.33%
Morgan Stanley	2.86%

Source: Euromoney FX survey

Stock market, generally referred to as (equity market) is a private or public market for the trading of company stock and derivatives of company stock at an agreed price; these are securities listed on a stock exchange as well as those only traded privately. The expression 'stock market' refers to the market that enables the trading of company stocks (collective shares), other securities, and derivatives. Bonds are still traditionally traded in an informal, over-the-counter market known as the bond market. Commodities are traded in commodities markets, and derivatives are traded in a variety of markets (but, like bonds, mostly 'over-the-counter').

The size of the worldwide 'bond market' is estimated at $45 trillion. The size of the 'stock market' is estimated at about $51 trillion. The world derivatives market has been estimated at about $480 trillion 'face' or nominal value, 30 times the size of the U.S. economy…and 12 times the size of the entire world economy. It must be noted though that the value of the derivatives market, because it is stated in terms of *notional* values, cannot be directly compared to a stock or a fixed income security, which traditionally refers to an *actual* value. (Many such relatively illiquid securities are valued as *marked to model*, rather than an actual market price.)

The stocks are listed and traded on stock exchanges which are entities (a corporation or mutual organization) specialized in the business of bringing buyers and sellers of stocks and securities together. The stock market in the United States includes the trading of all securities listed on the NYSE, the NASDAQ, the Amex, as well as on the many regional exchanges, e.g. OTCBB and Pink Sheets. European examples of stock exchanges include the Paris Bourse (now part of Euronext), the London Stock Exchange and the Deutsche Borse.

The bond market (also known as the debt, credit, or fixed income market) is a financial market where participants buy and sell debt securities, usually in the form of bonds. As of 2006, the size of the international bond market is an estimated $45 trillion, of which the size of the outstanding U.S. bond market debt was $25.2 trillion. Nearly all of the $923 billion average daily trading volume (as of early 2007) in the U.S. Bond Market takes place between broker-dealers and large institutions in a decentralized, over-the-counter (OTC) market. However, a small number of bonds, primarily corporate, are listed on exchanges.

References to the "bond market" usually refer to the government bond market, because of its size, liquidity, lack of credit risk and, therefore, sensitivity to interest rates. Because of the inverse relationship between bond valuation and interest rates, the bond market is often used to indicate changes in interest rates or the shape of the yield curve. Futures exchange is a central financial exchange where people can trade standardized futures contracts; that is, a contract to buy specific quantities of a commodity or financial instrument at a specified price with delivery set at a specified time in the future.

Nature of contracts

Exchange-traded contracts are standardized by the exchanges where they trade. The contract details what asset is to be bought or sold, and how, when, where and in what quantity it is to be delivered. The terms also specify the currency in which the contract will trade, minimum tick value, and the last trading day and expiry or delivery month. Standardized commodity futures contracts may also contain provisions for adjusting the contracted price based on deviations from the "standard" commodity, for example, a contract might specify delivery of heavier USDA Number 1 oats at par value but permit delivery of Number 2 oats for a certain seller's penalty per bushel.

Before the market opens on the first day of trading a new futures contract, there is a specification but no actual contracts exist. Futures contracts are not issued like other securities, but are "created" whenever Open interest increases; that is, when one party first buys (goes long) a contract from another party (who goes short). Contracts are also "destroyed" in the opposite manner whenever Open interest decreases because traders resell to reduce their long positions or rebuy to reduce their short positions. Speculators on futures price fluctuations who do not intend to make or take ultimate delivery must take care to "zero their positions" prior to the contract's expiry. After expiry, each contract will be settled , either by physical delivery (typically for commodity underlyings) or by a cash settlement (typically for financial underlyings). The contracts ultimately are not between the original buyer and the original seller, but between the holders at expiry and the exchange. Because a contract may pass through many hands after it is created by its initial purchase and sale, or even be liquidated, settling parties do not know with whom they have ultimately traded. Compare this with other securities, in which there is a primary market when an issuer issues the security, and a secondary market where the security is later traded independently of the issuer. Legally, the security represents an obligation of the issuer rather than the buyer and seller; even if the issuer buys back some securities, they still exist. Only if they are legally cancelled can they disappear.

Standardization

The contracts traded on futures exchanges are always standardized. In principle, the parameters to define a contract are endless (see for instance in futures contract). To make sure liquidity is high, there is only a limited number of standardized contracts.

Derivatives Clearing

There is usually a division of responsibility between provision of trading facility and settlement of those trades. While derivative exchanges like the CBOE and LIFFE take responsibility for providing efficient, transparent and orderly trading environments, settlement of the resulting trades are usually handled by Clearing Corporations, also known as Clearing Houses, that serve as central counterparties to trades done in the respective exchanges. For instance, the Options Clearing Corporation and the London Clearing House respectively are the clearing corporations for CBOE and LIFFE. A well known exception to this is the case of Chicago Mercantile Exchange, which clears trades by itself.

Central Counterparty

Derivative contracts are leveraged positions whose value is volatile. They are usually more volatile than their underlying asset. This can lead to situations where one party to a trade loses a big sum of money and is unable to honor its settlement obligation. In a safe trading environment, the parties to a trade need to be assured that their counterparty will honor the trade, no matter how the market has moved. This requirement can lead to messy arrangements like credit assessment, setting of trading limits and so on for each counterparty, and take away most of the advantages of a centralised trading facility. To prevent this, Clearing corporations interpose themselves as counterparties to every trade and extend guarantee that the trade will be settled as originally intended. This action is called Novation. As a result, trading firms take no risk on the actual counterparty to the trade, but on the clearing corporation. The clearing corporation is able to take on this risk by adopting an efficient margining process.

Margin and Mark-to-Market

Clearing houses charge two types of margins: the Initial Margin and the Mark-To-Market margin (also referred to as Variation Margin). The Initial Margin is the sum of money (or collateral) to be deposited by a firm to the clearing corporation to cover possible future loss in the positions (the set of positions held is also called the portfolio) held by a firm. In the simplest case, this is the rupee figure that answers a question of this nature: What is the likely loss that this firm may incur on its portfolio with a 99% confidence and over a period of 2 days? The clause 'with a 99% confidence' and 'over a period 2 days' is to be interpreted as that number such that the actual portfolio loss over 2 days is expected to exceed the number only 1% of the time, although how they know this is unknown. Several popular methods are used to compute initial margins. They include the CME-owned SPAN (a grid simulation method used by the CME and about 70 other exchanges), STANS (a Monte Carlo simulation based methodology used by the OCC), TIMS (earlier used by the OCC, and still being used by a few other exchanges like the Bursa Malaysia.

The Mark-to-Market Margin (MTM margin) on the other hand is the margin collected to offset losses (if any) that have already been incurred on the positions held by a firm. This is computed as the difference between the cost of the position held and the current market value of that position. If the resulting amount is a loss, the amount is collected from the firm; else, the amount may be returned to the firm (the case with most clearing houses) or kept in reserve depending on local practice. In either case, the positions are 'marked-to-market' by setting their new cost to the market value used in computing this difference. The positions held by the clients of the exchange are marked-to-market daily and the MTM difference computation for the next day would use the new cost figure in its calculation. Clients hold a margin account with the exchange, and every day the swings in the value of their positions is added to or deducted from their margin account. If the margin account gets too low, they have to replenish it. In this way it is highly unlikely that the client will not be able to fulfill his obligations arising from the contracts. As the clearing house is the counterparty to all their trades, they only have to have one margin account. This is in contrast with OTC derivatives, where issues such as margin accounts have to be negotiated with all counterparties.

References:

1. *http://www.investopedia.com;http://www.getobjects.com*
2. *http://www.investopedia.com/university/advancedbond*
3. *http://www.investopedia.com/articles*
4. *http://en.wikipedia.org/wiki/Black-Scholes*
5. *http://www.moodyskmv.com/products/pc_portfolioManager.html*
6. *http://stattrek.com/;http://mathworld.wolfram.com*
7. *http://en.wikipedia.org/wiki/Derivatives_market*

Index